M000279002

GREAT CITIES

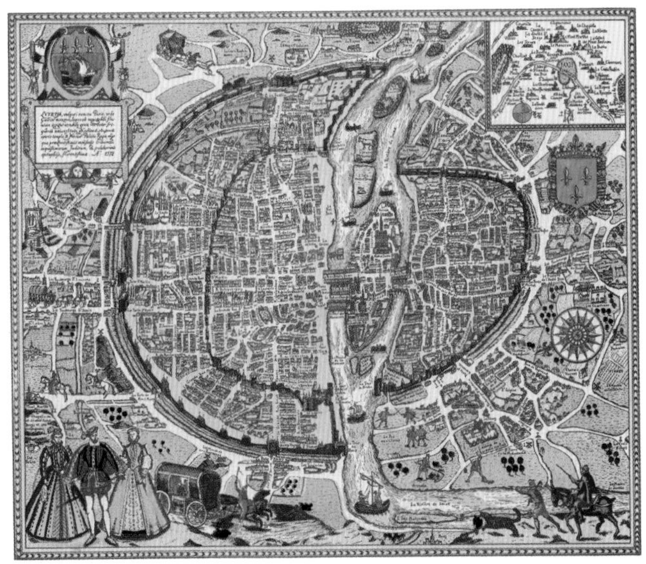

THE STORIES BEHIND THE WORLD'S MOST FASCINATING PLACES

GREAT CITIES

THE STORIES BEHIND THE WORLD'S MOST FASCINATING PLACES

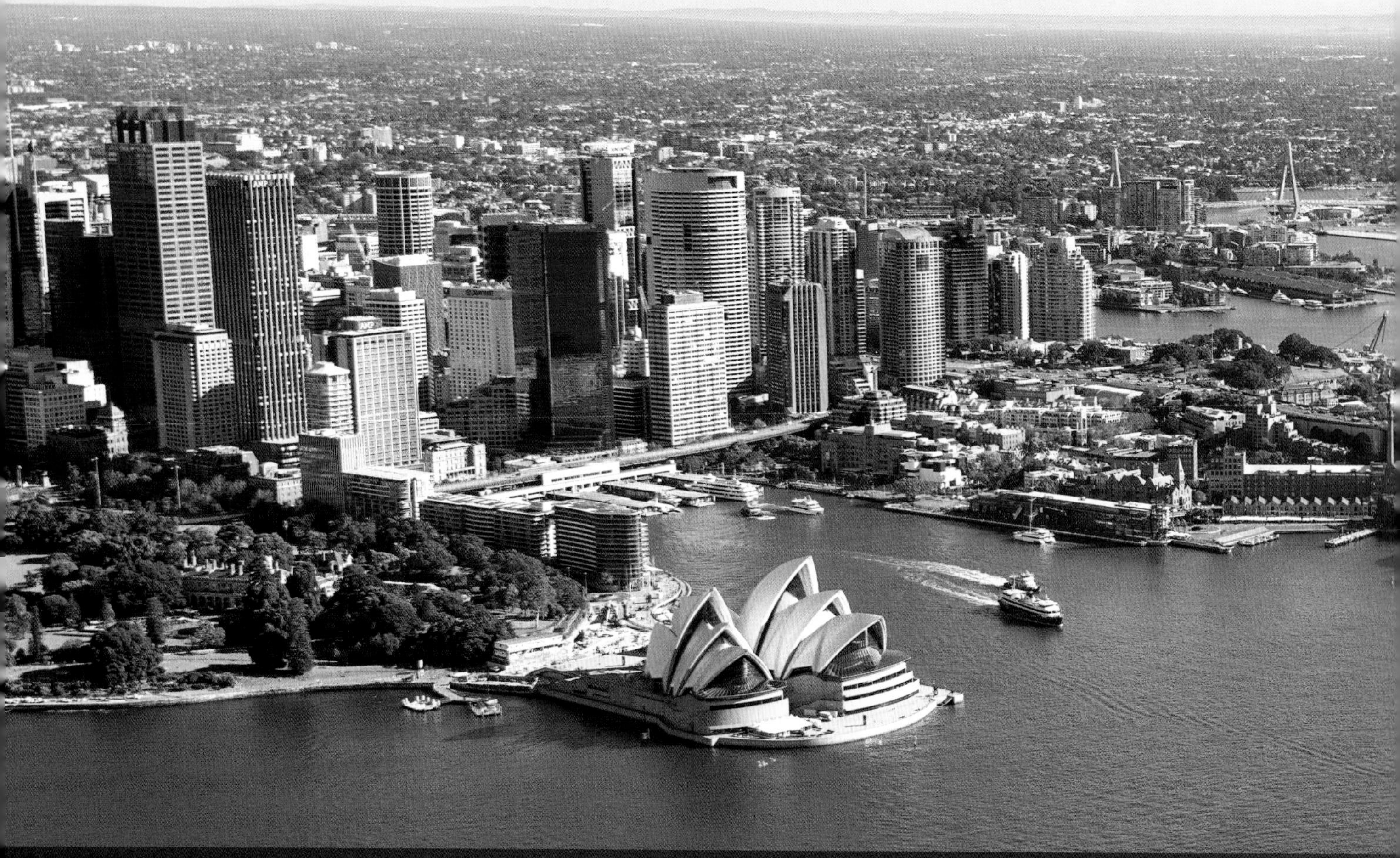

DK LONDON

Senior Editor Dora Whitaker
Senior Art Editor Jane Ewart
Editors Edward Aves, James Smart, Polly Thomas, Monica Woods
US Editor Megan Douglass
Designer Clare Shedden
Managing Editor Christine Stroyan
Managing Art Editor Anna Hall
Production Editor Kavita Varma
Senior Production Controller Samantha Cross
Creative Technical Support Sonia Charbonnier
Jacket Design Development Manager Sophia M.T.T.
Jacket Designer Surabhi Wadhwa
Associate Publishing Director Liz Wheeler
Publishing Director Jonathan Metcalf
Art Director Karen Self

This book was made with Forest Stewardship Council ™ certified paper—one small step in DK's commitment to a sustainable future.

DK DELHI

Senior Art Editor Vikas Sachdeva
Art Editors Shipra Jain, Noopur Dalal
Assistant Art Editors Adhithi Priya, Ankita Das
Senior Editor Janashree Singha
Editors Nandini D. Tripathy, Devangana Ojha
Assistant Editor Ankita Gupta
Managing Editor Soma B. Chowdhury
Senior Managing Art Editor Arunesh Talapatra
Jacket Designer Tanya Mehrotra
Jackets Editorial Coordinator Priyanka Sharma
Senior DTP Designer Vishal Bhatia
DTP Designers Rakesh Kumar, Nand Kishor Acharya
Project Picture Researcher Aditya Katyal
Picture Research Manager Taiyaba Khatoon
Pre-Production Manager Balwant Singh
Production Manager Pankaj Sharma
Editorial Head Glenda Fernandes
Design Head Malavika Talukder

First American Edition, 2021
Published in the United States by DK Publishing
1450 Broadway, Suite 801, New York, NY 10018

21 22 23 24 25 10 9 8 7 6 5 4 3 2 1
001-322067-Aug/2021

Published in Great Britain by Dorling Kindersley Limited

A catalog record for this book is available from the Library of Congress.
ISBN: 978-0-7440-2922-2

DK books are available at special discounts when purchased in bulk for sales promotions, premiums, fund-raising, or educational use. For details, contact: DK Publishing Special Markets, 1450 Broadway, Suite 801, New York, NY 10018
SpecialSales@dk.com

Printed and bound in the UAE

For the curious

CONSULTANTS

Peter Chrisp is a historian with a particular interest in the ancient world. He has written more than 90 books, many for DK, including *Ancient Greece*, *Ancient Rome*, and *Alexander the Great: Legend of a Warrior King*.

Amy Fuller is a historian of colonial Mexico and senior lecturer at Nottingham Trent University. Her research interests include narratives of conquest and conversion, religious drama, festivals, and folklore. Her first book was on Sor Juana Inés de la Cruz, and she has written and presented for both academic and popular audiences; appearing at history festivals and on the radio.

Philip Parker is a historian with wide-ranging interests, from the late Roman city, to the Viking establishment of trading settlements, and the history of world trade. He has been a contributor and consultant for numerous DK titles and is the author of *The A–Z History of London*.

Reza Masoudi Nejad is a research associate at SOAS University of London (The School of Oriental and African Studies). He is an urbanist with a cross-disciplinary background focused on urban history and transformation, crowds and protests, urban violence and conciliation, and religious rituals in urban context. He received his PhD from the Bartlett School of Built Environment, UCL. He is the author of *The Rite of Urban Passage*.

CONTRIBUTORS

Andrew Humphreys
Tharik Hussain
Anirban Mahapatra
Rebecca Milner
Brendan Sainsbury
Philip Parker
Phillip Tang
Philip Wilkinson
Nicola Williams

CHAPTER 1

CENTERS OF ANCIENT AND LOST CIVILIZATIONS

CHAPTER 2

GREAT RIVER CITIES

CONTENTS

CHAPTER 3

MARITIME CITIES

CHAPTER 4

CITIES BY DESIGN

CHAPTER 5

MODERN METROPOLISES

Page 1 Map of Paris showing the city walls, 1580
Page 2 The ancient ruins of the Acropolis, Athens, including the Parthenon and the Theatre of Dionysus
Pages 4–5 Sydney Opera House and Harbour Bridge
Page 6 Poster for Trans World Airlines featuring San Francisco's cable cars, 1950s

Introduction

Cities have been at the heart of human life since their first appearance 7,000 years ago. These centers of political, economic, and cultural power continue to shape the world we live in today.

△ LAW CODE OF UR-NAMMU
This c. 2100 BCE cuneiform tablet from Ur contains the world's oldest surviving law code. Clauses dealing with enslaved people seeking freedom and disputes over irrigation demonstrate the preoccupations of the rulers of the first cities.

Cities are the engines of human history. Within them, great buildings and artistic movements have arisen, vital scientific discoveries and fortunes have been made, and political leaders have emerged who went on to wage wars and win empires. All these achievements have been fueled by the labor, grit, and ingenuity of the ever-growing ranks of city-dwellers.

Today, around 55 percent of us live in urban areas. The very largest, such as Tokyo, New Delhi, and Shanghai, have over 20 million inhabitants—more than the entire global population in 5000 BCE. At that point, humanity had only just started its journey from small, widely dispersed groups of hunter-gatherers to the global megacities of today.

Agriculture and the first cities

Agriculture first developed in a crescent of fertile land centered on Mesopotamia around 10,000 BCE. People in South Asia, China, parts of Africa, and the Americas subsequently discovered this transformative practice, which allowed areas to support larger populations and communities to produce a surplus of food beyond their immediate needs. It also made the Neolithic peoples who practiced it less mobile, as they were now tied to tending and defending their fields. Specialists began to appear, such as craftsmen who made pottery for the storage of agricultural produce and jewelery from bone, wood, stone, or horn for the richer classes who were emerging in the increasingly sophisticated villages.

By around 7000 BCE, the villages had begun to turn into towns, such as Çatalhöyük, in what is now southern Turkey. Its population of around 5,000 lived in tightly packed mud-brick houses; followed a religion that centered on a bull cult and the veneration of the dead; and made a living from growing wheat and barley, herding sheep, and trading in obsidian obtained from a nearby volcano.

Some 930 miles (1,500 km) to the east, by around 4500 BCE, true cities were emerging. The fertile land of Mesopotamia between the Tigris and Euphrates Rivers, in modern-day Iraq, supported a thriving agricultural population. The need to construct irrigation ditches to transport water from the great rivers and their tributaries to the fields encouraged large-scale cooperation. Some places, particularly those that were the centers of cults for local gods, became the bases for rulers who came to monopolize the distribution of the agricultural surplus.

▽ ROYAL STANDARD OF UR
This panel, called "Peace," shows the wealth of a king (top row, third from left) as he receives fish and other agricultural goods, while lyre-players entertain him. It was made around 2500 BCE.

Specialist warriors defended the surplus and preyed on neighboring groups. Over time, the rulers grew powerful enough to erect the first monumental buildings—temples and palaces—and the latter became centers for the increasingly complex business of civic administration. Scribes employed the newly invented technique of writing to create archives documenting royal decrees. They also recorded the transactions that brought goods to an urban population that no longer farmed the land.

Uruk, established around 4500 BCE, was the first of the Mesopotamian cities, but it was surpassed by Ur, founded about five centuries later, which grew to be the most powerful of a network of city-states. Ur's 50,000 people were ruled by dynasties whose sway extended as far as modern Syria and Iran. Its merchants sailed to the south in search of wood and copper for the growing city's needs. They reached as far as Dilmun (modern Bahrain) and may have made contact with another early center of urban civilization, the Indus Valley culture, whose cities lay in modern-day Pakistan and northwest India. Unlike their Mesopotamian counterparts, Indus Valley cities such as Mohenjo-Daro and Harappa, founded around 2500 BCE, did not appear to build lavish palaces or wage war upon each other, but they did possess sophisticated sewage systems, the earliest known example of such sanitation, and a sign that rulers were for the first time becoming concerned about the health of their subjects.

Ur was the world's largest city for about 1,000 years, until it was overtaken by Mari in Syria around 2500 BCE.

▽ THE GREAT ENCLOSURE
This monumental structure was the centerpiece of Great Zimbabwe, one of sub-Saharan Africa's greatest premodern cities. Between the 11th and 15th centuries CE, its rulers grew rich on gold and ivory.

Grid-plan cities

△ Founded as a military colony by Trajan around 100 CE, Timgad, in modern Algeria, has a classic Roman grid, its *cardo* and *decumanus* forming a clear T (center).

◁ This postcard shows Timgad's *decumanus maximus*, with the triumphal Arch of Trajan at its western end.

The very earliest cities were largely unplanned, their shape dictated by chance, royal whim, or the contours of the land. Regular grid patterns of rectangular blocks were developed first by the Greek city-states, and were reputedly invented by the architect Hippodamus of Miletus in the 5th century CE. The Romans laid out new settlements throughout their empire based on Hippodamus's principles and on the regular grid plan of the camps made by legionaries each night, with two central spines, the *decumanus maximus* (running east–west) and the *cardo maximus* (north–south). Grid patterns were also common in Chinese cities such as Xi'an, and, though they fell into disuse in the chaotic sprawl of medieval European cities, they were revived in the modern era. Major North American cities such as New York, Chicago, and Washington, D.C., were laid out on a grid, while in planned cities such as Brasília, grids helped zone cities in an orderly fashion into business, retail, leisure, and residential districts. Such arrangements often helped the freer flow of traffic, but sometimes lacked the aesthetic appeal of older, less regular centers.

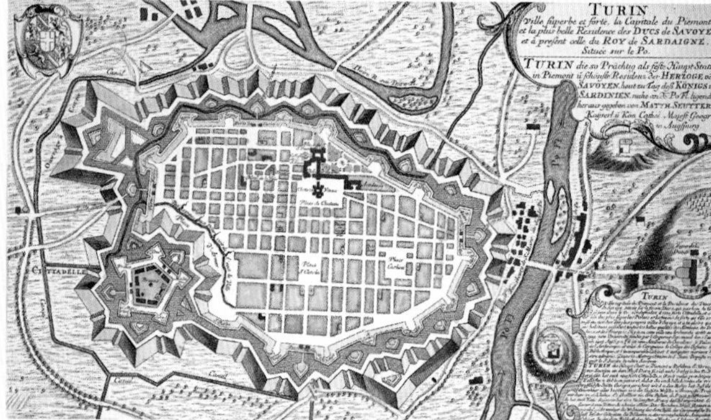

◁ Urban grids were less common in the Middle Ages but, as this 1720 plan of Turin by German cartographer Matthaeus Seutter shows, some northern Italian cities retained their Roman pattern.

A world of ancient cities

Although cities provided protection for their inhabitants, and an environment in which crafts could flourish and goods be traded, not all areas of the world were suitable for early urban growth. In some, the climate was too harsh or the soil not fertile enough to permit the agriculture necessary to support a higher population; in others, there was a lack of building materials. Even where cities did take root, other qualities were needed for them to truly thrive: an advantageous position astride trade routes, strong rulers who could guarantee stability, and protection from marauders were all prerequisites.

Such advantages enabled the rise of China's first cities, in the fertile Yellow River Valley, first at Erlitou around 2000 BCE and then, by 1500 BCE, at larger urban centers such as Anyang and Luoyang, which became the capitals of the earliest Chinese dynasties. By then, Egypt's first cities were almost a millennium old. They owed their existence, just as in Mesopotamia, China, and the Indus Valley, to a great river. The "gift of the Nile" allowed the cities of the pharaohs, such as Memphis and Karnak, to prosper. More ceremonial complexes than population centers—dotted with temples such as the pillared Hypostyle Hall of Amun-Re at Karnak—Egypt's cities found an echo in those of Mesoamerica, such as Teotihuacan, with its massive pyramids of the sun and moon at either end of a vast ceremonial way.

By the 1st century CE, urbanization had spread to most regions of the globe: the history of South America's cities began with the Caral-Supe complex in modern-day Peru around 3500 BCE, while Crete became the site of Minoan palace-cities around 2000 BCE. A thousand years later, new city-states appeared on the mainland. One of these, Athens, developed the concept of citizenship and became the earliest functioning democracy.

Imperial cities

As city-states grew into kingdoms and then empires, a new age of larger urban centers began. The city of Rome, whose empire stretched from Europe's far north to the deserts of North Africa, reached a population of around a million at the height of its power in the 1st century CE. The taxation revenues it extracted funded huge building projects such as the Colosseum, while its main port at Ostia brought in vast quantities of grain and wine for its people.

Rome was a maritime city, a military hub, and a cultural and scientific powerhouse. Its poets, playwrights, orators, and doctors would be remembered for centuries, and it endures as a modern capital. Other imperial cities fared less well. The Maya cities of Mesoamerica, such as Tikal and Palenque, were abandoned in the 9th century, probably because their growing populations had stretched the fragile rainforest environment beyond its capacity to regenerate. The trading port of Palmyra in modern-day Syria, with its marble colonnaded streets, dwindled into insignificance from the 4th century, while the temple-city of Angkor in Cambodia, which was largely abandoned in the 15th century, fell victim to shifts in political power and outside raiders. These magnificent metropolises became "lost cities," rediscovered by outsiders centuries later, their brooding ruins testament to once-mighty civilizations.

Trade and the Middle Ages

The collapse of a series of great empires—the Roman, Han Chinese, Sassanian Persian, and Indian Gupta—between the 3rd and 7th centuries did not lead to an end of urbanism. Although cities diminished in size or in some cases disappeared, the 9th and 10th centuries witnessed a fresh urban age, particularly in Europe, as new states began to consolidate and trade revived. Trading cities that escaped the stifling clutch of ambitious monarchs experimented with developing their own political institutions and plowed the profits from their trade back into the city. The Italian maritime republics of Pisa, Genoa, and above all Venice, were most successful, and by the 13th century the Venetians had acquired an extensive maritime empire in the eastern Mediterranean.

Royal and imperial capitals, such as Paris, Stockholm, Xi'an, and Kyoto prospered, too. The immense wealth brought in by taxation and trade allowed the building of new palaces and public buildings such as temples and theaters, so that they began to rival the great monumental cities of the ancient world. By 1650, the population of China's capital, Beijing, stood at 500,000, exceeding those of its nearest European rivals, Paris and London. But both those cities, and Amsterdam, were on the cusp of acquiring large maritime empires, fueled by trade across the Atlantic and into Asia, in spices, textiles, and enslaved people.

> "Every **seaman** ... is **not only a navigator**, but a **merchant** and also a **soldier**."
>
> SIR WILLIAM PETTY, ENGLISH ECONOMIST, MID-17TH CENTURY

▽ **HANSEATIC PORT**
This late-15th-century manuscript shows merchants waiting to receive ships docking in the harbor of Hamburg. The city was a leading member of the Hanseatic League, which united ports around the Baltic Sea in a mutually supporting network that traded in fish, grain, textiles, and luxury goods.

◁ *BRIDGE TOWER*, 1929
Glenn Coleman's oil painting shows John Roebling's innovative Brooklyn Bridge, which opened in 1883, linking Manhattan and Brooklyn across New York's East River.

> The **skyscraper** and the **20th century** are **synonymous;** the **tall building** is the **landmark of our age.**
>
> ADA LOUISE HUXTABLE, ARCHITECTURE CRITIC, 1982

The great age of trading cities gathered pace in the 18th century, with maritime empires supplying produce that the cities could not provide for themselves. A European agricultural revolution, with the discovery of new forms of crop rotation, increased productivity, but it was the Industrial Revolution that really accelerated progress. Factories powered by James Watts's steam engines (first patented in 1769) provided work for rural laborers, who streamed into cities. London's population reached a million in 1801, and three million by 1860. Areas with access to commodities such as iron or coal, or which could be linked by canals or the newly invented railroads, became attractive sites for cities. Those on steamship routes, like Cape Town, Mumbai, Buenos Aires, or Hong Kong, became part of a new network of global cities.

New facilities for growing cities

Yet such helter-skelter development was not without cost. Growth gave rise to health and social problems as laborers crowded into unsanitary slums and crime rates increased. Diseases such as cholera became rife, with outbreaks sweeping across London, Tokyo, Chicago, and many other cities during the 19th century. City authorities began to provide public facilities such as sewage systems, street lighting, and transit systems (the London Underground opened in 1863, the New York Subway in 1904).

The social structure of cities changed, too, with a rising middle class demanding better housing and a share in political power. Workers organized into labor unions and lobbied for improved conditions in factories, education for their children, and the right to vote. Historically, cities' growth had often been held back by high death rates. Better conditions meant lower mortality, and as migrants flocked to cities such as New York and Buenos Aires, further expansion ensued.

The rise of the megacity

The first third of the 20th century saw a golden age of urban architecture in which planners such as the Swiss-French Le Corbusier sought to reinvent the city in the age of Modernism (see box). New civic and corporate buildings in the geometric Art Deco style exemplified by New York's Empire State Building appeared in Napier in New Zealand, Shanghai, and Moscow. Cities grew upward, too. New York's Flatiron Building had been erected in 1902, and skyscrapers soon became a familiar feature of many urban skylines, breaching 1,300 ft (400 m) by the 1970s. Yet cities were not utopias. After World War II, problems of pollution, overcrowding, and aging infrastructure led to a flight from the

▷ WORLD'S TALLEST
At 2,717 ft (828 m), the Burj Khalifa has been the world's tallest building since its 2009 completion. Its 160 stories tower over a surging city: Dubai's population has increased tenfold since 1980.

The ideal city

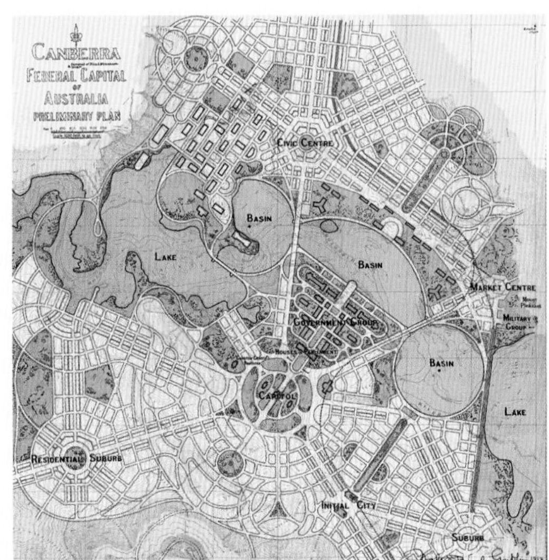

△ Walter Burley Griffin's 1913 plan for Canberra incorporated a string of lakes with geometrically laid out districts.

◁ Le Corbusier, here examining a city model, championed an urban vision in which high-rise blocks combined with abundant green space.

People have long dreamed of the ideal city. Greek philosophers such as Plato wrote about how it might be governed, while Chinese and Southeast Asian rulers laid out their capitals to mirror the heavens. In 1516, the English statesman Sir Thomas More's book *Utopia* provided a blueprint for a perfect city, and in 1593 the Venetian state constructed Palmanova, an elegant, star-shaped town in northeast Italy. Philanthropic ideals of equal opportunity for all citizens gave new vigor to the idea in the 19th century, leading to the construction of Garden Cities such as Letchworth, in England, and the laying out of Adelaide in Australia in 1836 on a grid plan surrounded by parkland. The theories of Modernist architects such as Le Corbusier that cities should be organized in a practical manner were implemented in places such as Chandigarh in India in the 1950s, which was divided into 47 self-contained sectors, each with its own educational, health, and retail facilities, separated by green spaces. Since then, planned capitals such as Abuja in Nigeria and Abu Dhabi in the UAE have risen, as the search for an ideal city that will combine beauty, utility, and livability continues. So far, none has quite reached the perfection its designers imagined.

> "The **problem** ... is this: how to make **our Garden City** experiment the **stepping stone** to a **higher and better** form of **industrial life.**
>
> EBENEZER HOWARD, *THE GARDEN CITIES OF TO-MORROW*, 1902

center and the hollowing out of some cities in Europe and North America, as their centers decayed. By contrast, in industrializing countries, many of them newly independent nations in Africa and Asia, rapid levels of population growth led to a drift into cities from agricultural areas. By 2020, the population of Lagos in Nigeria had reached 14 million.

While urban areas such as London and Los Angeles retain their role as 21st-century global cities, plugged into an increasingly interconnected world, they face new rivals. Some, such as Singapore or Beijing, enjoy the benefits of modern infrastructure. Other cities, like the DRC's capital of Kinshasa, have grown so fast that the residents of the informal, often poorly planned settlements that have sprung up in the suburbs far outnumber those in the official core.

Contemporary cities are as diverse as their predecessors. They are places of pilgrimage, entertainment hubs, industrial centers, and shipping ports. Cities like newly built Naypyidaw, Myanmar's capital since 2005, have an air of the ancient ceremonial complexes; others, such as Frankfurt and New York, serve as dynamic financial centers; and others still, such as Xi'an and Mumbai, have seen their populations soar as industry has replaced agriculture as the primary driver of prosperity.

The future of the city

Cities continue to reinvent themselves. In the last few decades, many have worked to reduce pollution and create appealing modern spaces by restricting polluting vehicles, encouraging energy-efficient buildings, and planting trees. In 2019, another impetus for change came in the form of COVID-19, which saw retail centers empty, businesses send workers home, and some question whether crowded cities were a safe environment. Yet cities have responded to changing circumstances in the past. Through the first kingdoms of Mesopotamia, global expansion, and the Industrial Revolution, they have evolved to remain at the heart of politics, economics, and culture. The history of the world is very much a history of great cities, and whatever future we build, these sites of trade, creativity, and transformation are likely to be at the heart of it.

It is predicted that by 2030 there will be 43 megacities with populations over 10 million.

Rome p.16

Athens p.24

Istanbul p.30

Tikal p.74

Damascus
Babylon
Leptis Magna
Timbuktu
Ephesus
Luxor
Petra
Great Zimbabwe
Lalibela

Mexico City p.66

Cusco p.78

Jerusalem p.36

Persepolis p.44

CHAPTER 1
CENTERS OF ANCIENT AND LOST CIVILIZATIONS

Delhi p.48

Xi'an p.60

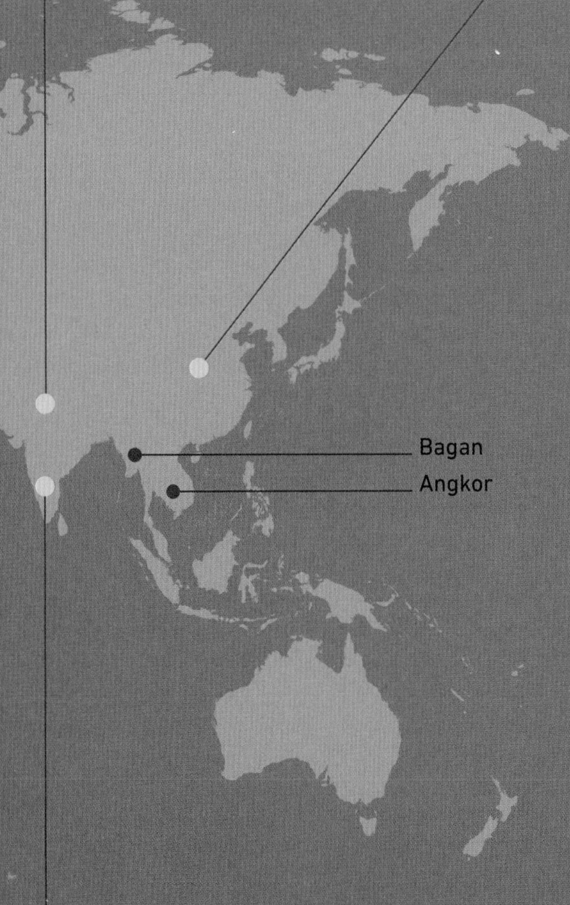

Hampi p.56

Rome

ETERNAL CITY

From a tiny hilltop settlement, Rome evolved to be capital of a great empire, seat of the Catholic Church, and a treasure trove of Western art.

Roman mythology credits the founding of Rome to the twin sons of Mars, Romulus and Remus, who were raised by a she-wolf after being discovered at the foot of the Palatine Hill. One of a group of seven hills, the Palatine was the site of a small settlement from around 1000 BCE. Myth notwithstanding, the location had clear advantages, being close to the sea and lying alongside the navigable Tiber River. Legend has it that Romulus became the first of seven kings, under whose rule local neighboring tribes gradually merged. Many of Rome's most venerable institutions were introduced under these kings, such as the Senate—the city's governing assembly, initially comprising 100 men—and the Cloaca Maxima, one of the world's first sewer systems.

Despite its diminutive size, ancient Rome became a powerful force, but was riven by social disputes. The last king, the Etruscan Tarquinius Superbus, was driven out in 509 BCE and a republic established, governed by two annually elected consuls. By the 2nd century BCE, Rome's armies had conquered the whole of Italy and territory beyond, while the city weathered a sack by the Gauls and came close to conquest by the Carthaginian General Hannibal. Wealth from territorial expansion funded public works, such as stone temples and baths, while housing for the growing populace colonized the hillsides and valleys.

VIEW OF THE COLOSSEUM, 1735 ▷
This painting by Giovanni Paolo Panini shows the Colosseum and the nearby Forum, including the Arch of Constantine, which was built in 312 CE to celebrate Emperor Constantine's victory over his rival Maxentius.

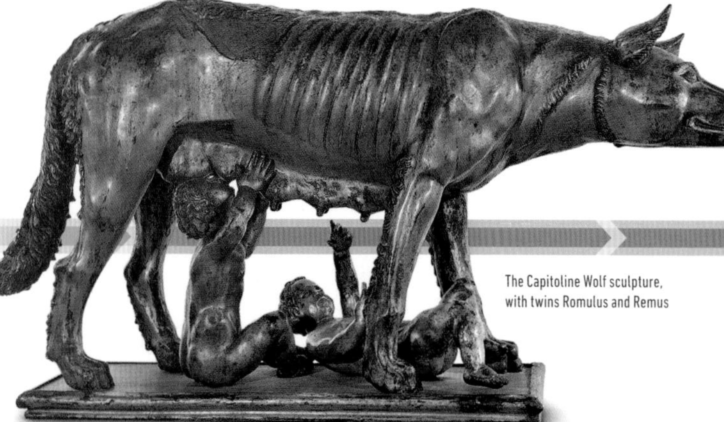

The Capitoline Wolf sculpture, with twins Romulus and Remus

753 BCE According to legend, Rome is founded on one of seven hills on April 21 by Romulus, who becomes its first king.

c. 650 BCE The Curia Hostilia is built—the first meeting place for the Senate, the council of elders that supervises Rome's government.

509 BCE King Tarquinius Superbus is overthrown and Rome becomes a republic.

390 BCE Rome is sacked by invading Gauls of the Senones tribe; when geese alert the soldiers, the garrison on the Capitoline Hill is saved.

> When falls **the Coliseum**, **Rome shall fall**;
> And when **Rome falls—the World**.

LORD BYRON, *CHILDE HAROLD'S PILGRIMAGE*, 1818

287 BCE The final secession of the plebeians, when Rome's poorer citizens threaten to abandon the city, leads to more political influence for them.

60–53 BCE The first triumvirate between Julius Caesar, Gnaeus Pompeius, and Marcus Crassus takes power in Rome, but breaks down into civil war.

In 45 BCE, Julius Caesar gave a feast in the Forum which was said to have been attended by 22,000 guests.

44 BCE Having won the civil war, Julius Caesar becomes dictator of Rome, but is killed by assassins who fear he might declare himself king.

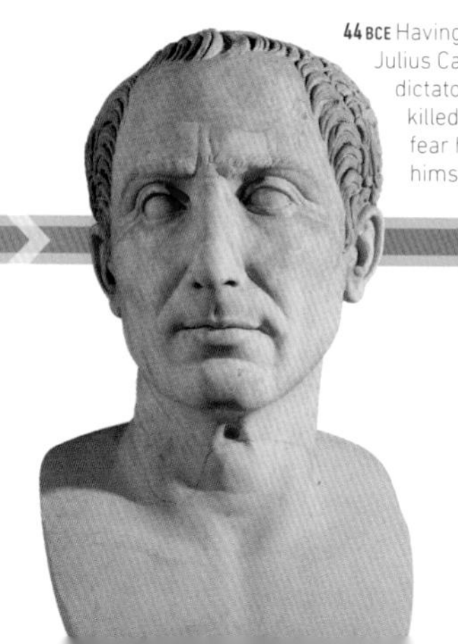

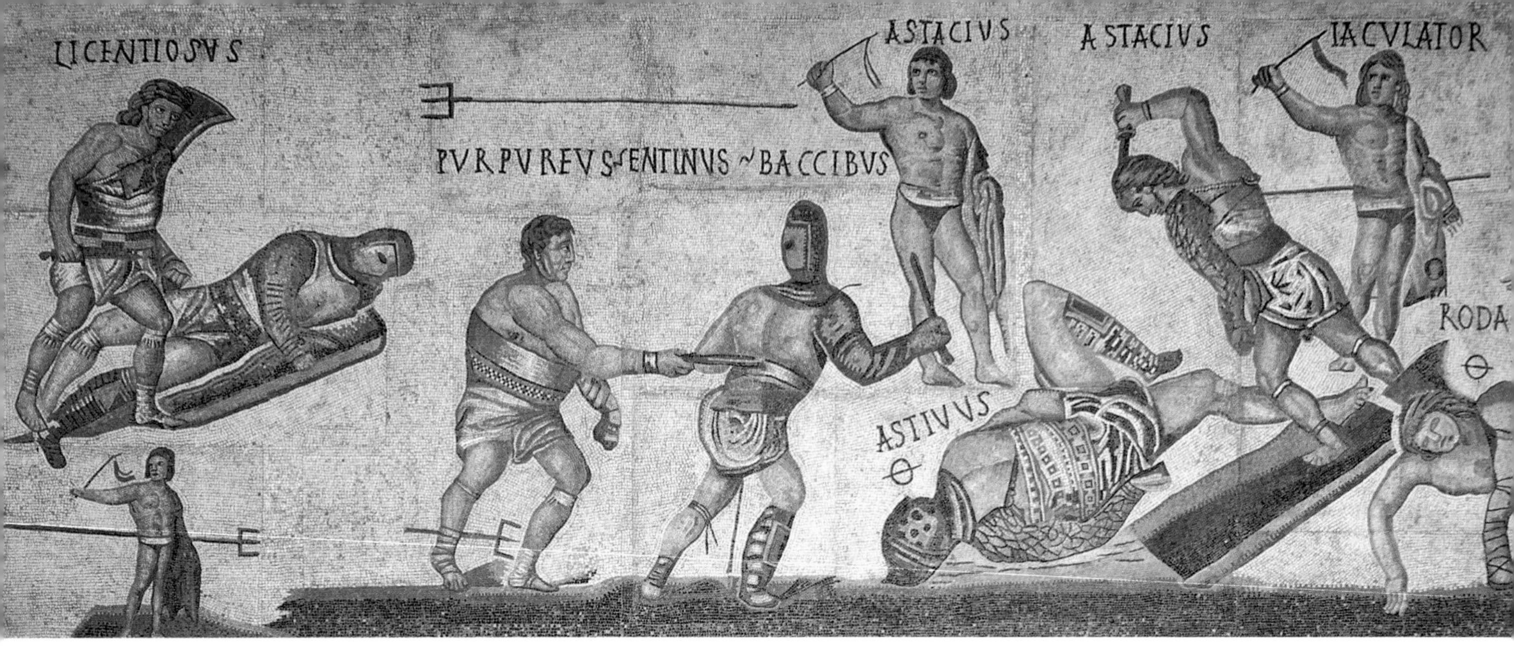

△ GLADIATORS
This 4th-century mosaic shows combat between a variety of types of gladiator, including the *retiarius*, who fought with a net and trident, and the *murmillo*, who carried a short sword and shield, and wore a helmet with a grille.

Rise of the Roman Empire

As a republic, Rome's population reached a million in the 1st century BCE, making it the largest city in the world. Its richer citizens dwelt in lavish villas on the surrounding hills, staffed by enslaved people and adorned with mosaics and frescoes. The poor lived in *insulae*, rickety apartment blocks, which were susceptible to frequent fires. Their ground floors housed merchants' stalls or *thermopolia*, taverns selling hot food and wine.

Rome's political scene was rambunctious, with elections for the consulship sparking street battles. Eventually, the conflict degenerated into civil war, but the assassination of the victor, Julius Caesar, on the steps of the Senate House in 44 BCE led to another spasm of violence. Caesar's great-nephew Octavian won this second civil war and put an end to both the bloodbath and the republic, having himself declared Emperor Augustus. The Roman Empire was born, with Rome as its capital. Augustus had grandiose ambitions, building a new forum, temples, and baths.

During the imperial period, Rome's political turmoil was tamed, but to keep its teeming population in check the emperors instituted the *annona*, a grain dole handed out to 200,000 poorer residents. They also held extravagant games in the Colosseum, an arena where up to 50,000 spectators could watch gladiatorial combats and organized hunts of wild beasts. In terms of disposition and aptitude, the emperors varied considerably. Caligula, who ruled from 37 to 41 CE, was capricious and cruel—fond of dressing up as a god, he executed or exiled many of those close to him—while Nero famously did nothing as Rome blazed in a great fire in 64 CE, pleased at the prospect of rebuilding its center. Trajan, by contrast, conquered Dacia (encompassing parts of present-day Romania, Hungary, and Serbia) and used the spoils to build a new forum and triumphal column.

In the late 3rd century, Emperor Aurelian built a wall to protect Rome from the threat of barbarian invasion. By this point, the city's population had dwindled, while civil wars raged once again and Mediolanum (Milan) took precedence over Rome. Emperor Constantine gave new hope, reuniting the empire and ending the persecution of Christians.

27 BCE Octavian, great-nephew of Julius Caesar, becomes the first Roman emperor, taking the name Augustus.

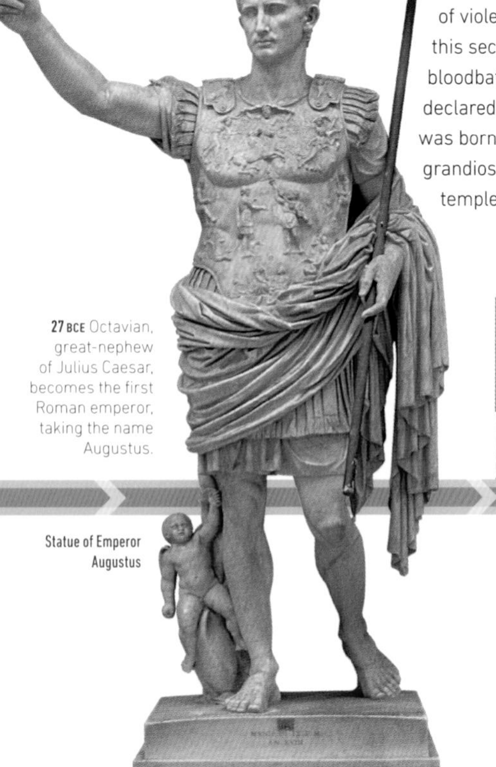
Statue of Emperor Augustus

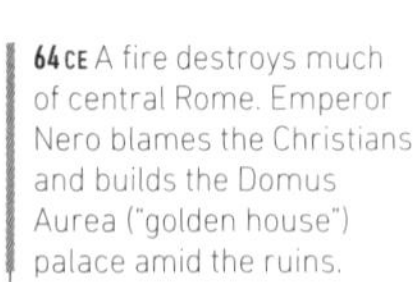
64 CE A fire destroys much of central Rome. Emperor Nero blames the Christians and builds the Domus Aurea ("golden house") palace amid the ruins.

80 Emperor Titus completes the Colosseum, which is inaugurated with gladiatorial games lasting over 100 days.

110 Trajan's conquest of Dacia is celebrated with a huge column in his forum showing episodes from the campaign.

Panel from Trajan's Column

125 The Pantheon temple, which still boasts the world's largest unsupported concrete dome, is remodeled under Emperor Hadrian.

The Roman Forum

△ Situated in the Forum, the Umbilicus Urbis Romae was the symbolic center of ancient Rome, from and to which all distances were measured. It was also said to mark an entrance into the Underworld.

> I found **Rome a city of bricks** and left it a **city of marble**.
>
> EMPEROR AUGUSTUS, QUOTED IN *THE TWELVE CAESARS*, 121 CE

Serving as market; meeting place; and administrative, legal, and political center, the Forum was the heart of Rome from its first development in the 6th century BCE. The oldest part, the Forum Romanum, which lay between the Palatine and Capitoline hills, contained the Curia or Senate House, the Temple of Saturn (which acted as the state treasury), and the House of the Vestal Virgins. During the late republic, new buildings were added, including several *basilicas* (aisled meeting halls) and the *tabularium* (record office). Later rulers made more additions—Emperor Augustus, for example, built a temple in 29 BCE to mark the spot where Julius Caesar was cremated. At the Forum's edges, the emperors Titus, Constantine, and Septimius Severus constructed triumphal arches to celebrate their victories in battle. During the Middle Ages, several structures survived by being converted into churches, but the rebuilding of Rome during the Renaissance led to the Forum being used as a stone quarry and much of it fell into ruins.

△ This 19th-century scene presents an idealized view of the temples, *basilicas*, and statues of the Forum.

▷ A postcard showing the ruins of the 5th-century BCE Temple of Saturn, which served as the state treasury.

313 Having defeated Maxentius at the Milvian Bridge outside Rome, Emperor Constantine I legalizes Christianity.

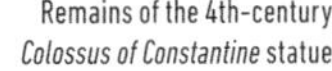
Remains of the 4th-century *Colossus of Constantine* statue

271 In response to a barbarian invasion of Italy, Emperor Aurelian orders the building of a 12-mile (19-km) wall to defend Rome.

402 Emperor Honorius moves the imperial capital from Rome to Ravenna.

410 Rome is sacked by the Gothic chieftain Alaric (and then in 455 by the Vandal King Gaiseric), sealing its decline.

△ SAN PAOLO FUORI LE MURA APSE
The 13th-century mosaic in San Paolo fuori le Mura, which survived a disastrous fire in 1823, shows Jesus Christ flanked by apostles. A diminutive figure of Pope Honorius III, who commissioned the work, crouches at Christ's feet.

Fall of the empire—Rome's dark ages

Yet this new dawn proved a twilight, as Rome was sacked successively by Goths and then Vandals. Most of its Christian churches (built under Emperor Constantine's patronage), however, were spared damage. The deposition of the last Roman emperor, Romulus Augustulus, by his Germanic army-chief in 476 CE left the city much-diminished. Italy's new Ostrogothic rulers used Ravenna as their capital. Crumbling, malaria-ridden, and depleted, Rome was saved only by the recognition of the bishops of Rome as popes, leaders of the Roman Catholic Church. Emperors in the Byzantine Empire—the remaining, eastern half of the Roman Empire—tried to reestablish Roman control in the West, but the results were often disastrous for Rome, with the city coming under siege repeatedly during the 6th century. It was the Roman Catholic Church that held most authority over Rome for the next 200 years, with Pope Gregory I paving the way by feeding the hungry and repairing the city's water supply. The threat of foreign invasion still lingered, leading the papacy to forge an alliance with the Franks. Large swathes of central Italy were granted to the papacy by the Franks and, in Rome in 800 CE, Frankish ruler Charlemagne was crowned Holy Roman Emperor by Pope Leo III.

Struggles between these two new powers—the Holy Roman Empire and the Papal States—defined life in Rome for centuries to come, with both aristocratic feuds and military clashes. Rome acquired its first university in 1303, but the transfer of the papal seat for nearly 70 years to Avignon, and a subsequent schism between rival popes, sapped the city's vitality. An earthquake in 1348 wrought so much destruction that it seemed that Rome was doomed.

Renaissance revival

The city's prospects changed during the Renaissance, from the 15th century. Trade had revived and patrons, both in the Roman Catholic Church and among rich nobles, sponsored artists and scholars. Old Roman manuscripts were unearthed and studied, and new artistic techniques flourished. Churches were restored and popes such as Julius II funded grand ecclesiastical buildings and artworks, notably a new St. Peter's Basilica and the frescoes of the Sistine Chapel, painted by Michelangelo over four back-breaking years. The city's jumbled maze of medieval streets was replaced by impressive avenues, such as the Via Giulia.

Religious and dynastic wars broke out in the early 16th century and ravaged Italy. In 1527, an army in the employ of the Holy Roman Emperor Charles V sacked Rome, the first

Ostrogothic brooch, c. 500

536 The Eastern Roman General Belisarius recaptures Rome for the Roman Empire, ending rule by the Ostrogoths.

590–604 Pope Gregory I strengthens the papacy and establishes its political control over Rome.

800 The Frankish ruler Charlemagne is crowned Holy Roman Emperor in St. Peter's Basilica.

A fleet of Arab pirates managed to sail up the Tiber in 846 CE and plunder St. Peter's Basilica and San Paolo fuori le Mura.

1108 The basilica of San Clemente is rebuilt on the site of an early medieval church and a Roman temple to Mithras.

1144 Rome becomes an independent commune, beginning a period of dominance by rival aristocratic families.

◁ SISTINE CHAPEL
Michelangelo's fresco on the Sistine Chapel ceiling shows God stretching out to touch the hand of the newly created Adam.

▽ ST. PETER'S PLAN
This 1569 engraving by Etienne Dupérac shows Michelangelo's design for a hemispherical dome for St. Peter's.

> "No one who has not seen the **Sistine Chapel** can have a clear idea of what **a human being can achieve**.
>
> JOHANN WOLFGANG VON GOETHE, 1786

time the city had suffered such a fate for nearly a thousand years. The Counter-Reformation saw ecclesiastical reforms and Rome adorned with buildings in the lavish and dramatic Baroque style. Particularly innovative were master architect Borromini and architect and sculptor Bernini, who designed the spectacular *baldacchino*, a bronze canopy that is the centerpiece of St. Peter's Basilica. Under Pope Sixtus V in the 1580s, streets were cleaned, old aqueducts restored, and monumental Egyptian obelisks erected in public spaces, including St. Peter's Square.

Despite the political and religious turmoil of the preceding two centuries, Rome entered the 1700s in a more confident mode. The Baroque style evolved in its final flourish into Rococo, which featured ornate decoration, as displayed in the extravagant, curved frontage of the Church of Santa Maria Maddalena near the Pantheon. Rome welcomed magnificent new secular monuments, such as the throng of marble sea creatures in the Trevi Fountain, completed in the 1760s and later beloved of gelato-eating and coin-tossing tourists.

The original St. Peter's Basilica was built around the shrine marking the burial place of the apostle Peter.

1347 A revolution led by Cola di Rienzo overthrows papal power but fails in its attempt to unify Italy.

1506 Work begins on the new basilica of St. Peter's, designed by Donato Bramante, but only finally completed and consecrated in 1626.

1527 Rome is sacked by the troops of Holy Roman Emperor Charles V.

1600 The philosopher and former Dominican friar Giordano Bruno is convicted of heresy and burned alive in the Campo dei Fiori.

The Sack of Rome by Pieter Bruegel the Elder, 16th century

◁ *BRITISH GENTLEMEN IN ROME*, c. 1750
This painting of the English School shows six aristocratic visitors resting in the shadow of the Colosseum, a customary stop on the Grand Tour, undertaken to enhance their education.

The Capitoline Museums, opened by Pope Clement XII in 1734, hold the world's oldest public art collection.

The Spanish Steps, another gathering place for the fashionable and rootless, was opened in 1725 and admired by a new breed of visitors. "Grand Tourists"—young men from northern Europe, such as the Scottish diarist James Boswell—came to admire the remains of the classical past and the newer trove of artistic and architectural riches that the Renaissance had bequeathed to Rome. The city even acquired its own Protestant cemetery to receive the mortal remains of foreigners who expired there, such as the English Romantic poet John Keats.

Rome and the Risorgimento

Yet beneath Rome's ever more gilded facade, resentment seethed against the papacy's millennium-long rule. Occupation by Revolutionary France between 1798 and 1814 inspired a generation of Italian nationalists such as Giuseppe Mazzini and the flamboyant Giuseppe Garibaldi, whose red-coated troops took to the barricades during an uprising in 1849, resulting in an independent Roman Republic being declared. It lasted barely a year before being ousted by the French—their own monarchy restored—leaving liberals and nationalists to plot fruitlessly in establishments such as the Caffè Greco on Via dei Condotti.

In the final years of papal rule, Rome slowly modernized, as street lighting arrived and the first train left the central station in 1860. Yet the popes stubbornly refused to come to terms with the movement campaigning for the unification of Italy, the Risorgimento. When a united Kingdom of Italy was declared in 1861, under King Vittorio Emmanuel II, most of the Papal States were included, but not Rome. Garibaldi led two unsuccessful attempts to capture the city before troops of the royal government breached the Aurelian Walls in 1870. After a token resistance by the Swiss Guard, the papacy's diminutive army, a white flag was hauled up to the cupola of St. Peter's and the Pope surrendered.

Italy was now free from papal rule, though the popes continued to occupy the tiny enclave of the Vatican. To house the army of bureaucrats who descended on the new capital, the government sequestered palaces for its offices. It also commissioned the Vittoriano, an extravagant, white-marble homage to the royal liberator of Italy—now a busy traffic island in the Piazza Venezia. Meanwhile, interest in the past was on the rise, with the first scientific excavations of the Colosseum conducted in the 1870s.

The Fascist era

Rome's population tripled in its first half-century of freedom to 650,000 in 1921. The rural poor who came in search of a better life, but found instead only poverty and urban squalor,

1762 The Trevi Fountain is completed by Giuseppe Panini, 30 years after Nicola Salvi began work on it.

1798 The French under Napoleon capture Rome and declare it a republic.

1849 A nationalist uprising centered on Rome, jointly led by Giuseppe Garibaldi, declares a republic, but papal rule is soon restored.

1871 Rome is taken by the forces of newly unified Italy and becomes its capital.

Caffè Greco counted among its clientele artistic and intellectual grandees such as Charles Dickens, Franz Liszt, and Henry James.

1893 Babington's Tea Room opens near the Spanish Steps to cater for Rome's British visitors.

LA DOLCE VITA, 1960 ▷
In this famous scene from Federico Fellini's masterpiece of Roman life, actors Marcello Mastroianni and Anita Ekberg wade into the moonlit Trevi Fountain.

"There is **no end**. There is **no beginning**. There is only the **infinite passion of life**.

FEDERICO FELLINI, DIRECTOR OF *LA DOLCE VITA*, 1976

proved a captive audience for Benito Mussolini's Fascist movement, which promised a return to the glory days of ancient Rome. His March on Rome, flanked by black-shirted supporters, began a 20-year experiment that ended in the disaster of World War II. Known as Il Duce ("the leader"), Mussolini planned to sweep away Rome's medieval center and replace it with a streetscape of modern skyscrapers. Fortunately his rhetoric outpaced reality and he confined himself to draining the outlying Pontine Marshes, finally solving Rome's malaria problem, and gifting the city a collection of muscular architecture, including EUR, a new suburb which featured Fascist takes on Classical style, including the Palazzo della Civiltà Italiana, a bizarrely square version of the Colosseum.

La Dolce Vita

Rome was declared an "open city" in 1943 and so escaped the wholesale destruction wrought on other European urban centers in the war's closing stages. In the 1950s, it bounced back as Italy's economic miracle raised morale and provided money for its reconstruction. These were the years of *la dolce vita* ("the good life"), as locals and foreign tourists rediscovered Rome's delights and the city became the backdrop to iconic films, such as *Roman Holiday* and *La Dolce Vita*, as well as being a playground for stars like Audrey Hepburn and Sophia Loren.

In 1957, the foundation treaty of the European Economic Community, the predecessor of the European Union, was signed in Rome. Three years later, the coming of the Olympic Games, which were held in historic venues such as the Roman Baths of Caracalla, set the seal on the city's second renaissance.

Rome's reinvention continues. Although over four million tourists descend each year to wonder at the Colosseum, St. Peter's, and the Vatican Museums, many of them also detour to admire its contemporary architecture, such as the cantilevered curves of MAXXI, the national museum of modern art, designed by Zaha Hadid. Over 2,500 years since its foundation, Rome is proving that it really is an eternal city.

△ ***ROMAN HOLIDAY* POSTER**
The 1953 romantic comedy starred Audrey Hepburn and Gregory Peck, with many of the key sights of Rome taking a supporting role.

1922 Fascist leader Benito Mussolini makes his March on Rome, after which he is appointed prime minister.

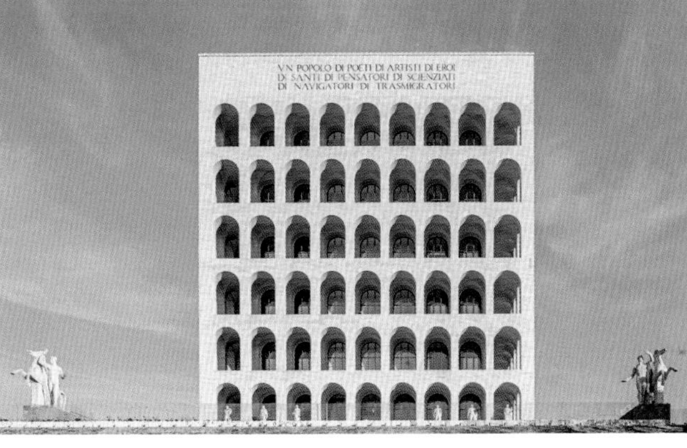

1938–1943 Building of the Palazzo della Civiltà Italiana, centerpiece of Mussolini's new EUR business district.

1960 Rome hosts the Olympic Games, during which Italy wins 13 gold medals.

1981 Pope John Paul II is subject to an assassination attempt in St. Peter's Square.

2021 Plans are announced for the restoration of the Colosseum.

Athens

CITY OF THE VIOLET CROWN

The birthplace of theater, democracy, and Western philosophy, the city-state of Athens was ruled by successive empires before winning independence, leaving Europe's most ancient capital with a rich legacy.

Athens's situation on Greece's Attica peninsula, within easy reach of the Aegean Sea, made it a magnet for settlers. Its craggy Acropolis—meaning "high city" in Greek—had a supply of drinkable water and provided a defensible position on which chieftains from the warlike Mycenaean culture built a fortified palace around 1250 BCE. Its construction is traditionally ascribed to heroes such as the minotaur-slaying Theseus, but Athenians also trace their origins to Athena, the city's patron goddess, who was said to have gifted it an olive tree as a promise of its future peace and prosperity.

By the 8th century BCE, power had shifted from kings to aristocratic *polemarchs*, or war-leaders, and *archons*, who administered the city's life. The first *agora*, or communal marketplace, was built northwest of the Acropolis and, with its control spreading out to the Attic countryside, Athens became one of the leading Greek city-states.

◁ ACROPOLIS PANORAMA
The Classical heritage of Athens still looms large, with the hill of the Acropolis and its ancient ruins, notably the Parthenon (center) and Theater of Dionysus (bottom), dominating its skyline.

> "**Athens**, the **eye of Greece**, mother of arts and eloquence.
>
> JOHN MILTON, *PARADISE REGAINED*, 1671

A reforming city-state

In the mid-7th century BCE, a nobleman named Cylon sought to become the city's sole ruler. His attempt at tyranny prompted reforms. The legislator Draco drew up Athens's first code of law, written on public tablets so any literate Athenian could consult it—its severe penalties gave us the term "draconian." Meanwhile, a prosperity born of trade saw new stone temples replace wooden shrines.

KORE ▷
This statue of a *kore* (young woman) from around 530 BCE was found on the Acropolis, where it was buried after the Persian destruction of the city.

c. 1250 BCE The Mycenaeans fortify the Acropolis with Cyclopean (huge unmortared stone) walls.

594 BCE Solon revises the Athenian law code to abolish the scourge of debt bondage—in which debtors could be enslaved in exchange for the money they owed.

547 BCE Peisistratos becomes *tyrant* (non-royal sole ruler) of Athens. He is succeeded by his sons; one is assassinated, the other driven from office.

534 BCE Modern drama is created when Thespis becomes the first actor to play an individual role during a festival of the god Dionysus.

530s BCE The red-figure style of pottery, which allows for greater detailing than the older black-figure style, is invented in Athens.

◁ PORCH OF THE ERECHTHEION TEMPLE
These *caryatids* (female figures acting as pillars) probably represent priestesses of Artemis. The temple was built around 406 BCE.

The word "ostracize" comes from the *ostraka*, or broken pottery, on which Athenians wrote the names of politicians they wanted to exile.

The confident city built a grand new temple to Athena Polias ("the protector") on the Acropolis, its pediments carved with scenes of battles between gods and giants. Yet Athens was fearful of a return to tyranny, and tensions over the exclusion of the poor from political power threatened to tear the city apart. Finally, at the end of the 6th century BCE, a new *archon*, Cleisthenes, established the world's first democracy. He set up a council, elected by 10 tribes drawn from geographical districts called *demes*. The council's agenda was set by an *ecclesia*, a broader assembly that also made key military and civic decisions. All free Athenian men, regardless of wealth, could attend the *ecclesia*—women, migrants from the rest of Greece, and enslaved people were excluded. To spread power more widely, office-holders and trial juries were chosen by lot.

Athens's prosperity was threatened when the Persian Empire invaded Greece in 492 and 480 BCE. A stunning naval victory at Salamis helped a Greek alliance push the Persians back, but not before the Athenians had to evacuate their city and watch while the Persians burned Athens and destroyed the buildings of the Acropolis.

The golden age

A victorious Athens established the Delian League, which began as an alliance of city-states but became an Athenian empire. Tribute from the states enabled the general and statesman Pericles to rebuild the city. Spaces for worship and performance were erected and Athens's theater—the world's first—hosted the work of great playwrights such as Aeschylus, Euripides, and Aristophanes. The Parthenon, a glorious temple to Athena, was completed in 433 BCE. Built of white marble, its soaring columns were capped with a frieze showing mythological scenes, and its interior held a great gold and ivory statue of the goddess.

This was the golden age of a creative, cosmopolitan city. Merchants brought goods from across the eastern Mediterranean, and the *agora* bustled with market-goers. Life was not luxurious: many citizens lived in small houses, their diets confined to such staples as bread, olives, cheese, figs, and beans. But poorer men at least could participate in

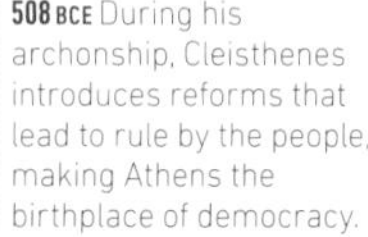

508 BCE During his archonship, Cleisthenes introduces reforms that lead to rule by the people, making Athens the birthplace of democracy.

490 BCE Athenian hoplites (heavily armored citizen infantry) defeat the Persians at Marathon, ending the first Persian invasion.

Detail from a Greek cup depicting a hoplite soldier

480 BCE The Athenian fleet defeats the second Persian invasion of Greece at Salamis, but the Acropolis is burned.

478 BCE Themistocles orders the building of a new defensive wall around Athens.

447–433 BCE The Parthenon is built on the urging of the Athenian statesman Pericles.

the assembly alongside their richer peers. Athens's riches and ambition attracted the jealousy of rivals and entangled it in the 27-year Peloponnesian War with Sparta in 431 BCE. Orators gave rousing speeches and poor citizens took their turns at the oars of the Athenian *triremes* (warships), but Sparta won, occupied the city, and demolished its walls. Rule by pro-Spartan cliques ensued, and even when democracy returned, Athens was a shadow of its former self.

An occupied city

In the 4th century BCE, Athens fell into the hands of the Macedonian conquerors Philip II and Alexander the Great. Yet it remained an intellectual powerhouse. Plato established the Academy, in an olive grove west of the city, while his pupil Aristotle founded the rival Lyceum school. However, by the time the Roman General Sulla captured Athens in 86 BCE, the city was a provincial, if revered, backwater.

△ AGORA OF ATHENS
The *agora*, built in the 5th century BCE below the Acropolis, included a circular *tholos*, the residence of the council president, and the *stoa*, or colonnades, which encircled the marketplace.

429 BCE Pericles dies of the plague, weakening Athens' leadership and contributing to its eventual defeat against Sparta in the Peloponnesian War.

404 BCE Sparta defeats Athens and installs a pro-Spartan regime.

399 BCE Socrates is tried on the charge of corrupting the youth of Athens and executed by being made to drink hemlock.

338 BCE The Macedonian King Philip II conquers Athens, beginning a long period of foreign domination.

100-50 BCE The octagonal Tower of the Winds monument, which acts as a sundial and weather vane, is built.

BYZANTINE CHURCH ▷
The 10th-century Church of the Holy Apostles, with its dramatic setting in the ancient *agora*, is among Athens's earliest Christian buildings.

> **Time** and **envy** have dealt with **Athens more barbarously** than ever the **Persians** did.
>
> MICHAEL CHONIATES, ARCHBISHOP OF ATHENS, *LETTERS*, c. 1185

The Tower of the Winds was used as a Christian church in Byzantine times; the Ottomans believed it was the tomb of Socrates.

The Romans were great admirers of Greek culture, and built new structures—the Emperor Hadrian completed the temple of Olympian Zeus in 131 CE and constructed a new library. Athens survived the fall of the Western Empire in the 5th century CE and became part of the Byzantine Empire, but ravages by Goths and Slavs impoverished it, and the coming of Christianity dented the prestige of its pagan philosophical schools.

Some prosperity returned in the 10th and 11th centuries, when exquisite churches such as the Kapnikarea and the Church of the Holy Apostles were built. But in 1204, the army of the Fourth Crusade wrested Athens from the Byzantines, and the Acropolis became the fortress of a succession of Western European dukes. Poverty and insecurity drove out much of the population.

When the Ottoman Turks took the city in 1458, they converted the Parthenon into a mosque. Even the *agora* was outside the reduced city, and sheep grazed in the sanctuaries of Olympian gods.

As the Ottomans in turn came under threat, they sited a gunpowder store on the Acropolis, where in 1687 besieging Venetian artillery scored a direct hit, reducing much of the Parthenon to rubble. The British diplomat Lord Elgin controversially transported around half of the Parthenon's frieze to Britain, beginning with 50 large pieces in 1801. He was one of many foreign visitors to Athens, increasing sympathy for the Greeks. When they revolted in 1821, their struggle was supported by the European powers.

Independence and renewal

During the Greek War of Independence, the city seesawed between Ottoman and Greek control. When it became capital of an independent Greece in 1833, the population had been reduced to just 2,000 people. But a determined renewal, helped by a resilience bred of centuries of occupation, saw the National University built in 1837 and a royal palace five years later, all in a lavish Neoclassical style. A grand new square, Syntagma, was joined by broad avenues, bringing a sense of space to the city's medieval jumble. In 1896, a new stadium was built for the first modern Olympics, a revival of

124–132 CE Roman Emperor Hadrian visits Athens three times, restoring temples and building a new library, gymnasium, and aqueduct.

529 Byzantine Emperor Justinian shuts down Plato's Academy and bans the teaching of pagan philosophy.

Irene, the first female Byzantine emperor, who reigned from 797 to 802 CE before being exiled to the island of Lesbos, was born in Athens.

1205 After the Fourth Crusade captures Constantinople, the Burgundian Crusader Otto de la Roche becomes Duke of Athens.

1311–1402 Athens is occupied successively by Catalans, Florentines, and Venetians.

1458 The Ottoman Turks capture Athens. The Parthenon becomes a mosque and the Tower of the Winds (pictured) is used as a meeting house by the Mevlevi Order.

an ancient tradition which brought glory when Greek athlete Spyridon Louis won the marathon. By the 1920s, Athens was a lively city, reverberating to the sound of *bouzouki* (Greek lute) players in the tavernas of the Plaka district.

There were more trials to come: Athens was occupied by the Germans during World War II, then ravaged by post-war street fighting between government forces and communist insurgents, while democracy was disrupted by military rule in the 1960s and '70s. But economic growth continued. Old districts were flattened and new quarters built, while open spaces disappeared as the city spread and joined up with its port, Piraeus. Through it all, Athenians retained a pride in their heritage, a sense reinforced when Athens again played host to the Olympics in 2006. The city that has given the world democracy, philosophy, and graceful architecture still hums with life.

△ ACROPOLIS MUSEUM
The Acropolis Museum includes a gallery for the Parthenon Marbles removed by Lord Elgin (and currently in the British Museum in London), should they be returned to Greece.

◁ ALEXANDER THE GREAT
This marble head of Alexander, one of Athens's conquerors, now sits in the city's Acropolis Museum.

1687 Much of the Parthenon is destroyed after a Venetian bombardment strikes an Ottoman gunpowder store.

1801 The Parthenon Marbles are removed from Athens, after Lord Elgin gains access to the Acropolis.

1833 The Ottomans evacuate Athens and it becomes the capital of an independent Greece.

1896 Baron Pierre de Coubertin organizes the first modern Olympic Games, held in Athens.

1940–1944 Athens is occupied by the German army during World War II, bringing appalling suffering.

2004 The 28th Olympic Games are held in Athens; Greece wins six gold medals.

2009 The Acropolis Museum opens just below the Acropolis. It contains over 4,000 objects from the ancient Greek, Roman, and Byzantine eras.

Istanbul

THE NEW ROME

For over two millennia, Greek, Roman, Turkish, Christian, and Muslim cultures have met and mingled in a melting-pot metropolis that borders two seas and straddles two continents.

The Bosporus, a strait linking the Black Sea with the Sea of Marmara and the Mediterranean, was one of the world's great trade routes by the start of the first millennium BCE. Colonists from Megara and other Greek cities saw an opportunity to control this trade, and founded a city on its western shore around 667 BCE. They called it Byzantium, after one of their leaders, Byzas, and it prospered.

Romans and Christians

In the 1st century CE, the Romans took over Byzantium, which grew to become one of the richest cities in the empire. Although it was badly damaged in a war between rival emperors in 195 CE, it recovered and the Emperor Constantine, recognizing its wealth and strategic site, made it his capital, Constantinople, in 330 CE. Constantine converted to Christianity, and several early ecclesiastical councils took place in the city. The presence of many educated churchmen made Constantinople an intellectual center as well as a political and commercial one, and rulers continued to develop the city with churches, aqueducts, and fortifications. Its cosmopolitan, stone-paved streets rang with Aramaic, Coptic, Armenian, and Latin, though the language of the ruling and educated classes was Greek. When the empire was divided in two in the 4th century, the city became capital of its eastern half. The west declined, but the Eastern Roman Empire, which became known as the Byzantine Empire, endured for over 1,000 years.

◁ ISTANBUL'S WATERSIDE SETTING, c. 1840
Hubert Sattler's 19th-century view of Istanbul shows the city's elegant mosques and imposing site on the Bosporus, which separates Europe from Asia.

> “If the **Earth** were a single state, **Istanbul would be its capital.**”
>
> NAPOLEON BONAPARTE

c. 667 BCE The settlement of Byzantium (also known by its Greek name, Byzantion) is founded, probably by Greeks from Megara.

196 CE The city is virtually destroyed by Roman troops loyal to Septimius Severus in his battle for the throne.

203 Septimius Severus rebuilds Byzantium, improving structures such as the hippodrome (racetrack).

330 Constantine refounds the city as Constantinople and starts work on its Great Palace.

381 Christian bishops meet at the First Council of Constantinople to agree a creed and other matters of belief and doctrine.

395 The Roman Empire divides in two; Constantinople becomes the eastern capital.

Justinian's Byzantine city

△ Hagia Sophia, before its conversion to a mosque.

> "The **emperor**, **disregarding** all **questions** of expense, eagerly pressed on to **begin the work** of **construction**, and began to **gather** all the **artisans** from the **whole world**.
>
> PROCOPIUS, ON JUSTINIAN'S REBUILDING OF THE CITY, c. 550 CE

△ The Emperor Justinian (left) offers a model of the Hagia Sophia to Mary and the infant Christ in this 10th-century mosaic from its south entrance.

When Justinian became emperor in 527 CE, his ambition was to recreate the old Roman Empire in all its glory, and he soon took over Italy and parts of North Africa. The growing kingdom needed a great capital, and Justinian set about beautifying Constantinople. He improved the city's water supply by building a vast underground reservoir held up by a forest of stone columns (known today as the Basilica Cistern), made the imperial palace grander and more luxurious, and strengthened the city walls.

But Justinian was not always a popular ruler. His advisers were often controversial and his wife, the former actress Theodora, was criticized for her reforming instincts and alleged past as a prostitute. In 532 CE, a crowd of protesters started a revolt against him and threatened to overwhelm the city. Theodora advised him to use an army of mercenaries to quell the disturbance. Their response was ruthless: some 30,000 people were slaughtered and the area around the Hippodrome suffered severe damage. However, in the next 30 years of his reign, Justinian continued to build and improve the city, leaving its buildings more lavish, and creating a suitably grand home for the officials, merchants, and travelers who came to the city from all over the empire. One of the casualties of the revolt had been the church of Hagia Sophia ("divine wisdom"), and Justinian rebuilt it in 537 CE, embellishing it with a vast dome and stunning mosaics. Now a mosque, it remains one of the world's most awe-inspiring buildings.

527 Justinian becomes emperor and begins to plan a grand new church, to designs by architects Anthemius of Tralles and Isidore of Miletus.

532 The palace is besieged during the Nika Revolt, and Justinian and Theodora turn to mercenaries to crush the rioters.

537 The new church of Hagia Sophia is completed and dedicated by Justinian.

Gold coin depicting Emperor Leo III

730 Emperor Leo III bans the veneration of religious icons, increasing tension between the Orthodox and Catholic churches.

843 A church council held at Hagia Sophia reverses the ban on icons.

At its height, the Byzantine Empire was vast, encompassing southern Spain, Italy, Greece, Turkey, the Balkans, the eastern Mediterranean, and parts of North Africa. Its capital was suitably grand: under Justinian (see box), Constantinople was probably the world's most populous city. Its libraries were centers of learning, and its markets traded goods from all over the world.

A city under threat

With its enviable wealth and influence, Constantinople was a frequent target for attacks. Slavs, Russians, Arabs, and Persians all failed in bids to conquer the city, largely due to its massive walls and strong navy. In the 11th century, the Seljuk Turks had more success, launching fierce attacks that drove the Byzantines out of Anatolia (Asian Turkey), reducing the empire's size and wealth. It proved a turning point: while the city recovered under a series of talented emperors, an attack by a Crusader army in the early 1200s left it in ruins. Constantinople suffered a slow decline, although the creative arts flowered under Emperor Michael VIII Palaeologus and his family. The Palaeologi attracted many foreign artists and scholars, restoring some of the once-vibrant atmosphere, but the days of Roman rule were numbered.

△ FRESCOES IN THE CHORA CHURCH
Theodore Metochites, a 14th-century imperial adviser, commissioned a lavish set of frescoes and mosaics for this remarkable church. Their vivid portrayals of saints and biblical scenes make them some of the best examples of the Palaeologan Renaissance.

1176 In the Battle of Myriokephalon, Seljuk Turks destroy the Byzantine army and end the city's control of most of Anatolia.

1204 Constantinople suffers major damage during the Fourth Crusade, beginning a period of rule by Western invaders.

After the Crusaders' sack, buildings were stripped and many locals left, reducing the city to a few scattered communities.

1261 Emperor Michael VIII Palaeologus recaptures the city, and begins a revival of art and scholarship known as the Palaeologan Renaissance.

1362 After further conquests, the Ottomans control large parts of the Byzantine Empire, leaving only Constantinople and a few outposts.

This double-headed eagle symbolizes the Byzantine emperors' dominion of east and west

△ BLUE MOSQUE
The Sultan Ahmet Mosque is widely known as the Blue Mosque because of the thousands of predominantly blue tiles that cover its interior. It can hold up to 10,000 people, and contains Ahmet I's tomb.

The Ottoman capital

In 1453, Ottoman forces under Sultan Mehmed II laid siege to Constantinople. The Turks were hampered by a great iron chain that the defenders had laid across the Golden Horn estuary to block enemy ships. Undeterred, Mehmed had his ships dragged over land on greased logs, bringing them into the Golden Horn, within reach of the city's sea walls. After weeks of fighting, the city was finally taken by the Ottomans.

Many people were killed, buildings were destroyed, and the pillage continued after the Ottoman victory. The sultan soon began a major rebuilding program, however. Hagia Sophia was turned into a mosque and adorned with four minarets; the construction of the vast imperial Topkapı Palace was begun; the city walls were rebuilt; and mosques and a vast Grand Bazaar, which would grow to accommodate some 4,000 shops, were established.

The sultan declared Constantinople his capital, and allowed many of the Greek-speaking people who had fled the city to return. It soon bustled with merchants again. They brought trade to a newly prosperous market, where there were plenty of rich Ottomans eager to buy imported silks and spices, as well as locally made carpets, ceramics, and metalware. Janissaries, traditionally

△ AHMET I AND HIS MOSQUE, 17TH CENTURY
This illustrated manuscript shows Ahmet I standing with his followers next to the Blue Mosque, with Hagia Sophia behind it. The city's mosques, with their towering minarets and gorgeous interiors, showcase the wealth and creativity of a great empire.

1453 Ottoman Sultan Mehmed II conquers the city and begins to transform it into his capital.

1478 Topkapl Palace is completed as the home of the ruler and his family, the center of government, and a meeting place for key officials.

1520 Süleyman I ("the Magnificent") becomes emperor, enlarges the Ottoman Empire, and commissions the architect Sinan to build new mosques.

1616 The Sultan Ahmet Mosque, also known as the Blue Mosque, is completed to a design by Sedefkâr Mehmed Ağa, a pupil of Sinan.

1807 The janissaries rebel, destroying much of the city, after Sultan Selim III tries to reorganize the army along Western lines.

1871 The construction of a tram network, initially with horse-drawn trams, greatly improves city transportation.

> **Islam** flourished; **mosques** ... were erected and a **peak of glory** was reached under the great **Süleyman the Magnificent.**
>
> DAVID TALBOT RICE, *CONSTANTINOPLE*, 1965

captive Christian boys who were converted to Islam and given elite training, formed the imperial guard, Europe's first standing army.

A golden age for the city had begun, and continued into the reign of Süleyman I, who extended the empire in the 16th century. Süleyman was a noted patron of the arts, encouraging painters and craftsmen to beautify the Topkapı Palace and the homes of his officials, and employing the empire's greatest architect, Mimar Sinan, on projects across the city. Süleyman also promoted education, making his capital home to a highly literate population, where poetry flourished and calligraphy, used to create stunning copies of the Quran, reached a peak.

A slow decline

The Ottoman rulers after Süleyman were less able, and the reins of power were often held by Grand Viziers (ministers), the women of the court, or the janissaries. There was also corruption and sometimes terrifying violence. In 1621, a hard winter was followed by a famine. Discontent flared, and to assert his authority Sultan Osman II threatened to abolish the powerful janissaries. In response, they rebelled, took over the palace, and killed Osman. Other sultans and their viziers had more success restoring Constantinople's stability, building grand Baroque palaces in the 18th and 19th centuries. But the city became unstable and backward-looking. Trade declined, the city's once-magnificent wooden houses began to look disheveled, and Constantinople found itself capital of an impoverished empire dubbed "the sick man of Europe."

New beginnings

World War I wiped out the remains of the Ottoman Empire, but Turkey secured its independence under the command of former soldier Mustafa Kemal Atatürk, who became president in 1923. He modernized the new nation, making Turkey a secular state and Ankara his new capital. The old capital, renamed Istanbul (from the Greek for "to the city"), thrived. New railroads and bridges improved access, and districts such as Ümraniye filled with new apartments, shopping malls, and mosques. The rolling back of religious strictures also gave more freedom to citizens, especially women, although conservative President Recep Tayyip Erdoğan has restricted media in recent years. This historic melting pot still bubbles with energy, mixing elegant palaces with glass-hewn skyscrapers, and combining a love of life's finer things with a beguiling bustle.

Hagia Sophia was a church until 1453, a mosque until 1935, and a museum until 2020. It is now a mosque again.

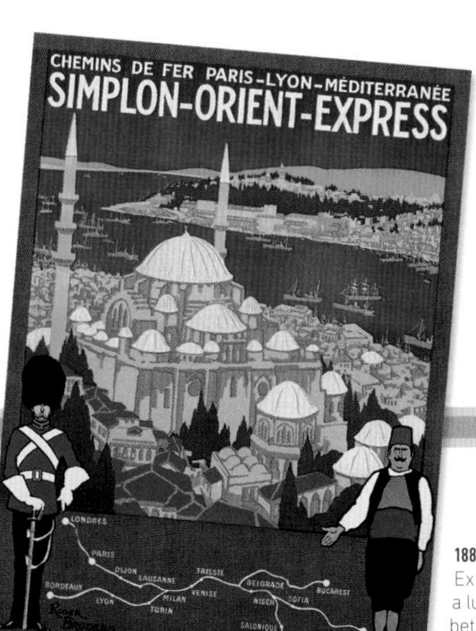

1888 The Orient Express establishes a luxury rail link between Paris and Constantinople.

1922–1923 Atatürk abolishes the Sultanate and separates religion and state. Ankara replaces Constantinople as capital of the Turkish Republic.

1930 The city is renamed Istanbul.

1973 The Bosporus suspension bridge, the first permanent crossing of the strait, is completed.

2004 The Yeşilvadi mosque, designed by Adnan Kazmaoğlu, is constructed in Ümraniye, on the Asian side of the Bosporus.

Jerusalem

THE HOLY CITY

Jerusalem has been a sacred place for three major world faiths for thousands of years, its ancient streets witness to a turbulent history of religious rivalry and division.

Situated on the slopes of a hill-ringed plateau west of the Jordan river, Jerusalem is one of the world's most ancient cities. It was established around 3200 BCE by Canaanite tribes who named it Rushalimum ("Shalem has founded it"), after one of their gods.

The City of David

According to Biblical tradition, the Israelites arrived in Canaan after fleeing oppression in Egypt. At first, they were just one small group in a region that had been bitterly contested between Hittites and Egyptians, but around 1000 BCE their king, David, captured Jerusalem from its Canaanite rulers. His successor, Solomon, built the First Temple to house the Ark of the Covenant, which contained the tablets of the Ten Commandments.

◁ SUNSET OVER JERUSALEM
The Temple Mount, surrounded by the old city walls, dominates Jerusalem, just as it has done since ancient times, with the golden cupola of the 7th-century Dome of the Rock its most visible feature from afar.

Lavishly constructed from Lebanese cedarwood, the temple became a sacred center of the Jewish religion, and an enduring focus of its rituals and law.

Solomon's achievements were short-lived, though. The kingdom's unity fractured under his successor and Jerusalem, now capital of Judah (the southern part of Palestine), became a vassal of the Assyrians. It was eventually destroyed in 586 BCE after a revolt against the new Babylonian overlord Nebuchadnezzar, and its people were deported to Babylon.

Jerusalem after the exile

That exile lasted 50 years until the Persian King Cyrus took Babylon and permitted the Jews to return home. A Second Temple was built, but Jerusalem suffered a series of foreign overlords—first Alexander the Great, then the Ptolemies and Seleucids. The Jews reestablished their independence after the Jewish priest Judas Maccabeus repelled Seleucid attempts to suppress Judaism, but in 63 BCE the Roman General Pompey took Jerusalem after intervening in a dispute between two religious factions.

c. 1000 BCE King David captures Jerusalem from the Canaanite King Araunah and moves the Ark of the Covenant to the city.

An 8th-century account of the taking of Jerusalem by Nebuchadnezzar

586 BCE Nebuchadnezzar of Babylon captures Jerusalem, destroying the First Temple and removing Jerusalem's population to Babylon.

c. 970 BCE King Solomon builds the First Temple on the Temple Mount.

167–160 BCE The Maccabean revolt drives out the Seleucids and leads to the establishment of the Hasmonean Kingdom.

63 BCE Roman General Pompey the Great enters Jerusalem, beginning the period of Roman dominance.

◁ SITE OF THE RESURRECTION
The Rotunda in the Church of the Holy Sepulchre is said to mark the site of the tomb where Christ was buried after the crucifixion, and of his subsequent resurrection from the dead, giving the church its original name of Anastasis (Greek for "resurrection").

To rebuild the Second Temple, Herod used 1,000 priests trained as craftsmen so as not to violate its sanctity.

Initially, the Romans exercised control through Jewish rulers, the most effective of whom was Herod the Great. In 19 BCE, Herod remodeled the Second Temple in grand style, cladding its walls in red- and blue-veined marble. At the edge of the plateau that became known as the Temple Mount, he also built a massive fortress called the Antonia, chiefly to protect the temple.

When Herod died, the Romans imposed direct rule and installed the prefect Pontius Pilate to govern the region. In 30 CE, he was forced to give way to Jewish traditionalist demands for the execution of a troublesome preacher named Jesus Christ. Jewish discontent exploded in 66 CE after a Roman attack on the temple treasury. The revolt ended in tragedy with the slaughter of 6,000 Jewish Zealots and the destruction of the Second Temple in 70 CE. Another revolt in 135 CE led Emperor Hadrian to expel the Jewish population and refound Jerusalem as a pagan city.

When religious life returned, it was Christian, not Jewish, after the decree in 313 CE by Emperor Constantine tolerating Christianity. Pilgrims started to visit, following the example of Constantine's mother Helena, who claimed to have discovered the True Cross on which Jesus was crucified. She founded the first version of the Church of the Holy Sepulchre, accelerating the transformation of Jerusalem into a Christian landscape.

The Muslim conquest

Tensions between rival forms of Christianity weakened the Roman Empire's hold, and when a Muslim army captured Jerusalem in 638 CE, resistance was muted. Caliph Umar ordered the conversion of churches to mosques and monasteries to madrasas. In 688 CE the Umayyad Caliph Abd al-Malik ibn Marwan built the Dome of the Rock on the site of the Second Temple, its great golden cupola dominating the Haram ash-Sharif ("the noble sanctuary"), the Muslim term for the Temple Mount. But by the 9th century, the new Abbasid caliphs began to neglect the city and its population shrank. The unstable Caliph al-Hakim ordered the destruction of remaining Christian churches. After the Seljuk Turks cut off Christian pilgrimage routes, the Christian rulers of Europe formed a crusade in 1096 to rescue the Holy City (see box).

70 CE Following a Jewish revolt, the Romans destroy Jerusalem, including the Second Temple.

135 Emperor Hadrian remodels Jerusalem as a pagan city, and proscribes the Jewish religion.

326 Empress Helena orders the construction of the Church of the Holy Sepulchre.

638 Caliph Umar captures Jerusalem after a short siege. He builds a small prayer house on the Temple Mount.

688 Caliph Abd al-Malik builds the Dome of the Rock shrine and expands the prayer house into the al-Aqsa Mosque (completed in 705).

The Crusader kingdom

> “In the Temple and the **Porch of Solomon**, men **rode in blood** up to their **knees and bridle reins**.
>
> RAYMOND OF AGUILERS, *HISTORIA FRANCORUM*, c.1100

The armies of the First Crusade took three years to complete the long overland journey from Europe to Palestine, but after a five-week siege they finally stormed Jerusalem on July 15, 1099, slaughtering Muslims, Jews, and local Christians indiscriminately. The Crusaders turned the al-Aqsa Mosque into a barracks, the Dome of the Rock into a church, reconsecrated the Church of the Holy Sepulchre, and expelled the surviving Muslim and Jewish inhabitants. Yet the new kingdom they established struggled to retain military manpower or attract Christian settlers. It also suffered perpetual factional struggles and weak leadership. Even with a second Crusade and the foundation of military orders such as the Knights Templar and Hospitallers to defend it, Jerusalem was taken by the Ayyubid Sultan Salah ad-Din ibn Ayyub (known as Saladin) in 1187. This time there was no massacre, and Muslims trickled back into the city. Despite a brief Crusader reoccupation, 150 years of conflict in the Crusades had served only to reduce Jerusalem to a smoking ruin.

△ This map from the *Historia Hierosolymitana* (*History of Jerusalem*), a 12th-century chronicle of the First Crusade by Robert the Monk, shows important Christian holy sites, including the Church of the Holy Sepulchre.

◁ A seal of the Crusader Kingdom of Jerusalem prominently shows the Church of the Holy Sepulchre, the city walls, and the former Dome of the Rock, which had been converted into a church.

Muslims believe the Angel Gabriel took the Prophet Muhammad on his “Night Journey” from Mecca to Temple Mount.

969 The seizure of Jerusalem by the Egyptian Fatimid caliphs ends decades of Abbasid neglect.

1099 The army of the First Crusade captures Jerusalem. Its Muslim inhabitants are massacred.

1149 A new Church of the Holy Sepulchre is built, to replace the building destroyed by Caliph al-Hakim.

1187 The Ayyubid Sultan Saladin defeats the Crusader army at Hattin and takes Jerusalem.

1229–1244 Crusaders regain control of Jerusalem before losing it to a Muslim Khwarezmian army.

The Mamluk city

In 1260, after more than 150 years of Crusader campaigns, Jerusalem was conquered by the Mamluks—former slave-soldiers who had risen to become Egypt's ruling class—beginning a six-century period of Muslim rule, which imprinted itself on the city's streets with mosques, madrasas, and ornamental tombs. The labyrinth of the Old City became differentiated more clearly into the four Quarters—Muslim, Jewish, Christian, and Armenian—into which it is still divided today.

Life, though, was far from peaceful. Despite the work the Mamluks carried out on the Haram ash-Sharif (Temple Mount), the city was in danger of becoming a backwater. However, the Crusaders' loss of the coastal town of Acre in 1291, which marked their final expulsion from the region, revived Jerusalem's fortunes.

With the danger of Christian attack gone, the Catholic Franciscans were allowed back in 1300 and given a church on the Mount of Zion. The Mamluk Sultan an-Nasir Muhammad turned his energies to works on the buildings of the Haram ash-Sharif, commissioning a splendid new colonnade and regilding the Dome of the Rock. He also built a new market—the Suq al-Qattanin (Cotton Merchants' Market)—and soap and linen manufacture grew as foreign traders flocked to the city. New religious buildings sprang up in the crowded Old City, many, such as the Manjakiyya madrasa, having to be wedged into small spaces over porticoes and the city gates. This growth came to an end when the city was ravaged by the Black Death in 1348, and raids by nomadic Bedouins choked off trade.

◁ OTTOMAN ISTANBUL
This late-19th-century tinted photograph shows a busy street leading to the Tower of David in the citadel, and the Jaffa Gate. The vendors and the merchants' camels laden with goods are a sign of the city's renewed commercial prosperity.

1246 The Egyptian Ayyubid sultans recapture Jerusalem from the Khwarezmian Turks.

Mamluk gold coins

1260 Baybars, the Mamluk Sultan of Egypt, takes control of Jerusalem.

1317 Mamluk Sultan an-Nasir Muhammad commissions the regilding of the Dome of the Rock.

1516–1517 The Ottoman conquest of Palestine; Sultan Selim I makes a pilgrimage to Jerusalem.

1541 Süleyman the Magnificent issues an edict allowing Jews to worship at the Western Wall.

The Ottoman revival

The entrance of the Ottoman Sultan Selim into the city on December 1, 1516, heralded great change. The Ottomans restored law and order, and under Süleyman the Magnificent (r. 1520–1566) there was a cultural revival. He ordered the rebuilding of the city walls and erected the imposing Damascus Gate—its turret stood guard over the city until it was toppled in 1967. In the 1540s, Süleyman allowed Jews to have a place of prayer along a narrow strip at the Western Wall of the former Second Temple, where the custom began of inserting petitions on pieces of paper slipped between the stones. After Süleyman's death, however, the political climate darkened. Although the Dome of the Rock was restored several times, the sultans and their governors were weak and authority in the city increasingly fell to local notable families.

By 1800, Jerusalem had shrunk again, with its 9,000 inhabitants, half of them Muslim, making their living from soap-making and ceramics, and the city dotted with apricot and mulberry orchards. When a fire broke out in 1808, gutting the Church of the Holy Sepulchre, recriminations flared up among the Christian denominations. These became so vicious that the authorities enforced a settlement under which the Greeks gained control of the main building, the Armenians were confined to the St. Helena crypt, the Copts to a small chapel, and the Ethiopians were left with the roof. To keep the peace between them, a Muslim family was given the main keys.

◁ **THE WESTERN WALL** The Western Wall (or Wailing Wall), the last surviving part of the Second Temple, became a place of Jewish worship in the 1540s.

The Zionist movement

In the 1830s, Jerusalem began to stir once more. The Egyptian reformer Muhammad Ali briefly occupied the city and established a modern administration. Sephardim and Ashkenazi Jewish communities built new synagogues. Christian missionaries began to arrive, and the British established the first European consulate in 1839. It was the Jewish community that grew most robustly, however, helped by foreign philanthropists such as the Rothschild family. New Jewish suburbs started to appear outside the crowded warren of the Old City, and by 1890 there were nine of them. They were populated by new waves of Jewish migrants from Eastern Europe, driven out by pogroms in the Russian Empire. Many of them, such as Theodor Herzl, were inspired by the new vision of Zionism, which called for Jews to establish a state in the Biblical land of Israel based on socialist foundations. By 1900, the Jewish population had grown so much they were a majority, heightening tensions with the now outnumbered Muslims.

In the mid-17th century, Jerusalem had 43,000 vineyards, 2,045 shops, 17 Quranic schools, and two synagogues.

1703–1705 The Naqib al-Ashraf revolt against oppressive Ottoman taxation establishes brief autonomy for Jerusalem.

1831 Muhammad Ali of Egypt captures Jerusalem, but the Ottomans retake it in 1840 with British assistance.

1860 The first modern Jewish neighborhoods are built outside the Old City.

1897 The first Zionist Congress is held, led by Theodor Herzl, who argues that Jews of the diaspora should return to Jerusalem and establish a Jewish state.

Commemorative postcard of the first Zionist Congress

1917 The British army under General Allenby enters Jerusalem.

△ **BRITISH GARRISON SOLDIERS**
British troops stand guard at a road junction in Jerusalem in 1939. The year saw riots by Arabs demanding independence and increased attacks by Jewish militant groups, such as the Irgun.

> “Our **Jerusalem** is a **mosaic of** all the **cultures**, all the **religions**, and all the **periods** that **enriched the city**.
>
> *OUR JERUSALEM* PETITION BY ISRAELI WRITERS, ARTISTS, AND KNESSET MEMBERS, MAY 1995

The British mandate

The Arab population of Jerusalem hoped that General Edmund Allenby's entry into the city in December 1917 would bring them the independence they believed Britain had promised them. They soon found that the British had been making equal and contradictory promises to the Jewish community, including a letter from Foreign Secretary Arthur Balfour declaring support for a Jewish homeland in Palestine.

Consequently, the British League of Nations Mandate over Palestine began in bitterness. The British tried to promote communal harmony by reestablishing the municipal council with a Muslim mayor and Jewish and Christian deputies, and repairing the decaying infrastructure. New Jewish suburbs sprang up to the west of the Old City, with Arab equivalents to the east, and the new King David Hotel and Central Post Office gave Jerusalem the appearance of a rapidly modernizing city. Yet old hatreds festered beneath the surface. The Muslim nationalist Mohammed Amin al-Husayni, whom the British appointed Grand Mufti, clashed with the Jewish Agency for Israel, which encouraged a rising tide of Jewish immigration. Riots occurred in 1929, an Arab general strike in 1936 escalated into a widespread uprising, and Jewish militant groups targeted both Arabs and the British authorities, including a devastating bomb attack on the King David Hotel in 1946.

Jerusalem divided and reunited

When the United Nations' proposals to partition Palestine between Arab and Jewish states foundered and the British withdrew, Jewish nationalists declared the State of Israel. The war that then erupted with their Arab neighbors was ended by a truce in March 1949. This left Jerusalem divided for the next two decades: the Old City, in Muslim hands, was crammed with Palestinian refugees; the west of the city, captured by Israel, teeming with new Jewish migrants. The fractured city was only finally reunited, but definitely not healed, when Israeli forces took East Jerusalem (including the Old City) in the Six-Day War in May 1967.

1920 Jerusalem comes under the control of the British League of Nations Mandate.

1929 Rioting is sparked by a Muslim-Jewish dispute over access to the Western Wall.

At the end of World War II, thousands of Jewish refugees attempted to settle in Palestine. Many were turned back by the British.

1946 An attack on the King David Hotel, temporary headquarters of the British authorities, kills 91 people.

Eyewitness Story of Life in Amazing Poland--Page 2
CHICAGO DAILY NEWS
RED STREAK
SET UP NEW JEWISH STATE
Fighting Rages In Jerusalem
Call Troops in St. Paul Strike
Sunny News from the Weatherman
CUBS WIN

1948 The State of Israel is declared; the first Arab-Israeli War erupts.

The city's Muslim population found itself beleaguered, as the Israeli government built new blocks for Jewish settlers around East Jerusalem and radical Jewish groups sought to buy Old City properties. Terrorism blighted Jerusalem as members of the Palestine Liberation Organization (PLO) fought back. In 1987, the First Intifada, a sustained Palestinian protest movement, broke out.

All attempts to bring peace have been in vain. The Oslo Peace Accords in 1993 between Israel and the PLO promised a final determination of Jerusalem's status, but this never came to pass, and a Second Intifada erupted in 2000. The Israeli government responded with even harsher security measures and declared Jerusalem as capital of Israel, a move which was generally unrecognized until the US relocated its embassy there in 2018.

Like most modern cities, Jerusalem is a multicultural and vibrant place. Yet it is a city like no other, one in stasis, with Palestinian suburbs outside the center sectioned off by a security wall, and few illusions that faith and politics can be reconciled or the wounds of centuries of hurt healed. Amid it all, Jerusalem remains a profoundly potent symbol for Jews, Christians, and Muslims, and a city where the ancient and modern coexist in proximity, if rarely in harmony.

△ **YAD VASHEM HALL OF NAMES**
The Yad Vashem Holocaust Memorial was given this striking new home in 2013, a building described by its architect as "a volcanic eruption of light and life," in which the Hall of Names honors the memory of the six million Jews killed in the Holocaust.

1949 A truce is declared between Jordan and Israel. Jordan takes over the running of East Jerusalem and the West Bank.

1953 Yad Vashem Holocaust Memorial is established.

1967 In the Six-Day War, Israel takes East Jerusalem, including the Old City.

1980 Israel declares Jerusalem its capital (not recognized internationally).

1993 The Oslo Peace Accords are signed but the status of Jerusalem remains disputed.

2000 Pope John Paul II becomes the second-ever pope to visit Jerusalem.

Persepolis

CITY OF THE PERSIANS

Persepolis was the majestic center of Persia, a ritual site boasting magnificent buildings that for 200 years hosted elaborate ceremonies to glorify its Achaemenid rulers.

Half temple, half grand audience chamber of its rulers, Persepolis—the name is Greek, meaning "city of the Persians"—was founded in the early 6th century BCE. Situated in the Persian heartland in the southwest of modern-day Iran (30 miles/50 km northeast of Shiraz), it replaced the original Persian royal capital at nearby Pasargadae and then for nearly two centuries served as a potent symbol of the power of the Achaemenid kings.

Building a royal city

Cyrus the Great established the Persian Empire in 550 BCE by conquering the previously dominant Medes, but it was left to his successor Darius to choose a capital suitable for this vast domain. While Darius I governed for much of the year from Susa, further to the south, he lavished most of his efforts on the construction of Persepolis, bringing in laborers as well as skilled masons, carpenters, and artists to erect the first of a series of spectacular buildings.

The glory of Darius's achievement at Persepolis was the Apadana, a raised audience chamber with 36 columns soaring to over 66 ft (20 m), topped with bulls' head capitals. A procession of carved figures adorns the eastern stairway, representing 23 groups of people from throughout the empire, each dressed in their national costume and bearing gifts of tribute from their homeland: the Ethiopians bring elephant tusks and an okapi, the Greeks carry beehives, and the Bactrians lead a camel.

A clay tablet found in the Treasury mentions 55 stoneworkers who were brought in specially from Egypt to work on Persepolis.

◁ FRIEZE ON THE APADANA STAIRCASE
A procession of Lydians, from the far west of the Persian Empire, bring vases as part of their tribute to Darius, which also includes metal rings adorned with griffin heads and a chariot drawn by two stallions.

> "May **Ahuramazda protect this country** from **foe**, from **famine**, and from **falsehood**.
>
> INSCRIPTION ON THE PALACE OF DARIUS

529 BCE Cyrus the Great is buried at Pasargadae.

c. 518 BCE Darius I begins construction of Persepolis.

c. 515 BCE Building of the Apadana at Persepolis commences, with the construction of the main audience hall.

c. 510 BCE The frieze of tribute-bearers is carved on the Apadana staircase.

480–470 BCE The Palace of Xerxes is built, decorated with reliefs showing servants carrying food for the king and trilingual inscriptions in Old Persian, Elamite, and Akkadian.

In the Middle Ages, Persepolis was also known as Chehel Minar ("40 columns"). Today, only 13 columns remain.

▷ *DESTRUCTION OF PERSEPOLIS*
This painting, by American artist Tom Lovell, shows Alexander the Great's Macedonian soldiers bearing flaming torches. The Greek historian Diodorus Siculus said that the first torch was cast by Thaïs, a courtesan from Athens, in revenge for the Persian King Xerxes' burning of her home city.

Persepolis was not a major city and did not have a large residential population, but each spring, when the Persian kings visited for the New Year ceremony, it came to life. On ascending the great double staircase, the tribute-bearers would reach the impressive Apadana, its roof made of timber beams up to 213 ft (65 m) in length, the exterior decorated with polychrome glazed brick depicting guards and nobles, and the interior, which could hold thousands of onlookers, furnished with intricate wall-hangings.

Banquets and audiences

To the south of the Apadana, Darius built his own private palace, the Tachara. Doubling as a banquet hall, where the king could enjoy respite from the demands of court and sip wine from elaborate rhytons (conical drinking vessels with animal head fixtures), the Tachara also had its own garden. Darius's son Xerxes I continued his father's work at Persepolis, despite the distraction of an ultimately unsuccessful invasion of Greece in 480 BCE. He enlarged the Apadana and added a new throne hall, the Hall of a Hundred Columns. Its 10 rows of 10 columns were accessed by a grand portico flanked by colossal stone bulls. Xerxes also constructed his own personal palace at the highest point of the platform. To round off the complex, he built an intimidating entrance to the palace—a huge portal guarded by monumental winged bulls, known as the Gate of All Nations.

Darius had already built a small treasury to house regalia and gifts from foreign envoys. Xerxes supplemented this with an open courtyard and another

c. 475–465 BCE Xerxes adds the Hall of a Hundred Columns to the Apadana, its portico adorned with enormous carved stone bulls.

465–424 BCE Artaxerxes I makes additions to the Hall of a Hundred Columns, the last major building work at Persepolis.

333–330 BCE Alexander the Great invades and conquers the Persian Empire, ending the Achaemenid dynasty.

330 BCE Alexander the Great's troops burn and loot Persepolis, leaving it in ruins.

It was said that Alexander the Great's troops looted 2,500 tons of gold and rescued 800 captive Greek artisans from Persepolis.

columned hall, storing the court's most valuable treasures there in a kind of private museum. The items left behind by long-ago looters give an indication of its riches: an alabaster bowl inscribed with the name of the Egyptian Pharaoh Necho; a lion-handled granite vessel dedicated to the Assyrian King Ashurbanipal; and piles of royal tableware stamped with Xerxes' name.

In the mid-5th century BCE, Xerxes' son, Artaxerxes, made some additions to Persepolis, including the extension of the Hall of a Hundred Columns, but by this point the royal city was substantially complete. The Achaemenid kings continued to visit annually for over a century more, and they were buried in a complex of cliff tombs 6 miles (10 km) away at Naqsh-e Rostam, where carvings show them standing to the side of Zoroastrian fire altars.

Destruction and restoration

Disaster struck in 330 BCE when the Macedonian ruler Alexander the Great, having defeated the Persian King Darius III, arrived at Persepolis. In a drunken rage—and, it was said, in revenge for the destruction of the Old Temple of Athena a century and a half earlier—he ordered his troops to burn and loot the city. The timbered roofs fell, the columns collapsed, and most of the inhabitants fled.

In the 3rd century CE, under the Sasanians, the center of Persian power shifted to Estakhr, on the plain below, which had probably once been the residential settlement for the servants and soldiers who worked in Persepolis. The Sasanians added their own inscriptions below the Achaemenid tombs at Naqsh-e Rostam, including one of their king, Shapur I, humiliating the defeated Roman Emperor Valerian. Later rulers treated Persepolis as a quarry for their own projects: in the 930s CE, the Buyid ruler Amir Abu Shuja carted away four grand doorways to enhance his palace at Shiraz. The original purpose of the site was slowly forgotten, and it became known as Takht-e Jamshid ("the throne of Jamshid") after a legendary Persian king. European travelers came to wonder at the ruins, beginning with Odoric of Pordenone, an Italian Franciscan monk, who visited in the early 14th century. At the start of the 18th century, the Dutch artist Cornelis de Bruijn made a series of drawings of the site which brought it to wider attention and attracted even more foreign tourists, many of whom carved their names on its stones.

In the 1930s, modern excavations began, first under the German archaeologists Ernst Herzfeld and Erich Schmidt, who also initiated reconstruction. Gradually some sense of Persepolis's grandeur was restored, and in 1971 Shah Mohammed Reza Pahlavi hosted a lavish celebration to mark 2,500 years since the foundation of the Persian Empire. Foreign rulers, royalty, and dignitaries descended for what was dubbed "the party of the century," an attempt to recapture a sense of Darius's ceremonial capital at its height.

> "The man who has **respect for that law** which **Ahuramazda** [Zoroastrian deity] has established ... he both becomes **happy while living**, and becomes **blessed when dead**.
>
> INSCRIPTION ON THE PALACE OF XERXES

◁ DRINKING VESSEL
A golden rhyton in the shape of a monstrous lion. Such luxury items, used at feasts, were an important part of the display of Achaemenid royal power at Persepolis.

△ DOOR JAMB
A relief on an entrance door to the Palace of Xerxes shows the king served by two attendants, one of whom carries a parasol.

260 CE Sasanian rock carving at Naqsh-e Rostam celebrates Shapur I's victories over three Roman emperors, Gordian III, Philip the Arab, and Valerian.

933 Buyid ruler Amir Abu Shuja removes four monumental doors from Persepolis.

1704 Dutch artist Cornelis de Bruijn visits Persepolis and makes sketches of the site.

1971 The Shah of Iran holds grand ceremonies to celebrate the 2,500th anniversary of the Persian Empire.

1979 UNESCO inscribes Persepolis on the World Heritage List.

Delhi

CITY OF SEVEN CAPITALS

The epicenter of political power in the Indian subcontinent for most of the last millennium, Delhi is said to have seen the rise and fall of seven capital cities. The current Indian capital, New Delhi, is the eighth.

Delhi finds legendary mention in the ancient Indian epic *Mahabharata* as Indraprastha, the capital city built by the Pandavas, the story's heroes. Excavations suggest that the area has been inhabited since at least 1000 BCE, though the first reference to "Delhi" doesn't appear until the 1st century BCE, when a local chieftain named Dhilu is said to have named the settlement he built there after himself.

The Delhi Sultanate

Delhi began to emerge as a political stronghold in the 11th century CE, when the Tomara dynasty founded a citadel called Lal Kot (Red Citadel) on the southwestern fringes of the modern metropolis. In the 12th century, the rival Chauhans ousted the Tomaras and extended the fort with massive ramparts, the ruins of which still stand today, and renamed it Qila Rai Pithora. Then, in 1192, the Chauhans were defeated by Muhammad Ghori (from modern-day Afghanistan) in a decisive battle that paved the way for Islamic dynasties to conquer the Indian subcontinent. Following Ghori's death in 1206, the first of these dynasties was founded by Qutb ud-din Aibak, a formerly enslaved soldier, or Mamluk, who had risen to the position of general within Ghori's army. Aibak built his new capital on the site of Qila Rai Pithora, and named it Mehrauli.

Through the next three centuries, Delhi served as the center of power for a succession of Islamic dynasties. The Khiljis, who followed the Mamluks, fortified themselves in Siri, near present-day Hauz Khas. The Tughlaqs came next, and moved their capital within Delhi several times—as well as decamping briefly, under the capricious Muhammad-bin-Tughlaq, to Daulatabad in western India. Muhammad's successor, Feroz Shah Tughlaq, founded Ferozabad (Delhi's fifth capital) in 1354, where the Feroz Shah Kotla fortress is the most notable of several surviving Tughlaq bastions. The brief reign of the Sayyids was followed by the Lodis, whose legacy lives on in a series of fine tombs at the Lodhi Gardens, in today's New Delhi.

THE RED FORT AND SALIMGARH FORT, c. 1830 ▷
The seat of power for the Mughal emperors, Delhi's iconic Red Fort is connected to the earlier Salimgarh Fort by an arched bridge, which formerly spanned a channel from the Yamuna River.

c. 1052 Anangapala of the Tomara dynasty builds Lal Kot, establishing the first city of Delhi.

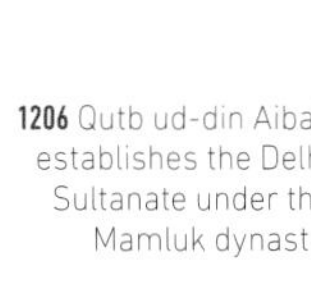
1206 Qutb ud-din Aibak establishes the Delhi Sultanate under the Mamluk dynasty.

1220 Work on the Qutub Minar, commissioned by Qutb ud-din Aibak c. 1199, is completed by his son-in-law Iltutmish.

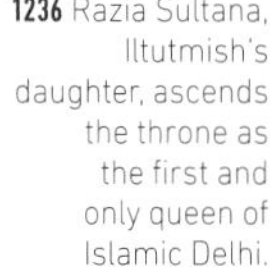
1236 Razia Sultana, Iltutmish's daughter, ascends the throne as the first and only queen of Islamic Delhi.

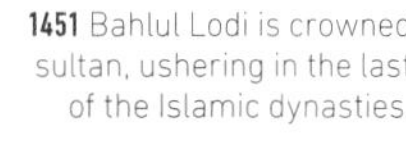
1451 Bahlul Lodi is crowned sultan, ushering in the last of the Islamic dynasties.

“I asked my soul: **What is Delhi?**
She replied: The world **is the body** and **Delhi its life**.

MIRZA GHALIB, URDU POET, 19TH CENTURY

◁ PURANA QILA
The massive fortifications of the Purana Qila were built on the site of the mythical city of Indraprastha. It was the seat of power for Humayun and Sher Shah Suri.

△ SHER SHAH SURI
Sher Shah Suri reigned over the subcontinent for just five years but in that time set up a postal system, introduced a currency (the rupiya), and laid down the Grand Trunk Road spanning his entire kingdom from modern-day Bangladesh to Afghanistan.

Rise of the Mughals

Ibrahim Lodi, the third Lodi sultan, inherited a divided kingdom, and his tyrannical leadership only made him more enemies. One of his governors invited Babur, a descendant of the Mongol Emperor Genghis Khan, to intervene. In 1526, Babur defeated Ibrahim to take his throne, establishing Mughal rule over the Indian subcontinent. During his short reign Babur based himself at Agra (which had been founded under the Lodis three decades earlier), but in 1533 Babur's son and successor, Humayun, returned to Delhi and set up a new capital called Dinpanah on the banks of the Yamuna River. Seven years later, Sher Shah of the Suri dynasty seized power and strengthened Dinpanah, which he renamed Shergarh. The ramparts, now known as Purana Qila, still stand today.

Humayun recaptured Delhi in 1555 but his successors chose to rule the empire from Agra, and Delhi went into decline. The coronation of Shah Jahan, the fifth Mughal emperor, in 1628, however, was the beginning of a new golden age for the city. An inveterate and extravagant builder—most famous for the Taj Mahal—the new emperor turned his back on Agra, and commissioned the construction of a brand new city, Delhi's seventh capital, on the Yamuna river. Work began on Shahjahanabad—named after its creator—in 1638, and eleven years later the emperor and his retinue moved in.

Shahjahanabad

Shah Jahan's metropolis was a masterpiece of Mughal architecture. He commissioned the massive Red Fort, which became the city's administrative core. Built of red sandstone, the emperor's palace complex displayed his lavish tastes. Within its ramparts were lush lawns and gardens, marble pavilions, mosques, apartments, and royal baths, as well as a marketplace where traders dealt in precious jewelery, gemstones, silk, and other goods. The royal court received visitors in the Diwan-i-Aam ("hall of public audience"), a magnificent sandstone pavilion supported by elegant columns and faced with lime stucco. At its back wall, on a marble pedestal, sat the emperor's bejeweled Peacock Throne. He would hold court with his most senior nobles at the Diwan-i-Khas ("hall of private audience"), the walls of which were embellished with fine marble filigree and intricately inlaid with lapis, jade, and mother-of-pearl, the ceiling molded entirely in silver.

1526 Babur establishes the Mughal dynasty in India after defeating Ibrahim Lodi in the Battle of Panipat.

1530 Babur dies in Agra, and is succeeded by his son Humayun as the emperor of the Mughal Empire.

1540 Sher Shah Suri briefly wrests control of Delhi from the Mughals.

1556 Humayun dies,a year after recapturing Delhi. His son Akbar transfers his capital to Agra.

1569 Humayun's widow, Bega Begum, commissions Humayun's Tomb in honor of her late husband.

SHAH JAHAN'S COURT ▷
In the time of Shah Jahan, the Hall of Public Audience was festooned with tapestries and laid with silk carpets. Here, his son Aurangzeb salutes him from among the noblemen below.

Beyond the Red Fort, the walled city of Shahjahanabad radiated westward in the shape of a quarter-circle sector, with the Yamuna River a natural fortification to the east. The city's commercial heart was a wide bazaar that stretched for more than a mile (1.5 km) on either side of the Chandni Chowk, originally a half-moon-shaped square (on the site of today's Town Hall). The bazaar was cut through by a central water channel (later built over by the British) and lined with stores and stalls trading in exotic merchandise such as spices, perfumes, textiles, porcelain, jewelery, and medicinal supplies. To the south was the city's main mosque: the triple-domed Jama Masjid, rendered in red sandstone and white marble, and able to accommodate up to 25,000 worshippers; it still holds its reputation as the largest mosque in India.

After Shah Jahan's demise, Shahjahanabad continued to serve as the Mughal capital, except for a period during the reign of his son, Aurangzeb, but repeated incursions from the Maratha Empire from western India and Afghan invaders from the northwest frontier weakened the Mughals' grip on the city. In 1739, Delhi was brutally sacked by the soldiers of Nadir Shah, the Shah of Persia, who slaughtered more than 20,000 men, women, and children in a mere six hours and pillaged the city's treasures, taking away the Peacock Throne and the famed Koh-i-Noor diamond. The defenseless Mughals had little option but to appoint the Marathas as the protectors of the throne, with the Mughals retaining nominal control only in Delhi itself. Further raids by the Afghans in the 1750s paved the way for the Marathas to consolidate their grip over Delhi in 1757, leaving the Mughal dynasty to wallow in political and military ignominy.

> "If there is a **paradise on earth**, it is this, it is this, **it is this.**
>
> INSCRIBED ON THE ARCHES OF THE DIWAN-I-KHAS, RED FORT

1638 Shah Jahan commissions a new capital in Delhi for the Mughal Empire, and names it Shahjahanabad.

1650 Jahanara Begum, eldest daughter of Shah Jahan, conceives and plans the construction of Chandni Chowk, the city's main square.

Shah Jahan's son Aurangzeb seized the throne in 1658, executed his brothers, and had his father imprisoned.

1681 Aurangzeb moves his capital to the city of Aurangabad, in southern India.

1707 Delhi once again becomes capital after Aurangzeb's death, but begins to slip into decline as the Marathas gain ground in the subcontinent.

Jantar Mantar observatory

1724 Jai Singh II, a subordinate of the Mughals, builds the Jantar Mantar in Delhi. The open-air observatory consists of giant astronomical instruments, used to calculate time.

1739 Nadir Shah of Persia invades Delhi, massacres its inhabitants, and carries away vast amounts of treasure.

△ **EID IN DELHI**
The Islamic festival of Eid was a focal point of the Mughal calendar. In this painting from the 1840s, Emperor Bahadur Shah Zafar leads a procession seated atop his caparisoned elephant, with his family following behind.

Delhi under British rule

In 1803, British forces defeated the Marathas at the Battle of Delhi, and the city came under the administration of the British East India Company. The Mughals kept nominal access to the Delhi throne, shorn of virtually all power. In 1857, after years of being throttled by a tyrannical British administration, Indian soldiers in the ranks of the British armed forces joined hands in a nationwide rebellion. United in revolt, thousands of soldiers marched to Delhi, where there was no British garrison stationed. There, they hastily declared the elderly Bahadur Shah Zafar, the last reigning Mughal, as the emperor of India.

The uprising—immortalized in history books as the First War of Independence—was short-lived. British forces soon regrouped and attacked Delhi, recapturing the city after a three-month siege. The aftermath of the revolt was brutal: Company soldiers pillaged the city in reprisal, killing thousands of Indian soldiers and civilians and looting their properties. Bahadur Shah Zafar was taken prisoner, and two of his sons and a grandson were murdered on the site where traitors and state enemies had been routinely executed by Delhi's previous emperors.

The revolt marked the formal end of the Mughals, and the beginning of direct rule of India by the British Crown—the period known as the Raj. The British moved their capital to the less volatile Calcutta (now Kolkata), and administered Delhi from the leafy Civil Lines district, where their palatial mansions and hotels became the hub of British social life. The once-thriving area of Shahjahanabad (Old Delhi), meanwhile, was left to fade into obscurity.

By the early 20th century, Calcutta had become a focal point for agitation against British rule, and at the Imperial Durbar of 1911, King George V announced that the Indian capital would once again move back to Delhi. Construction of the new imperial city, visualized by the architect Edwin Lutyens (see box), began the following year. In 1931, New Delhi—designed as a grand statement of British imperial might—was inaugurated as the new capital. Yet British confidence was short-lived. Within 16 years, they'd be gone.

1803 The Marathas are defeated by the British. Delhi comes under the East India Company's control.

1857 Bahadur Shah Zafar, the last Mughal emperor, is arrested by British troops after the Siege of Delhi.

Following his arrest, Bahadur Shah Zafar was tried at the Red Fort, charged on four counts, and imprisoned in Burma (now Myanmar), where he died in 1862.

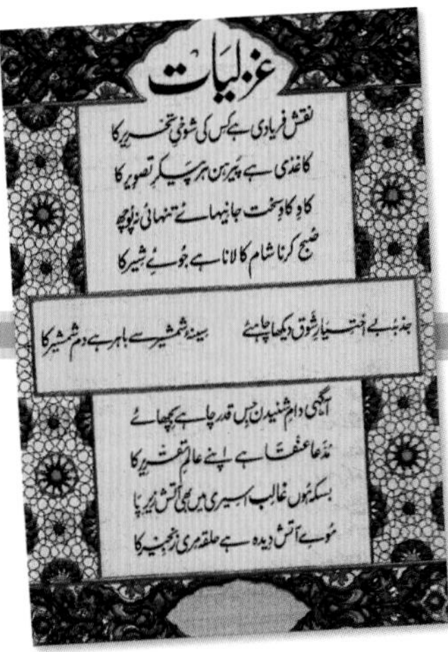

غزلیات

نقش فریادی ہے کس کی شوخیِ تحریر کا
کاغذی ہے پیرہن ہر پیکرِ تصویر کا
کاوِ کاوِ سخت جانی ہائے تنہائی نہ پوچھ
صبح کرنا شام کا لانا ہے جوئے شیر کا
جذبۂ بے اختیارِ شوق دیکھا چاہیے
سینۂ شمشیر سے باہر ہے دم شمشیر کا
آگہی دامِ شنیدن جس قدر چاہے بچھائے
مدعا عنقا ہے اپنے عالمِ تقریر کا
بسکہ ہوں غالب اسیری میں بھی آتش زیرِ پا
موئے آتش دیدہ ہے حلقہ مری زنجیر کا

Mirza Ghalib's "Naqsh Faryaadi," the first couplet of *Diwan-e-Ghalib*

1869 Mirza Ghalib, one of the most celebrated poets of the Mughal era, dies in Delhi.

1911 King George V visits Delhi and is crowned Emperor of India in the presence of Indian royalty and dignitaries.

1912 Construction of New Delhi begins, and continues for nearly two decades.

Lutyens' Delhi

> "Whoever has **built a new city** in Delhi has always **lost it** ... We [**the British**] were **no exception**.

WILLIAM DALRYMPLE, QUOTING IRIS PORTAL, *CITY OF DJINNS*, 1993

◁ The grand new city of "Imperial Delhi" was built to the southwest of the city's former heart, Shahjahanabad.

△ The circular design of New Delhi's Parliament House is said to be based on an 11th-century temple. It is slated to be converted into a museum when parliament moves to a new building, scheduled for 2024.

Born in London, England, Edwin Lutyens already had a reputation as one of Britain's leading architects by the time he was invited to lead a planning committee for the construction of a new imperial capital in Delhi in 1911. Taking some inspiration from Pierre Charles L'Enfant's designs for Washington, D.C. (see p. 260), Lutyens and his team devised the new district on a monumental scale. Its heart was the Kingsway (now the Rajpath), a grand, tree-lined mall which linked the triumphal India Gate to the majestic, pink-sandstone Viceroy's House (now the Presidential Palace), an elegant blend of Neoclassical form with elements of India's own architectural traditions. Beyond lay broad, shady avenues lined with spacious white bungalows; at the district's northern corner was Connaught Place, designed by Robert Tor Russell, as the hub of commercial activity. The new city took nearly 20 years to build, and is often cited as one of the finest architectural ensembles in the world. Lutyens himself was knighted in 1918, and in tribute to him, New Delhi's administrative core, still the heart of India's government, is sometimes called Lutyens' Delhi.

1922 The University of Delhi is established.

1931 Delhi is formally inaugurated as the new administrative capital of British India.

1935 Jamia Millia Islamia, a university founded in Aligarh (in Uttar Pradesh), is moved to Delhi. It becomes a premier institute for the arts and sciences.

1947 The ceremony for India's Independence is held in New Delhi. Jawaharlal Nehru becomes the first prime minister.

△ **REPUBLIC DAY PARADE**
A spectacular parade is held in New Delhi on January 26 every year to commemorate India's birth as a republic in 1950. The parade showcases the country's military prowess and vast cultural diversity.

> **I met** a hundred men **going to Delhi** and **every one** is **my brother.**
>
> POPE PAUL VI, 1964

Delhi after independence

When Prime Minister Jawaharlal Nehru announced the fruition of India's "tryst with destiny" to the Indian parliament in Delhi on the eve of the nation's independence in 1947, celebrations across the city were widespread. Yet the cost of freedom was Partition, as India was split along religious lines and (predominantly Muslim) Pakistan came into being. Sectarian violence broke out between Hindu and Muslim communities, thousands of Muslims were killed, and many more were driven from the city—by 1951, the Muslim population had fallen from a third of Delhi's total to a mere 5 percent. The exodus was matched by an even greater influx of refugees from the northwest, for which the city was ill-equipped. Dozens of refugee "colonies" were set up on the outskirts, which in time developed into new neighborhoods, but the city's growth was haphazard. In 1957, the Delhi Development Authority was established to plan future growth, but even though the Master Plan for Delhi that resulted acquired large areas of new land, the city still struggled to meet its housing needs.

Meanwhile, the commercial life of the city began to change as it transitioned from a trading center to an industrial powerhouse. Many of the newcomers found work in the factories that spilled out in satellite cities such as Ghaziabad and Faridabad, which in due course were absorbed into Delhi's expanding limits. The staging of the Asian Games in 1982 heralded a new phase in the city's development, spurring economic activity and a further wave of inward migration. High-rises started to appear on the skyline around Connaught Place in New Delhi, the city's central business district, and the leafy suburbs of South Delhi began to flourish.

By the late 1980s, the city had a population of almost 10 million people. The pace of change picked up again after the sweeping economic reforms of the early 1990s, which resulted in a wave of foreign investment and laid the platform for the unprecedented economic growth that has underpinned the city's transition into a modern global metropolis.

Mahatma Gandhi in Delhi, 1939

1948 Amid post-Partition unrest, Mahatma Gandhi, who led India's campaign for independence, is assassinated in New Delhi.

1950 India becomes a republic on January 26, with New Delhi as the national capital.

1965 Doordarshan, India's national television channel, begins daily transmissions from New Delhi.

1973 The Delhi Agreement is signed between India, Pakistan, and Bangladesh in the aftermath of the Bangladesh Liberation War.

Postage stamp issued for the 9th Asian Games

1982 New Delhi hosts the 9th Asian Games. The city undergoes significant urban development for the occasion.

1991 New Delhi is designated a National Capital Territory, a status exclusive from other Indian states and union territories.

◁ THE LOTUS TEMPLE
Built in 1986 for followers of the Baha'i faith, the Lotus Temple consists of 27 marble "petals," unfolding like a lotus flower. Open to people of any (or no) religion, it is one of the most visited buildings in the world.

A world city

Today, the city of Delhi is home to nearly 30 million people, with an urban sprawl that stretches from the congested lanes of Old Delhi—where life still continues with an unhurried 19th-century lilt—to the skyscrapers of Gurgaon's Cyber City, where *Fortune* 500 giants spin the great Indian dream. A cosmopolitan hub, with arguably the richest culinary scene of all Indian cities, the capital has cemented its place as the nation's cultural center, home to sophisticated art galleries and markets selling handicrafts curated from across the country. In recent times, some of the city's medieval villages have been restored and reinvented as cultural districts—among these are Hauz Khas, a hamlet built around a reservoir dating back to the Khilji era, which is now one of Delhi's top hipster areas, and Lodhi Art District, a hub for contemporary street art that has taken shape not far from the tomb of Sikandar Lodi.

Of course, rapid urbanization has also caused problems. The increasing population continues to put tremendous pressure on the city's infrastructure and electricity shortages are routine during summer months, and—despite the still-expanding Delhi Metro—the 11-million-plus motor vehicles plying the city's streets often bring traffic to a near standstill. Pollution poses a serious health hazard to the city's residents.

Nonetheless, as the country's premier location for government offices, public institutions, and private enterprises, Delhi continues to hurtle down the one-way street of growth and development. As new areas of the city develop, and futuristic experiments in glass and steel thrust skyward, Delhi takes its place confidently among rival global megalopolises, a force to be reckoned with for its cosmopolitan ethos, multicultural character, and enduring historic and artistic appeal.

According to the UN, Delhi's urban population of 29 million is the second highest in the world, behind Greater Tokyo.

2002 The Delhi Metro enters active service, and dramatically alters public transportation in the city.

2005 The vast Akshardham Temple complex opens, becoming the largest temple in Delhi.

2010 The 19th Commonwealth Games are held in New Delhi, as the city is given yet another face-lift.

2014 The World Health Organization declares New Delhi to have the most polluted air of any city in the world.

2016 Delhi implements the odd-even scheme to reduce traffic congestion, whereby vehicles with even-numbered plates are allowed to run only on even dates, and odd-numbered plates on odd dates.

▽ LODHI ART DISTRICT
Set up in 2014, the Lodhi Art District showcases the best of New Delhi's contemporary street art and graffiti.

Hampi

CITY OF VICTORY

Over a brief but glorious period of around 230 years, Hampi rose to become the biggest and most dazzling city of medieval India, before being brutally sacked and fading into oblivion until the modern era.

In the heart of the Deccan plateau in South India, the ethereal, boulder-strewn landscape around Hampi has long been held sacred for its central role in the ancient Hindu epic *Ramayana*. It is known in the story as Kishkindha, the mythical kingdom of monkeys that lends support to Lord Rama in his battle against the demon King Ravana. By the 10th century, Hampi was well established as a pilgrimage center called Pampa Kshetra, from which its name derives, and it developed further over the following centuries under the Hoysala dynasty as a hub for religion and education.

Dawn of an empire

By the early 14th century, the armies of the powerful Delhi Sultanate to the north were aggressively making incursions south. With the reigning Hoysala Empire on the verge of collapse, two brothers, Harihara and Bukka—commanders placed in charge of repelling the invasion—raised a small army and in 1336 set up a new capital at Hampi, a naturally fortified site on the Tungabhadra River. They named it Vijayanagar—"city of victory."

The early kings of Vijayanagar ambitiously pushed the boundaries of their kingdom in all directions. By the early 1400s, the empire had expanded to include almost all of peninsular South India. The city itself was made almost impregnable, surrounded by huge stone walls. Successive kings developed the city's infrastructure, building palaces and temples, roads and markets, as well as a sophisticated irrigation system of water tanks and canals.

Historians believe that during its heyday in the early 16th century Hampi was the second largest city in the world, after Beijing.

◁ VIRUPAKSHA TEMPLE
The nine-tiered, 160-ft (50-m) *gopura* (entrance tower) of the Virupaksha Temple dominates Hampi's ruins. The temple has been a place of active worship for more than a thousand years.

> "The city of **Vijayanagar** is such that the pupil of the eye has **never seen a place like it**, [nor has] there existed **anything to equal it** in the world.
>
> ABD-AL-RAZZĀQ, PERSIAN TRAVELER, 1443

1326 Armies of the Delhi Sultanate defeat the last of the Hindu kingdoms in South India.

1336 Harihara and Bukka establish a new kingdom at Hampi, and begin expanding their domain.

1356 On Harihara's death, Bukka takes the throne. He is credited with developing the city's irrigation system.

Before being seated in Hampi, Vijayanagar's capital was briefly located in Anegundi, a village across the Tungabhadra River.

1509 Krishna Deva Raya, the greatest of Vijayanagar's emperors, is enthroned.

The court of Krishna Deva Raya

◁ MYTHICAL HAMPI
The Hampi region features in the *Ramayana* as the fabled monkey kingdom of Kishkindha, depicted here in an illustrated manuscript from 1653.

“Vijayanagar is **as large as Rome**, and **very beautiful** to the sight. It is the **best provided city** in the world.

DOMINGO PAES, *CHRONICLE OF THE KINGS OF VIJAYANAGAR*, 1520

By 1509, when Krishna Deva Raya was crowned king of Vijayanagar, Hampi had grown to become India's richest city as well as its biggest, with a population estimated to be around 500,000. It was now the military and political nerve center of the entire Deccan region, and a formidable entrepôt for intercontinental trade.

Age of gold

Krishna Deva Raya ruled for a brief but eventful period of 20 years, an era that marked Hampi's apogee. The city went through unprecedented development and beautification. Many of the city's showcase temples, statues, and pavilions were completed during this period, and others were embellished with intricate designs—most famously the extraordinary stone columns at the Vittala Temple commonly referred to as the Sa-Re-Ga-Ma (Do-Re-Mi-Fa) pillars, which, when gently tapped, produce individual musical notes like a xylophone.

When Domingo Paes, a chronicler hailing from the nearby Portuguese colony of Goa, visited Hampi in 1520, he found the city to be of striking beauty. “There are many groves within it, in the gardens of houses, many conduits of water which flow into the midst of it, and in places there are lakes,” he wrote in his journal. He went on to describe elaborate festivities featuring bejeweled elephants, dancing women, and lavish feasting, held on an astounding scale.

Traders from faraway lands arrived in chariots laden with exotic merchandise—jewels from Sri Lanka and Myanmar, pearls from the Straits of Hormuz, Chinese brocade, and Malabar spices—to sell in the colonnaded shophouses of the sprawling Krishnapura street market. The Portuguese writer Barbosa commented on the city's cosmopolitan, egalitarian air, where “great equity and justice is observed by all, not only by the rulers, but by the people to one another.” At this time, the city secured almost exclusive ownership—paid for in gold—of the finest Arabian horses, an advantage that underpinned the empire's military might.

1509–1529 Many of Hampi's iconic monuments, including the 22-ft (7-m) monolithic statue of the deity Narasimha, are completed during Krishna Deva Raya's reign.

1542 Aliya Rama Raya takes power. His aggressive treatment of neighboring sultanates leaves Vijayanagar isolated.

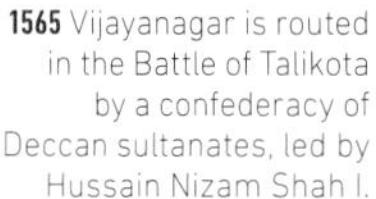

1565 Vijayanagar is routed in the Battle of Talikota by a confederacy of Deccan sultanates, led by Hussain Nizam Shah I.

Hussain Nizam Shah I on horseback, 16th century

A city lost and found

Yet the death of Krishna Deva Raya in 1529 marked the beginning of the end for Hampi. The tyrannical and interfering King Aliya Rama Raya united the Vijayanagar Empire's enemies against him, and in 1565, a confederacy of Deccan sultanates sought revenge. At the Battle of Talikota, Aliya Rama Raya was captured and beheaded, and Hampi was invaded, sacked, and laid to waste by the invading armies. In a matter of days, the once-glorious city was reduced to a pile of rubble, which according to legend remained ablaze for six months.

While local chiefs fought over the remnants of the empire, the city itself was never repopulated after the war. The ruins were gradually reclaimed by wilderness, and remained obscured from public sight for more than 200 years. In 1800, after the British East India Company assumed control over the Deccan region, Hampi was formally surveyed for the first time. Since India's independence in 1947, the government of India has focused attention on restoring and preserving many of its monuments, and today the ruins cast a spell over tourists and scholars from around the world—indeed, many visitors find it hard to leave.

△ **VITTALA TEMPLE RUINS**
Dedicated to Vishnu, the Vittala Temple is the grandest of Hampi's shrines. The exquisitely carved stone chariot in front of the temple features on India's Rs 50 note.

1646 The Vijayanagar Empire finally comes to an end, as several kingdoms break away and declare independence.

1799 Tipu Sultan of Mysore is defeated by an army of the British East India Company. The Deccan plateau comes under British rule.

1800 The Surveyor General of India makes the first study of Hampi's ruins.

1856 British officer Alexander Greenlaw takes the first photographs of Hampi's ruins. The pictures soon go missing, resurfacing only in 1980.

1900 Robert Sewell's *A Forgotten Empire*, an account of the Vijayanagar dynasty, turns the spotlight on Hampi and piques the interest of modern historians.

1986 The Group of Monuments at Hampi, comprising more than 1,600 remains, is inscribed as a UNESCO World Heritage Site.

Xi'an

CITY OF PERPETUAL PEACE

The capital of 10 Chinese dynasties, Xi'an was once the world's largest city, a huge and bustling trading center at the end of the Silk Road, adorned with magnificent Buddhist pagodas and imperial palaces.

Xi'an's history goes back a long way: the Neolithic Yangshao people built a village near the present-day city in the 5th millennium BCE. They chose a prime site, ringed by mountains and close to the Yellow and Wei rivers. The fertile, easily defended spot attracted the Zhou, the first really powerful Chinese dynasty, who built their capital, Fenghao, here in around 1000 BCE. Two centuries later, they moved their capital to Luoyang, and the city slipped back into obscurity, setting a pattern of glory, decline, and renewal that would echo down the centuries.

The First Emperor and the Han

Qin Shi Huangdi, the First Emperor, united China in 221 BCE, and revived the city. He migrated thousands of rich provincial families to populate a walled city that he named Xianyang, divided into wards where drums sounded a night curfew. His splendid residence, the Er Fang (or "nearby palace"), was the largest palace China had seen, with a terrace where 10,000 people could gather. But his rigid rule—he imposed standardized measurements and a uniform script, and executed dissenting scholars—led to opposition. He died in 210 BCE, and his dynasty ended just three years later. Only his grand mausoleum survived, its sealed interior hiding the magnificent, life-size Terra-Cotta Army (see box, p.64). It would not be seen again until 1974.

The new Han dynasty chose a site about 12 miles (20 km) southeast of Xianyang as its capital under Emperor Gaozu in 202 BCE, and named it Chang'an. The Han control of rich

> "It is the most **impregnable** refuge in **heaven** and **earth**."
>
> PAN GU ON THE ADVANTAGES OF CHANG'AN, 1ST CENTURY CE

◁ THE EMPEROR'S ARMY
Each of the 8,000 life-size Terra-Cotta Warriors buried in the mausoleum of Qin Shi Huangdi was carved with a different face, a sign of the enormous care taken in the preparation of an entourage that would serve the emperor in the afterlife.

Zhou-era bronze harness ornament

4500 BCE The Neolithic village of Banpo flourishes in a fertile valley of the Yellow River.

c. 1000 BCE The Zhou establish their capital, Fenghao, in the area southwest of modern Xi'an. Bronze-working reaches a peak.

770 BCE The Zhou move their court to Luoyang, and Fenghao declines.

221 BCE The area becomes the site of Xianyang, the capital of the first united Chinese state, under the Qin.

212 BCE Qin Shi Huangdi orders the building of the Er Fang ("nearby palace"), the largest palace yet constructed in China.

agricultural lands and the city's position at the start of the Silk Road, the trade route connecting East Asia with Europe, provided the emperors with enormous financial resources. Emperor Gaozu's minister Xiao He gave the city an armory and state-controlled market, and began to fill in the urban grid with lavish projects that earned him an imperial rebuke for his extravagance. It is said that it took 145,000 laborers to construct the grand Changle and Weiyang palaces and complete the city walls.

The next emperor, Hui, continued this pursuit of luxury, and built an icehouse to preserve delicacies in the royal residence. In the late 2nd century BCE, the Emperor Wudi added a park with a boating lake where festivals and pageants were held, and an imperial menagerie, which boasted a rhinoceros and an elephant.

The Han grip on power gradually slackened, and discontent led to the elevation of a usurper, Wang Mang, in 9 CE. His 14-year rule was distinguished by its grandiose projects (nine temples were built for the worship of the spirits of past emperors) and the chaos of its ending, a violent sacking of Chang'an by the resurgent Han.

Tang flowering

After the Han dynasty collapsed in the 2nd century CE, China broke up into several warring kingdoms, and Chang'an dwindled in importance. It found renewed favor as the capital of the short-lived Sui dynasty, which reunited the country in the 6th century, before reaching the height of its glory in the 8th century under their successors, the Tang. During the Tang dynasty, this great Silk Road city bustled with merchants hawking precious spices, fine

◁ **REMEMBERING HOME**
This painting, by an 18th-century artist, shows a section of Chang'an that was modeled on Feng, the hometown of Gaozu, the first Han emperor. Gaozu reputedly ordered the reconstruction of Feng's streets in the capital for his homesick father.

Emperor Gaozu, meaning "founder"

206–202 BCE After the Qin collapse, the Chu and Han battle over a divided kingdom, until the Han gain the upper hand under Emperor Gaozu.

202–200 BCE Emperor Gaozu commissions the Changle and Weiyang palaces.

◁ ALONG THE SILK ROAD
This 15th-century silk scroll shows traders carrying a cargo of precious goods on the long journey from Chang'an across the Silk Road through Central Asia.

> Now the **mansions** have **new owners**. Another **generation** dons the caps and robes of **high office**.
>
> *AUTUMN MEDITATIONS*, DU FU, c. 760 CE

textiles, exotic woods, and jewelery. Its 108 wards were filled to bursting with over a million people. Its scale was astonishing: the main avenues were up to 330 ft (100 m) wide, lined with trees and edged with drainage ditches, while its walls were 40 ft (12 m) high, and pierced with 12 city gates. A new palace, the Daming, was built to the north, its walls enclosing huge halls, flower gardens, and the headquarters of the vast imperial bureaucracy.

This was a city of faith and learning, packed with Buddhist shrines, Confucian temples, and Nestorian churches. Soaring over them all was the 10-story, relic-packed Wild Goose Pagoda, built to house the precious manuscripts collected by the monk Xuanzang during a 17-year pilgrimage to India. But there were warning signs. Powerful eunuchs stirred up intrigue in court; too much wealth was concentrated in the hands of the Buddhist monks; and the city grew less diverse—the gardens of the rich, in the eastern part of the city, became so large that an edict was passed to restrict their size.

Destruction and renewal

Late Tang Chang'an suffered successive sackings by rebels and Tibetan raiders in the 8th century. Poets still sang Chang'an's praises, but in increasingly melancholy tones. Weak emperors such as Wu Zong, who had pharmacy owners beaten if they did not stock the drugs he thought would give him everlasting life and who built a terrace 150 ft (45 m) high from which to commune with the immortals, did little to arrest its decline.

The city's Tang-era gates were so wide that three or four carriages could pass through at once.

TANG TRADER ▷
A merchant rests on his camel in this delicate polychrome ceramic, typical of many Tang sculptures showing Silk Road traders.

194–190 BCE The city walls and Han palaces are built, requiring the work of 145,000 laborers.

9–23 CE The city is largely destroyed during violence at the start and end of the usurper Wang Mang's reign.

25 The Eastern Han move the capital of the empire from Chang'an to Luoyang.

300–581 Chang'an serves as capital in 313–316, 534–537, and 556–581, under the Western Jin, Wei, and Zhou dynasties.

584 Now named Daxing, the city becomes capital of a reunited China under the Sui dynasty.

634 The Daming Palace, the world's largest royal residence, is built.

The Terra-Cotta Warriors

Qin Shi Huangdi, the First Emperor, was obsessed with immortality, seeking out elixirs created by Daoist sages that promised longevity. When death finally claimed him in 221 BCE, he was buried in a 20-sq-mile (50-sq-km) compound, his tomb set inside a massive mound.

It was here, in 1974, that a farmer stumbled across the first of what turned out to be 8,000 terra-cotta warriors, which were intended to serve the emperor in the afterlife. This ceramic army, once brightly painted, faced east as though toward an imagined foe, and was equipped with bows and crossbows, and accompanied by charioteers. The site was looted in ancient times, and archaeologists found no trace of the lake of mercury that was also reputed to have protected the tomb, although they did find the skeletons of several people and horses, who may have been buried alive with their ruler.

◁ Archaeologists restore the army: piecing together the original fragments, stopping paint flaking, and retarding mold development is a painstaking process.

> “They built **models of palaces, pavilions, and offices**, and filled the tomb with **fine vessels, precious stones**, and **rarities**.
>
> SIMA QIAN, *RECORDS OF THE GRAND HISTORIAN*, c. 90 BCE

◁ The Terra-Cotta Army included officers, like this general, some up to 6½ ft (2 m) tall.

652 The Wild Goose Pagoda is built as a translation center for the Buddhist monk Xuanzang.

715 The Hanlin academy is established to train scholars to serve in the imperial bureaucracy.

755 Chang'an is sacked during a revolt led by rebel General An Lushan.

781 Erection of the Nestorian stele, which details the flourishing of a version of Christianity in Chang'an.

When smuggler-turned-revolutionary Hung Chao's rebels sacked Chang'an in 880 CE, the city was doomed. The Tang collapsed, and the new emperor, Zhu Wen, founder of the Later Liang dynasty, ordered the city's wooden buildings to be moved en masse to his new capital, Luoyang.

Although the stone structures became ruined and the once orderly grand avenues were choked with small shops, Chang'an continued as a commercial center and its prosperity briefly revived during the time of Marco Polo's travels in the 13th century. A restoration came under the Ming in the 14th century. They built a new city wall (enclosing a far smaller urban space) and the imposing Bell and Drum Towers to sound the curfew, but the city then lapsed into comparative obscurity. It was renamed Xi'an ("western peace") in 1900, when the empress and her court fled there during the Boxer Rebellion. China's industrial growth in the late 20th century injected the city with new life—it's now home to 12 million people, with several universities and a large manufacturing base. But above all it is Xi'an's past that has renewed its fortunes, in the shape of the million tourists who come each year to marvel at the Terra-Cotta Army, giving the First Emperor the immortality he craved.

△ SOUND AND LIGHT
The Ming walls and towers of Xi'an are beautifully highlighted during an evening sound and light show, featuring traditional Chinese dragon dancers. The walls have become one of the modern city's main tourist attractions.

882 The Daming Palace is destroyed during the Hung Chao rebellion, as the Tang dynasty enters its final decline.

907 Chang'an's wooden buildings are moved to Luoyang, a former ancient capital.

It took 20,000 carpenters to dismantle Chang'an's wooden buildings and reassemble them in the new capital, Luoyang.

1370 A new city wall is built during a partial restoration of the city by the Ming.

1900 The city is renamed Xi'an ("western peace") by the Qing court, which shelters here during the Boxer Rebellion.

1974 The pits containing the Terra-Cotta Warriors are discovered by a local farmer.

2014 The Yongning, the southern gate of the Ming walls, is restored and opened to the public as a museum.

Mexico City

CITY OF PALACES

Born as Aztec Tenochtitlan, whose temples were destroyed by the Spanish and reshaped into a colonial settlement of palaces and churches, Mexico City grew through independence and revolution into the megacity of today.

Around 1248, a nomadic warrior-tribe called the Culhua-Mexica—more commonly known as the Aztecs—migrated to the Valley of Mexico. They entered an area, surrounded by mountains and volcanoes, with a rich history that took in peoples such as the Toltecs, whose civilization had collapsed over a century earlier, and ancient cities such as Teotihuacan, the largest in the pre-Columbian Americas.

According to an Aztec origin myth, they had journeyed from a place called Aztlan, and were instructed by Huitzilopochtli, the sun and war god who was their patron, to settle where they saw an eagle resting on a nopal cactus. They made their home by Lake Texcoco and here, from around 1535, they started to build Tenochtitlan.

This island city was connected to the mainland by three causeways, one of which had an aqueduct running along it. On the eastern side, the Aztecs built a dyke for flood protection. Floating gardens, or *chinampas*, were created to grow maize and other staples. The ceremonial precinct in the center of Tenochtitlan housed palaces, ball courts, and temples—notably the Huey Teocalli ("great temple"), today best known by its Spanish name, the Templo Mayor. This huge stepped pyramid was dedicated to Huitzilopochtli and the god of rain, Tlaloc. The Aztecs began as mercenaries and rose to prominence, allying with neighboring Texcoco and Tlacopan. They eventually became the dominant force in the region, controlling a vast empire.

◁ ***THE GREAT CITY OF TENOCHTITLAN*, 1945**
Mexican artist Diego Rivera's mural portrays the vibrancy of an Aztec market, with the city's causeways, *chinampas*, and palaces, and the Templo Mayor, visible in the background.

> “Some of our **soldiers** even asked whether **the things we saw** were not **a dream.**”
>
> BERNAL DÍAZ, *THE TRUE HISTORY OF THE CONQUEST OF NEW SPAIN*, 1568, ON THE SPANISH FIRST SEEING TENOCHTITLAN

750 CE The city of Teotihuacan, which at its peak had 200,000 inhabitants and was for centuries Mesoamerica's largest city, is abandoned. It will be revered by the Aztecs as a sacred place.

1248 The Aztecs arrive in the Valley of Mexico at Chapultepec. Their stories say they came from Aztlan, a mythical homeland to the north.

1325 The Aztecs found Tenochtitlan on the site where they see an eagle perching on a nopal cactus.

1428 The Aztec Emperor Itzcoatl forms the Triple Alliance with the neighboring cities of Texcoco and Tlacopan. The alliance becomes the basis of Aztec power.

1487 The Templo Mayor is completed in its final form, and tens of thousands are sacrificed over four days in celebration.

Aztec sculpture from Tenochtitlan's Templo Mayor

◁ AZTEC SUNSET
The 16th-century Aztec *Codex Borbonicus* depicts Xolotl (who helps guide the sun through the underworld) as the companion of the setting sun, Tonatiuh.

At its height, the Aztec Empire consisted of a network of almost 400 subject and allied cities, stretching from the Gulf of Mexico to the Pacific. It supplied Tenochtitlan with tribute, including goods and produce, but also captives for sacrifice.

Aztec daily life

By 1500, Tenochtitlan was home to more than 200,000 people. Tlatelolco, on the city's northern outskirts, was the site of the great market, held every fifth day and attended by over 40,000 people buying and selling goods such as food, jaguar skins, quetzal feathers, knives, and ceramics.

Order and balance were of the utmost importance in Aztec society. Roles fulfilled by men and women were mostly separate and complementary, with women generally tending to the home, but also carrying out important religious duties. Although men could work in a number of professions, society was geared toward war, and all men were expected to fight for the *tlatoani* (emperor). Children were taught to contribute to the family from a young age, initially by their parents. Boys were also formally trained in schools where they learned to fulfill religious duties and become warriors or priests. Elite Eagle or Jaguar Warriors were chosen from the best fighters.

Religion permeated all aspects of life, and there were many festivals dedicated to the gods. Human sacrifice was often central to these events, but ritual violence, such as bloodletting and self-mutilation, was also part of everyday life. The city's sacred precinct was dominated by the Templo Mayor, atop which the hearts of captives or slaves would be cut out of their chests as an offering to ensure the sun would have the energy to battle with the darkness and rise again the next day.

> "There is **one square** ... where are **daily assembled** more than **60,000 souls** ... buying and selling.
>
> HERNÁN CORTÉS, *SECOND LETTER TO EMPEROR CHARLES V*, 1520

1502 A massive flood hits Tenochtitlan; the Aztec *tlatoani*, Ahuitzotl, is killed and Montezuma II becomes ruler.

1503 The stone of the five suns bears the date July 15, which some historians believe to be the date of Montezuma II's coronation.

Skull carvings, displayed at the base of the Templo Mayor

1509 Aztec myths record that fire is seen in the sky, the first of eight omens of evil foretelling the arrival of the Spanish 10 years later.

November 1519 Hernán Cortés arrives in Tenochtitlan with 500 Spanish troops and tens of thousands of Indigenous allies.

June 1520 La Noche Triste: the Spanish are forced to retreat from Tenochtitlan, and 860 Spanish soldiers, 5 Spanish women, and more than 1,000 Tlaxcalan warriors are killed.

1520 May Pedro de Alvarado orders the massacre of thousands of unarmed Aztec celebrants taking part in the sacred Toxcatl festival.

The coming of the Spanish

This world was devastated by the arrival of Europeans. In February 1519, Spanish conquistador Hernán Cortés left Cuba against the orders of its governor, Diego Velázquez, to follow in the footsteps of two previous expeditions, the second of which had met Aztecs and learned of the great court of the *tlatoani*, Montezuma II. Cortés landed on the coast of the Gulf of Mexico, where he founded the town of Veracruz. He forged alliances with Indigenous groups, including the Tlaxcalans (enemies of the Aztecs), and marched to Tenochtitlan with 500 Spanish troops and tens of thousands of allies, most of whom waited outside the city.

In November, the Spanish were received peacefully by Montezuma II. Gifts were exchanged and the *tlatoani* welcomed them into Tenochtitlan. The conquistadors responded by taking Montezuma hostage, and attempted to rule through him. Meanwhile, a force of 1,100 men had been sent by Velázquez to arrest Cortés, landing in Veracruz in April 1520. Cortés left Tenochtitlan with only 226 soldiers, but captured the expedition's leader and persuaded the men to join him. In the meantime, Cortés' second-in-command, Pedro de Alvarado, had ordered the massacre of thousands taking part in the Toxcatl festival, and Cortés returned to a compound under siege. The Spanish brought Montezuma to a rooftop to appeal to the Aztecs, but he was struck down and then probably murdered by the conquistadors.

The Spanish left at midnight, loaded with gold, but were discovered and fiercely attacked. They made it to Tlaxcala and, with the help of their Indigenous allies, they regrouped and returned in May 1521 to lay siege to Tenochtitlan, which had been ravaged by smallpox.

The Aztecs, led by their last *tlatoani*, Cuauhtémoc, fought bravely. But by August 1521, it was over. The city was pillaged, its temples and palaces were destroyed, and Cuauhtémoc was tortured and eventually executed. Cortés became the first governor of New Spain and, in 1524, 12 Franciscans arrived to begin the "spiritual conquest" of the new territory.

Despite his efforts in the conquest, Cortés fell out of favor with Charles V of Spain. The man who had crushed the Aztecs was removed from office in 1527.

△ THE FALL OF TENOCHTITLAN
This 17th-century painting shows Cortés crossing a causeway into the city during the final assault.

One conquistador estimated that 136,000 human skulls were affixed to the *tzompantli* (rack) at the Templo Mayor's base.

Aztec terra-cotta Eagle Warrior

April 1521 Cortés begins the siege of Tenochtitlan, taking lakeside towns, and launching ships built in Tlaxcala onto the lake to stop the Aztecs resupplying.

August 1521 The Spanish and Indigenous auxiliaries launch a final attack on the defenders hemmed into Tlatelolco. After the capture of Cuauhtémoc, Aztec resistance collapses.

1522 Cortés is named Captain-General of New Spain, but is removed five years later after falling out of favor with the Spanish king.

1535 Antonio de Mendoza is appointed the first viceroy of New Spain.

◁ MEXICO CITY CATHEDRAL
The Metropolitan Cathedral looms over the Zócalo, the city's main square, in this 19th-century painting. Work on the bell towers was only finished in the 1790s, over 200 years after construction began.

Mexico City Cathedral weighs approximately 127,000 tons, and is gradually sinking into the mud of the old lake bed beneath it.

The colonial city

A court was created in the city to give Spain more direct control of its new colony, with Antonio de Mendoza becoming the first viceroy in 1535. The transformation of Tenochtitlan into a Spanish colonial city soon began in earnest. This "New Spain" was to be an improved version of its Old World counterpart, a place where the Spanish hoped to create a Catholic utopia away from what they viewed as the heresy plaguing Europe. The city was rebuilt in a grid system, and old temples were replaced by churches, monasteries, and convents, often using the old Aztec bricks. The Spanish Crown ordered Mendoza to provide an explanation of the Aztec political and tribute system, so he commissioned Nahua scribes at the Franciscan college, Tlatelolco, to create the *Codex Mendoza* around 1541. The Aztec nobility were allowed to govern two districts of the capital. Many of the conquistadors and settlers took Indigenous concubines, and out of these unions grew a considerable *mestizo* (mixed-race) population.

Expansion and independence

Mexico City (which took its name from Culhua-Mexica, the Aztecs' name for themselves) expanded steadily on the back of Indigenous and African enslaved labor. In 1551, Spain decreed the establishment of the Royal and Pontifical University of Mexico, which opened its doors in 1553. In 1573, construction started on the cathedral, replacing the city's original church, which the Spanish had built immediately after the conquest. This became a center of regal ceremony, involving the upper echelons of the court and clergy.

The colonial era gave Mexico a hierarchical society based on class and race, as well as grand residencies that led to Mexico City's nickname, "the city of palaces." At the top of the social pyramid were the *peninsulares*, or Spanish-born settlers. By the mid-17th century they were far outnumbered by *criollos*, but these Mexican-born descendants of Spanish settlers lacked the status or political influence of the *peninsulares*, and this became a major factor in Mexico's independence movement. The *criollo* community included many culturally significant figures, such as the writer and philosopher Sor Juana Inés de la Cruz, and they started to forge their own identity, calling themselves Mexicans and

1539 New Spain's first printed book, a Christian catechism, is produced in the city.

1551 The Royal and Pontifical University of Mexico is founded under a charter granted by King Charles I of Spain.

1648 Priest Miguel Sanchéz writes an account of a vision of Our Lady of Guadalupe, the Virgin Mary. Her image, found on a cloak, is now a renowned artifact.

1692 A revolt breaks out after a drought, famine, and rises in corn prices. The viceroy's residence is set on fire.

1749 The Jesuit College of San Ildefonso is enlarged, and becomes Mexico City's most prestigious educational institution.

1790 The Aztec Sun Stone is discovered in the Zócalo while repairs are being carried out on the cathedral.

The Aztec Sun Stone, in 1914

◁ *RETABLO DE LA INDEPENDENCIA*, 1960–1961
Juan O'Gorman's mural, depicting *El Grito de Dolores*, shows the priest (and later general) Miguel Hidalgo leading revolutionary figures, one of them bearing the icon of the Virgin of Guadalupe.

drawing on Aztec imagery to separate themselves from Spain. The *criollos* were also instrumental in the creation and growth of the cult of Our Lady of Guadalupe. In 1648, *criollo* clergyman Miguel Sanchéz published an account of the saint appearing to an Indigenous Nahua man a century earlier, and leaving her image on his cloak. Sanchéz's story was widely accepted, and Our Lady of Guadalupe eventually became Mexico's patron saint—her cloak is visited by millions of modern pilgrims every year.

The French invasion of Spain in 1808 and the capture of Charles IV created a power vacuum in New Spain. In 1810, *criollo* priest Miguel Hidalgo rang the bell of his church in the small town of Dolores, northwest of Mexico City, in a protest against the injustices of Spanish rule. His *Grito de Dolores* ("Cry of Dolores") marked the beginning of an independence war, which in 1821 saw the capture of the city by nationalist forces. Exactly three centuries after Cortés had conquered it, Mexico City became the capital of an independent nation.

1799 Anger at favoritism toward Spanish-born residents prompts the Conspiracy of the Machetes, a revolt against Spanish rule that is rapidly crushed.

1803 Prussian naturalist Alexander von Humboldt visits, staying in a house on República de Uruguay. His writings on Mexico's heritage and geology are hugely influential.

1810 Miguel Hidalgo's *Grito de Dolores* ("Cry of Dolores") sparks the Mexican War of Independence.

Mexico's coat of arms shows an eagle and a snake

1821 Mexico declares independence from Spain, and Mexico City becomes its capital.

1838 The looting of a French-owned bakery in Mexico City leads to the "Pastry War," in which ports including Veracruz are occupied by the French.

◁ BASILICA OF OUR LADY OF GUADALUPE
Mexico's national shrine, built in 1974, houses the cloak containing the image of Our Lady of Guadalupe. It replaced the 1709 shrine, built where the Virgin Mary was supposed to have appeared in 1531.

Mexico City's metro system, the STC, carries 1.6 billion people a year on its 12 lines.

In the 200 years since independence, Mexico City has seen violence, revolution, and invasion. Augustín de Iturbe was proclaimed president in 1821 and Emperor of Mexico in 1822, only to be exiled in 1823 as Mexico became a republic. Tension with the US led to war, and an 1847 assault on the capital that saw the heavily outnumbered Niños Héroes, teenage military cadets, hold off the Americans for several hours at Chapultepec Castle.

Revolution and modernity

The mid-19th century saw the political pendulum swing between Conservatives and Liberals. In the 1850s one of the latter, Benito Juárez, implemented the Reform Laws, which curtailed the powers of the Catholic Church and the military, and oversaw the confiscation of Church land. The French invaded in 1863 and installed Maximilian von Hapsburg as emperor the following year, but he was executed in 1867 as the republic returned. Stability finally came under Porfirio Díaz, who promised "order and progress." He served as president for seven terms, a period known as the "Porfiriato" that saw Mexico City transformed. New hospitals, schools, roads, and factories were built, as well as extravagant buildings that rivaled those of Europe, such as the Palacio de Correos and Palacio de Bellas Artes.

Díaz's policies stirred up resentment, however. He favored large landowners and deprived the rural poor of land, which, along with opposition to his authoritarian government, sparked the Mexican Revolution in 1910. The capital escaped the worst of the violence, though thousands died during La Decena Trágica when a coup successfully ousted the short-lived government of Francisco Madero, and the armies of Emiliano Zapata and Pancho Villa entered the city in 1914.

Out of the turmoil emerged the PRI, the Institutional Revolutionary Party, which took power in 1929. Mexico City modernized, with skyscrapers, a new motorway, and the enormous Ciudad Universitaria, a campus and cultural center that was made a UNESCO World Heritage Site in 2007. The 1968 Summer Olympics showed off the new city, but with the population surging to nearly 10 million by 1980, cracks were showing, and the city suffered severe pollution. In 2000, a now-stagnant PRI finally lost power. Today, Mexico's capital is a confident place, where evocative relics and backstreet taco joints rub shoulders with vibrant modern art and cutting-edge dining. The sun once worshipped by the Aztecs now shines down on a sprawling, creative economic powerhouse.

1867 The Austrian Archduke Maximilian is executed by firing squad after a three-year reign as emperor of Mexico.

1877 Porfirio Díaz seizes power, beginning the period known as the "Porfiriato," in which he serves seven terms as president.

1910 The Mexican Revolution begins as a result of the increasing unpopularity of the Porfirio Díaz regime.

1913 Thousands are killed in the city during La Decena Trágica, 10 days of fighting during a coup that deposes new president Francisco Madero.

1914 After Madero's replacement Victoriano Huerta is deposed, Pancho Villa (center) and Emiliano Zapata briefly occupy the presidential palace.

1929 The PRI (Institutional Revolutionary Party) is established. It will rule until 2000.

Frida Kahlo

> "I **paint self-portraits** because I am **so often alone**, because I am the **person I know best**.
>
> FRIDA KAHLO, ARTIST, 1907–1954

One of Mexico's greatest artists, Frida Kahlo was born in Coyoacán, in the south of Mexico City. She was disabled by polio as a child and was almost killed at 18 when her bus collided with a tram, leaving her spine broken in three places among other horrific injuries. Using a special easel, she began painting from her bed, with a mirror above it so she could create self-portraits. Her blend of Indigenous imagery with Surrealism brought her international acclaim. She had a tempestuous relationship with fellow Mexican artist Diego Rivera, and joined the Mexican Communist Party in 1927, hosting Soviet revolutionary Leon Trotsky in the 1930s. Her creative output and activism secured her reputation as a feminist icon, and her former home of Casa Azul is now a museum.

◁ *The Two Fridas*, from 1939, is a double portrait of Kahlo, one in European and the other in traditional Tehuana dress. The blood reflects her injuries and Aztec ritual sacrifice.

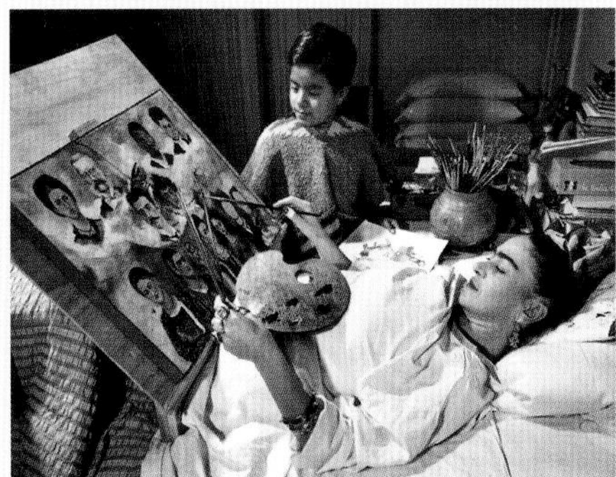

△ Kahlo's 1925 bus accident left her spine so damaged she was immobilized for long periods. Confined to her bed for months, she began to paint from it.

1956 The Torre Latinoamericana is completed. At 545 ft (166 m), it is the tallest building in Latin America at the time, and remains Mexico's highest for 26 years.

1978 Electrical workers digging near the Zócalo find a stone monolith depicting the goddess Coyolxauhqui.

1985 Mexico City is hit by a massive earthquake, registering 8.1 on the Richter Scale—around 10,000 people are killed.

Greater Mexico City's population reached 21 million in 2020, making it North America's largest city.

2000 Andrés Manuel López Obrador of the left-wing PRD party becomes Mexico City's second elected mayor. In 2018, he becomes Mexican president.

2011 The Museo Soumaya art gallery opens in an ultra-modern building covered with 16,000 hexagonal aluminum tiles.

Tikal

PLACE AT THE WELL

Carved out of the Central American jungle, the pyramid-temples of Tikal were the heart of a Maya city-state that dominated the neighboring region until its mysterious abandonment in the early 10th century CE.

The Maya established a series of cities in Mesoamerica from around 500 BCE. Tikal (its name means "at the well"), which lay in the Guatemalan lowlands close to Lake Petén Itzá, was one of the smallest of these. When most highland cities (such as the larger nearby El Mirador) were abandoned around 100 BCE, perhaps due to drought or deforestation, Tikal survived, growing to become a huge complex of palaces and pyramid-like temples set around a Great Plaza. Its ruler, the *ajaw*, was a war-leader and spiritual conduit to the gods, conducting ceremonies that the Maya believed ensured the city's continued well-being.

Rulers and empire

The most important of these ceremonies marked the *k'atun*, a 20-year cycle in the Maya sacred calendar. At the end of each cycle, the *ajaw* set up altars and stone stelae with inscriptions in the Mayan glyph writing system, which glorified their deeds and showed them making sacrifices of their own blood using strings of sharp maguey thorns. Each time, they also built a new set of double pyramids near the Great Plaza.

From the stelae we know the names of 33 *ajaws*, beginning in the late 1st century CE. Over the next two centuries, Tikal expanded, until at the time of Chak Tok Ich'aak I it was one of the most prosperous Maya cities.

In 378 CE, Siyaj K'ak', an outsider from Teotihuacan, over 620 miles (1,000 km) away in what is now Mexico, overthrew Chak Tok Ich'aak. He installed Yax Nuun Ayiin, the son of a Teotihuacano noble, as *ajaw*. The invaders' influence grew, and carvings show their distinctive *atlatls* (spear throwers) and goggle-eyed rain god Tlaloc. Expansion continued under Siyaj Chan K'awiil II, who presided over a very important *baktun* ceremony (marking 20 *k'atuns* or 400 years) in 435 CE, and was buried in a sumptuous tomb under Temple 33.

◁ PANORAMA OF TIKAL
Around the Great Plaza are Temple I (on the right) and Temple II (on the left). Below them is the Central Acropolis and at the top the North Acropolis, where many early *ajaws* were buried.

350 BCE Building of temples around the North Acropolis of Tikal begins.

c. 90 CE Yax Ehb Xook, Tikal's first recorded king, comes to the throne.

292 Stela 29, the first dated stela at Tikal, is set up, showing an *ajaw* in Maya dress with his father looking down from the heavens.

378 The arrival of Siyaj K'ak' begins a "New Order" of Teotihuacan influence on Tikal.

411 Accession of Siyaj Chan K'awiil II ("Sky Born"), whose 25-year reign sees Tikal's power reach a new peak.

Stela 31, dedicated to Siyaj Chan K'awiil II

The tallest pyramid at Tikal is Temple IV, also known as the Temple of the Two-Headed Serpent, which is 213 ft (65 m) high.

Tikal experienced a troubled period in the 6th century CE, and in 562 CE was overrun by forces from Calakmul, from the north. For 130 years there were no more stelae set up. Tikal's territory split in two, with rival rulers based in the city and in nearby Dos Pilas. Nuun Ujol Chaak managed to reunite the two in the 670s CE, but was defeated by a coalition backed by Calakmul.

Tikal's revival

Nuun Ujol Chaak's son, Jasaw Chan K'awiil I, won a decisive battle against Calakmul in 695 CE; a victory celebrated in carved wooden lintels, painted tableaux, and stelae inscriptions. Tikal once again became a major regional power, fighting wars with Naranjo in the east and Dos Pilas to the south. Jasaw Chan K'awiil engaged in massive construction projects, including three twin pyramids to mark the *k'atun* endings of his reign and a court for playing the ball game that was common throughout the region, in which players wearing elaborate harnesses had to propel rubber balls through goal hoops. He also built the massive Temple II near the Great Plaza, which may have served as his wife's tomb. Most impressive was Temple I, which stood 180 ft (55 m) in height and was built on the site of an older shrine. There the king was buried together with a huge trove of jade and shell jewelery, painted ceramics, and bones engraved with tiny glyphs showing Maya gods.

▷ FUNERARY MASK
The Maya placed masks, such as this one of jade and mother-of-pearl, over the faces of their royal dead. These preserved the ruler's legacy by replacing their own face after death.

◁ MAYA ALTAR
The carving on Altar 5, found near Temple III, shows two Maya nobles—one of whom may be Jasaw Chan K'awiil I—performing a ritual involving the reinterment of the skull and leg bones of an important woman.

Under his son Yik'in Chan K'awiil, Tikal reached the height of its power. The population may have exceeded 100,000, most living hard lives in wooden platform dwellings far from the grandeur of the Great Plaza, and relying on the inadequate water supplies of the city's 10 reservoirs. The king rebuilt most of the ceremonial causeways linking important parts of the city; ordered the construction of Temple IV (the Temple of Inscriptions), which he had carved with a history of the city; and conducted campaigns against the Naranjo kingdom.

These wars overextended Tikal, and by the time Jasaw's grandson Yax Nuun Ayiin II came to the throne in 768 CE, rival cities such as Naranjo and Caracol were reviving. Tikal was still rich enough for him to construct twin-pyramid complexes to celebrate two *k'atun* endings, but these were the city's last grand monuments.

The decline of the city

After Stela 24, which commemorates the 810 CE *k'atun* ending, the record is silent until a solitary stela is erected in 869 CE by a ruler who called himself Jasaw Chan K'awiil II, in a reference to the city's glory days. However, by then the city's population had shrunk and its political power was broken. Soon it was almost totally abandoned.

Tikal's collapse was not an isolated occurrence. Most major Maya cities suffered similar catastrophes around 900 CE as the Classic Period of Maya history ended. It is unclear why the civilization suffered such a setback,

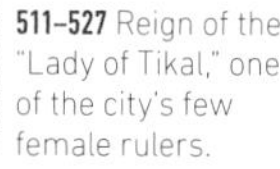

511–527 Reign of the "Lady of Tikal," one of the city's few female rulers.

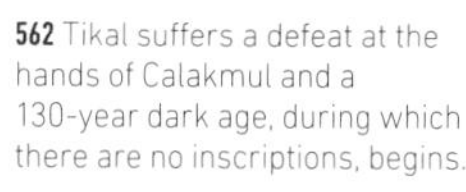

562 Tikal suffers a defeat at the hands of Calakmul and a 130-year dark age, during which there are no inscriptions, begins.

657 Nuun Ujol Chaak is expelled from Tikal by forces from Calakmul.

672 Nuun Ujol Chaak returns to Tikal, but seven years later is killed in battle and buried in a remodeled Temple 33.

695 Jasaw Chan K'awiil I defeats Calakmul, takes its king prisoner, and restores Tikal's power.

c.700 Temple II is built as a funerary monument for Jasaw Chan K'awiil I's queen, Lady Kalajuun Une' Mo'.

▷ ARCHAEOLOGISTS AT WORK
Modern excavations began at Tikal in the 1920s, and discoveries are still being made. Here, archaeologists work on the interior of a building on the site in the 1950s.

but overpopulation and the environmental stress caused by the need to feed growing cities when only rain collected in reservoirs was available for drinking and watering crops, combined with the impact of constant warfare, may have made cities like Tikal unviable.

Gradually Tikal was reclaimed by the jungle, its temples and pyramids covered by foliage, its buildings undermined by tree roots. Only in the mid-19th century did the first outsiders rediscover its splendor. The British diplomat Alfred Percival Maudslay cleared much of the site in the early 1880s, and major excavations were carried out from 1956 to 1969 by the Tikal Project, originally led by American archaeologist Edwin Shook. The monuments of Tikal could now be clearly seen, yet its history remained obscure until the deciphering of most of the Mayan glyph system in the 1970s and 1980s. Only then could the conquests and triumphs of Tikal's *ajaws*—and the purpose of their magnificent temples and pyramids—be truly understood.

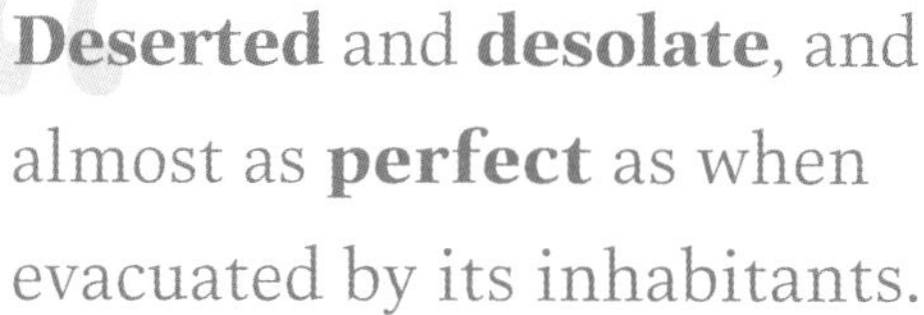

“**Deserted** and **desolate**, and almost as **perfect** as when evacuated by its inhabitants.

A PRIEST QUOTED IN *INCIDENTS OF TRAVEL IN CENTRAL AMERICA, CHIAPAS, AND YUCATAN*, BY JOHN LLOYD STEPHENS AND FREDERICK CATHERWOOD, 1841

Vase from the Temple of the Jaguar

c. 732 Temple I (the Temple of the Jaguar) is built as a funerary temple for Jasaw Chan K'awiil I.

743 Yik'in Chan K'awiil defeats Naranjo and takes its King Yax Mayuy Chan Chaak captive. He builds Temple IV in celebration.

768 The last great king of Tikal, Yax Nuun Ayiin II, ascends to the throne, as the city's decline begins.

The dynasty of Tikal, from its first known king to the last, included 33 *ajaws* and lasted for 779 years, nearly three centuries longer than the Western Roman Empire.

810 An *ajaw* named "Dark Sun" erects Stela 24 outside Temple III to celebrate a *k'atun* ending.

869 The last dated monument at Tikal is set up in the Great Plaza.

Cusco

CITY OF THE PUMA

The Inca adorned their imperial capital with grand palaces and temples before the Spanish conquerors refashioned a colonial city of churches and plazas, creating a dual heritage that lives on today.

Cusco stands at an elevation of 11,150 ft (3,399 m) in the Peruvian Andes, ringed by mountains. The area's defensible position led to its settlement as early as 800 BCE by people of the Chanapata civilization. By 700 CE, organized states had emerged, with sophisticated towns and skilled artisans. The region was rich in metals and semiprecious stones, and it attracted the Wari people, then the Killke, who established the first urban center in Cusco itself, at the confluence of the Saphy, Huatanay, and Tullumayo rivers. Its name in Quechua, the Indigenous language of the Andes, means "the navel of the world."

A sacred center

The Inca arrived in the region around 1200 and took control of Cusco. For them this was a sacred place of pilgrimage. Under Manco Cápac, the first Sapa Inca (Inca ruler), and his successors, the city grew slowly, sectioned into *hanan* (upper) and *hurin* (lower) districts. Its layout was oriented along *ceques*, sacred lines which radiated through the city, linked by 328 *huacas*, or sacred spots.

In 1438, the ninth Sapa Inca took the throne. Pachacuti (Earth Shaker) defeated the neighboring Chanca people and began a massive extension of the empire, which eventually stretched north to modern-day Ecuador and south to Chile's Atacama desert. Cusco, the capital of this realm, was remodeled in the form of a puma to symbolize strength, its spine marked by the Tullumayo river, and its head by Sacsayhuamán fortress. Grand buildings were constructed using vast stone blocks fitted together without mortar, a characteristic of Inca architecture. In the center were the palaces and *kancha* (compounds) of the nobles, set around the Huacaypata square, where ceremonies were held and a perpetually lit brazier burned sacrificial llamas. Craftsmen and farmworkers lived in the surrounding villages in mud-brick houses. They cultivated terraces of maize and potatoes and tended to flocks of llamas.

◁ ENGRAVING OF CUSCO, 1572
This work by Frans Hogenberg and Simon Novellanus features the Sapa Inca, carried in a palanquin, while, to the left, Sacsayhuamán is rendered as a three-ringed fort.

Inca myths tell of siblings who were guided by the sun god Inti to the site of Cusco; it's more likely the Inca took the area from the Killke by force.

c. 800 BCE People of the Chanapata civilization are the first settlers in the Sacred Valley around Cusco.

c. 750 CE The Wari, who build a large city at Pikillaqta, 12 miles (20 km) to the east of Cusco, control the area.

Llama-shaped Wari pot, 7th–11th century

c. 1100 The Killke people build the Sacsayhuamán fortress.

c. 1200 Manco Cápac, the first Inca emperor, founds the Inca city of Cusco.

1438 Pachacuti remodels the city in the form of a puma, with Huacaypata square as its navel.

"**Nowhere** in this kingdom of **Peru** is there **a city** with the **air of nobility** that **Cusco** possessed.

CRÓNICAS DEL PERÚ, PEDRO CIEZA DE LEÓN, 16TH CENTURY

◁ THE GOLDEN GLORY OF AN INCA EMPEROR
In this 18th-century Spanish portrait of Atahualpa, the Inca ruler wears a golden coronet in the form of two intertwined serpents and a richly ornamented cape, and bears a staff tipped with a golden sunburst.

Cusco, with a population of around 450,000, receives approximately 3 million tourists a year, many of them on their way to visit the Inca ruins at Machu Picchu.

The most splendid of Cusco's buildings was the Coricancha, or sun temple, its walls adorned with sheets of beaten gold symbolizing the sweat of the sun god Inti. Inside lay a garden crafted from precious metals and jewelery, including a field of corn with golden stalks. The Punchao, a golden statue of the infant sun god, received offerings of burned food and *chicha* (a maize-based drink) brewed by the *aqllakuna*, virgins dedicated to the god. The Coricancha was flanked by shrines to the moon goddess Mama Quilla (decorated with silver, representing her tears) and Illapa, the thunder deity.

The Spanish conquest

In 1524, disaster struck. Smallpox, transmitted along trade routes after the Spanish arrival in the Caribbean in 1492, devastated the empire and was the likely cause of the death of the Sapa Inca, Huayna Cápac. His sons Atahualpa and Huáscar each claimed the throne, and a bloody civil war broke out just before Spanish conquistador Francisco Pizarro arrived in 1532. Pizarro kidnapped Atahualpa, stole the vast ransom of gold collected by his subjects, and then murdered him. In May 1533, Pizarro marched into Cusco with his small force, installed Manco Cápac II as puppet ruler, and proceeded to loot the temples and palaces. The new ruler escaped and subjected the city to a 10-month siege, at whose height the straw roofs of the city's buildings were set ablaze, reducing most of Cusco to ashes.

With the aid of Indigenous allies, Pizarro retook the city, and the remaining Inca nobility fled to the jungle city of Vilcabamba, where they resisted for nearly 40 years. The Spanish rebuilt Cusco in their own image, replacing the palaces and shrines with new churches and convents faced with limestone. Some Inca nobles became integrated with the Spanish elite, who lived in villas in the city. The common people were forced into *reducciones*, new settlements established to control them better, and had to at least nominally convert to Christianity.

1527 After the death of Huayna Cápac, his son Huáscar claims Cusco.

January 1532 Atahualpa captures Cusco from Huáscar and becomes Sapa Inca.

November 1532 Spanish conquistador Francisco Pizarro captures Atahualpa at Cajamarca and holds him for ransom.

1533 The Spanish under Pizarro take control of Cusco, appointing Manco Cápac II as Sapa Inca.

A 1535 account of the conquest of Peru by Francisco Xerez

1534 Cusco is refounded as a Spanish city, ending over three centuries of Inca rule.

1537 After a 10-month siege, Manco Cápac II takes most of Cusco, but retreats to Vilcabamba after the Spanish fight back.

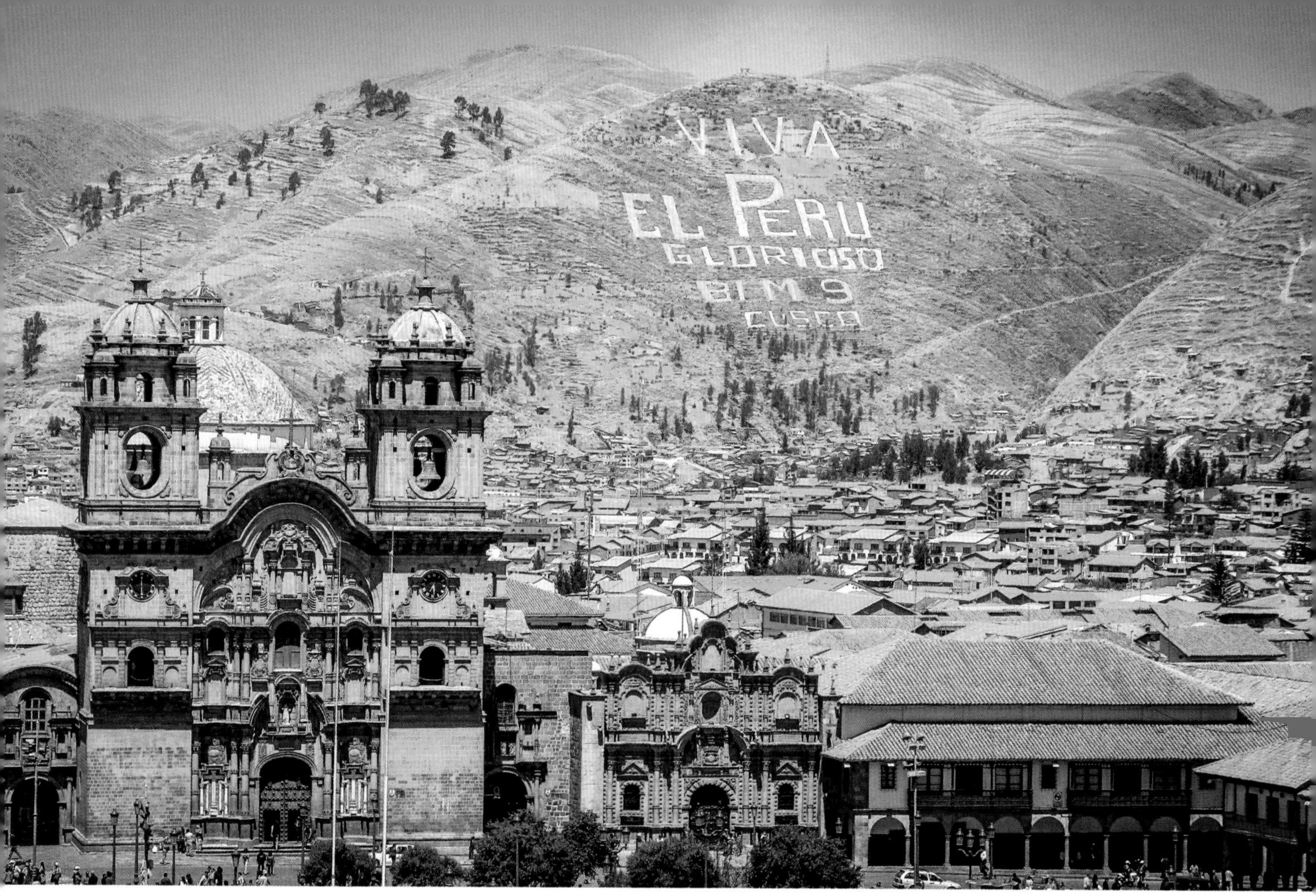

The rediscovery of the past

The following centuries saw periodic rebellions against the Spanish, such as that of Túpac Amaru II, which ended in 1781 with his execution in the Plaza de Armas. Over time Cusco faded in prominence, until an earthquake in 1950 damaged many Spanish-era buildings, revealing Inca foundations that had resisted the tremor's violent shaking. Gradually the old Inca city was rediscovered and its Indigenous culture treasured once more. The city became a UNESCO World Heritage Site in 1983 and tourists came in increasing numbers to wonder at Cusco and walk the nearby Inca Trail to the splendid ruins of Machu Picchu. Tradition remains strong among Cusco's Indigenous people, who still speak Quechua and continue to weave and wear traditional brightly colored textiles, and drink *chicha*. In 1995, local authorities adopted the Quechuan spelling Qosqo for the city. Five centuries after Pachacuti, the earth had shaken once more, and revived Cusco's Inca roots.

△ CUSCO TODAY
The surrounding hills tower above modern Cusco, as they did in Inca times, but colonial buildings now dominate, such as the Baroque Iglesia de la Compañía de Jesús, built on top of the palace of Huayna Cápac.

1572 Execution of Túpac Amaru I, the last Inca emperor, in the Plaza de Armas, the old Inca Huacaypata.

1650 A major earthquake destroys many of Cusco's buildings.

1780–1781 Revolt by Inca leader Túpac Amaru II. He meets the same fate as his forebear, and is executed in the Plaza de Armas.

The ransom for Atahualpa comprised a large room filled with gold and silver worth approximately $350 million today.

1950 Another major earthquake destroys many buildings in central Cusco, exposing their Inca foundations.

1983 UNESCO declares Cusco a World Heritage Site.

▽ SANTA CATALINA CONVENT WALLS
This Spanish convent was built over an Inca temple, and some Inca masonry remains.

MORE GREAT CITIES

Ephesus

City of Artemis

Situated on the west coast of Turkey, Ephesus was founded by Greek settlers in the 10th century BCE. It became known for the richness of its trade, its philosophers, and the Temple of Artemis, one of the Seven Wonders of the Ancient World. Under Roman rule, the city became a large and vibrant hub and received a splendid new forum, triumphal arch, and the magnificent Library of Celsus, today its most well-known remains. An early center of Christianity, it was visited by St. Paul, but as its harbor silted up over time its importance dwindled, and by the 15th century it was abandoned.

Luxor

City of the Dead

Once called Thebes, Luxor, in southern Egypt, contains an extraordinary number of monuments from its time as ancient Egypt's capital. During the New Kingdom era, from 1550 BCE, the pharaohs built temples on the east bank of the Nile, at Luxor and neighboring Karnak, with a grand avenue of sphinxes between them. The west bank was reserved as a necropolis—pharaohs such as Queen Hatshepsut built funerary temples where bodies of the dead were laid to rest in hidden tombs. The only one to survive looters was that of boy-king Tutankhamen, whose treasures were excavated by Howard Carter in 1922.

Petra

Rose-Red City

Protected behind the Siq, a narrow cleft through a ravine in southern Jordan, Petra was the capital of the Nabataeans, an ancient Arabian people. They grew wealthy on the tolls extracted from the caravans that carried valuable spices through the desert, and used these riches to carve ornate temples and tombs for their rulers. The merchants who carried their wares through the Siq were greeted by the Khazneh (Treasury), an extravagant facade cut into the rose-red stone that gave Petra its nickname. A thriving city in the 1st century CE, Petra was conquered by the Romans in 106 CE and it gradually lost its role as a trading center. It was abandoned in the 12th century and only discovered again by outsiders in 1812.

Damascus

City of Jasmine

The capital of modern Syria, Damascus lays claim to being one of the oldest continuously inhabited cities in the world. Founded in the 3rd millennium BCE, it was ruled by the New Kingdom of Egypt before becoming the capital of an Aramaean state. It was then ruled by Assyrians, Greeks, and Romans. It reached its peak as the capital of the Umayyad caliphate from 661 CE, during which time its Great Mosque was built, fusing Greek and Islamic workmanship; it is still one of the largest (and oldest) mosques in the world. When the caliphate moved to Baghdad in the 750s, Damascus became neglected. However, it flourished once more under Ayyubid rule in the 11th century, when it became a center of Islamic thought and was adorned with new madrasas and mosques. A major cultural center, Damascus was chosen as the capital of Syria in 1946 when it gained independence from France.

Babylon

Gate of the Gods

Its ruins around 50 miles (80 km) south of Baghdad, in modern Iraq, Babylon was one of the richest and most powerful cities of the ancient Near East. Founded around 2000 BCE, its Amorite rulers grew rich from its grain trade, building city walls and temples. One of them, Hammurabi, decreed one of the world's earliest law codes and conquered much of southern Mesopotamia. The city's great stepped ziggurat temple, the Etemenanki, was so renowned that it inspired the biblical story of the Tower of Babel. The city had a resurgence in the 7th century when its Neo-Babylonian rulers, among them Nebuchadnezzar II, built new palaces, ornate city gates, and the Hanging Gardens of

△ **Petra** The Theater at Petra was carved into the mountainside in the 1st century CE.

△ **Damascus** A 16th-century depiction of a Mamluk governor and his retinue.

Babylon, one of the Seven Wonders of the Ancient World. Alexander the Great made it his capital and died there in 323 BCE, after which the city went into decline.

Leptis Magna

The New City

Lying on the Libyan coast, Leptis Magna contains one of the finest surviving Roman cityscapes. Founded by the Phoenicians in the 7th century BCE, under the Romans it became a modestly prosperous town based on olive oil production. Only when local boy Septimius Severus became Roman emperor in 193 CE did it achieve real wealth. He funded a new forum, a huge triumphal arch, and colonnaded streets, making Leptis one of the grandest cities in North Africa. Attacks by local tribes and then the Vandals in the 5th century destroyed its prosperity, and when the Arabs conquered it in 647 CE, only a few inhabitants remained.

Timbuktu

Pearl of the Desert

Its towering mosques for centuries a landmark on the edge of the Sahara Desert, Timbuktu was founded around 1100 CE. Situated on a trade route for salt and gold, it rapidly prospered, becoming a key center of the Mali Empire in the 1300s. Mali's greatest ruler, Mansa Musa, endowed it with the fortresslike mudbrick Djinguereber mosque in 1327, and the city became a center of Islamic scholarship, with madrasas, a university, and libraries packed with precious manuscripts. When a Moroccan army wrested it from the Songhai Empire in 1591, Timbuktu diminished, becoming, for Westerners, an archetype of an impossibly distant place.

Lalibela

City of Rock-Cut Churches

Situated in northern Ethiopia, Lalibela is composed of a dozen remarkable churches, excavated into the rock and divided by a labyrinth of channels. Work was begun in the late 12th century on the orders of the Christian Ethiopian ruler Lalibela, who wanted to build a new Jerusalem following that city's capture by Muslims. Although some of the buildings may have been royal houses, it remained a holy site and is still populated by monks, priests, and pilgrims.

Great Zimbabwe

The Great Stone House

In the southeast of modern Zimbabwe, Great Zimbabwe's extensive ruins make it one of the most imposing ancient sites in sub-Saharan Africa. The center of a thriving empire based on the gold trade, it originated around 900 CE when its Shona rulers built a vast acropolis and the huge Great Enclosure. Trade in ivory, copper, and shells to the coast made Great Zimbabwe's rulers rich. Overworking of the gold mines, deforestation, and drought may all have led to its downfall in the 15th century, when it became a ruin. A carved soapstone bird, discovered at the site in 1891, has become a symbol of the country, appearing on its coins and flag.

Bagan

City of Four Million Pagodas

Covering a vast plain on the east bank of the Irrawaddy River in Myanmar, Bagan is a complex of more than 2,000 surviving temples. From 1044 to 1287, Bagan was the capital of the Pagan Empire, the first united Burmese kingdom, and during this time its rulers turned it into a royal capital of fabulous wealth, its skyline studded with the tapering bell-shaped towers of its temples and pagodas (reputed to be more than four million in number). Mongol attacks in the late 13th century shook the Burmese kingdom and Bagan went into decline, although it has continued to be the object of religious and secular pilgrimage.

Angkor

City of Temples

Around 4 miles (6 km) north of Siem Reap in Cambodia, Angkor was the capital of the Khmer Empire from the 9th century. A holy as well as a royal city, the massive towers of its main temple, Angkor Wat, were built in the 12th century to represent Mount Meru, the sacred Hindu five-peaked mountain. Its walls were adorned with a riot of scenes from Hindu mythology. Successive monarchs built other temples and it became a place of pilgrimage. When the Khmer Empire weakened, Angkor deteriorated, and after the capital was sacked by the Siamese in 1431 it was abandoned, its thousands of temples eventually claimed by the jungle. Restoration began in the early 20th century.

△ **Timbuktu** *The North Side of Timbuktoo* by explorer Heinrich Barth, 1857.

△ **Bagan** The temples and pagodas of Bagan, in Myanmar's Mandalay region.

London p.86

Berlin p.118

Prague p.108

Moscow p.124

Kraków

Bratislava

Québec City p.146

Minneapolis

Reno

Detroit

Montréal

Bordeaux

Munich

New Orleans p.150

Paris p.94

Florence p.102

Vienna p.114

Cairo p.130

CHAPTER 2
GREAT RIVER CITIES

Varanasi p.136

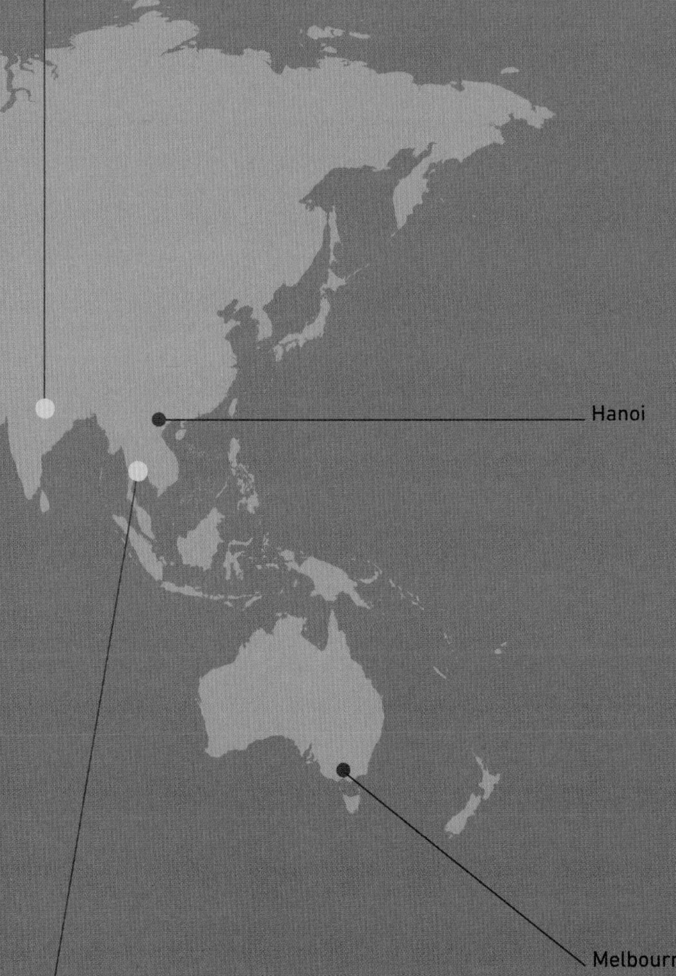

Bangkok p.140

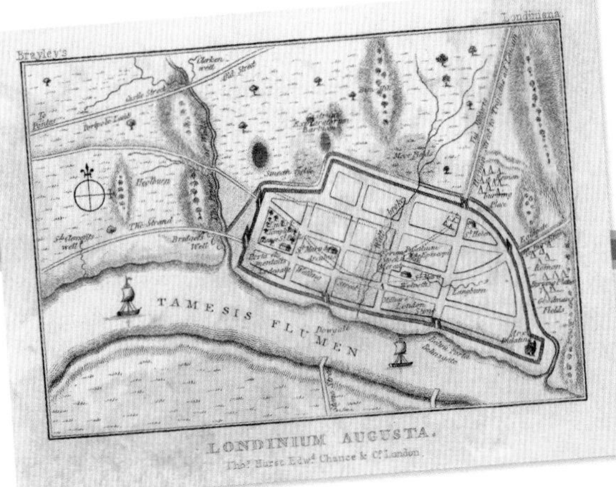

Map showing the extent of Roman London

c. 47 CE Roman invaders establish a settlement called Londinium on the banks of the Thames.

c. 61 Rebels led by Queen Boudicca attack and partly destroy Londinium.

240 A temple is built to the god Mithras, who was worshipped by many Roman soldiers.

604 Construction of the first St. Paul's Cathedral begins, probably on the same site as the present cathedral.

London

THE BIG SMOKE

From dynamic medieval city to imperial capital and global metropolis, London has always looked out from its riverside site to a wide world of opportunity.

The Romans invaded England in the 1st century CE, crossing the Thames as they fought their way into what is now Essex. Recognizing the river's strategic value and potential for trade, the Romans built a walled town there and called it Londinium. Around a decade after their arrival, a rebellion led by East Anglian Iceni people under Queen Boudicca ravaged the city. But for most of the Roman occupation, London thrived, and a forum, basilica, and baths were built, alongside a military fort.

A developing capital

After the Romans left around 400 CE, the area became home to the Anglo-Saxons, a newly arrived Germanic people from northern Europe. They repelled Viking incursions and held London until the Normans conquered England in 1066. The Norman kings, and the Plantagenets who followed them, built the Tower of London and the first stone bridge over the Thames, and made London the seat of England's first parliament. The city, still confined to its Roman walls, became England's capital and developed as a river port, building links with foreign cities such as Hamburg and Bremen. London was also a major religious center, with links to Canterbury—the headquarters of the English Church—and a palace for the archbishop.

◁ A CITY OF TRADE, 1751
Thomas Bowles' view of London shows the Thames busy with shipping. Beyond the Tower of London (lower right), the steeples of Sir Christopher Wren's churches rise among streets of closely packed red-brick houses.

871 A large Viking raid on London sees the Norse army camp inside the city walls for much of the winter.

1065 Westminster Abbey, outside the city walls, is completed.

Henry II ordered a stone-built London Bridge in 1176, replacing the timber structures of the Romans, Saxons, and Normans. It was eventually replaced in 1831.

c. 1100 The White Tower, the tallest part of the Tower of London, is finished as a key element in the city's military defenses.

1170 Archbishop Thomas Becket is murdered in Canterbury. He is canonized and later becomes London's patron saint.

Pilgrim badge depicting St. Thomas Becket, 14th century

1157 The Hanseatic League, a powerful group of European merchants, gains the right to trade without tolls in London.

1264 The first parliament to sit in London takes place, monitoring and controlling royal power.

▷ **THE GLOBE THEATRE**
The original Globe was built in 1599 for the Lord Chamberlain's Men, the theater company for whom Shakespeare acted and wrote plays. The wood-framed theater had an open courtyard.

▽ **WILLIAM SHAKESPEARE**
Born in Stratford, Shakespeare had moved to London by 1592. He wrote some 39 plays and is widely regarded as the world's greatest playwright.

> "The **sight of London** to my exiled eyes, is as **Elysium** to a **new-come soul**.
>
> CHRISTOPHER MARLOWE, *EDWARD II*, 1593

Peace and prosperity

London's rise continued in the 13th and 14th centuries, but was threatened in the 15th century by the Wars of the Roses, a civil war between rivals for the throne. The conflict was eventually won by Henry VII, who became the first Tudor king—and the last English king to win his throne on the battlefield. The resulting stability allowed commerce to thrive again, and London to regain some of the prosperity it had lost during the wars. The settlement of Westminster, just west of the city walls and home to royal palaces and Westminster Abbey, expanded.

In London itself, buildings were upgraded and links with mainland Europe strengthened. The resulting revenue helped usher in a creative golden age, especially in poetry, music, and theater. Playwrights such as Christopher Marlowe, Ben Jonson, and William Shakespeare entertained large audiences of every social class at theaters sited mostly on the south side of the river. The rich had their portraits painted by world-class artists such as Hans Holbein, and sublime choral and instrumental music was performed in their homes and at church during Mass.

In the 1530s, there was a religious upheaval caused by a dispute between King Henry VIII and the Roman Catholic Church over the pope's refusal to grant the king a divorce. Henry severed the country's links with the Church and its Latin rituals, throwing the country and city into turmoil. London's merchants continued to trade, however, and in 1571 opened the Exchange. Modeled on a similar building in Antwerp, it provided a vital place for deals to be made, especially in the wool and cloth trades, and was a powerful advertisement for London's status as a mercantile capital—especially when Queen Elizabeth I granted the use of the name "Royal Exchange." The quays along the Thames were busy with ships, sailors, and merchants from all over Europe. Many streets held markets where customers pushed their way through dense crowds, the air thick with the cries of traders and ripe with the smells of fish and livestock.

1485 Henry VII, the first Tudor king, takes the crown and ushers in a period of peace and prosperity.

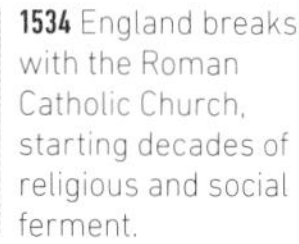

1534 England breaks with the Roman Catholic Church, starting decades of religious and social ferment.

Portrait of Elizabeth I, painted in the 1560s

1559 Elizabeth I is crowned in Westminster Abbey and is welcomed by Londoners as a defender of England against Catholicism.

1580 Local laws limiting the building of new houses lead to the overcrowding of existing homes in the city.

Elizabethan theaters were sited outside the city walls for fear their audiences would cause disorder and spread the plague.

1592 William Shakespeare is first recorded working as an actor and dramatist in London.

△ THE GREAT FIRE
This view of the 1666 fire, based on an original by the artist Waggoner, shows it burning most fiercely in front of Old St. Paul's Cathedral on the left.

"It **begun this morning** in the **King's baker's house** in Pudding-lane and ... **hath burned** St. Magnus's Church.

THE DIARY OF SAMUEL PEPYS ON THE GREAT FIRE, 1666

War, fire, and rebirth

In the 1640s, the atmosphere in the city changed. A civil war began in which Parliament and the monarchy clashed for power. Parliament won the war and London was briefly the capital of a republic led by austere Protestants known as Puritans. The king was beheaded outside the royal Banqueting House, the city's theaters were closed, and pastimes such as dancing were banned. London's relaxed cultural life came to an end, and even the prevailing fashions became more somber. Yet after just over a decade of Puritan rule, the monarchy was restored. The theaters were soon open again, an observatory was built at Greenwich, and tea and coffee became fashionable. Disaster struck in the 1660s, in the form of an outbreak of bubonic plague and the devastating Great Fire. The fire began at a bakery and raged for five days through the city's mostly timber-framed buildings. Even stone structures such as churches and the Royal Exchange were burned out. The rich moved out to the country and normal life came to a standstill as London faced its greatest crisis since the Roman period.

Fire destroyed the Royal Exchange, the Guildhall, 87 churches, and over 13,200 houses, and made 100,000 people homeless.

1600 The British East India Company is set up in London to trade with Asia.

1649 After his defeat in the English Civil War, Charles I is executed in Whitehall; royal rule is replaced by that of Parliament.

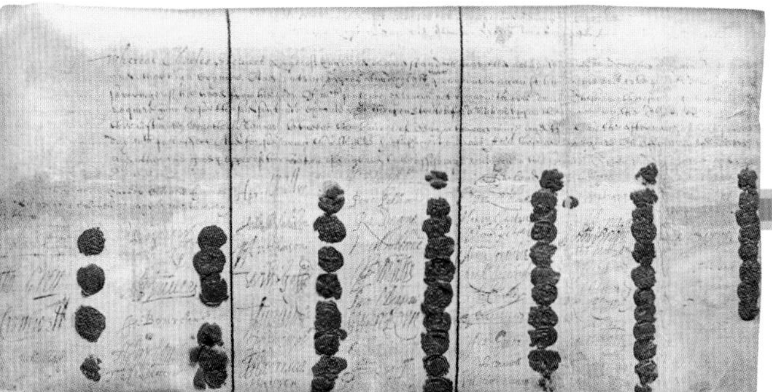

Charles I's death warrant, signed by 59 commissioners (judges), including Oliver Cromwell

1660 A group of scholars sets up the Royal Society, an association and academy devoted to science.

1665–1666 An outbreak of bubonic plague hits London, killing around 100,000 people and leading many to flee the city.

1666 The Great Fire of London destroys the majority of the city's buildings.

Sir Christopher Wren

◁ Wren's former house near Hampton Court Palace is marked by a blue plaque.

△ Louis Dodd's painting of the Thames shows how St. Paul's dominated London's skyline before the tall office buildings of the 20th century. The much-lauded structure, designed by Wren in the English Baroque style, was completed in 1710.

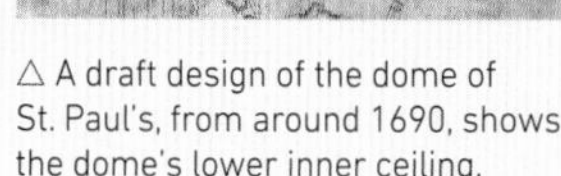

△ A draft design of the dome of St. Paul's, from around 1690, shows the dome's lower inner ceiling.

Born in 1632, Sir Christopher Wren trained as a professor of astronomy and was one of the founders of London's Royal Society. But he was increasingly drawn to architecture, and by the 1660s was advising on the restoration of a dilapidated St. Paul's Cathedral. His plans were interrupted: in 1665 plague struck London, followed in 1666 by the Great Fire. Wren was asked to rebuild the ruined cathedral and at least 50 other fire-damaged churches. His work transformed London, with elegant, practical churches whose steeples towered over the rebuilt city. With its huge dome, St. Paul's remains one of the city's most outstanding buildings. The inventive Wren, who combined a mastery of geometry with European Baroque influences, also designed a new wing of the royal palace at Hampton Court and a vast complex of buildings at the naval hospital (now the Old Royal Naval College) in Greenwich.

> "The **extent** and **variety** of the ... works of **Sir Christopher Wren** can hardly be **rivaled**.
>
> MARGARET WHINNEY, *CHRISTOPHER WREN*, 1971

1669 Sir Christopher Wren begins rebuilding city churches gutted by the Great Fire.

Fire Courts were set up to decide who should bear the costs of the Great Fire; some building owners received compensation, paid for by a coal tax.

1675 The foundation stone for the new St. Paul's Cathedral is laid.

1717 The development of London's West End begins with the construction of Hanover Square.

Great Pagoda, Kew Gardens

1759 Kew Gardens is founded, quickly becoming famous for its collection of plants and its ornate buildings.

1801 After years of informal stock trading at the Royal Exchange and other venues, a regulated Stock Exchange is born.

Immediately after the fire, plans were made to rebuild London. Sir Christopher Wren (see box) drew up a new grid-based plan for the city, but landowners wanted to rebuild their houses in their original positions, so this and other similar plans were rejected. Rebuilding quickly got underway, with a new law banning flammable timber structures. The work took over a decade, and London became a transformed city of brick and stone, with a new Royal Exchange, a rebuilt cathedral, and churches designed by Wren. By the late 1680s, with the reconstruction virtually complete, businesses back on a sure footing, and the security provided by brick houses and the city's first fire insurance companies, optimism and prosperity returned.

High culture and hard lives

The 1700s saw London expand beyond its old boundaries. To the west, Westminster was still a separate settlement, surrounded by tracts of land owned by aristocrats who had built houses there to be close to the royal court. Some sold their land to developers, who built new streets and squares, joining Westminster to London and creating the area still called the West End. The new developments were carefully planned, mostly made up of long rows of houses, some arranged in squares with a public space in the center. These impressive residences, with light, wood-paneled living rooms and attic rooms for servants, attracted rich merchants and their families, who liked the spacious streets and elegant architecture. The city was becoming more sophisticated, and the mid-18th century saw the foundation of Kew Gardens and bodies such as the Royal Academy of Arts, whose first president was the portrait painter Joshua Reynolds. But the city was a place of great contrasts: not far from the refined squares were alleys where beggars, drunks, and sex workers lived hard lives.

The Thames had long been used for transportation and trade, and in the first half of the 19th century, land transportation took huge steps forward. The first horse-drawn omnibuses carried workers around the growing city and, in the 1830s, railroads arrived. The new connections brought visitors to attractions like the 1851 Great Exhibition and helped businesses prosper, leading to more arrivals, including many Irish people in the 1840s. Housing was built as the city spread out in every direction, but growth brought challenges. Poor sanitation spread disease and, with the Thames used as an open sewer, drinking water became contaminated. There was a cholera epidemic in 1832, and by the 1850s London's stench was greater than ever.

△ *GIN LANE*, 1751
William Hogarth's print took aim at the damage caused by cheap spirits. It was published as a pair with *Beer Street*, in support of the 1751 Gin Act. Disease, poor housing and sanitation, alcoholism, and crime were rife in 18th-century London.

1829 Horse-drawn omnibuses provide public transportation in London.

1837 Euston station, the first of London's major railroad termini, opens, offering links to northwestern cities such as Liverpool.

1845 The Great Famine in Ireland brings many refugees to the city.

1847 The House of Lords is the first part of the new Houses of Parliament to open by the Thames.

1858 The smell of Thames sewage reaches its worst level, penetrating the Houses of Parliament, an event dubbed "The Great Stink."

A Punch cartoon of The Great Stink

◁ PARLIAMENT BLITZED
Prime Minister Winston Churchill stands in the ruined House of Commons in May 1941, after London and other cities had suffered months of bombing raids.

The city cleans up

The city responded to the 1858 Great Stink by commissioning engineer Joseph Bazalgette to build a network of sewers to take the waste outside London and deposit it in the river at high tide, so it would be washed away. There was a huge improvement in public health as a result.

These vital changes beneath the city streets were matched by a soaring economy. The Stock Exchange made London the financial center of the world, while the manufacture of furniture, clocks, clothing, and luxury goods gained hugely from the city's status as the capital of a worldwide empire. Thousands of workers made the daily journey from new suburbs to their offices and factories. From the 1860s onward, more and more traveled on the world's first underground rail system, which helped relieve congestion on crowded overground trains.

Another beneficial development was that both surface and underground trains were being converted to electric power by the 1890s, reducing the fumes that saw the city dubbed "the big smoke." London's population had reached six million by 1900, encompassing everyone from the government of the world's largest empire to workers living in slum housing, and it was as famous for the serial killer Jack the Ripper as for the novelist Charles Dickens.

About 43,000 civilians were killed in the London Blitz—around half the country's total civilian casualties in the war.

London and the World Wars

During World War I, many Londoners lost their lives at the front, but the city itself escaped widespread damage. In the interwar period London quickly embraced the new, from the manufacture of electrical goods and cars to recreations such as the cinema. There was further suburban expansion, with new districts forming as the city expanded into the counties of Middlesex, Essex, and Kent. Many of these new districts were linked to the center by new Underground lines. However, World War II was devastating for London, with a German bombing campaign known as the Blitz reducing parts of the docks, factories, and countless houses to rubble.

The post-war era was a period of austerity, relieved by the optimism of the 1951 Festival of Britain, staged in London as an uplifting "tonic to the nation." The city's air quality remained a problem. Especially in winter, smoke from coal fires mixed with fog to cause dense smog, making it impossible to see and causing respiratory illnesses to soar. The government responded with the 1956 Clean Air Act, which imposed smokeless fuels in the capital, making the city a more comfortable and healthier place to live.

Booms and challenges

In the 1960s, London emerged as a center of popular culture. Worldwide success by British bands (many, like the Beatles, recording in the famous Abbey Road Studios) and fashion designers such as Mary Quant and Barbara Hulanicki sent news of "swinging London" around the globe and brought waves of tourists to the city, making up economically for the decline of London as a port. Gaps in the labor market were filled by immigrants from the former British Empire—especially from the Caribbean and the Indian subcontinent—as London became increasingly multicultural. There were setbacks in the 1970s and early '80s, with a series of terrorist attacks related to the sectarian "Troubles" in Northern Ireland, together with riots in Brixton, south London, when Black protesters clashed with police.

1863 The Metropolitan Railway, London's first Underground line, opens between Paddington and Farringdon.

1864 The Peabody Trust builds its first apartments, providing decent accommodation for the poor.

1875 Joseph Bazalgette's vast sewage system is completed, making London a far healthier place.

1908 The first official map of London's subterranean rail lines is published, and the term Underground is used as part of its advertising.

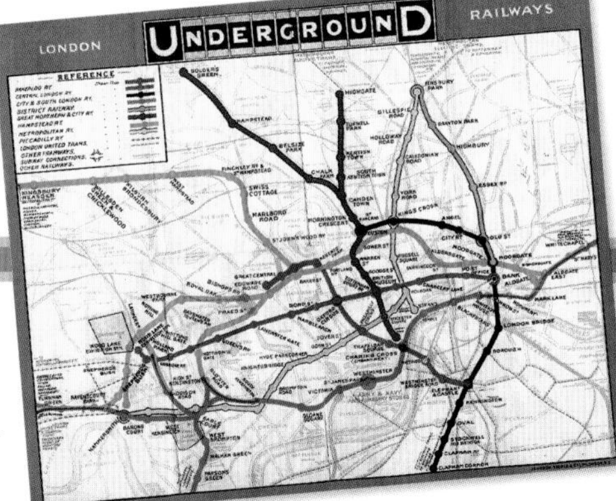

1940 The London Blitz begins, and German bombs kill many Londoners and destroy buildings.

1951 The Festival of Britain is held; its main legacy is the Royal Festival Hall on the South Bank.

1960s "Swinging London" becomes a center of fashion and youth culture.

◁ CARNABY STREET IN 1970
This West End street became the heart of "swinging London" in the 1960s. Malcolm English's illustration shows the vividly painted boutiques that stocked the latest fashions.

▽ BUS ADVERTISEMENT
Fashion designer Mary Quant, who advertised on London buses, popularized the mini skirt in the 1960s, and brought bold, colorful clothes to millions of young women.

> "In a decade **dominated by youth, London** has **burst into bloom**. It **swings**; it is **the scene**.
>
> *TIME* MAGAZINE, APRIL 15, 1966

By the end of the 1980s, however, London was booming again as a successful financial center with a modernized stock exchange. Waves of new office developments such as Canary Wharf in the former Docklands area brought skyscrapers to London, transforming the city's appearance. London quickly looked more modern, and Wren's elegant churches were dwarfed by the new developments. Prosperity has brought challenges: gentrification has spruced up many neighborhoods and seen food markets flourish, but people with lower incomes are often squeezed out as a result. Yet this dynamic city continues to face its future with optimism. Visitors flock to a reconstructed Globe Theatre and the gleaming London Eye observation wheel, while the 2012 Olympics saw the city bask in the limelight and show off its many assets, from its royal parks and Georgian streets to great pubs, fine museums, and the great sweep of the Thames where it all began almost 2,000 years ago.

▽ THE SHARD
The tallest of London's wave of modern skyscrapers is the Shard (left), a 72-story tapering tower near London Bridge.

1977 An explosion of punk rockers, including the Sex Pistols and the Clash, emerge from the city's thriving music scene.

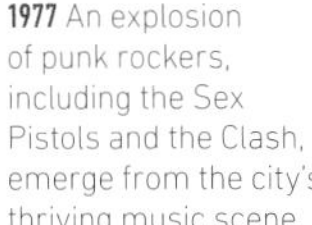

1991 The Canary Wharf development opens, beginning a building boom that transforms London.

2000 The Millennium Dome (now the O2 Arena) provides a focal point for the celebrations of the new millennium.

2012 The Olympic and Paralympic Games are held in London.

Paris

CITY OF LIGHT

From a Celtic encampment on the banks of the Seine, Paris grew to become one of the most influential and dazzling capitals of the late 19th century. Its tale is woven from a love affair with art, architecture, and the avant-garde.

The heart of Paris was pinpointed in the 3rd century BCE when a nomadic tribe of Celtic Gauls known as the Parisii settled on an island—Ile de la Cité today—in the Seine River. These early warriors lived in simple wattle-and-daub huts. They buried their dead with their chariots and were sophisticated enough to mint gold coins for trading.

But the flooding Seine proved unpredictable. When invading Romans conquered the area in 52 BCE, they destroyed the island settlement and chose to build a new town—Lutetia—on higher land across the water on the river's left bank. Lutetia was laid out in a typical grid pattern with a central axis leading to a bridge spanning the river. By the 1st century CE, the town had become a prosperous river port with 5 to 10 thousand inhabitants and a guild of *nautes* (boatmen) whose early sailing vessels appear on the Paris coat of arms. Gladiatorial combats and other entertainments filled the amphitheater and a parade of shops sold, among other wares, perfumed oils and plant essences to enjoy in three public baths.

◁ *LE CARREAU DES HALLES*, 1880
Les Halles was established as the city's main marketplace in the 12th century. It has taken many forms, including the fresh produce market shown in this painting by Victor Gabriel Gilbert.

Medieval Paris

The city's position at an important crossing on the Seine proved advantageous, and medieval Paris flourished. After the collapse of the Roman Empire, the town was occupied by Frankish King Clovis I who made it the seat of his new kingdom. It was now firmly known as Paris, after its original settlers. By the 11th century, political stability was achieved and cobblers, cloth-makers, apothecaries, and shipbuilders formed guilds, creating a powerful collective voice for the city's earliest artists and artisans.

The establishment of the University of Paris in around 1170 gave the city an academic cachet it would never lose. An influx of scholars from around Europe mingled on the left bank, communicating in Latin and lending the area a new nickname, the "Latin Quarter." This was a period of frenetic construction and development. The *marais* (swamp) on the right bank was drained and became a hub of commerce, while city walls—replaced centuries later by a ring of boulevards—were built and reinforced with a garrison fortress at the Louvre. Many other landmarks appeared at this time. On Ile de la Cité, construction began in 1163 of a magnificent Gothic cathedral—Notre-Dame de Paris—and in 1248 extraordinary stained-glass windows in a newly erected Sainte-Chapelle were the most glorious thing Paris had ever seen.

250 BCE A Celtic tribe known as the Parisii settle on the Ile de la Cité in the Seine River.

Gold coin of the Parisii

52 BCE The Romans conquer the area and build a new town called Lutetia.

360 CE Lutetia changes its name to Paris.

509 King Clovis I makes Paris the capital of his unified kingdom of the Franks.

1163 Construction begins on Notre-Dame de Paris, a Gothic masterpiece that takes nearly 200 years to complete.

▷ WALLED PARIS
As Paris expanded during the Middle Ages, successive rings of walls were constructed to defend the city, as shown in this map of 1578. Beyond the walls to the north, Catherine de' Medici's Jardin des Tuileries had just been landscaped.

Much of the important and valuable artwork in Paris is kept in underground storage rooms. If it is forecast that the Seine will flood, the pieces are moved to higher ground.

The French Renaissance

After the devastation of the Hundred Years' War (1337–1453), the Renaissance in the 15th and 16th centuries rebooted the city intellectually and artistically. At the Sorbonne, the first university printing press opened in 1470, kicking off a book trade that would rival Venice.

French kings fell under the spell of the Italian Renaissance. François I, a zealous ambassador of exploration and artistic discovery, invited Italian painters, sculptors, and craftspeople to work in court under his patronage. Among them was Leonardo da Vinci who brought several of his masterpieces with him, including the *Mona Lisa*. The king's art collection was the start of a world-renowned depository at the Louvre. Royal architects made the first attempts at town planning, creating elegant, uniform buildings, and open urban spaces like the magnificent Place Royale (Place des Vosges), a setting for extravagant jousting displays well into the 17th century.

Grandiose architecture reflected the monarchy's quest for glory. The Louvre fortress was transformed into a Renaissance pleasure palace, while the Palais des Tuileries and the Hôtel de Ville were also commissioned.

1578 Henri III lays the first slab of Pont Neuf, the first stone bridge in Paris to be built without houses on top.

1643 Four-year-old Louis XIV ascends the throne, but only assumes absolute power in 1661.

1667 Paris becomes the first capital to introduce public street lighting.

Bouquinistes (booksellers), with their racing-green stalls, have sold their wares along the Seine since 1891; in the 16th century, they were itinerant.

1682 Louis XIV moves his royal court to his lavish, out-of-town palace in Versailles.

1686 Café Procope opens and becomes a locale for intellectuals to philosophize over coffee and sorbet.

Age of Enlightenment

Paris was nicknamed *la ville lumière* ("city of light") for its role in the Enlightenment. Years of religious feuding between Catholics and Protestants under Henri IV and the stifling absolutism of Louis XIV (the Sun King) meant 18th-century Paris keenly embraced the principles of individual thought and religious tolerance. Intellectuals gathered at cafés to discuss equality, liberty, and other radical new ideas put forward by the likes of Voltaire, Montesquieu, and Rousseau. Literary salons allowed aristocratic men and women in Paris to respectfully socialize together—many were hosted by female socialites.

A burst of dramatic activity saw new theaters open, including the Comédie Française, still one of the most prestigious theaters in the world. The fashion industry boomed, serving aristocrats keen to be seen in the latest styles worn by Marie Antoinette and the royal court. On the streets, meanwhile, butchers boiled up broth from meat scraps and sold it to workers as carry-out. From 1786 tables were allowed and, according to urban legend, the world's first restaurant was born.

Revolution and redesign

The French Revolution in 1789 changed the course of Paris forever. At this time, most Parisians were still living in squalor and poverty, as they had since the Middle Ages. Resentment at these inequalities, rising inflation, and food shortages fueled opposition to Louis XVI, which culminated in a revolutionary mob storming the Bastille, the king's prison, on July 14. Four years later, cheering crowds on Place de la Concorde would watch as Louis XVI and Marie Antoinette were executed by guillotine. During the subsequent Reign of Terror, 17,000 people were killed by official execution and looted churches became "temples of reason." The Revolution rid France of the monarchy and feudal social system, and laid the foundations for a modern society based on equality, separation of church and state, and election of legislative assemblies.

In 1804, Napoleon I crowned himself emperor and set out to reform the country and make Paris the most beautiful city in the world. Triumphal arches and Neoclassical architecture, inspired by imperial Rome, were added to the city landscape, and more bridges were built across the Seine. Canals were constructed to transport goods and provide Parisians with fresh drinking water. Later in the century, further industrialization ushered in gas street lighting and the first public buses, as well as the first passenger railroad, a precursor to the Paris Métro. During the Second Empire, Napoleon III and Baron Georges-Eugène Haussmann masterminded the greatest urban redesign in history (see box, p. 98).

> **The secret of freedom** lies in **educating** people, whereas the **secret of tyranny** is in keeping them **ignorant**.
>
> MAXIMILIEN ROBESPIERRE, 1792

1689 The curtain rises on the world's longest-operating theater, the Comédie Française, at Palais Royal.

1751 Denis Diderot publishes his first encyclopedia.

1789 On July 14, an armed mob storms the Bastille prison, sparking the French Revolution.

1793 The Musée du Louvre opens. Four years later it acquires Leonardo da Vinci's *Mona Lisa*.

1795 "La Marseillaise" is adopted as the new Republic's national anthem. It is named after the volunteer troops from Marseille who sang it on their march to the capital.

Haussmann's redesign

△ Twelve avenues radiate from L'Etoile ("the star").

> **I want** to be a **second Augustus** ... because Augustus ... made Rome **a city of marble.**
>
> NAPOLEON III, 1842

△ Haussmann's redesign of Place de l'Etoile (now Place Charles de Gaulle) was typical of his vision: a meeting point of broad, tree-lined avenues, which give access across the city.

Baron Georges-Eugène Haussmann, under instruction from Napoleon III, undertook the most radical task of the 19th century: to redesign Paris and transform the outdated capital into a sublime modern metropolis.

In 1852 the oldest part of the city was a medieval hangover of small overcrowded houses hemmed into dark labyrinthine lanes. Narrow congested streets were completely inadequate for the increasing cart and carriage traffic. Over the following 17 years, Haussmann razed the city's chaotic old quarters and some 20,000 buildings to engineer a city with imperious boulevards, ornate fountains and squares, train stations, leafy parks, a sewage system and clean water supply, and even monumental public lavatories. So visionary was the design that Paris has changed little since.

1836 The Arc de Triomphe is inaugurated, honoring those who fought and died in the French Revolutionary and Napoleonic Wars.

The stone used for the Romano-Byzantine Basilica Sacré-Coeur, at Montmartre's highest point, turns white on contact with rainwater.

1860 Napoleon III annexes suburbs into Paris, including Montmartre.

1869 An opera house named the Folies Trévise opens. It would later become the Folies Bergère, the cabaret hall renowned for its extravagant performances during the *belle époque*.

1874 Renoir, Monet, and other Impressionist painters break free of the French Academy's formal annual Salon with their own solo art exhibition.

▷ *DANCE AT LE MOULIN DE LA GALETTE*, 1876
No artwork celebrates the exuberance of the *belle époque* quite like this Impressionist masterpiece by Pierre-Auguste Renoir.

The *belle époque*

Prussian troops lay siege to Paris for four months from September 1870 during the Franco-Prussian War. Starving Parisians in the barricaded city resorted to eating exotic animals from the Jardin des Plantes zoo, including two elephants named Castor and Pollux. Horsemeat, introduced a few years earlier by city butchers for the poor, also became widespread. Alsatian war refugees opened brasseries serving beer and sauerkraut.

When peace came in 1871, it fell to the new government to reconstruct the city and bring about what was a slow economic recovery. The Third Republic in Paris was synonymous with the *belle époque* ("beautiful age"), a dizzying period of creativity and style. It spawned the Moulin Rouge and can-can girls, the red-light district of Pigalle, and bohemian Montmartre with its popular taverns and artists' squats. At the Impressionists' third solo exhibition in 1877, Renoir unveiled his painting of a party at the Moulin de la Galette, a festive *guinguette* (outdoor dance hall) where artists lunched, danced, and drank far too much *guinguet* (cheap wine). Later, Pablo Picasso, Henri Matisse, Georges Braque, and Gertrude Stein, among others, dreamed up Cubism, Fauvism, and other new artistic styles in the unheated studios of the Bateau-Lavoir in Montmartre. They paid for food and drink at the Lapin Agile cabaret club with paintings. At the luxury Ritz hotel, French chef Auguste Escoffier created some of the recipes that would become the basis of French gastronomy. In 1903, he published his classic cookery tome, *Le Guide Culinaire*.

Art Nouveau left its indelible mark on Paris with brasseries sumptuously decorated in ceramics, mosaics, painted glass, and polished wood. The first Métro line opened in 1900 and Art Nouveau architect Hector Guimard designed wildly flamboyant entrances to Métro stations in curvaceous cast iron and glass. Art Nouveau's zenith coincided with the 1900 Exposition Universelle at the Grand Palais. Telescopes, kaleidoscopes, a 360 ft (110 m) Ferris wheel, a hot-air balloon simulator, and screenings of the world's first motion picture by the Lumière brothers were eye-popping attractions. Forty countries had their own national pavilion.

There are 6,100 streets in Paris. The shortest, Rue des Degrés in the 2nd arrondissement, is just 18.9 ft (5.75 m) long.

1889 The Moulin Rouge opens in Pigalle, thrilling Parisians with flamboyant cabaret shows and its showpiece can-can.

1898 Building begins on the first Métro line, inaugurated two years later with Art Nouveau station entrances by architect Hector Guimard.

1900 Some 50 million visitors flock to the Exposition Universelle at the Grand Palais, a World's Fair showcasing the city's technological brilliance.

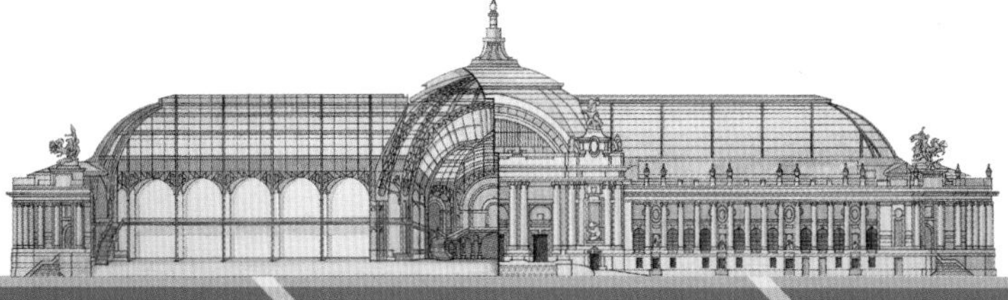

1905 Lurid paintings exhibited at the fall Salon are slammed by art critics as the work of *fauves* (wild cats). Fauvism is born.

1919 Ernest Hemingway, F. Scott Fitzgerald, and other expat writers make Sylvia Beach's English-language bookshop, Shakespeare & Company, their hangout.

> **Fashion is not** something that exists in **dresses only**. Fashion is **in the sky**, **in the street**, fashion has to do with **ideas**, **the way we live**, **what is happening** ...
>
> COCO CHANEL, FASHION DESIGNER

△ FASHION CAPITAL
Paris has had a major influence on fashion trends since the era of Louis XIV. In the post-war period, names such as Dior, Chanel, and Yves Saint Laurent became known the world over.

During the Fair, the second-ever modern Olympic Games were held, with swimming events taking place in the murky Seine. Gustave Eiffel also designed the Eiffel Tower as a temporary structure for the events; it was vilified by art critics at the time and described as a "metal asparagus," but proved popular with the public.

War and all that jazz

Paris was bombarded during World War I and occupied by the Germans during World War II. Between the two wars, the city thrived as a center of the arts and avant-garde. Pioneering fashion designer Coco Chanel opened her first boutique on Rue Cambon in 1910. She liberated women from corsets, dressed in trousers, and gave the world the little black dress. Long associated with Paris, Chanel left the city at the end of World War II when her involvement with the Nazis came to light, returning nine years later.

In the *années folles*, or Roaring Twenties, the capital's crazy creativity and liberalism lured expatriate writers like Ernest Hemingway, F. Scott Fitzgerald, and James Joyce, who sought inspiration in the nightlife and Art Deco brasseries of Montparnasse. The population of Paris peaked at this time, hitting 2.9 million in 1921.

Jazz clubs in the 1930s resounded with the swing music of Black musicians, such as saxophonist Sidney Bechet, while Edith Piaf revived the *chanson française* in

PARIS 1924
VIIIe OLYMPIADE
JEUX OLYMPIQUES

1924 Paris hosts the Summer Olympic Games for the second time, becoming the first city to host the Olympics twice.

1926 Coco Chanel's little black dress appears on the front cover of *Vogue*.

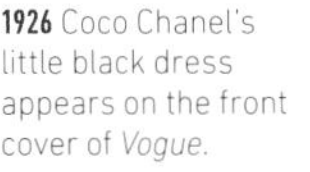

1940 Paris is occupied by German forces during World War II. Half the population flees to the countryside. Nazis take over the opulent Ritz hotel.

1944 Allied forces liberate Paris on August 25.

The Grande Arche de La Défense stands at one end of a historical axis, aligning with the Arc de Triomphe and Arc de Triomphe du Carrousel.

1950 French photographer Robert Doisneau immortalizes Parisian romance with his black-and-white shot of a kiss between two lovers by the Hôtel de Ville.

1968 Students occupy the Sorbonne amid nationwide protests.

music halls. Existentialists Jean-Paul Sartre, Simone de Beauvoir, and Albert Camus righted the world over coffee at Café de Flore in Saint-Germain-des-Prés.

Modern times

The wildly popular love song "La Vie en Rose," written by Edith Piaf on a Champs-Élysées café terrace in 1945, boosted low morale in post-war Paris. Equally sensational—albeit more risqué—was the arrival of the bikini, designed by French engineer Louis Réard and launched at a Paris public pool in 1946.

In May 1968, the Latin Quarter was taken over by young people and workers. What began as a protest against the war in Vietnam became an expression of discontent with the government that spread throughout the country.

In the 1970s and '80s, French presidents commissioned huge public buildings with ground-breaking architecture known as *grands projets*. The topsy-turvy Centre Pompidou featured interior pipes and workings on its facade. When the iconic glass pyramid at the Louvre was unveiled in 1989, Parisians gasped in horror. Landmark 21st-century architecture includes the Philharmonie de Paris and the resurrected Gare d'Austerlitz, both by French architect Jean Nouvel.

In 2019, fire broke out at Notre-Dame and heartbroken Parisians wept as the spire of their cathedral—the spiritual heart of Paris—tumbled to the ground. The French president promised to rebuild it in time for the Paris Summer Olympics in 2024.

Paris has inspired countless photographs, paintings, and stories. Its streets and bridges, which still conjure the charm of the "beautiful age," have formed the backdrop of films directed by the likes of Charlie Chaplin, Billy Wilder, Baz Luhrmann, and Julie Delpy, among many others. Creatively, the city still thrives, remaining a global influence in fashion and the visual arts, and adding stunning contemporary icons to its elegant skyline.

1985 Christo and Jeanne-Claude wrap Pont Neuf in golden fabric.

1991 The much-loved banks of the Seine become a UNESCO World Heritage Site.

2014 Spanish-born Anne Hidalgo is elected first female mayor of Paris.

2019 Fire engulfs Notre-Dame. Its spire collapses and the emblematic cathedral is closed to 14 million annual visitors for years to come.

▽ CONTEMPORARY ARCHITECTURE
The Fondation Louis Vuitton was opened as a cultural center and art museum in 2014. Designed by Frank Gehry, the museum reportedly cost €800 million ($963 m), eight times its initial budget.

Florence

CRADLE OF THE RENAISSANCE

Medieval prosperity paved the way for the small city-state of Florence to herald the Renaissance, and become a masterpiece in its own right.

The founding of Florentia ("the flourishing town") is usually credited to Julius Caesar, who built a settlement for military veterans by the Arno River in 59 BCE. Positioned at the narrowest crossing of the river, and overlooking a broad plain, the town grew and indeed flourished, as both garrison and commercial center. After the Romans departed, Florence was taken by Germanic barbarians—first Ostrogoths, then Lombards, with a spell of imperial control by a Byzantine army, and, eventually, by the great European Emperor Charlemagne in 774 CE.

A turning point came at the beginning of the 11th century, when Margrave Hugh of Tuscany made Florence his home, initiating several centuries of relative stability, prosperity, and increasing independence. While periodically entangled in disputes between factions of its noble families, who had gained power at the expense of trade guilds, medieval Florence was a dynamic, affluent city-state. Wool, silk, and leather merchants sold their wares along its winding streets. The cobbles rang with the clatter of packhorses loaded with raw wool or bales of finished cloth. Florentine families, in particular the Medici, dominated banking and merchant trade, using their fortunes to build *palazzi* (palaces), reconstruct the Ponte Vecchio over the Arno, and to support artists and poets.

◁ *DAVID*, 1504
The most famous Renaissance statue was created by Michelangelo for the facade of Florence cathedral, but placed instead in the Piazza della Signoria.

△ *THE SIEGE OF FLORENCE*, 1558
In this painting by Florentine Giorgio Vasari of the city under siege, the Arno River, domed cathedral, city walls, and numerous churches are all visible.

59 BCE The Romans found Florence (which they called Florentia) as a colony for retired members of the army.

250 CE Merchants from the east bring Christianity to Florence.

Florence was often fought over by rival rulers after the Romans left because of its strategic position near the adjoining plain.

c. 1000 Margrave Hugh of Tuscany makes Florence his principal city.

1115 The Florentines set up a governing commune, bringing a form of democracy to their city.

1216 Tuscany becomes mired in the conflict between rival Guelph and Ghibelline families.

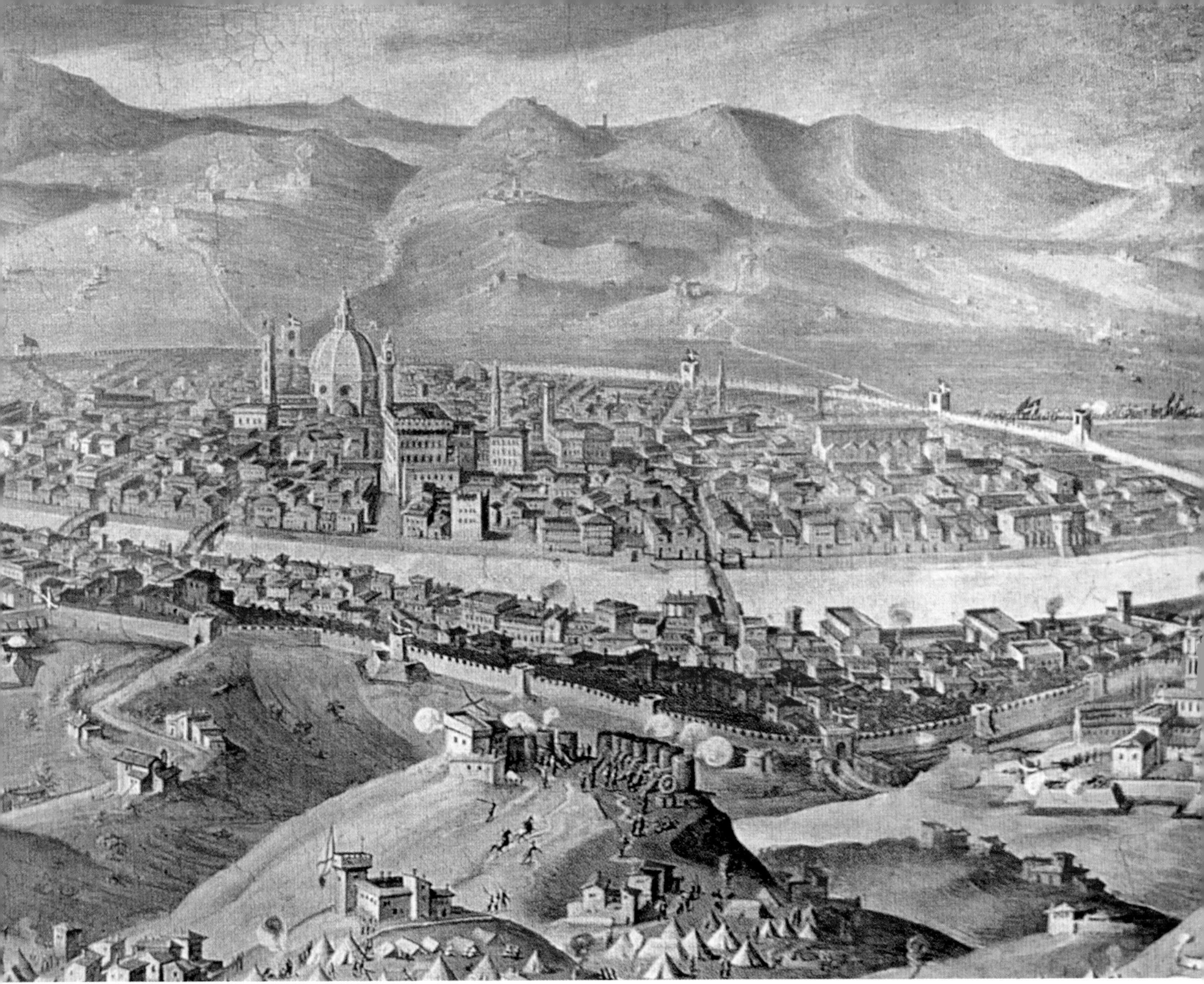

> You will begin to **wonder** that **human daring** ever **achieved** anything so **magnificent**.

JOHN RUSKIN, *MORNINGS IN FLORENCE*, 1875

1252 The gold florin, Florence's currency, is first minted; Florence becomes a republic.

1294 Work is begun on completely rebuilding the cathedral, a project that would last 140 years in total.

1302 Disputes between political factions lead to poet Dante Alighieri's expulsion from Florence.

1345 After severe flood damage, the Ponte Vecchio bridge and the shops along it are rebuilt.

1348 The Black Death reduces the city's population of 90,000 by almost half.

△ *RESURRECTION OF THE BOY*, 1483–1485
Domenico Ghirlandaio's masterpiece shows St. Francis miraculously bringing back to life a child who had died in a fall. The painting adorns a chapel in the church of Santa Trinità endowed by a rich Florentine banker, Francesco Sassetti.

City of art and learning

During the 14th and 15th centuries, Florence nurtured the great cultural revival, later known as the Renaissance, which gradually spread across the whole of western Europe. Chief among Florence's noble dynasties and wealthy patrons of the arts were the Medici, who ruled for almost 300 years from 1434, when Cosimo il Vecchio (the Elder) assumed power. He lived lavishly, evident in his commissioning of the Palazzo Medici with its highly intricate stonework, but he also patronized the careers of artists and architects such as Brunelleschi, Fra Angelico, and Donatello. This investment in the city's culture became a key feature of aristocratic life: the Medici and other distinguished families beautified their homes, built the Ospedale degli Innocenti (Europe's first orphanage), and remodeled many churches, employing the best Renaissance painters to create altarpieces and frescoes.

Florence fostered not only art and architecture, but also scholarship and science. At a time when most Europeans were illiterate, thousands of Florentine children (both boys and girls) benefited from a basic education and the rulers supported advanced scholars, many of whom studied and translated the works of the ancient Greeks and Romans—books that had been largely unknown for centuries. In the 1490s, much of this intellectual activity was interrupted when the Medici were expelled during an invasion by the French King Charles VIII, and the puritanical friar Girolamo Savonarola took control of Florence. In stark contrast to his art-loving predecessors, Savonarola destroyed works of art that offended his extremist views.

1402 Sculptor Lorenzo Ghiberti wins a competition to produce bronze baptistery doors for the cathedral.

1406 The Florentines defeat their long-standing rivals, the city of Pisa.

1419 Work begins on the Ospedale degli Innocenti, designed by Filippo Brunelleschi.

1434 Cosimo il Vecchio becomes the first Medici ruler of Florence.

1436 Brunelleschi sees his design for the octagonal cathedral dome come to fruition.

1475 Botticelli paints *The Adoration of the Magi*, in which the Magi are portraits of members of the Medici family.

Medici coat of arms

1498 The dictatorial Girolamo Savonarola, ruler of Florence from 1494, is executed in Rome.

1513 Giovanni de' Medici becomes Pope, increasing the family's power.

Lorenzo de' Medici

> Nor was there ever in **Florence**, or even in Italy, one so **celebrated for wisdom** ...

NICCOLÒ MACHIAVELLI ON LORENZO DE' MEDICI, *FLORENTINE HISTORIES*, 1520–1525

△ This portrait of Lorenzo de' Medici, by Giorgio Vasari, was painted posthumously.

▷ Lorenzo and his brother Giuliano feature front left in Botticelli's *Madonna of the Magnificat* (1481).

Known as "the Magnificent," Lorenzo de' Medici (1449–1492) became ruler of Florence in 1469, following his father, Piero I. The young Lorenzo was educated by some of the most advanced scholars of his time, and became a keen collector of books, as well as an accomplished poet and musician. The writers and scholars he supported included humanist intellectuals who tried to reconcile the writings of ancient philosophers with contemporary Christian beliefs. He had a deep fascination with the visual arts, and among the great painters he sponsored were Botticelli, Leonardo da Vinci, Michelangelo, and several lesser masters. Michelangelo and others even spent time living in his household. Lorenzo ruled for longer than many of the Italian dukes and was able to cement Florence's status as the most powerful of all the independent city-states in Italy.

1527 Republicans expel the Medici from the city.

1532 *The Prince*, a handbook for rulers by Florentine statesman Niccolò Machiavelli, is published.

1537 Cosimo de' Medici (known as Cosimo I) becomes Duke of Florence and begins a major building program.

1557 In September, catastrophic floods overwhelm the city.

1579 Artists Giorgio Vasari and Federico Zuccari complete the frescoes that adorn the interior of the cathedral's great dome.

△ *THE TRIBUNA OF THE UFFIZI*, 1772–1777
When German artist Johann Zoffany painted the Tribuna, a room in the Uffizi, he included a crowd of 18th-century visitors discussing and admiring the paintings. Florence was a major stopping place on the Grand Tour.

Alliances and upheavals

The rulers of Florence's Renaissance heyday managed to combine great political power with their love of the arts, an openness to new philosophical ideas, and a talent for subduing the other Italian city-states and maintaining wide influence in northern Italy. Many of the later leaders, including Cosimo I, who became Grand Duke of Tuscany in 1569, continued this tradition. Over time, however, the city was neither so culturally rich, nor the dukes so powerful. They did manage to make alliances with other European powers; a strong link with France began in 1533, when Catherine de' Medici married the Duke of Orléans, who was soon to become King Henri II. While this helped bolster Medici power, it did not significantly benefit Florence, which slipped into a slow decline in the 17th and 18th centuries, its golden age seemingly consigned to the past. The 17th-century Grand Dukes did still show an interest in science, sponsoring the astronomer Galileo Galilei and the physicist Evangelista Torricelli. They also put together a superb art collection in the Uffizi Gallery, which was later bequeathed to the city.

With the death of the last of the male Medici line in 1737, the Grand Duchy was inherited by an Austrian, Francis Stephen, husband of the Austrian Empress Maria Theresa. The end of the century saw Florence under attack by Napoleon, who drove out Austria, and for a few years Tuscany was ruled by the French. These conflicts between outside rulers sent Florence into political turmoil, making day-to-day life uncertain for tradespeople and workers. Construction of new buildings was scaled back, meaning Florence's historic streets were preserved for posterity, but more and more houses emptied as citizens sought work elsewhere. Meanwhile, momentum gathered for Italy to create an independent, unified state. The struggle for independence reached a climax with the creation of a new Kingdom of Italy, and Florence briefly became its capital between 1865 and 1870, before that role passed to Rome.

A design destination

Throughout the 18th and 19th centuries, Florence was a prime destination for foreign tourists, principally aristocrats embarking on the European Grand Tour. Many young noblemen rounded off their artistic circuit in Florence, where they would come to admire Roman remains and Renaissance art, and to buy paintings and sculptures to take home. While the city's political power had ebbed away, its cultural influence was enormous, and soon attracted a wave of middle-class tourists, together

Galileo was tutor to Grand Duke Cosimo II and dedicated his book about his astronomical discoveries (*Starry Messenger*, 1610) to Cosimo.

1737 The Medici line comes to an end and Francis Stephen of Austria takes over, becoming Grand Duke of Tuscany.

1796 Napoleon launches his first Italian campaign, reaching Florence on July 1.

***The Baptistery, Florence* by John Ruskin**

1840 John Ruskin visits Florence to draw the city's buildings, study the works of art in its collections, and research its history.

1865 Florence briefly becomes the Kingdom of Italy's capital.

1870 Florence is part of a fully reunified Italy; the capital returns to Rome.

◁ **MUSEUM-CITY**
Central Florence still has the character of a Renaissance city, dominated by the cathedral and the nearby church of San Lorenzo.

△ **TRAVEL POSTER**
In the 1920s, when this poster was printed, Florence was actively promoting itself as a tourist destination.

with artists and architects. Visiting writers, such as British art critic and social reformer John Ruskin, and poets Robert and Elizabeth Barrett Browning, spread the city's fame still more widely. By the late 19th century, when many Florentines had abandoned their city, more than 1 in 7 of Florence's residents were from Britain.

The 20th century saw Florence facing mixed fortunes. Respect for the city's history generally defeated plans to erect modern buildings (with the exception of a Modernist railroad station), but bitter fighting around Florence during World War II left its mark. Retreating German forces blew up all the bridges across the Arno, except the Ponte Vecchio, necessitating a huge post-war reconstruction campaign. Further setbacks came when the city was overwhelmed by severe flooding in 1966, causing irreparable damage to its artistic heritage, with many masterpieces destroyed. The Arno's banks have held fast since then, and Florence has found its feet once more, with a thriving industrial and commercial life, including a strong design sector. The city's medieval artisanal legacy is clear to see in the homegrown design talents of Gucci, originally a purveyor of leather luggage; the luxury goods company Salvatore Ferragamo; and print and pattern supremo Emilio Pucci. The other main pillar of the economy is, of course, tourism. Today's "grand tourists" throng the fragile historical center and marvel at Brunelleschi's mighty cathedral dome, rising above a terra-cotta and cream tableau barely changed since the Renaissance.

1943 Florence suffers from Allied bombing. The historical monuments are spared but 200 people are killed.

1944 The German occupation of Florence ends.

1966 Major flooding is the cause of much damage to the city. Volunteers nicknamed "mud angels" clear away mud and refuse and carry works of art to safety.

1988 Cars are banned from the center of the city.

2016 As part of ongoing modernization, the Uffizi Gallery increases capacity to 101 rooms.

Prague

CITY OF A HUNDRED SPIRES

Having flourished in the Middle Ages and shined briefly during the Renaissance, in the 19th century Prague became a melting pot of ideas—and a cultural center where the Czech people found their identity.

The valley of the Vltava River lies in the heart of Europe, in the area known as Bohemia, now part of the Czech Republic. By around 500 BCE it was occupied by Celtic tribes, but over the next millennium other groups arrived, including Germanic peoples and Franks, followed in the 6th century CE by Slavs, who won the upper hand.

According to legend, Prague was founded by two of these Slavs, Princess Libuše and her husband Přemysl, who became the first rulers of a dynasty that would last over 400 years. The Přemyslids first settled on the craggy hill at Vyšehrad, on the right bank of the Vltava, and later built Prague Castle on the opposite bank. One of their number was the pious Duke Václav. His younger brother, Boleslav, was jealous of his power and—perhaps under the influence of his mother—murdered Václav at a religious feast. Václav, seen as a Christian martyr, was made a saint. He is now best known by his Western name, St. Wenceslas, and his legendary piety is celebrated in the carol "Good King Wenceslas." It would not be the last time Prague would celebrate faith—or see blood shed for it.

◁ *VIEW OF THE OLD TOWN OF PRAGUE WITH THE CHURCH OF OUR LADY BEFORE TYN,* 1866
This view of Prague's Old Town Square is by Ferdinand Lepié. The Old Town Hall is visible on the left.

God and empire

The Přemyslids oversaw the growth of a bustling town, with a bridge over the river and a market in a vast square on the right bank, in the area now called the Old Town. The market attracted merchants from Germany, who traded along the river or traveled on roads that met in the Old Town Square. Prague also became home to a substantial Jewish community.

However, the Přemyslid dynasty ended in 1306, when Václav III died leaving only an illegitimate daughter. Prague soon became part of the Holy Roman Empire, and Emperor Charles IV boosted the importance of the city by making it his capital. Charles, the most revered of Prague's medieval rulers, also rebuilt the castle, began work on the cathedral, constructed a new stone bridge over the river, and, in 1348, founded the Charles University. Prague had become one of Europe's finest cities. However, soon its people's reforming instincts would spark war.

> "I see a **vast city**, whose **glory** will **touch** the **stars**!"
>
> ATTRIBUTED TO QUEEN LIBUŠE, 9TH CENTURY

c. 800 CE The Přemyslid dynasty is founded by the legendary Libuše and Přemysl.

870 Prague Castle is built on high ground overlooking the left bank of the Vltava.

935 Václav the Good, also known as Wenceslas I, famous as a model of noble virtue, is murdered by his brother when about to attend church for Mass.

1091 A marketplace operates in the Old Town Square.

1270 The Old-New Synagogue is built in the Jewish quarter to the north of the Old Town.

△ DEFENESTRATION OF 1618
This engraving by Matthäus Merian the Elder shows the meeting of Protestant leaders with governors representing the Catholic Hapsburg emperor. In heated exchanges, the Protestants threw two of the governors out of the castle window, sparking the Thirty Years' War.

In the 15th century, Prague came under the influence of reformers, inspired by religious leader Jan Hus. He demanded an end to corruption in the Catholic Church, and some of his followers began to question Catholic practices. This was the beginning of a movement, later known as the Reformation, which was to transform Europe. The emperor resisted change, and the result was a religious war. The reforming Czechs had some success under their inspirational military leader, Jan Žižka, whose innovative use of firearms allowed small forces to overcome much larger armies. However, in 1415 Hus was burned at the stake, and religious tensions continued for more than a century, intensifying when the empire was taken over by the staunchly Catholic Hapsburg dynasty. In the 1550s, they invited Jesuits to settle in Prague in order to bring its people back to the old faith. The city's inhabitants proved stubborn, but the Jesuits would leave a grand legacy.

From Renaissance to war

One late-16th-century emperor, Rudolf II, turned his back on politics and poured his energy into culture. Prague became famous for its royal gardens, imperial art collection, and scientists. The emperor's interests were wide-ranging and eccentric by modern standards: he was patron not only to eminent Danish astronomer Tycho Brahe, but also to alchemists searching for the elixir of life.

1348 Charles University, one of the oldest in Europe, is founded.

1410 The Prague Astronomical Clock is installed on the Old Town Hall. It still operates today, making it one of the world's oldest clocks.

Crown of Emperor Rudolf II

1583 Rudolf II bases his court in Prague.

1620 Czech forces are defeated at the Battle of White Mountain, outside Prague.

1627 New laws are brought in by Ferdinand II to promote Catholicism and restrict Protestant practices.

1653 Work on building the Jesuit college of the Clementinum begins.

1714 Statues on the Charles Bridge are completed.

In addition, Rudolf produced a charter for religious freedom, giving the city's Protestants hope that they might one day be free of Hapsburg rule. But tensions continued. In 1618, a group of Protestant nobles threw two royal governors out of a window in the castle; the following year the nobles removed the emperor, Ferdinand II, from the Bohemian throne and installed their own candidate. These events sparked the Thirty Years' War, which pitted Protestant against Catholic across Europe. A year after the 1619 coup, the Protestant Czechs were brutally defeated by the Hapsburg army at the Battle of White Mountain, just outside Prague. There followed 27 executions in the city's Old Town Square.

Building a Baroque beauty

During the conflict, Ferdinand II moved the imperial capital to Vienna. Prague fell into decline and Protestants still suffered persecution. The Jesuits, prominent in the city, played a major part in the discrimination, but by the mid-17th century, when European life became more settled, they gave Prague a more positive legacy. To bolster their power and create platforms from which they could preach, the Jesuits began a major building program, remodeling most of the city's churches and constructing an enormous monastic college called the Clementinum. Around its five main courtyards were St. Clement's church, other churches and chapels, lecture halls, and a vast library. These facilities, combined with the Jesuits' formidable teaching skills, made the complex an important European center of learning. Like many of Prague's late-17th- and 18th-century buildings, the Clementinum was built in the ornate Baroque style. Prague's Baroque buildings were grand on the outside, but their true glory was their interior decoration and layout, featuring huge columns, much carving and gilding, dramatic lighting effects, painted ceilings, and statues that were often larger than life.

Prague became a grand and sophisticated city, home to some of Europe's finest musicians and an elegant social scene, with Mozart a rapturously received visitor. Yet while its center projected wealth and harmony, there was brutal poverty—in 1771, a sixth of the population died from famine, some in streets just a few feet from the ornate doors of abbeys and palaces.

A cultural capital

By the beginning of the 19th century, the city was expanding, with the development of its first suburb, Karlín, to help accommodate a population that had more than doubled in the 18th century. Although many of the new arrivals were Czechs, Prague was still part of the Hapsburg Empire, and its rulers, the educated class and manufacturers who were beginning to develop the city's industry, spoke German. The bureaucracy was complex, and this "Germanization" caused resentment, and a rise in nationalist sentiment.

Prague's Žižkov district is named after Jan Žižka, who defended the city from imperial forces in 1420, and whose use of armored wagons anticipated modern tank warfare.

> "... it was not freedom that **most influenced** the **shape and spirit of Prague**, it was the **unfreedom**, the life of **servitude**, the many ignominious **defeats** and cruel **military occupations**.
>
> IVAN KLÍMA, *THE SPIRIT OF PRAGUE*, 1994

1755 Building finishes on the Baroque church of St. Nicholas.

1784 Prague's four towns (Old Town, New Town, Little Quarter, and Hradčany) unite to create one large city.

1817 Karlín, Prague's first suburb, is established.

Czech Art Nouveau

△ Poster by Mucha for a youth sports festival.

> "His art ... reflects with tender nonchalance the **fluid beauty** of form and the delicately veiled **secrets of the soul**.
>
> CHRISTIAN BRINTON, AMERICAN ART CRITIC, ON ALFONS MUCHA

△ Alfons Mucha designed stained glass for the restoration of St. Vitus Cathedral in the 1920s; this detail shows his fascination with curved lines and natural features.

Prague's late-19th-century heyday coincided with the Art Nouveau style, which peaked between 1890 and 1914. Some Czechs, such as artist Alfons Mucha, went to Paris to work, and were attracted there to the style's sinuous lines, portrayal of idealized female beauty, and use of flowers and foliage. But many worked in Prague—where Mucha eventually returned—making colorful mosaics, prints, posters, and sculptures. Art Nouveau artists decorated Prague buildings with murals and plaster, often working both inside and out, lending a new color to city streets. Designers of public buildings such as the Obecní Dům (Municipal House) and the main railroad station adopted the style, too. This made Art Nouveau hard to miss, helping it spread further, as well as stimulating civic and national pride.

1818 The Czech National Museum is founded in Prague.

1848 A Czech nationalist uprising against the imperial rulers is unsuccessful.

1883 The National Theater is opened after a long delay due in part to a disastrous fire.

1891 The Jubilee Exhibition (World's Fair) is held in the city.

1897 Slum clearance begins in the old Jewish ghetto.

1912 The Obecní Dům arts and civic center opens.

1918 The Republic of Czechoslovakia is founded. Nationalist Tomáš Masaryk is its first president.

The 19th century saw Prague's growth continue; as the population rose, industry expanded with the exploitation of coal and iron in the nearby countryside, and railroad and tram lines were built. As the middle class became richer and more numerous, they longed more than ever to see Prague as the capital of an independent state.

Knowing they stood no chance in a military struggle, they focused on culture and education, reviving the literary use of the Czech language and encouraging the study of Czech history. A monumental new National Museum and other grand civic buildings were constructed. Czech architects and artists designed and decorated them in a range of styles, from Renaissance to Art Nouveau (see box), making Prague a world-class cultural center. The venues attracted writers and musicians, while composers such as Bedřich Smetana, and Antonín Dvořák wrote music that brought Czech history to life. Perhaps the greatest of all the new buildings was the Obecní Dům (Municipal House), its auditorium and exhibition halls gloriously decorated with Art Nouveau murals, tiling, and plasterwork.

A nation again

World War I saw the defeat of the Hapsburgs' Austro-Hungarian Empire, and Prague was made the capital of the new Republic of Czechoslovakia. The city was now home to a government that ran a small but successful democracy. Prague remained welcoming to new trends in art and design, and Modernist, flat-roofed buildings sprang up on Prague's streets. For 20 years, the city prospered, but it was occupied during World War II by the Nazis, who extended their repressive regime across the country.

The war was followed by a 40-year period of totalitarian communist rule, when the city was cut off from the capitalist world. The population had many of their human rights removed and there were shortages of essential goods. In 1968 came the Prague Spring, a brief period of liberalization under communist leader Alexander Dubček that was brutally suppressed by Soviet Russia. Later, Prague played a key role in the defeat of communism in the peaceful 1989 uprising that became known as the Velvet Revolution. Since then, the city has become vibrant again. Visitors have poured in to discover one of Europe's most beautiful cities, and exiled Czechs have returned. Prague continues to balance historic beauty and modern life, valuing above all its rich cultural legacy.

△ **PRAGUE SPRING**
In August 1968, Soviet Russian troops invaded Czechoslovakia to put an end to the Prague Spring and reimposed totalitarian rule. Young Czechs waving the Czechoslovak national flag staged a protest in Wenceslas Square.

Politician and philosopher Tomáš Masaryk, the first Czech president, remains a symbol of democracy in the country.

1939 German troops invade Prague, which becomes the capital of the Nazi Protectorate of Bohemia and Moravia.

1948 The Czech Communist Party takes power after winning a landslide election result.

1955 The world's largest statue of Stalin is erected in Letná Park; it is destroyed in 1962.

1989 Velvet Revolution takes place in Prague; Václav Havel becomes president.

1993 Prague becomes capital of the Czech Republic after the Czechs and Slovaks agree a Velvet Divorce.

Vienna

IMPERIAL CITY

For over 600 years, Vienna lay at the heart of the vast Hapsburg Empire. The city was celebrated for its grand buildings and fine music, and later for cultivating radical advances in art, design, science, and philosophy.

Vienna's position on the Wien River in the fertile Danube basin made it attractive to many incoming peoples, from the ancient Celts to the Romans. It was the Celts who called the place Vindobona, the origin of the name Vienna. The Romans adopted this title when they established a garrison at the site in the 1st century CE, drawn by its location on the ancient Amber Road trading route.

Other Central European tribes followed, including the Slavs and Avars, but the invaders with the most lasting impact were the Franks. They appointed dukes from outside Austria to govern border areas (marches), such as the land around Vienna. In the early 9th century, their king, Charlemagne, brought Vienna into the Holy Roman Empire, where it remained for over 1,000 years. It became an increasingly important city under the Hapsburg dynasty, who began their long rule with Rudolf I in 1278.

Hapsburg Vienna

Vienna grew and prospered under the Hapsburgs. They rebuilt the cathedral, remodeled other churches, founded the university, and made the city their capital. Emperor Maximilian I was a keen patron of the arts and sciences, and founded the Vienna Boys' Choir in 1498, beginning a tradition of fine music-making. One of his successors, Ferdinand I, gave the imperial court a magnificent new home, the Hofburg, and the court attracted some of Europe's best artists and craftsmen.

Hapsburg forces repelled an Ottoman invasion in 1683, leaving Vienna free to thrive as an imperial city and center of commerce. It was transformed in the 18th century with the construction of streets of Baroque townhouses, ornate courtiers' mansions, and the glorious Belvedere palaces. This building boom was led by Emperor Charles VI and then by his daughter, Maria Theresa, both of whom were enthusiastic patrons of musicians. One of their favorites was Mozart, who composed many of his greatest operas and orchestral pieces in Vienna, including *The Marriage of Figaro*. He had first visited the city as a six-year-old musical prodigy, performing in the glittering Mirrors Room of the Schönbrunn Palace. Many others followed Mozart, giving the city a reputation as Europe's musical capital.

CORNER OF KOHLMARKT ▷
This painting of the Kohlmarkt at the end of the 19th century shows its rows of fashionable shops, some with elaborate Baroque facades, extending toward the Hofburg.

Albrecht V, painted in 1828

c. 212 CE The Romans develop Vindobona into a self-governing town.

1156 The Frankish Babenberg dynasty begin their rule over Vienna, capital of the Eastern March duchy.

1160 The main structure of St. Stephen's Church (later cathedral) is completed.

1438 Albrecht V gives Vienna the title of *Kaiserstadt* ("imperial city").

1556 Vienna becomes capital of the Hapsburg Empire, under Ferdinand I.

Vienna's Pestsäule ("plague column") was commissioned by Leopold I to beg for mercy from the 1679 plague epidemic.

1683 Vienna withstands a lengthy siege by the Ottoman Turks, thanks in part to its strong fortifications.

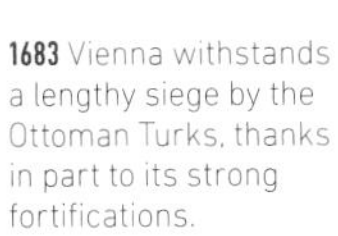

1714 The 18th-century rebuilding of Vienna in the Baroque style begins, with the construction of the Lower Belvedere Palace.

Empress Maria Theresa's gold carriage

1740 Empress Maria Theresa comes to the throne.

1781 Wolfgang Amadeus Mozart moves to Vienna, where he composes and performs some of his greatest music.

▷ *CAFÉ GRIENSTEIDL*, 1896
Authors gathered at this renowned coffee house, painted here by Reinhold Völkel. Coffee culture thrived in Vienna in the 19th century; legend has it the trend began with some Turkish coffee beans plundered during the 1683 Siege of Vienna.

Vienna has over 40 palaces, several of which belonged to the imperial family, one to the archbishop, and many to the empire's highest-ranking noble families. Nearly all are in the Baroque style.

The dawn of the 19th century signaled more turbulent times. Occupation by Napoleon, in both 1805 and 1809, was followed by a period of authoritarian rule presided over by a powerful chief minister, Prince Metternich. In 1848, as revolutions swept through Europe, the Viennese middle classes rose up, demanding liberal reform. Metternich was removed during the March Revolution and a less oppressive regime ensued. However, a final rebellion, the Vienna Uprising in October of the same year, saw bloodshed and harsh suppression by imperial troops.

Portrait of Eugenia Primavesi, Gustav Klimt, 1913

Ringstrasse grandeur

Under Emperor Franz Joseph (r. 1848–1916), the modern city began to take shape. With the plan of connecting the suburbs with the imperial center, the old fortifications were razed and replaced with a broad new street—the Ringstrasse, inaugurated in 1865. Circling the city, the Ring featured Vienna's first public park and a number of stately museums. Beyond were streets of new houses to accommodate an expanding population, which included immigrants and traders from all over the empire.

The grand Neoclassical style of the Ring was soon so widespread that many people began to look down on it as old-fashioned. Despite this traditional setting, Vienna was still a center for the latest in music (Brahms, Bruckner, and the Strauss family all worked in the city, while Mahler was conductor at the opera). Sigmund Freud developed his theory of psychoanalysis while a resident. Vienna's coffee houses were popular places to meet and share ideas, frequented by businessmen, writers, and artists alike.

1848 Sympathy with revolutionary Hungary sparks October's Vienna Uprising.

1857 The building of the Ringstrasse development begins.

1897 A group of artists found the Vienna Secession; painters like Gustav Klimt transform art.

1899 The ornate Majolikahaus opens, exemplifying Jugendstil.

> Vienna is a **handsome, lively city**, and pleases me exceedingly.

FREDERIC CHOPIN, *LIFE AND LETTERS*, 1906

Revolution in the arts

By the end of the century, many of Vienna's artists, designers, and architects were dissatisfied with the work of their forebears. Baroque or Neoclassical architecture were deemed unfit for modern life, and 19th-century Realism seemed dull and unadventurous. Architects such as Alfred Loos began to design buildings shorn of overblown decoration, while Gustav Klimt and other artists took painting in a radical new direction, creating work that could be startlingly colored, stylized, or shockingly explicit. In 1897, a group of them broke away (seceded) from the conservative art establishment, creating their own group, the Secession, which soon found followers all over Europe. They held exhibitions in a groundbreaking new gallery, the Secession Building, designed by Joseph Maria Olbrich and topped with an unmissable golden openwork dome.

The geometric style developed by Viennese designers was influential, too. Jugendstil ("young style"), as it became known, informed the work of the progressive Wiener Werkstätte ("Vienna workshop"). Founded by Secession member Josef Hoffmann, the cooperative was inspired by the British Arts and Crafts movement and aimed to bring art into the home, via anything from tea sets to textiles.

Political upheavals

Although Vienna's culture flourished in the late 19th and early 20th centuries, the city fared less well politically. The Hapsburg emperors lived grandly but their influence was waning, and the empire was on the losing side in World War I, leading to its eventual collapse in 1918. For the next two decades, Vienna was the scene of long political struggles between right and left, culminating in the rise of fascism and Adolf Hitler's takeover of Austria in 1938.

Intellectual life continued during this time, with the development of a formidable group of logical-positivist philosophers and scientists, the Vienna Circle, and a revolutionary group of composers, centered on Arnold Schoenberg. But many of these people were Jewish, and either left Austria or lost their lives in the Holocaust, leaving Vienna greatly diminished.

After World War II, Austria and its capital were occupied by the Allies for 10 years, until 1955 when Vienna once more became a capital city—of the independent Austrian Republic. A steady recovery followed, with the city chosen as a key location for the United Nations and as the site of political summits. Vienna is regularly ranked as one of the world's most livable places—thanks to its green spaces, efficient public transportation, and low crime—and it remains a city of stunning beauty that has preserved an unparalleled heritage of music and art.

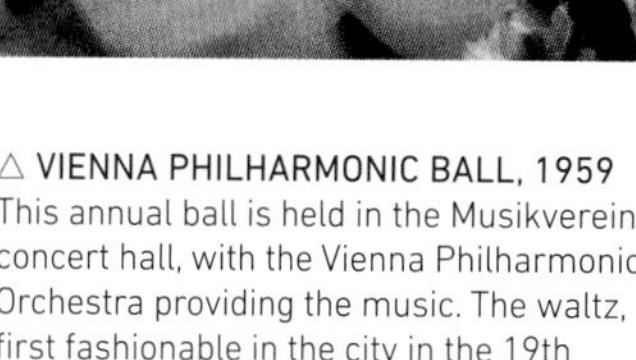

△ **VIENNA PHILHARMONIC BALL, 1959**
This annual ball is held in the Musikverein concert hall, with the Vienna Philharmonic Orchestra providing the music. The waltz, first fashionable in the city in the 19th century, features prominently.

1903 The Wiener Werkstätte is set up, inspired by the ideas of William Morris.

1938 Hitler gives a speech in front of the Hofburg Palace announcing the annexation of Austria into Nazi Germany.

1944 The Allies bomb Vienna during World War II.

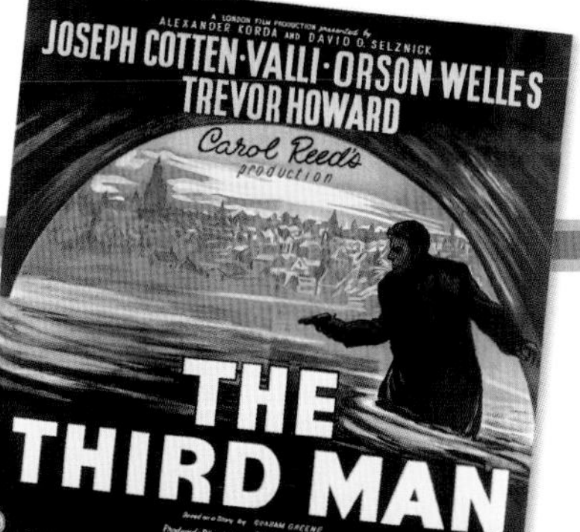

1949 Orson Welles stars in the film *The Third Man*, set in war-damaged Vienna.

1979 Vienna becomes a major HQ of the United Nations, alongside New York City, Nairobi, The Hague, and Geneva.

1985 Completion of Hundertwasserhaus, a striking building combining features of Modernist architecture with Vienna's decorative tradition.

2019 Vienna tops the Mercer Quality of Living Index for the 10th year running.

HOTEL ATLANTIC
HOTEL
PASSAGE
GRAND MERC

Berlin

ATHENS ON THE SPREE

In its passage from Prussian preeminence to foreign occupation, economic boom town to city divided—and eventually reunited—Berlin has shown an unrivaled ability to rise from its ruins.

Legend attributes the founding of Berlin to a figure known as Albert the Bear. He was a margrave, or nobleman, who ruled the area of Brandenburg, in what is now northeast Germany, from 1157 to 1170. Whether Albert truly did found the future capital is disputed, but a bear emblem still features on the city's coat of arms. The first historical mention of Berlin occurs in 1237. At that time it was conjoined with Cölln, on the opposite bank of the Spree River. Within a century, the two had merged into a single town, gaining sufficient status to become a member of the Hanseatic League of free-trading northern European cities.

In 1411, the region of Brandenburg came under the governorship of Friedrich of Hohenzollern, who established Berlin as his capital. Just over 30 years later, the Hohenzollerns built Berlin Castle on what is now Spree Island. Despite the fortifications, Berlin suffered heavily during the Thirty Years' War between Catholic forces loyal to the Holy Roman Emperor and Swedish-backed Protestant armies. The city's neutrality meant it was plundered and pillaged by both sides. Reconstruction was carried out by Friedrich Wilhelm, who encircled the city with new defenses, created new neighborhoods, and laid out the Lustgarten and Unter den Linden. He also encouraged the settlement of refugees, including Jews from Vienna and Huguenots expelled from France.

◁ *METROPOLIS*, 1917
Scarred by his experiences as a soldier, George Grosz completed this hellish vision of a Berlin gone mad and doomed to its own destruction at the height of World War I.

The rise of the Prussian capital

Friedrich Wilhelm's successors assumed the title of kings of Prussia. His great-grandson, Friedrich II (also known as Frederick the Great), took Prussia into a series of wars with Austria and Russia, but also initiated ambitious projects in his royal capital, including the Staatsoper (State Opera) and the palace that now houses the Humboldt University. By the late 18th century, such was Berlin's military and economic might, and so highly was it regarded as a center of Enlightenment thinkers and religious freedoms, that citizens referred to the city as "Athens on the Spree."

1157 Albert the Bear becomes Margrave of Brandenburg, a major principality of the Holy Roman Empire, corresponding to what is now northeast Germany.

1237 The first historical mention of the twin settlements Berlin and Cölln appears in church records.

1307 Berlin and Cölln merge into a single town.

1648 The Thirty Years' War ends and Friedrich Wilhelm undertakes reconstruction of the city, including the creation of Unter den Linden, connecting the Tiergarten Park and the Palace.

1701 Friedrich III has himself crowned King Frederick I of Prussia. Berlin becomes the capital of the Prussian Empire.

1740 Frederick the Great begins his 46-year reign, during which time Berlin is transformed into one of Europe's great intellectual, military, and economic capitals.

△ *PORTRAIT OF THE JOURNALIST SYLVIA VON HARDEN*, 1926
Artist Otto Dix was a key figure in the 1920s *Neue Sachlichkeit* ("New Objectivity") movement. Its artists rejected romantic idealism and shared a commitment to exposing the truths underlying contemporary ills.

> “**Berlin** was a **skeptical, sober city** of quick-witted, sharp-tongued people, **leading** all **German cities** in **sarcasm and insolence**.
>
> GEORGE GROSZ, *AN AUTOBIOGRAPHY*, 1946

Frederick the Great's death precipitated a decline in Berlin's fortunes. His successor, Friedrich Wilhelm, did endow Berlin with its most famous landmark, the Brandenburg Gate; however, nine years after his death in 1797, the monument served only to symbolize the city's humiliation when it framed the procession of Napoleon Bonaparte into Berlin after he defeated the Prussian army.

Birth of an imperial capital

Prussia resumed self-rule in 1813, initiating an era of reform and reconstruction that saw the foundation of the Friedrich Wilhelm University by minister of education Wilhelm von Humboldt (for whom the university was later renamed), and the unveiling of many Neoclassical buildings, including the Altes Museum and Neue Wache. Away from the grandeur, however, much of the rapidly swelling populace was suffering in poverty. Berlin had a first popular uprising in 1830, culminating in the bloody revolution of 1848 that left over 200 dead.

In 1862, King Wilhelm I appointed Otto von Bismarck as his prime minister. Neither figure was popular in liberal Berlin—attempts on both men's lives were made in the city—but Bismarck masterminded a series of military

1806 Napoleon conquers Berlin and removes the statue of Victory from the top of the Brandenburg Gate, sending it to Paris.

1830 A first museum opens on Museumsinsel (Museum Island), the Königliches Museum, later renamed the Altes Museum (Old Museum).

1866 Otto Von Bismarck, prime minister of Prussia, is attacked by a would-be assassin on Berlin's Unter den Linden.

Helmet worn by Otto Von Bismarck

1871 As Wilhelm I is proclaimed German Kaiser ("emperor") at Versailles, Berlin becomes the capital of a newly unified Germany.

1894 Following 10 years of construction, the Neo-Baroque Reichstag is opened as the new Berlin home of the German parliament.

1905 Kaiser Wilhelm II's imposing Protestant cathedral, the Berliner Dom, is completed.

1918 With the end of World War I, Berlin becomes the capital of the Republic of Germany.

BOMBED-OUT BERLIN ▷
In April 1945, Soviet leader Josef Stalin sent 2.5 million troops, 7,500 aircraft, 6,250 tanks, and 41,600 guns in an assault on Berlin, reducing much of the city to piles of smoldering rubble.

victories against Denmark, Austria, and France that forged an empire to dominate central Europe and promoted the Prussian king into the German Kaiser, or "emperor." Thousands of people poured into the imperial capital to fuel its rising industries: the population rocketed from 969,000 in 1875 to over two million by 1905.

Metropolis

Berlin became one of the greatest cities in Europe, a true *Weldstadt*, or "world city." Electric trams zipped along crowded streets, past the Hotel Excelsior—with 600 rooms, the continent's largest hotel—and the recently completed Berliner Dom, a cathedral designed to rival even the splendor of St. Peter's in Rome. This was a city of modernity, industry, and power, lit up by electricity, with giant zeppelin airships drifting overhead. American humorist Mark Twain visited and likened Berlin to Chicago: he called it the "newest city I have ever seen."

While Berlin seemed to welcome the outbreak of war in 1914, euphoria eventually gave way to the despair of defeat. The Kaiser abdicated in 1918 and Germany became a republic with a constitution forged in the town of Weimar, where politicians had fled from the chaos of the capital. By 1924, however, thanks to an American-led aid plan, Berlin had managed to bounce back. Once again bursting with energy, it was a center of industry and science, radical art and decadent entertainment, a mix exemplified in the Expressionist science-fiction film *Metropolis* (1927), with its scenes of toiling workers and humanoid robots.

Just as the United States had helped start the party, the US stock market crash of 1929 threw Berlin into economic depression. Huge job losses and hyperinflation resulted in mass poverty. The threat of anarchy enabled the rise of political extremism that ultimately led to Adolf Hitler being sworn in as chancellor on January 30, 1933. Four weeks later, an unknown arsonist burned the Reichstag, home of the German parliament in Berlin, to the ground.

Berlin was devastated by the war that Hitler instigated. The Battle of Berlin saw Britain's RAF, later joined by the US Air Force, launch 314 air raids on the city. In April 1945, Soviet soldiers encircled the city, fighting their way to the

In 1923, Berlin businesses paid their employees twice a day to keep pace with inflation.

Albert Einstein rose to international prominence while working in Berlin between the wars, winning the Nobel Prize in Physics in 1921.

1919 The internationally influential Bauhaus design school, founded by Walter Gropius, opens in Weimar; it moves to Berlin in 1932.

1920 Berlin is swollen as the city expands to incorporate seven towns and 59 villages. The population surpasses four million.

1927 Fritz Lang's startling vision of modernity, *Metropolis*, is released. Shot in Berlin, the film costs over five million Reichsmarks.

1933 Adolf Hitler is appointed Chancellor of Germany. Weeks later, the Reichstag is burned down.

1936 Berlin hosts the Olympic Games, centered on the newly built Olympiastadion.

The Berlin Wall

△ Crowds celebrate the opening of the crossings in the Berlin Wall, which took place on November 9, 1989.

When it was completed, the Berlin Wall extended 96 miles (155 km) around West Berlin; 23 miles (37 km) of that ran through the city center. Largely constructed of concrete and studded with watchtowers, the Wall was the scene of many daring escape attempts, including some involving hot-air balloons and aerial wires. Over time, the barrier was modified in various ways to make crossing more difficult. Nevertheless, up to 100,000 people tried to escape over the Wall, and at least 140 died in the attempt. The last of these fatalities occurred in March 1989, only seven months before the Wall came down amid a wave of revolutions across Eastern Europe and mass protests in East Berlin. Today, only a small portion of the Wall remains. Most prominently, a series of painted segments is preserved as the East Side Gallery, a reminder of the city's divided past and also its triumphant reunification.

center. In his bunker behind Wilhelmstrasse, Hitler committed suicide and the Red Army raised the Soviet flag above the gutted Reichstag.

East and West

At the Yalta Conference in 1945, the Allies carved Berlin into four zones of occupation: American, British, French, and Soviet. When relations between Soviet Russia and the Western Allies chilled, the Soviets began a blockade of what was now collectively known as West Berlin. All transport routes were cut off. In response, the Allies created three "air corridors" to deliver food and essentials. The Soviets called off the blockade after 11 months, in May 1949, but five months later created the German Democratic Republic (GDR) with its capital in East Berlin.

During the 1950s, East and West Berlin evolved separately as the Cold War between the US and its allies and the Soviet Union intensified. The Soviets reshaped their sector of Berlin, creating vast Moscow-style avenues and socialist housing blocks, while the US channeled money into West Berlin. Despite border checks, citizens were free to pass between the two zones and many East Berliners

1945 At the end of World War II, the four occupying powers divide Berlin into American, British, French, and Soviet zones.

1948 The Soviet Union begins a blockade of the city to which the Western Allies respond with the Berlin Airlift.

1949 Charlottenburg resident Herta Heuwer invents the *currywurst*, which will become the signature street food of Berlin.

1949 The Americans, British, and French create the political entity of West Germany with Bonn as its capital and seat of government.

1953 On June 17, Soviet tanks roll into East Berlin to crush a workers' uprising.

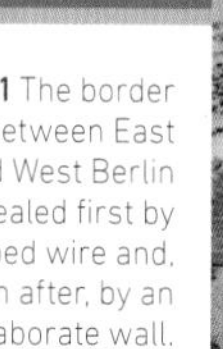

1961 The border between East and West Berlin is sealed first by barbed wire and, soon after, by an elaborate wall.

1961 West Berlin invites mass Turkish immigration to replace lost East German labor.

1968 Berlin experiences wide-scale student protests resulting in a number of deaths.

▷ THE REICHSTAG REBUILT
Badly damaged by fire in 1933 and stranded for decades beside the Wall, the German seat of Parliament was finally renovated in the 1990s to a design by Foster + Partners.

commuted across to work. As the disparity between the two halves of the city grew, East Germans increasingly moved to West Berlin (the border with West Germany was sealed in 1952). By the end of the decade, it seemed East Germany would cease to function because of the flight of skilled laborers to West Berlin.

Divided and reunited

In August 1961, East German police began to drag barbed wire across Potsdamer Platz. Within 24 hours the crossing between East and West Berlin was closed. Days later the construction of a wall began (see box). West Berliners and their allies were powerless to do anything. American and Soviet tanks faced off at Checkpoint Charlie and US President Kennedy delivered a speech of solidarity that ended with the famous words, *"Ich bin ein Berliner."*

Almost as shocking was the fall of the Wall in November 1989. The subsequent dissolution of the Soviet Union allowed for the reunification of Berlin and, the following year, of Germany itself. In 1990, Berlin once again became the seat of government.

Since then, the city has continued to exert a fascination, as a leading influence in European politics and as a capital for creatives from around the world. Potsdamer Platz—once the busiest intersection in Europe, then a no-man's-land between East and West Berlin—has been redeveloped as a showcase for international architecture. Meanwhile, artists, DJs, and influencers throng gallery openings, clubs, and pop-up restaurants, ensuring Berlin's legacy as a city that combines industry with hedonism.

1969 The East Germans inaugurate the Fernsehturm ("TV tower"), intended to be both a symbol of Communist power and of the city.

1971 The Four Powers meet and sign an agreement formally recognizing Berlin's divided status.

1989 Following mass protests, on November 9 East German authorities open the barriers in the Berlin Wall.

1999 The German federal parliament relocates from Bonn to Berlin's newly reconstructed Reichstag.

2005 The city inaugurates a Memorial to the Murdered Jews of Europe, otherwise known as the Holocaust Memorial.

Moscow

THE THIRD ROME

From its beginnings as a provincial fortress, Moscow went on to shape the world through great art and literature, and later with an uncompromising politics born of proletarian revolution.

Moscow began as a remote trading post on the Moskva River, between the cities of Novgorod in the north and Kiev to the south. In the early 12th century, the Grand Prince of Kiev sent his son, Yuri Dolgoruky, to govern the northeastern Vladimir-Suzdal province. He built fortresses to defend the region and, in 1156, fortified Moscow with a stockade (*kremlin*) encircled by a moat. Although Moscow was already a small town when he arrived, Dolgoruky is often described as the city's founder.

Ivans Great and Terrible

In the 13th century, the Mongols swept westward, sacking Kiev. They would rule the region for over a century, during which they empowered Moscow's Grand Prince Ivan I, who became their chief tribute collector in 1328. In time, Moscow was able to raise its own army and defeat the Mongols, giving birth to Russia. Under Ivan III, "the Great," Moscow secured an empire stretching east to the Urals. He imported Italian architects, who built the Kremlin's massive walls and landmark Trinity Tower in 1495. The Cathedral of the Assumption, where princes were crowned and patriarchs buried, was rebuilt. Ivan also married the niece of the last Byzantine emperor and declared himself the defender of Orthodox Christianity—making Moscow the heir to Rome and Constantinople. Moscow's princes claimed the title "czar," a Russian derivation of "caesar."

In the 16th century, Ivan's grandson Ivan IV, "the Terrible," transformed himself from Grand Prince of Moscow to "Czar of all the Russias." He graced Moscow with St. Basil's Cathedral, and Russia expanded into Siberia. But he also established the *oprichniki*, Russia's first political police force, and killed his one competent son in an argument, leaving a mentally unstable son to rule. Thus began the Time of Troubles, a period of rival claimants and foreign interventions, notably by the Poles, who occupied Moscow between 1610 and 1612. The upheavals ended in 1613, when leading citizens placed 16-year-old Mikhail Romanov in power, initiating the 300-year rule of the Romanovs.

▷ **RED SQUARE**
Facing the State Historical Museum, Moscow's colourful 16th-century St. Basil's Cathedral is a symbol of Russia..

Russian Coat of Arms

1156 CE Moscow's first *kremlin* is built. The structure is wooden, with a moat.

1453 Constantinople falls, and Moscow claims the role of protector of Orthodox Christianity.

1462 Ivan the Great comes to power, unifies Russia, and uses Italian architects to rebuild the Kremlin.

1552 Ivan the Terrible commissions St. Basil's Cathedral to celebrate the capture of the Mongol stronghold of Kazan.

1610 A Polish and Lithuanian army occupies Moscow during the Time of Troubles; following a siege by the Cossacks, the city is liberated in 1612.

> “**Moscow ...** so much **flows together** in that **one sound** for **Russian hearts**! What **store of riches** it imparts!
>
> ALEXANDER PUSHKIN, *EUGENE ONEGIN*, 1833

△ *AUDITORIUM OF THE BOLSHOI THEATER*, 1856
The Bolshoi Ballet Company was founded in 1776, but had no permanent home until the Bolshoi Theater—captured here by painter Mihály Zichy—opened in the 1820s.

Reborn from the flames

Mikhail's grandson, Peter I, "the Great," transformed Russia from a landlocked state into one of Europe's greatest empires. But he had no love for Moscow, which he viewed as a city of antiquity, superstition, and prejudice. Instead, beginning in 1703, he built a brand new capital that looked to the West: St. Petersburg. For the next 200 years, Moscow was Russia's second city.

It took an invasion by Napoleon in 1812 to reinvigorate the city. When the French general took up residence in the Kremlin, defiant Muscovites razed their own city. Napoleon retreated, harried by a harsh early winter and pursued by the Russian army. Flush with victory, Muscovites embarked on a great rebuild. Vast areas were developed, with new avenues fanning out from Red Square and Alexander Gardens laid out beside the Kremlin's walls. Several planned complexes were created, notably Theater Square, with the Bolshoi Theater at its center. Noble families rebuilt their ancestral homes, and Moscow rose again with fantastic speed. Fittingly for a capital whose domain stretched from Baltic coasts to Central Asian steppes, the architecture mixed classical facades with oriental domes.

Many of the biggest merchant and industrial families assigned money to philanthropy and artistic patronage. Writers, artists, and composers explored Moscow's heritage in works such as Leo Tolstoy's *War and Peace* (1869) and Modest Mussorgsky's opera *Boris Godunov* (1874). The popular view was that Moscow had been saved by peasants who had taken up arms to defend the mother city, and a movement to emancipate serfs from indentured agricultural labor saw them flock to Moscow to fuel an economic boom. Within 60 years, Napoleon's ruins had been transformed into a bustling city of palatial residences, grand thoroughfares, and sprawling industrial suburbs.

1712 Peter the Great moves the capital from Moscow to St. Petersburg and the Kremlin is abandoned.

1755 Poet and scientist Mikhail Lomonosov founds Moscow University.

1770 Moscow is devastated by bubonic plague and more than 50,000 die.

1812 Napoleon invades Moscow and its citizens set the city ablaze rather than see it occupied.

1824 During a building boom, the Bolshoi Theater is built on Theater Square.

1861 Czar Alexander II's Emancipation Reform frees thousands of peasants to move to the city.

1877 Premiere of Tchaikovsky's *Swan Lake* ballet at the Bolshoi Theater.

1883 The Cathedral of Christ the Savior is consecrated.

The Russian Revolution

> **History** will **not forgive** us if we do not **assume power** now.
>
> VLADIMIR LENIN, LETTER TO THE RUSSIAN SOCIAL DEMOCRATIC LABOR PARTY, 1917

By 1900, more than half of Moscow's population were first-generation migrants living in slums and discontent on the fringes of the city. A Russian war with Japan in 1904 only increased unrest, triggering strikes and demonstrations the following year, first in St. Petersburg and then in Moscow. The 1905 revolution was quashed, but 12 years later, in February 1917, the hardships and losses of war sent Russian citizens back out into the streets. A weakened Nicholas II was forced to abdicate and his family was placed under house arrest. He was replaced by a provisional government.

Unable to restore order, the provisional government was itself overthrown in a coup that October, orchestrated by Vladimir Lenin's Bolshevik Party. In the wake of the Revolution, Lenin ordered that the capital be returned to Moscow. From here, Lenin and his Communist "Red" army fought a civil war against "White" supporters of the Romanov regime. When it appeared as if the royal family might be rescued by the Whites, they were killed. The civil war ended in 1920 with the Bolsheviks in control of a transformed nation: Soviet Russia.

△ Children gaze at the bronze head of a smashed statue of Czar Alexander III in 1917, during the Russian Revolution. Alexander's son, Nicholas II, was Russia's last czar.

▷ "Have you volunteered for the Red Army?" asks this 1920 recruitment poster.

Anton Chekhov reads *The Seagull* with actors from the Moscow Art Theater, 1899

1899 Premiere of Chekhov's *Uncle Vanya* at the Moscow Art Theater.

1905 The unpopular Russo-Japanese War provokes the Moscow Uprising.

When the monumental Upper Trading Stores opened along the east side of Red Square in 1893, it housed 1,200 stores. Today it is the GUM shopping mall.

1917 Revolution begins in St. Petersburg and spreads to Moscow, where street fighting leaves more than 1,000 dead.

◁ PALACES OF TRANSPORTATION
Not just a transportation system, Moscow's Metro employed some of the Soviet Union's finest architects and artists to create a showcase for socialist achievements.

Seeing red

The late 19th century may have seen great architecture and art being created in Moscow, but the city's slums were poverty-stricken. Discontent flamed into an attempted revolution in 1905, and a successful one 12 years later (see box, p.127). In 1918, Vladimir Lenin's Bolshevik Party made Moscow the capital of Soviet Russia, although it was hardly a place of triumph: as well as those killed in the war, hundreds of thousands had fled turmoil in the city and returned to their villages. A population of over 1.8 million in 1915 had almost halved to 1 million by 1920. From this, the Bolsheviks began to remold Moscow into a new center of progressive socialism. For a few years, in the early 1920s, Moscow became a workshop of the avant-garde, nurturing artists such as Kazimir Malevich, graphic designer Alexander Rodchenko, architect and stage designer Vladimir Tatlin, and director Sergei Eisenstein, maker of revolutionary films including *Battleship Potemkin* (1925).

Lenin died in 1924, and his embalmed corpse was put on display in Red Square in a sarcophagus designed by the radical architect Konstantin Melnikov. He was replaced as the head of the Communist Party by Josef Stalin, who continued the work of reshaping Moscow. A 1935 Moscow Master Plan decreed that new development had to proceed by whole "ensembles," not by individual buildings, and increased city-block sizes and building heights. This was city planning by sledgehammer. A vast new parade route was bulldozed through the city center, while below ground, construction began on the Moscow Metro. Churches were demolished, notably the massive Cathedral of Christ the Savior, which was destroyed to make way for a colossal Palace of the Soviets, which was never built. (Following the dissolution of the Soviet Union, the cathedral was rebuilt between 1995 and 2000.) At one point there were even plans to blow up St. Basil's Cathedral because it was considered an obstruction to military processions. The most distinctive monuments of Soviet Moscow went up in Stalin's final years. Collectively known as the Seven Sisters, these wedding-cake-like Gothic skyscrapers were built between 1947 and 1953, and were the tallest buildings in Europe at the time.

1918 Lenin names Moscow the capital of the Russian Soviet Federative Socialist Republic.

1921 Moscow exhibition 5x5=25 presents the work of five avant-garde artists proclaiming the "death of art."

1924 Lenin dies and is succeeded by Stalin. Lenin's embalmed body goes on display in Moscow.

1931 Stalin orders the dynamiting of the Cathedral of Christ the Savior to make way for a never-built Palace of the Soviets.

1935 The first line of the Moscow Metro opens.

1937 The monumental stainless-steel, Socialist-Realist sculpture *Worker and Kolkhoz Woman* is created for the year's World's Fair in Paris. It is subsequently moved to Moscow.

World War II and the Battle of Moscow

Under Stalin's command, Muscovites had to defend their city once again. In October 1941, German tanks and infantry advanced on the Russian capital. By December, the Germans were on the outskirts of the city and the Russians counterattacked. Over weeks of fighting, with Muscovites bringing food to their soldiers and carrying the wounded away to care for them in their homes, the Red Army managed to drive the Germans back—today, giant tank traps on the road out to Sheremetyevo Airport mark the point where the Germans were halted. The Battle of Moscow was one of the largest battles in World War II and, according to one estimate, Russian losses equaled the combined number of Americans, British, and French who died during all of World War II.

The post-Stalinist city

Through the Communist era, the city saw a rapid expansion of its suburbs, which became densely populated thanks to massed high-rise tower blocks, and were linked to the center by extended Metro lines. Otherwise, Moscow slowly stagnated until Mikhail Gorbachev came to power in 1985. He sought to revitalize the ailing socialist system through *glasnost* ("openness") and *perestroika* ("restructuring"), but could not prevent the breakup of the USSR.

In the early 1990s, Boris Yeltsin presided over an exhilarating but lawless period of economic liberalization, in which a new Russia emerged. Private enterprise took over state assets, and the country charged into a piratical form of capitalism. Much of the wealth flowed to Moscow, which became a city of bling. A clique of "New Russians" shopped in exclusive malls and sipped champagne while clubbing. A joke summed up the free-spending attitude: "What do you think of my watch? It cost me $1,000," says one businessman. "That's nothing," replies his friend. "I bought the same one last week for $2,000." Most Muscovites, however, struggled to put food on the table.

In 1999, Yeltsin handed power to his new prime minister, Vladimir Putin, who was confirmed as president in March 2000. Since then, as the capital of a stable and increasingly powerful Russia, Moscow has expanded to the extent that it is not so much a large city as a small state. There are now over 20 million residents in the metropolitan area, making Moscow the most populous urban area in Europe; it is officially classed as a megacity. And while Soviet-era statues look on, the population continues to swell with aspirational Russians seeking the good life in the country's capital and model of new urbanism; a city which is technologically advanced, surprisingly green in all senses, and full of the promise of fast living and fortune.

▽ **FLOATING BRIDGE**
Developed in 2013, Zaryadye Park marries 21st-century architectural wonders, such as the V-shaped Floating Bridge over the Moskva, with lessons from the past, in the form of a museum of Russian history.

1940 Mikhail Bulgakov completes his Moscow-set novel *The Master and Margarita*. It is not published in Russia until 1967, after the writer's death.

1953 Stalin dies and is replaced by Nikita Khrushchev, who initiates the construction of mass housing estates around the city outskirts.

1985 Mikhail Gorbachev becomes general secretary of the Communist Party and institutes policies of *glasnost* and *perestroika*.

1990 The first McDonald's in Russia opens in Moscow.

1993 Boris Yeltsin sends in troops to deal with protesters at Moscow's White House (the home of the Russian parliament).

2000 The newly rebuilt Cathedral of Christ the Savior is consecrated.

2011 President Dmitry Medvedev announces a plan to expand the territory of Moscow by 155 percent, by annexing a vast tract southwest of the city.

Cairo

UMM AL-DUNYA ("MOTHER OF THE WORLD")

When Arab armies conquered the Roman fortress of Babylon-of-Egypt, they lay the ground for the city of al-Qahira, "the victorious." Known in the West as Cairo, it was destined to grow into a modern megacity.

Following the death of the last of the Ptolemaic pharaohs, Cleopatra, in 30 BCE, the Romans took control of Egypt. They occupied its Mediterranean capital, Alexandria, and established military outposts throughout the country. One such fortress was built at an ancient river crossing, near the site of the Old Kingdom capital of Memphis, and just south of the point at which the Nile fanned out to form a wide delta. The river was the country's main highway and the fortress controlled the passage between the delta and the populous Nile valley. A key frontier stronghold and a busy port, it was known as Babylon-of-Egypt.

The Roman fortress became the nucleus of a small but prosperous town, and a base for a legion. When Christianity arrived in Egypt during the 1st century CE, Babylon became the seat of a bishopric, but Egypt's Coptic Christians were subject to persecution. Even after Christianity was adopted as the official religion of the Roman Empire in 380 CE, theological differences between Egypt and Rome meant that Copts were branded as heretics. The persecution came to an end in 640 CE with the arrival of an army originating in the Arabian deserts and bearing the flag of another new religion, Islam.

Egypt's Islamic capital

Babylon surrendered to the conquering Muslim Arabs, who were welcomed by the Egyptian people as liberators. The Muslims set up a tent city, Fustat, north of the Roman walls. Here they built Egypt's first mosque, naming it after their victorious leader, 'Amr ibn al-'As. The tent city was soon replaced by one of mudbrick, which grew in size, spreading ever further north. As politics shifted in the wider Islamic world, this new Arab city—and, by extension, the whole of Egypt—became subject to rule from Damascus, then Baghdad. Home to waves of immigrant officials and soldiers, it was already a cosmopolitan and wealthy outpost when, in 969 CE, an army belonging to the North African Fatimid dynasty swept in and took control.

> He who has **not seen Cairo** has **not seen the world.**
>
> *THE THOUSAND AND ONE NIGHTS*

▷ *VIEW OF CAIRO*, c. 1872
Using wealth accrued through conquest and trade, the medieval Mamluk rulers of Egypt endowed Cairo with a spectacular array of mosques, palaces, and mausoleums, as shown in this study in oils by Louis Comfort Tiffany, better known for his stained glass.

1st century BCE The Romans build a fortress on the east bank of the Nile called Babylon-of-Egypt.

33 CE The apostle Mark the Evangelist introduces Christianity to Egypt.

3rd century The first churches are founded in Babylon-of-Egypt. Several survive today in an area that is still known as Coptic Cairo.

640 A Muslim Arab army led by its commander 'Amr ibn al-'As conquers Egypt and establishes a base on the future site of Cairo.

969 The Fatimid dynasty of North Africa wrests control of Egypt from Baghdad and creates a new capital, which will become Cairo.

The Pyramids of Giza

> From the **heights** of these **pyramids**, **forty centuries look down** on us.
>
> NAPOLEON BONAPARTE ADDRESSING HIS TROOPS, 1798

Although the modern city laps at the base of the Pyramids, which stand on the Giza Plateau 5½ miles (9 km) from the Nile, Cairo did not exist in the pharaonic era. The Pyramids were part of the necropolis attached to the Old Kingdom capital of Memphis, which was founded prior to the 31st century BCE. These monumental resting places of kings were constructed around 2580–2510 BCE, at which time the site of the future Cairo was just a crossing on the river. From the 10th century CE onward, stones from nearby ancient sites, including the Pyramids, were recycled to build the medieval city.

◁ The Great Sphinx of Giza and the Pyramid of Khafre, stripped of its outer stone casing, except at the very top, c. 1920–1922.

△ Aerial view of the Giza Plateau showing the Great Pyramids, and Cairo encroaching.

The city victorious

Continuing the trend begun by 'Amr ibn al-'As, the Fatimids established a new city immediately to the north of the existing settlement. They named it al-Qahira, meaning "the victorious"; non-Arabic speakers would pronounce it as "Cairo." The new city was protected by walls and entered through one of several great fortified gates. It contained grand squares, palaces, and numerous mosques, including al-Azhar, which quickly became a renowned center of Islamic learning (and continues to be so in the 21st century, as the University of al-Azhar).

In 1168, fearing the advance of the European Crusaders then rampaging around the eastern Mediterranean, the Fatimids appealed for help from their fellow Muslims. The Seljuk dynasty of Damascus saw off the immediate Christian threat but, once in Cairo, deposed the rulers they

972 The Fatimids found the Mosque of al-Azhar, which becomes a major center for Islamic learning.

1171 Salah ad-Din ibn Ayyub, otherwise known as Saladin, becomes sultan in Egypt.

1176 Saladin constructs a citadel and new city walls to defend Cairo from Crusaders.

1250 Following the death of the eighth Ayyubid sultan, the *emirs* (leaders) of the Mamluk army seize control of Egypt.

1260 Highly trained Mamluk horsemen contribute to the defeat of a Mongol army at Ain Jalut.

1260 Baybars becomes sultan, beginning an age of Mamluk military dominance in the eastern Mediterranean.

had supposedly come to help. The new master of Egypt was Salah ad-Din ibn Ayyub, better known in the West as Saladin. He built a fortress at the western edge of the city, where he sired a short-lived dynasty, the Ayyubids, which ran to four sultans before their attendant slave warriors, the Mamluks, seized control of Egypt for themselves.

City of 1,001 nights

Under the Mamluk regime, Cairo became the capital of an empire that extended into what is now Turkey. The militaristic Mamluks also proved to be keen patrons of the arts. For more than 250 years, the riches that came from controlling East–West trade routes were lavished on Cairo. The city was adorned with fantastic architectural complexes, embellished with exquisite stone carving, marble inlays, and ivory- and woodwork. Bazaars were filled with exotic wares from distant lands, from African ostrich feathers to Chinese silks. In 1481, a visiting Italian rabbi wrote in his journal, "I swear that if it were possible to put Rome, Venice, Milan, Padua, Florence, and four more cities together, they would not equal in wealth and population half that of Cairo." This was the city that inspired many of the tales in *The Thousand and One Nights*.

When, in 1498, Vasco da Gama discovered a route around Africa, it freed European merchants from the duties imposed by Cairo. Less than 20 years later, a new power, the Ottoman Turks, crushed the Mamluks in battle. Cairo's years as a glittering capital were at an end.

▷ **MAP OF CAIRO FROM PIRI REIS'S *BOOK OF NAVIGATION*, 1525**
At the bottom (north) of this illuminated map, the Nile is shown splitting to form the delta. The walled city is on the east bank, separated from the river by a floodplain.

Mamluk glass lamp

1340 In Venice, the Doge's Palace is built, with architecture inspired by Mamluk Cairo.

1348 Cairo suffers up to 7,000 deaths per day at the height of the bubonic plague epidemic.

During the Mamluk era, the competition for control of the sultanate was so cutthroat that only a handful of sultans ever died of natural causes.

1474 Sultan al-Ashraf Qaitbay completes his mosque and funerary complex in Cairo, considered the zenith of Mamluk architecture.

1517 Following decisive military victories over the Mamluks the previous year, the Ottoman Turks capture Cairo and Egypt.

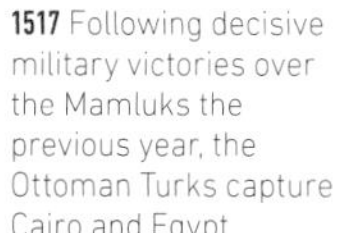

△ PARIS ON THE NILE
During the reign of Ismail (r. 1863–1879), the city's wealthy elite built a new European-styled Cairo, with grand hotels catering to curious foreign visitors.

Modernizing Cairo

As part of the Ottoman Empire, provincial Cairo stagnated as its revenues and taxes were channeled to Istanbul. The catalyst for change was an invasion by Napoleon Bonaparte. France's ploy to obstruct Britain's access to India was unsuccessful, and the occupation lasted only a handful of years, but the departure of the French created a power vacuum. This was filled in 1805 by an Albanian mercenary named Muhammad Ali, who established himself as the new ruler of Egypt. He was bold enough to wage war against the Ottomans, directly threatening Istanbul until the European powers forced him to retreat. He was also a modernizer, who introduced the cash crop of cotton and built an industrial base, as well as securing hereditary rule for his family. Under his descendants, Cairo spread beyond its medieval walls to fill the Nile floodplain with a new European-style city of tree-lined avenues and squares, modern apartment buildings, and villas. The world was invited to come and view this new Cairo during the festivities that accompanied the opening of the Suez Canal.

1798 Napoleon Bonaparte leads a French army in an invasion of Egypt and establishes his headquarters in Cairo.

1805 The Albanian Muhammad Ali seizes power following the departure of the French.

1863 Ismail, a grandson of Muhammad Ali, initiates the creation of the new European quarter of Cairo.

1869 Cairo hosts royalty and heads of state from around the world to celebrate the opening of the Suez Canal.

1871 The first-ever performance of Verdi's opera *Aida* takes place at the Cairo Opera House.

1908 The Egyptian Museum opens on Ismailia Square, now known as Tahrir Square.

1910 A Belgian industrialist creates the new suburb of Heliopolis, where attractions include a racetrack and flying displays.

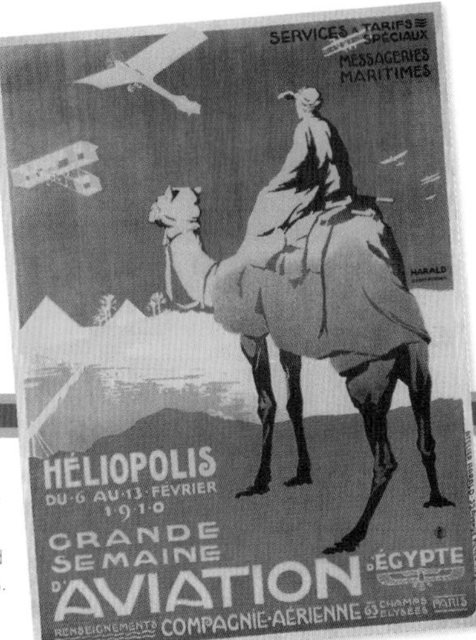

Europeanizing Cairo

For the next 10 or 15 years, Cairo almost had the character of a gold rush town, as investors and entrepreneurs raised increasingly grand hotels, banks, mansions, and even palaces. Egypt's rulers spent similarly lavishly, but much of their money came from loans by European powers. When Europe called in the debts, Egypt could not pay and, in 1882, the British colonial authorities stepped in to take control. Cairo became outwardly more European, as not only Britons but also people from France, Italy, Greece, and others took up residence, establishing their own communities and businesses. These incomers lived subject to their own national laws rather than the laws of Egypt. As a concession to growing nationalist sentiments, the British granted Egypt its "sovereignty" and the *khedive* (hereditary ruler) became a king, but foreigners still kept hold of the reins.

Capital of the Arab world

Smoldering resentment of foreign rule flared up in January 1952, when Cairo was set on fire in anti-British demonstrations; six months later, a group of young army officers seized power. The king was deposed, and in 1956 Colonel Gamal Abdel Nasser became president of the Republic of Egypt. As mass nationalization got underway, Cairo's substantial foreign community sold up and left. Under the charismatic Nasser, Egypt became a beacon of nationalism for countries throwing off the yoke of colonization throughout the Middle East and Africa, and Cairo assumed the status of a capital for the whole Arabic-speaking world. Major projects changed the face of the city, including huge new districts with names like Engineer City and Victory City. On central Tahrir Square, the old British Army barracks were torn down and replaced with an Egyptian-owned international hotel and the headquarters of the Arab League.

△ MURAL OF UMM KULTHUM, KOM-AL GHURAB SUBURB
Known as the "Voice of Egypt," Umm Kulthum held monthly radio concerts, recorded in Cairo and broadcast from 1934, which were listened to across the Arabic-speaking world.

In the 21st century, the ever more populous city is shifting again. An army of developers is creating a vast city extension in the desert that will house five million people. Meanwhile, the Pyramids continue to watch over Cairo from their vantage point at the edge of the desert, providing a sense of permanence and imperturbability that extends to Cairo itself, a powerful but steady and culturally significant center in an often volatile region.

Considered the world's fastest-growing city, Greater Cairo is projected to be home to 40 million by 2050.

1952 Rioting across Cairo destroys foreign-owned businesses; in July a revolution unseats the king.

Cairo is 90 percent Muslim and 10 percent Christian. Most Christians belong to the Coptic Orthodox Church.

1961 President Nasser inaugurates the Cairo Tower as the symbol of a new Egypt.

1972 A global "Treasures of Tutankhamen" exhibition channels millions of dollars back to Egypt.

1988 Cairo writer Naguib Mahfouz wins the Nobel Prize in Literature.

2011 Tahrir Square becomes a center of protest during the Arab Spring Revolution.

2021 Projected opening of the new Grand Egyptian Museum at the Giza Plateau.

Varanasi

CITY OF SHIVA

On the banks of the sacred Ganges, 3,000-year-old Varanasi is revered as Hinduism's holiest city. Closely associated with both Shiva and Buddha, it's a temple-packed place of pilgrimage and a creative center.

Varanasi is a site of huge religious importance, and one of the world's oldest living cities—continually inhabited, never abandoned. According to Hindu myth, Varanasi (also known as Benares) was established by the god Shiva more than 10,000 years ago. Archaeological evidence suggests that the city has been lived in since at least 1800 BCE, and has been progressively built upon until the present day.

The city sprang up in the floodplains of the Ganges basin, and the river proved vital for trade and transportation. Varanasi became a major hub for craft and commerce, and by the 6th century BCE, its bustling markets brimmed with merchants dealing in coveted goods such as silk, muslin, essential oils, and ivory. Some traditional trades from the era thrive today, and dozens of perfumeries still line many of the old town's lanes.

Age of enlightenment

As its economic importance grew, Varanasi flourished as a regional center for religion, education, and art. In 528 BCE, Buddha chose Sarnath, just outside the city, as the site for his first sermon. By then, Varanasi had become the capital of the kingdom of Kashi—literally "a place of radiance that ensues from knowledge and enlightenment." The city is still known as Kashi, and the name is the origin of its nickname, "city of light."

In the 4th century BCE, the Maurya Empire of eastern India grew to control most of the country and, around 260 BCE, Emperor Ashoka renounced Hinduism for Buddhism, turning the spotlight on Varanasi (due to the city's proximity to Sarnath). The city began attracting religious leaders, academics, and philosophers from across Asia. The Chinese monk Xuanzang, who played a crucial role in spreading Buddhist ideas between India and China, visited in 635 CE and noted that the thriving city stretched for 3 miles (5 km) along the Ganges' western bank. Then, in the 8th century, the great Indian spiritualist Adi Shankaracharya arrived in Varanasi, and founded a sect of the Hindu deity Shiva.

VARANASI'S *GHATS* ▷
Ghats are stepped riverside piers where rituals of worship, including ablutions, offerings, and cremation, are performed. Most were built between the 14th and 18th centuries.

1800 BCE Excavations suggest the presence of habitation around present-day Varanasi.

528 BCE The Buddha delivers his first sermon in nearby Sarnath.

635 CE Chinese monk and scholar Xuanzang visits Varanasi during his tour of Buddhist sites across Pakistan, India, Nepal, and Bangladesh.

8th century Hindu philosopher Adi Shankaracharya establishes a sect of Shiva in Varanasi.

"Benares is **older than history**, older than tradition, **older even than legend**, and looks **twice as old** as all of them put together.

MARK TWAIN, *FOLLOWING THE EQUATOR*, 1897

◁ INSIDE THE KASHI VISHWANATH TEMPLE
This 1862 pencil sketch depicts pilgrims and priests in an inner courtyard. The temple has been repeatedly destroyed and rebuilt over the centuries—the current structure dates from 1780.

The sect's foundation, alongside the legend of the city's divine creation, meant Varanasi grew in spiritual importance for Hindus. In the centuries that followed, thousands of shrines were built to the Hindu gods, from modest riverside altars to grand centers of worship like the Shiva-dedicated Kashi Vishwanath Temple. Varanasi became known as the "city of temples."

Swinging fortunes

In the 12th century, the Islamic Sultanate of Delhi expanded across India, and the Kashi Vishwanath Temple was desecrated by the invaders in 1194. Varanasi's glory dwindled, but the city retained its status as a religious and educational center, and played a critical role in the birth of new sects and beliefs. The Bhakti movement, which emphasized worship through music and dance and broke away from Hinduism's rigid caste and gender structures, had its origins here in the 15th century, and some of the tradition's leaders, such as the mystics Kabir and Ravidas, were born in the city. The Sikh leader Guru Nanak traveled here in 1507, and his embracing of the Bhakti tradition was instrumental in the development of Sikhism as a major Indian religion. The 15th and 16th centuries were a period of artistic fertility, too, and numerous artisans and musicians emerged from Varanasi—*kathak*, one of India's most iconic classical dance traditions, was born here.

Varanasi reached another high point during the reign of Mughal Emperor Akbar, who was crowned in 1556. His 50-year reign was broadly tolerant of different faiths, and the city saw new Hindu temples built, older temples rebuilt or restored,

Varanasi is home to an estimated 20,000 temples, some of which date back more than 800 years.

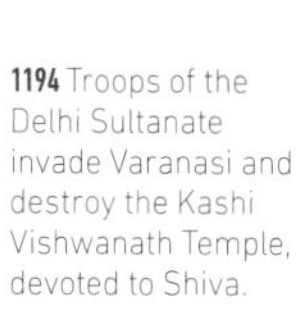

1194 Troops of the Delhi Sultanate invade Varanasi and destroy the Kashi Vishwanath Temple, devoted to Shiva.

1507 Guru Nanak, who goes on to found Sikhism, visits Varanasi.

1556 Upon being crowned Emperor of Mughal India, Akbar sponsors a cultural revival of Varanasi that continues throughout his five-decade reign.

1659 Aurangzeb, Akbar's great-grandson, succeeds to the throne. He destroys temples across the nation, including many in Varanasi.

1737 As the Mughals decline, the city wins kingdom status under the rule of the maharajas of Benares.

The royal throne of the maharajas of Benares

△ SADHUS IN VARANASI
Varanasi is a gathering place for sadhus, Hindu ascetics who have renounced a worldly life. Sadhus live off donations and are respected for their holiness.

bridges laid, and the riverside promenade paved for the first time. But not every Mughal ruler was as even-handed, and Akbar's great-grandson Aurangzeb ordered many Hindu temples to be destroyed during his reign, commissioning mosques to be erected in some of the demolished sites.

Following the demise of Aurangzeb in 1707, the Mughal Empire slipped into decline and the Hindu Maratha Empire expanded out of western India. Varanasi and the surrounding area became a kingdom, ruled by the maharajas of Benares. Sustained Maratha patronage led to much of modern Varanasi's urban landscape taking shape through the 18th century, with the building or restructuring of many of its iconic temples and *ghats*.

Colonial era to modern times

The British East India Company monopolized trade in India in the 18th and 19th centuries. Following the unsuccessful Indian Rebellion of 1857, the British governed the nation directly. Varanasi's civic fortunes grew exponentially during the years of British rule. A number of pioneering educational institutions were established in Varanasi, preserving and furthering the city's centuries-old academic heritage. The Sanskrit College was established in 1791, dedicated to the study of the Sanskrit language. The Central Hindu College, which was founded in 1916, evolved into the prestigious Banaras Hindu University, and remains an important center for arts, languages, and sciences, attracting students from across the country.

After Indian independence in 1947, Varanasi became part of Uttar Pradesh state. Its religious traditions and creativity have ensured its continued prominence in the modern age. Musicians associated with the city include Bismillah Khan, who brought the oboe-like *shehnai* to concert halls; classical singer Girija Devi; and global sitar star Ravi Shankar. Benarasi silk, gorgeously decorated with gold and silver brocade, is highly prized by traditional stylists and contemporary fashion designers alike. Even the Banarasi *paan*, a juicy, chewable mixture of spices, nuts, and condiments wrapped in betel leaf, has gained legendary status among gastronomes, and makes a routine appearance at the end of menus across India.

Above all, Varanasi remains a unique destination, drawing millions of people every year. The city's *ghats* are a stage of relentless human activity where tens of thousands of pilgrims pay homage to gods and departed souls, penitents wash away their sins in the waters of the Ganges, photographers wait for the perfect shot, hawkers eye up opportunities, and tourists from around the world are overwhelmed by the splendor and bustle of this eternal metropolis.

Hindus believe that through being cremated in Varanasi and having their ashes released into the Ganges, they will reach Nirvana.

▽ BENARASI SILK
Woven from the finest silk produced in the region, the Benarasi weave is among India's most exquisite and expensive textiles, and Benarasi saris often feature in bridal outfits.

1750–1800 A rebuilding program starts, and many iconic river *ghats* are built or renovated.

1910 Benares is recognized as a princely state by the British. It continues to be administered by the maharajas of Benares.

1916 Ustad Bismillah Khan is born. He moves to Varanasi as a child, and goes on to popularize the oboe-like *shehnai*.

1920 Birth of Ravi Shankar, one of the world's foremost sitar exponents, in Varanasi.

1951 Varanasi district's population reaches one million—by 2021 it was around four times that figure.

2015 Varanasi is made a UNESCO City of Music for its musical heritage, schools, and festivals.

Bangkok

CITY OF ANGELS

Once famed as a floating city of houseboats, Buddhist priests, and godlike kings, Bangkok has been transformed into a high-rise metropolis where gilded temples rub shoulders with teeming malls.

Before Bangkok was an imperial capital, let alone one of the most visited cities on earth, it was a rural village in a loop of the Chao Phraya River. These humble origins may have given Bangkok its name: *bang* being a river village, *makok* a tree with an olive-like fruit.

By the mid-14th century, the most important city in Siam—as Thailand was formerly known—was Ayutthaya, which lay further up the Chao Phraya. Ships trading with Ayutthaya passed by Bangkok, and the community grew. When the Burmese sacked Ayutthaya in 1767, the Siamese regrouped under the general Phraya Taksin, who became king later that year and made Thonburi, a fortified town across the river from Bangkok, his capital. When Taksin was deposed in a coup, his successor Rama I decided to build a capital that could recreate Ayutthaya's glory. He chose Bangkok, on the river's east bank, which was less vulnerable to Burmese attacks from the west.

On April 21, 1782, laborers drove a pillar into the ground near the river, marking the founding of the royal city. All Thai cities feature such a pillar, housing guardian spirits. Its spirits would protect Bangkok's rulers for 150 years.

◁ THE GRAND PALACE AND CHAO PHRAYA RIVER
This 1864 mural shows the spires of the Grand Palace in the foreground. The elaborate, highly decorated complex, built under Rama I (r. 1782–1809), remains Bangkok's spiritual heart.

The floating city

After preparing the site, the Siamese built the Grand Palace, a fortified complex next to the river. Clustered around the palace were temples containing important Buddhist relics, the most prestigious of which was Wat Phra Kaeo, the Temple of the Emerald Buddha—named after its sacred Buddha image, crafted from gold and precious stones. This royal area, called Ratanakosin, was transformed into an artificial island by digging a series of moatlike canals. Noble households ringed the royal complex, while artisans and merchants congregated nearby to profit from their patronage.

> **Bangkok** ... is a **rejuvenating tonic**; the people seem to have found the **magic elixir**.
>
> BERNARD KALB, *THE NEW YORK TIMES*, 1961

1400s CE A settlement at Bangkok is mentioned in a document from the reign of Chao Sam Phraya (r. 1424–1448), who rules from the Siamese capital, Ayutthaya.

1685 King Narai commissions the French to build forts in Bangkok, as shown on this 1751 map.

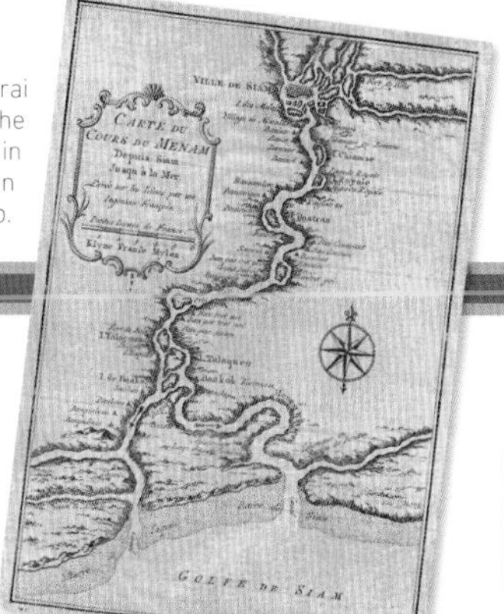

1768 Following the destruction of Ayutthaya, Phraya Taksin establishes a new capital at Thonburi, on the west bank of the Chao Phraya.

1779 Phraya Chakri captures Vientiane in Laos and removes the prized Emerald Buddha to Thonburi.

1782 Phraya Chakri becomes Rama I and establishes a grand new capital in Bangkok, across the river from Thonburi.

◁ ▷ **CELESTIAL GUARDIANS AND THE PALACE** Gaudy demons called *yaksha* (left) guard the precious Emerald Buddha at Wat Phra Kaeo, which is part of the Grand Palace complex (right) and is revered as the holiest Buddhist site in the country.

The royal city was given a grand official name, though its full 43 syllables were abbreviated to just two: Krung Thep, or "city of angels." To most of the populace, the city remained "Bangkok." Armies of laborers scored the land around Ratanakosin with a lattice of canals that soon filled with stilted buildings and houseboats anchored two or three rows deep—by the mid-19th century the city had a population of 350,000, most of them water-dwellers. The waterways were commercial highways, crammed with people fishing and rowing goods to the floating city markets; they were also the stage for ritual and pageantry, when the king and his court would take to the water in stunning barge processions marking religious events and royal anniversaries. The city became known as the Venice of the East; as one amazed British traveler wrote in 1865, it "seemed to have risen from the waters."

Most of its inhabitants lived on water out of necessity: the king owned all the land, and the right to reside on it was granted only to nobles and Buddhist monks. Exceptions were made—the Portuguese, with whom Bangkok traded, settled around the Santa Cruz church in Thonburi, while the Chinese had a settlement in the district of Sampheng, east of the royal complex. The city continued to thrive on trade, mostly with China, and enjoyed a long era of relative peace and prosperity.

From water to land

In the mid-19th century, Bangkok entered a new era under the rule of Rama IV. For many years the royal court had shunned contact with the West, but in 1855 the king entertained Sir John Bowring, governor of Hong Kong and emissary of Queen Victoria. The result was a treaty that shifted Siam's trade orientation away from China and toward the West. Its physical impact on the capital city was transformative. Opening the kingdom to increased foreign trade boosted the economy, precipitating rapid expansion, particularly to the east of Ratanakosin, while also introducing new ideas from the West.

One such European innovation came about after the city's foreign consuls signed their names to a petition requesting a road on which they could ride in carriages or on horseback for pleasure. In 1857, Rama IV Road became the city's first public thoroughfare. This was followed by

1785 After the completion of the royal district, a three-day consecration ceremony sees the city given the new name of Krung Thep.

1786 Birth of Sunthorn Phu, who would become Thailand's best-known royal poet and whose epics remain popular today.

1832 Rama III turns Bangkok's oldest temple, Wat Pho, into a public center of learning—it's now considered Thailand's first university.

Stamp depicting the Sunthorn Phu epic *Phra Aphai Mani*

> **Bangkok** was a **wily** yet **guileless** city, always ready with **new surprises.**

ALEXANDER MACDONALD, FOUNDER OF *THE BANGKOK POST*, 1949

New Road (Charoen Krung), running straight from Ratanakosin through the Chinese district to the foreign settlements at Bang Kolem. Roads began to replace canals at pace, and by the mid-20th century, the water-world that was old Bangkok was almost completely gone.

After visiting Europe in 1897, Rama V commissioned a new royal district, called Dusit, as a showcase for the modern monarchy. The new royal residences were filled with European artwork, porcelain, and jewelery at such expense that other projects, such as Siam's first railroad line, were delayed for lack of funds.

The Thai capital

In April 1932, 150 years after the founding of the city, Rama VII inaugurated Memorial Bridge, the first bridge to span the Chao Phraya River and link Thonburi and Bangkok. While it was obviously practical, there was a more symbolic meaning. The royal court hoped that in uniting the spirits of the old and new capitals, they could bring a divine harmony to eclipse a dark prophecy that had been revealed to Rama I. The curse foretold that the Chakri dynasty he had founded would last for only a century and a half, and that time was nearly up.

Trouble was indeed brewing. Opposed to, among other things, the system of absolute monarchy, a group of mostly foreign-educated officers and students formed the People's Party and staged a bloodless coup in 1932.

Absolute monarchy was replaced by a constitutional monarchy on the English model, with the king as a figurehead. In 1938, to underline the changes, the name of the country was changed from Siam to Thailand. People's Party member Field Marshal Phibun would dominate the country's politics for most of the next 20 years. He may have kept a signed portrait of Benito Mussolini on his office wall, but he was strongly pro-American—a perspective that would shape Bangkok in the decades to come.

△ **THE AQUATIC CITY**
In old Bangkok, canals served as streets and the city was often referred to as the Venice of the East.

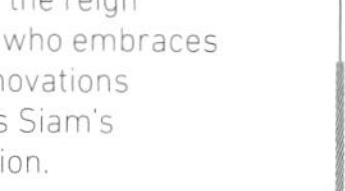

1851 Start of the reign of Rama IV, who embraces Western innovations and initiates Siam's modernization.

1855 Rama IV signs the Bowring Treaty with Britain, ushering in the European influences that ultimately transform Bangkok.

1862 English governess Anna Leonowens travels to Bangkok to teach English to Rama IV's 39 wives and 82 children. Her memoirs formed the basis for the 1956 film *The King and I*.

1893 France sends gunboats to threaten Bangkok, forcing the king to give up territories east of the Mekong River, setting the boundaries of modern Thailand.

1932 A bloodless coup unseats absolute monarch Rama VII. A constitutional monarchy is introduced with parliamentary government.

American influence

In the wake of World War II, Phibun welcomed an influx of American dollars and used them to fund rapid urban growth in the capital. Ties were strengthened during the 1960s when the US was involved in conflicts in Vietnam, Laos, and Cambodia, and used Thailand as a friendly site for military bases. American expertise was drafted in to create development plans for Bangkok that were subsequently criticized as a misguided attempt to turn the city into the Los Angeles of the East. During this time, the city was ravaged by superhighway projects that ripped concrete gullies through traditional neighborhoods.

▽ STUDENT PROTEST OF 1973
Popular demonstrations in October 1973 resulted in the end of the dictatorial Thanom regime and marked the growing influence of Bangkok university students in politics.

The Americans had other impacts. Selling sex had always been big business—the Chinese were operating floating brothels soon after Bangkok was founded. But the presence of American GIs saw the industry increasingly cater to foreigners. When they left the go-go bars of Patpong in the mid-1970s, crowds of curious visitors took their place. As global travel soared, Bangkok became a hugely popular stop-off en route to Thailand's beaches and islands, its glittering temples, sprawling markets, and street food eclipsing its seedy side.

Politics, prosperity, and rising water

Bangkok may never have been conquered, but it has rarely been quiet. Since the coup that abolished absolute monarchy in 1932, Thailand has experienced another

1941 Thailand forms an alliance with Japan. Bangkok is bombed by Allied air forces.

1946 Bhumibol Adulyadej becomes king, titled Rama IX. He restores discarded royal rituals, including the annual plowing ceremony in the main royal square in Bangkok.

1950 Rama IX marries Queen Sirikit; she would give birth to the future Rama X in 1952.

1965 Thailand accommodates US military bases during the Vietnam War. Bangkok is flooded by American soldiers on "rest and recuperation" leave.

1973 Left-wing demonstrations in Bangkok result in the death of 77 protesters, most of them students.

12 successful coups, plus a further nine that were unsuccessful—that's more military coup d'états in modern history than any other country. Between coups, there have been frequent periods of mass demonstrations—in 1973 and 1992, left-wing activists took to the city streets to protest against military dictatorship.

Yet amid all the business-as-usual political instability, Bangkok has visibly thrived. Its suburbs now stretch beyond the city boundaries into neighboring provinces, while its skyline abounds with the sort of glitzy, statement-making glass towers that characterize Asian metropolises from Shanghai to Dubai. Its citizens shop in multi-story mega-malls, which they whisk between on raised expressways or the ever-expanding Metropolitan Rapid Transit system.

At certain times of the year, however, passenger numbers drop steeply. Bangkok was built on marshland and the city remains prone to flooding. The annual monsoons transform many streets into streams, and see MRT stations raise barriers to stop the water getting into the system. By the end of the 21st century, much of the city could be underwater. Yet nostalgists might point out that it is no stranger to water—not for nothing was the old Bangkok of canals and floating markets known as the Venice of the East. And history has shown that Bangkok is a survivor, a city that has ridden out crisis after crisis, and absorbed influences from around the world. Today, its tower blocks look over the joyous hubbub of street life, as Bangkok adapts its rich Siamese heritage to the glass and steel age.

△ **COURSING THROUGH THE CITY**
Where once canals transported people and goods around Bangkok, elevated superhighways and bridges, such as the Bhumibol Bridge, which opened in 2006, carry road traffic in what is one of the world's busiest and most congested cities.

1997 After decades of prosperity, Asia is struck by a financial crisis. Construction halts, littering Bangkok with unfinished high-rise buildings, some of which remain abandoned today.

2004 The MRT, Bangkok's first underground public transit system, begins operation.

2010 Rot Fai open-air market launches in the north of the city. Specializing in antiques and vintage items, it is one of Bangkok's most popular tourist landmarks.

2011 Heavy monsoon rains flood large parts of Bangkok. Many outer neighborhoods are inundated.

2013 Bangkok is named the number-one destination for international visitors for the first time in the annual Global Destination Cities Index.

2016 Completion of the King Power MahaNakhon skyscraper, also known as the Tetris building, Thailand's tallest structure at 1,050 ft (320 m).

Québec City

LA VIEILLE CAPITALE ("THE OLD CAPITAL")

Mixing the charm of the old world with the promise of the new, Québec City straddles the mighty St. Lawrence River, from where it proudly proclaims its French-Canadian culture.

Long before the British and the French traded musket fire over the St. Lawrence River, the Indigenous Iroquoians inhabited a village-size precursor to Québec City called Stadacona. Putting down roots in the early 1300s, the Iroquoians lived in longhouses, grew maize, and fished in the majestic St. Lawrence using birchbark canoes.

Cartier and European contact

French explorer Jacques Cartier first arrived on Canada's eastern shoreline in 1534 in search of gold and a western passage to Asia. Intrigued by the vast uncharted land, he came back the following year, sailing all the way up the St. Lawrence to Stadacona. Cartier fostered relations with the local Iroquoian chief, Donnacona, but scurvy and frigid weather decimated his party. He kidnapped the chief and returned to France to recuperate, where Donnacona died.

◁ *SKATING ON THE ST. LAWRENCE RIVER*, 19TH CENTURY
While early pioneers struggled in Québec City's harsh climate, later inhabitants enthusiastically embraced winter sports to keep warm, including skating on the frozen St. Lawrence.

Cartier made a third voyage to the region in 1541, this time founding a small colony, Fort Charlesbourg-Royal, upstream from Stadacona. Within two years, illness and deteriorating relations with the Iroquoians meant it was abandoned.

New settlement and New France

More than 60 years passed before the French made another attempt to establish a permanent settlement in the Québec region. When French navigator Samuel de Champlain arrived in 1608, at the behest of Bourbon King Henry IV, he detected no trace of Fort Charlesbourg-Royal or the Iroquoians. Undeterred, he founded L'Habitation de Québec (its name derived from an Algonquin word meaning "where the river narrows").

Debuting as three diminutive buildings surrounded by a wooden stockade, the colonial outpost quickly developed into a trading center and fort. Nevertheless in 1629, after a brief naval blockade, the English seized the nascent settlement without firing a shot. The Québec region was restored to the French by the Treaty of Saint-Germain-en-Laye in 1632, but the bullish English resolved to return.

1300s The semi-nomadic village of Stadacona is established by the Iroquoians.

Iroquoian trumpet pipe

1534 French explorer Jacques Cartier, the first European to survey the St. Lawrence River, arrives in eastern Canada.

1547 map of Canada informed by Cartier's expeditions

1608 Samuel de Champlain founds L'Habitation de Québec.

1629 The fledgling settlement is seized by the Scottish Kirke brothers during the Anglo-French War.

From 1608 until 1791, Québec City was capital of the French and (later) British colony that ultimately became Canada, which accounts for its nickname "La Vieille Capitale."

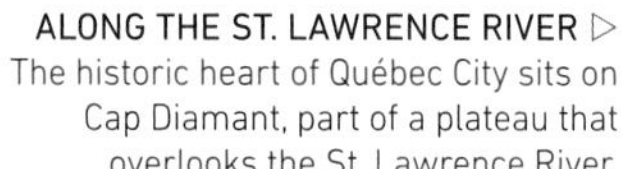

ALONG THE ST. LAWRENCE RIVER ▷
The historic heart of Québec City sits on Cap Diamant, part of a plateau that overlooks the St. Lawrence River.

Siege and surrender

The British made two more attempts to take Québec, but it was not until 1759, during the French and Indian War, that they finally wrested the city from French control.

Navigating the difficult currents of the St. Lawrence River, the British, under the command of General James Wolfe, laid siege to Québec for three months before the French were prised out of their heavily fortified city to engage in an open battle on the Plains of Abraham. Defeating the French in less than an hour, the British celebrated a decisive victory (although General Wolfe perished on the battlefield). Not only had they forced Québec City to surrender; they had sounded the death knell of French rule in Canada and allowed Britain to usurp France as a global power.

British rulers, French culture

The next decade was crucial in shaping the city's identity, which, despite prolonged British rule, would always cling to its French language, culture, and traditions.

In 1774, the British passed the Québec Act to appease their newly conquered subjects and ensure French loyalty. The pioneering legislation safeguarded the rights of French Catholics, permitted the continuation of the French style of law, and reestablished the traditional seigneurial system of land ownership. The concessions paid dividends: in 1775, Québec repelled a fierce attack by the American revolutionaries with French-Canadians electing to fight alongside the British rather than join the rebels.

After a second war with the Americans in 1812, the British strengthened the city's defenses, constructing La Citadelle, a star-shaped fort that blended seamlessly

1759 Québec City falls to the British; the victory is famously depicted in *The Death of General Wolfe* (1770), a painting by Benjamin West.

1763 Treaty of Paris ends the French and Indian War and cedes New France, including Québec City, to Britain.

1775 Rebels in America's revolutionary war invade Canada but are repelled by the British and French in the Battle of Québec.

1820 After the War of 1812, the British start building La Citadelle, their largest fort in the Americas.

1867 The British North America Act creates the Dominion of Canada, with Québec City as capital of Québec province.

with Québec's existing walls and bastions. Yet, despite its impressive array of European-style architecture, the city's fortunes were changing as its economic position began to be challenged by Montréal, 155 miles (250 km) upriver.

The dredging of the St. Lawrence, starting in the 1840s, meant that big ships were able to reach Montréal, and Québec City was increasingly bypassed for trade. Similarly, with the union of Canada into one federation in 1867, the city was replaced by Ottawa as national capital.

Grand projets

Civic projects in the late 19th and early 20th centuries reestablished Québec City in the national consciousness as a place of beauty and grandeur. In 1893, the Canadian Pacific Railway built the turreted Château Frontenac hotel atop the riverside Cap Diamant promontory, which became the pièce de résistance in Québec's handsome cityscape. Straddling the St. Lawrence, the Québec Bridge took shape two decades later, opening in 1919 as the world's longest cantilever bridge.

Two Allied conferences during World War II kept Québec City in the international eye, as did a 1985 UNESCO listing for Old Québec, with its ramparts and cobbled streets. To this day, the city has retained its Normandy-style architecture, French-influenced cuisine, and unique holidays like Saint-Jean-Baptiste Day (June 24). Around 4.6 million tourists a year pour in to marvel at the only walled city north of Mexico and the cradle of French civilization in North America.

△ **TRAVEL POSTER**
From the 1880s, the Canadian Pacific Railway began attracting wealthy tourists to Québec City.

1893 The Château Frontenac hotel opens, designed in homage to the monumental châteaux of the Loire Valley.

1919 The Québec Bridge opens after a 30-year construction period, in which two collapses had cost 88 lives.

1943 Québec City hosts the first of two Allied conferences that decide key issues in World War II.

After an exodus of British settlers in the late 19th century, French-speakers made up over 90 percent of the city's population by 1950.

1960 The Quiet Revolution spurs social and economic development under the liberal government of Jean Lesage.

1985 Old Québec is named a UNESCO World Heritage Site.

New Orleans

THE BIG EASY

Mixing influences from Europe, the Caribbean, and Africa with the spirit of the American South, New Orleans is a unique blend of grit, soul, effervescence, and improvisation anchored beside the Mississippi River.

The balmy river delta now occupied by New Orleans was inhabited for thousands of years before Columbus's maiden voyage. Notable among the area's Indigenous people were the Chitimacha, who lived in easily defended swamp villages. Following the arrival of Europeans in the 1500s, the Mississippi basin became a pawn on the colonial chessboard and the region gradually developed a hybrid Creole identity, forged by settlers from France, Spain, Haiti, Canada, and Africa.

Early explorers

In 1542, survivors of an abortive gold-seeking expedition led by Spaniard Hernando de Soto paddled through the delta, raising the ire of locals as they went. Over a century later, in 1682, French explorer René-Robert Cavelier, Sieur de La Salle, ushered another canoe party through the Mississippi basin, naming it "La Louisiane" and claiming it for France. By the early 1700s, French traders had begun settling along the lower Mississippi River, close to a well-used portage site between the river and Bayou St. John. A fort was built in 1701, but it was not until 1718 that Jean-Baptiste Le Moyne de Bienville officially founded La Nouvelle-Orléans on a sharp bend in the Mississippi that was protected by a natural levee. Four years later, the village became capital of French Louisiana.

Early French rule lasted just 45 years but left an indelible mark on New Orleans' emerging culture. Struggling against weather and disease, the region was ceded to Spain during the French and Indian War in 1762. After fires in the late 18th century, the compact "French Quarter" was rebuilt with the distinctive Spanish architecture that is still visible today.

> An American has **not seen the United States** until he has seen **Mardi Gras** in **New Orleans.**
>
> MARK TWAIN, LETTER TO PAMELA MOFFETT, MARCH 1859

400 CE Indigenous peoples use a trade route and portage site between the Mississippi and Bayou St. John.

1718 French colonist Jean-Baptiste Le Moyne de Bienville founds La Nouvelle-Orléans.

1722 New Orleans becomes capital of French Louisiana, an administrative district of New France.

1768 Six years after being ceded to Spain, a French-Creole revolt in New Orleans unsuccessfully tries to return Louisiana to France.

1788 A great fire destroys over 800 buildings in the fledgling city.

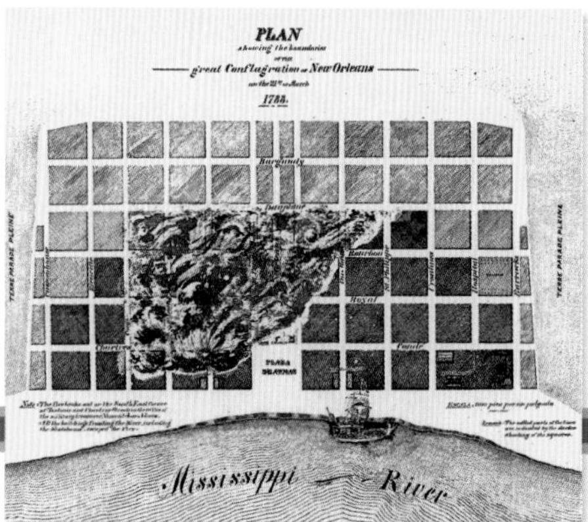

Plan showing the extent of the 1788 fire

▽ COLORS AND CROWDS
Parades, masks, costumes, and cakes mark Mardi Gras, the rambunctious pre-Lent carnival first held in New Orleans in 1837. It now attracts over a million participants.

> "Every time I close my eyes **blowing that trumpet of mine**, I look right in **the heart** of good old **New Orleans**.
>
> LOUIS ARMSTRONG, JAZZ MUSICIAN

Gumbo is a thick Creole soup made with stock, meat, shellfish, and vegetables, whose roots and ingredients are a culinary reflection of New Orleans' diverse culture.

THE BED CHAMBER OF MARIE CATHERINE LAVEAU, 2020 ▷
Artist Andrew LaMar Hopkins explores pre–Civil War New Orleans through the city's property-owning "free persons of color," who helped shape the look and feel of the French Quarter.

The 19th century

Enriching an already diverse melting pot, New Orleans passed from Spanish, to French, to American hands in quick succession in the early 1800s. Keen to offload France's American colonies after a brutal slave rebellion in Haiti, Napoleon cut the last European ties in 1803, selling Louisiana to the US for $15 million.

Despite its new American overseers, New Orleans' French culture continued to thrive with the arrival of both white and Black settlers from Haiti and Cajuns from northeast Canada. Imported French traditions included the city's famous Mardi Gras parade, a mask-wearing extravaganza that debuted in 1837.

Two decisive battles wracked New Orleans in the 19th century. In 1815, an army commanded by future US President Andrew Jackson defeated a numerically superior British invasion force in a late plot twist to the War of 1812. Fifty years later, the Union Army entered New Orleans unopposed during the Civil War. The early capitulation proved to be a turning point in the war, and meant the city escaped with little physical damage.

1803 Three years after secretly negotiating the transfer of Spanish Louisiana to France, Napoleon sells the colony to the US.

The ornate jacket of the Louisiana Purchase

1812 Louisiana, including New Orleans, is admitted to the United States as the 18th state.

1837 The first official Mardi Gras parade is held on the Tuesday before Ash Wednesday.

Despite handing governmental duties to Baton Rouge in 1849, New Orleans was briefly reinstated as state capital between 1865 and 1880.

1862 Confederate New Orleans is taken by the Union Army during the Civil War with minimal damage.

1897 New Orleans creates Storyville, a regulated zone for prostitution where jazz begins to flourish.

▷ NEW ORLEANS JAZZ & HERITAGE FESTIVAL POSTER
Also known as Jazz Fest, this annual festival was first held in 1970 and celebrates the music, culture, and cuisine of New Orleans. The inaugural lineup featured Duke Ellington, the Preservation Hall Jazz Band, Fats Domino, and Peter Fountain.

Between the wars, New Orleans grew in both size and stature, reaching its economic zenith. The Mississippi was packed with steamboats as the city prospered from both its cotton trade and as the largest slave market in the country. Though New Orleans was spared destruction in the Civil War, the defeat of the South checked the city's growth and precipitated sweeping societal changes. Plans for post-war reconstruction came into effect in 1863. In the decades that followed, river steamboats were superseded by railroads and, in the city's stratified class system, well-educated "free persons of color" fought vigorously against segregationist Jim Crow laws that disenfranchised African Americans.

The 1890s witnessed the birth of an exciting new form of music, christened jazz. First showcased in the clubs of Storyville—a rough urban district where prostitution was tolerated—jazz was a mashup of African drumming, marching band music, syncopated ragtime, and wild improvisation. The sound quickly became synonymous with the city and went on to have a profound influence both in the US and around the world.

Disaster and recovery

Long impacted by hurricanes and floods, from 1896 New Orleans endeavored to improve its drainage system. Six pumping stations and hundreds of miles of piping were installed over the next three decades, as 30,000 acres (12,140 hectares) of land were reclaimed from swamp. By the 1960s, only 48 percent of the city lay above sea level, a design feature that would come back to haunt it. In August 2005, Katrina, a Category 5 hurricane, lashed America's Gulf Coast, breaching New Orleans' storm defenses, and causing unprecedented flood damage. More than 1,800 people died. Recovery was slow, but over the next decade a $14.5 billion risk-reduction project worked to improve levees and floodwalls. After such tough times, a joyful Superbowl win in 2010 and booming tourism have marked an upturn in The Big Easy's fortunes.

△ PRESERVATION HALL JAZZ BAND
Formed in the early 1960s to safeguard and promote New Orleans' traditional music, the Preservation Hall's house band is a musical collective of 50-plus players.

1901 Trumpet player and singer Louis Armstrong is born in New Orleans.

1961 Founding of the Preservation Hall Jazz Band, which quickly goes on to become a city institution.

2005 Hurricane Katrina devastates New Orleans, with floods inundating 80 percent of the city.

2010 New Orleans Saints win the NFL Superbowl for the first time.

2016 A decade after Katrina, New Orleans rebounds with record-breaking numbers of visitors drawn to the still-thriving French Quarter.

MORE GREAT CITIES

Bordeaux

Port of the Moon

Stretching along the banks of the Garonne River in southwest France, Bordeaux is one of the world capitals of wine. It grew rich on the proceeds of the vineyards of the Gironde as far back as the 12th century. In the 18th century, it was the second busiest port in the world after London, shipping coffee, cocoa, sugar, cotton—and enslaved people. The wealth accrued shaped one of the most grandiose cities in Europe, full of noble facades and elegant urban spaces. Today, the city is home to over 350 historical monuments, as well as France's aeronautics industry and one of the most powerful research lasers in the world.

Munich

Village of a Million People

Deep in southern Germany, Munich traces its origins to Benedictine monks who established a marketplace beside a crossing of the Isar River; the name in German, München, means "by the monks' place." From the 13th century, it was residence to the Wittelsbach dynasty of Holy Roman emperors and kings of Bavaria. Under them, Munich was adorned with soaring churches and palaces and imposing civic buildings. Today, beyond the Baroque exterior, Munich is an economic and technological powerhouse, home to car manufacturer BMW and the all-conquering soccer team Bayern Munich.

Bratislava

Beauty on the Danube

The capital of Slovakia is unique in that the city has borders with both Austria and Hungary. Like their capitals, it also sits on the Danube, which historically aided its development as a commercial center. It was recognized as a township in 1291 and, when the eastern part of the Kingdom of Hungary was captured by the Ottomans in 1526, Bratislava became the Hungarian capital. With a population of around 500,000 today, it is a compact but endearing capital combining a medieval old town, Baroque palaces, and bald Soviet-era blocks.

Kraków

Little Rome

Legend attributes the founding of Poland's second city to Krakus, a mythical ruler said to have slain the Wawel dragon. The fairy tale fits well with Kraków's splendid medieval market square and Gothic-spired castle overlooking the Vistula River. However, historians credit the city's founding to the Vistulans, dating it to the 8th century. From 1038 to 1596, Kraków was the capital of Poland and flourished under Kazimierz the Great, who founded one of the oldest universities in Europe. Its professors were among those shipped to concentration camps when the Germans seized the city in 1939. The historic center survived World War II largely intact, and in 1978 it was made the world's first UNESCO World Heritage Site.

Hanoi

Between the Rivers

Ly Thai To, first ruler of the Ly dynasty of Vietnam, is generally credited with founding what would become Hanoi in 1010. He called it Thang Long ("rising dragon") and it became his nation's capital for almost 800 years. It was only after the last Vietnamese dynasty, the Nguyen, transferred the capital south that the city was renamed Ha Noi ("between the rivers"). It was occupied by the French in the 19th century, who left their stamp in the form of tree-lined boulevards and colonial buildings that combine French with Vietnamese architectural styles. During the Vietnam War of the 1950s to '70s, the city suffered massive damage from bombing by the US. These days, it is again the capital of Vietnam and a modernizing, increasingly high-rise metropolis built on more than 1,000 years of eventful history.

Melbourne

Australia's Second City

Forty-seven years after the founding of Australia's first European settlement of Sydney, in

△ **Bordeaux** Wine barrels being unloaded at the Port de Bordeaux, postcard c.1900.

△ **Munich** A view of the city from Hartmann Schedel's *Chronicle of the World*, 1493.

1835 colonists set up camp on the north bank of the Yarra River. Just 12 years later, it was recognized by Britain's Queen Victoria as the city of Melbourne. A gold rush in 1851 saw it overtake Sydney as Australia's most populous city. The demographics have since swung the other way, but as the home of Australian rules football and host to the Melbourne Cup, one of the world's most famous horse races; Formula One; and the Australian Open tennis tournament, Melbourne holds the mantle of sporting capital of Australia. It also claims cultural preeminence as home to the oldest and most visited gallery in the country (the National Gallery of Victoria), and more theaters than any other city in Australia. Since the 2010s, Melbourne has consistently been ranked as the world's first or second "most livable city" by the international *Economist* magazine.

Reno

Biggest Little City in the World

Reno sits at the base of the Sierra Nevada mountains in a fertile valley of the Truckee River. What started in 1859 as a log toll bridge officially came into being as a town in 1868, named after Civil War General Jesse Lee Reno. The arrival of the railroad in 1868 boosted the economy, as did the decision of the state of Nevada to legalize gambling in 1931. At the same time, the state's liberal divorce laws meant that across the US, "I'm going to Reno" became an alternative way of saying "I'm getting divorced." Changing laws saw the decline of both businesses and Reno is now better known as a center for outdoor recreation, due to its close proximity to mountains, lakes, and ski resorts.

Minneapolis

Mini Apple

The name is derived from the Sioux word *minne*, meaning "water," and the Greek *polis*, meaning "city." The city owes its existence to the Mississippi River and, specifically, the St. Anthony Falls, which were harnessed to power logging and flour mills in the mid-19th century. The population grew rapidly later that century with mass immigration, especially from Scandinavia and Germany. The modern city is the most-populous center and business hub between Chicago and Seattle, sitting in a region dense with lakes and wetlands, many connected by parks cut through with trails for hiking and biking. Minneapolis is also a creative hub, particularly when it comes to music, nurturing both Bob Dylan and Prince.

Detroit

Motor City

When French trader Antoine de la Mothe Cadillac built a fort on a river in 1701, he named it Fort Pontchartrain du Détroit in honor of his patron (the French word *détroit* means "strait"); later the British called it simply Detroit. Two hundred years later, Cadillac's own name was taken up by the car manufacturing industry as Detroit was establishing itself as the world's automotive capital. As cars and car parts were shipped in and out of the city, the Detroit river was heralded as the "Greatest Commercial Artery on Earth." During World War II, Detroit's industrial capacity was repurposed for the Allied war effort and 400,000 migrant workers flooded into the city. The city shaped global culture with the Motown sound (from "Motor Town") and later techno music. In the modern era, industrial restructuring saw huge job losses, population flight, and the city filing for bankruptcy, but subsequent revitalization has reversed Detroit's fortunes.

Montréal

Festival City

In 1642, colonists from France established a mission on an island at the confluence of the St. Lawrence and Ottawa Rivers, in territory belonging to native Iroquoians. This settlement became the trading center of New France (the area colonized by France in North America), before coming under British control during the Seven Years' War in the mid-18th century; the city has been split between the two identities ever since. Montréal's location on the St. Lawrence aided its growth as a transportation and manufacturing hub, and it was the largest city in Canada until it was overtaken by Toronto in the 1970s. French Canadians are the majority population in Montréal, and it is often said to be the second-largest French-speaking city in the world, after Paris. Like Paris, it excels in the arts and cuisine, and is one of North America's most cosmopolitan cities.

△ **Hanoi** The freshwater West Lake was formed from a curve in the Red River.

△ **Montréal** In winter, snow blankets the city and the St. Lawrence River freezes over.

New York City p.214

Dublin p.158

Amsterdam p.162

Stockholm p.168

San Francisco p.210

Copenhagen

Boston

Belfast

Vancouver

Miami

Naples

Marseille

Cartagena

Lagos

Rio de Janeiro

Havana p.222

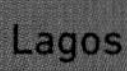

Lisbon p.172

Barcelona p.178

Buenos Aires p.226

Venice p.184

Cape Town p.192

Shanghai p.198

Sydney p.204

CHAPTER 3
MARITIME CITIES

Dublin

FAIR CITY

With its Viking origins, Georgian streets, and 20th-century rebirth, Dublin's influence on the international stage has been huge, thanks to its citizens' flair for words, drama, and music.

Before the Vikings came, the area around Dublin was home to farmers, fishermen, and an ecclesiastical settlement. But the founding of the modern city is traditionally credited to the Norsemen, who sailed their longships up the Liffey River in the 9th century CE and founded a base from which they sent raiding parties across Ireland. The dark tidal pool where the Poddle River entered the Liffey provided the name "Black Pool"—"Dyfflin" in Norse, "Dubh Linn" in Irish.

English rule

The Vikings dominated Dublin until the Anglo-Normans invaded in 1170. The new arrivals had been recruited by an exiled Irish king, but soon took over, making Dublin the center of English power in Ireland and reinforcing their presence with a castle and two cathedrals. In time, the conquerors integrated into Irish culture to the extent that many of them no longer recognized the sovereignty of the English king. Henry VIII's response was to bring Ireland under more direct control in 1537 and hand all of Dublin's Catholic institutions to the newly formed Anglican Church. The Irish countryside remained a place of unrest, with spells of outright war between the Crown and local nobles, but Dublin grew rich on trade in linen and wool, and later from the export of beef, pork, and dairy to the British colonies.

The city wore prosperity well. The gentry commissioned grand residences; a new parliament house (now the Bank of Ireland) was built in 1729; and a fine entrance and facade for the country's leading university, Trinity College, was completed in 1759. Around the same time, an Act of Parliament established the Wide Streets Commission, which reshaped the old medieval city with grand avenues, stately squares and parks, and elegant civic institutions.

> “**Dublin** can be **heaven**, with **coffee at eleven** and a **stroll** through **Stephen's Green**.
>
> POPULAR SONG "THE DUBLIN SAUNTER," BY LEO MAGUIRE, c.1950

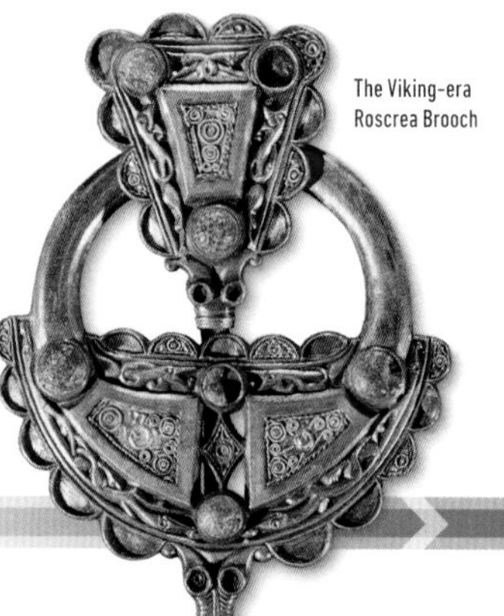

The Viking-era Roscrea Brooch

837 The Vikings raid settlements along the Liffey. They later return to conquer the region, founding a town that they call Dyfflin.

1170 Norman knight Richard "Strongbow" de Clare captures Dublin and makes it his capital.

1297 Dublin becomes the seat of the Irish Parliament, which has power over legislation and taxes.

1536 Henry VIII has himself declared head of the Church in Ireland, although outside Dublin Catholicism dominates.

1660 Financed by a globally successful export trade, Dublin enters a period of urban growth with magnificent new streets, squares, public buildings, and parks.

1758 The Wide Streets Commission is established by an Act of Parliament with the task of replanning Dublin.

▽ *THE LIFFEY SWIM*, 1923
Jack B. Yeats's much-loved oil painting makes the viewer part of an excited crowd, capturing the sense of collective celebration at this famous annual Dublin tradition.

> "**I always write about Dublin**, because if I can get to the **heart of Dublin** I can get to the heart of **all the cities of the world**.
>
> JAMES JOYCE, AUTHOR, 1921

△ THE LONG ROOM, IN TRINITY COLLEGE'S OLD LIBRARY
The 18th-century Long Room contains around 200,000 books. The Old Library also holds the beautifully illuminated *Book of Kells*, created by monks around 800 CE.

Poverty and pride

At the end of the 19th century, Dublin remained a compact city, barely 2½ miles (4.25 km) from west to east and 2 miles (3.5 km) from north to south. Although its elegant main commercial streets—Grafton Street south of the Liffey and Henry Street north of it—were filled with wealthy shoppers, the middle classes had by now forsaken the center. They were replaced by rural migrants, who had headed to the city

A Guinness poster from 1936

1759 Arthur Guinness founds the St. James's Gate Brewery in Dublin and gives his name to the classic stout still brewed on site to this day.

1800 The Act of Union dissolves the Irish Parliament and reintroduces direct rule of Ireland from London.

1845 Three years of potato blight results in the Great Famine, flooding Dublin with starving migrants from the countryside.

1904 Playwrights W. B. Yeats, Lady Gregory, and Edward Martyn found the Abbey Theatre, part of a revival of Celtic language and culture.

1916 Irish nationalists seize the General Post Office in Dublin and read out the Proclamation of the (Irish) Republic.

to escape poverty and starvation caused by the Irish potato blight of the 1840s. This influx made Dublin a majority-Catholic city again, and coincided with a revival of interest in Ireland's Gaelic heritage. Ireland had been ruled from London since it lost its parliament through the 1800 Act of Union, and Irish nationalism was a growing force. Literary talents flourished, such as poet and dramatist W. B. Yeats, who helped found the Abbey Theatre in 1904 and in later years served in the Irish Senate. This was the Dublin presented by the city's preeminent chronicler, James Joyce, in the short stories of *Dubliners* (1914) and the epic journey across the city that is *Ulysses* (1922).

On Easter Sunday 1916, frustrated nationalists rose up against the British, occupying the General Post Office where their leader, the poet Patrick Pearse, announced the Irish Republic. The British crushed the rebellion and executed 16 of its leaders. Violence continued in the years that followed: British patrols were attacked in the city and there were bloody reprisals. But by 1922, the Republic of Ireland had its independence.

Celtic tiger

In the 20th century, Ireland's capital was transformed. Slum clearance began in the 1930s and continued through the '40s and '50s. Large-scale redevelopment of the city center followed, some of it controversial as it involved the demolition of many lovely old Georgian buildings. In 1973, Ireland joined the European Economic Community (the forerunner of the European Union), and in the 1990s European grants funded development. The historic Temple Bar area was renovated, vast buildings went up around the docks, new museums were opened, and the city gained a new landmark in the slender, conical Spire of Dublin.

In the 21st century, Dublin feels more vibrant and youthful than ever. The city continues to renew itself, and writers such as Sally Rooney and Roddy Doyle and bands including U2 and The Script make an outsize contribution to world culture. Dublin's atmospheric pubs and historic attractions welcome ever-greater numbers of foreign visitors, while the city's burgeoning tech sector provides a European home for global companies. It's a mix that sums up Dublin today: a dynamic modern city that still holds its traditions close.

With around 2 million residents in 2021, the Greater Dublin area is home to 40 percent of Ireland's population.

▽ BORD GÁIS ENERGY THEATRE
Designed by Polish–American architect Daniel Libeskind, this canal-side theater is at the heart of an ambitious redevelopment of an area of city docks.

1922 *Ulysses*, James Joyce's evocation of Dublin, is first published. The novel is set entirely on June 16, 1904.

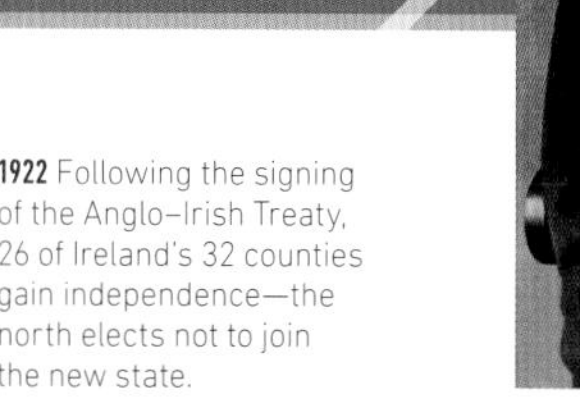

1922 Following the signing of the Anglo–Irish Treaty, 26 of Ireland's 32 counties gain independence—the north elects not to join the new state.

1973 Ireland joins the European Economic Community (EEC), forerunner of the European Union (EU).

1979 Little-known Dublin band U2 issue their debut release, a three-song EP called *Three*.

Royalties from the 1964 musical *My Fair Lady* (based on George Bernard Shaw's play *Pygmalion*) go to the upkeep of Dublin's National Gallery.

1988 Dublin celebrates its official millennium; in 988 an Irish king first received taxes from the townspeople.

1995 Ireland's period as a "Celtic Tiger" begins. The national economy soars, and a building boom transforms Dublin.

Amsterdam

VENICE OF THE NORTH

With its network of canals and success as a port, Amsterdam is a city defined by water. Maritime trade brought prosperity and an openness to new ideas that still distinguish the Dutch capital today.

A waterlogged area on the banks of the Amstel River was an unlikely place for a future city, but the Amstel could claim unrivaled access to sea trade. From the early 13th century, a small settlement of fishermen developed by the river. They built earth mounds to hold back the rising river, and used their skill in carpentry to construct both wooden houses and sturdy, high-sided, flat-bottomed ships, which performed well in shallow coastal waters and on the open sea. Shipbuilding was soon making them as much money as fishing. To prevent flooding, they blocked the Amstel with a dam, the feature that gave the place its name.

Built for trade

After 1275, Amsterdam's traders began to benefit from favorable exemptions from the tolls that rulers often charged merchants importing and exporting goods.

◁ *A VIEW OF AMSTERDAM*, 19TH CENTURY
Throughout much of its history, Amsterdam's canals were busy with cargo vessels, passenger boats, and activity on the quays, as portrayed here by French artist Charles Kuwasseg.

This attracted lucrative markets in salt herring, beer, timber, and grain—the city became the granary of the Low Countries. Around 1385, Amsterdam's first canals came into use, exploiting existing defensive moats, which had been built in the Middle Ages. With the river, harbor, and canals teeming with the ships of both fishermen and merchants, the city was beginning to boom. After a series of fires in the 15th century, houses and churches were gradually rebuilt in stone, making the place still more impressive. Amsterdam was set to become one of the most important ports of northern Europe.

> “... the most **busie concourse** of **mortall men** ... & the most **addicted to commerce**.
>
> *THE DIARY OF JOHN EVELYN*, AUGUST 1641

c.1200 Fishermen build a small settlement at the mouth of the Amstel River.

1264 Construction of a dam across the Amstel begins.

1275 The ruling Count of Holland grants the town, now called Amstelledamme, freedom from tolls.

c.1350 The city becomes an entrepôt (port and trading center) for grain and beer.

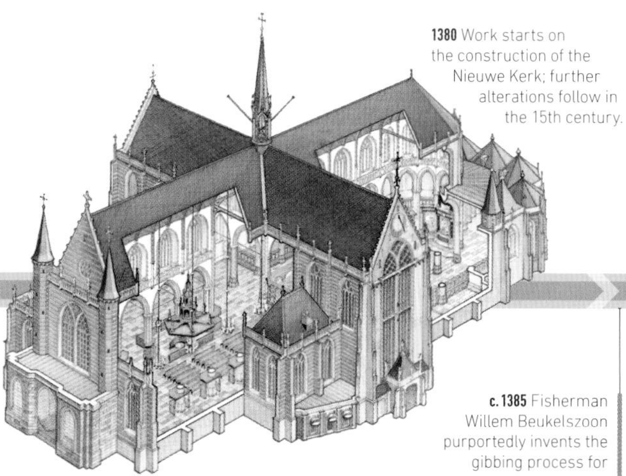

1380 Work starts on the construction of the Nieuwe Kerk; further alterations follow in the 15th century.

c.1385 Fisherman Willem Beukelszoon purportedly invents the gibbing process for preparing salt herring.

△ RETURN FROM THE INDIES
Hendrick Cornelisz Vroom's 1599 painting marks the return of the ships of a Dutch trading expedition to the East Indies, bearing cargoes of spices.

The construction of the two canal belts around Amsterdam made the city almost five times its earlier size.

In 1519, a combination of dynastic marriages and alliances brought Amsterdam into the Europe-wide Hapsburg Empire. The emperors were devout Catholics keen to impose their faith on their new subjects, many of whom were becoming Protestant and resented Catholic dominance and Church corruption. Religious conflict became violent in 1535, when a group of Anabaptists were killed in a battle with city guards. For 30 years, unrest was rife. After the Dutch revolted against their Hapsburg rulers in 1568, they took control of Amsterdam and a Dutch Republic was declared.

Canals and merchants

For about 100 years from 1580, Amsterdam enjoyed a golden age. Trade increased, Dutch-owned ships traveled the world, and the city's shipbuilders supplied the fleets of several European countries. The belt of canals that still defines the old center was dug, the imposing city hall was erected, and grand houses appeared on the canal banks in defiance of the city's boggy reclaimed ground. Merchants took up residence, many of whom were directors of the Dutch East India Company, founded in 1602. The company's trading and colony-building in Southeast Asia steered Amsterdam's success, making it a key center for importing precious spices into Europe. The city's streets thronged with international traders, and investors did business at the world's first stock exchange. Rich merchants spent lavishly on everything from furniture to highly prized, rare tulip bulbs, and bought paintings from great artists such as Rembrandt, who made Amsterdam the artistic capital of Europe.

1519 Amsterdam is brought into the Hapsburg Empire, under Holy Roman Emperor Charles V.

1535 The execution of many Anabaptists reflects years of persecution of the city's Protestants by the Catholic rulers.

1568 The Dutch revolt led by Protestant William of Orange begins.

1578 Catholics are expelled from Amsterdam, which becomes capital of the Dutch Republic in 1581.

1602 The Dutch East India Company is founded.

1610 Construction begins on the first phase of a canal belt, a triple ring of canals around Amsterdam.

1631 The artist Rembrandt van Rijn moves to Amsterdam from his native town of Leiden.

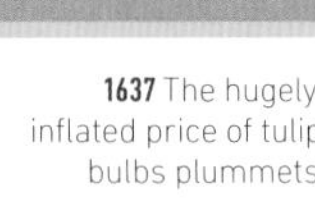

1637 The hugely inflated price of tulip bulbs plummets.

Golden Age of painting

△ In *The Night Watch*, Rembrandt displays his outstanding brushwork, use of light, and arrangement of figures to produce a large group portrait that is full of action and interest.

△ Rembrandt produced many self-portraits, chronicling his whole life from youth to old age. This etching was produced when the artist was 28 years old.

The peak of Amsterdam's prosperity coincided with a generation of painters who were among the most brilliant in the history of art. The Dutch Golden Age artists ranged from genre painters such as Pieter de Hooch and townscape specialists like Jan van der Heyden to the greatest and most versatile of all, Rembrandt van Rijn, whose mastery of light, atmosphere, and portraiture brought him fame throughout Europe. Most of these painters lived in Amsterdam, although other towns, such as Vermeer's home of Delft, also produced acclaimed artists. These painters responded to the taste of their wealthy clients, who favored images that reflected their status and sophistication and the glory of their city—elegant portraits, finely furnished house interiors, seascapes crammed with Dutch ships, and still-life images featuring plates loaded with realistically depicted food.

1648 Peace with Catholic Spain allows Amsterdam to dominate sea trade.

1652 The medieval city hall is destroyed in a fire; rebuilding soon begins.

For the foundations of the city hall (now the Royal Palace), the builders drove 13,659 33 ft (10 m) wooden piles deep into the ground.

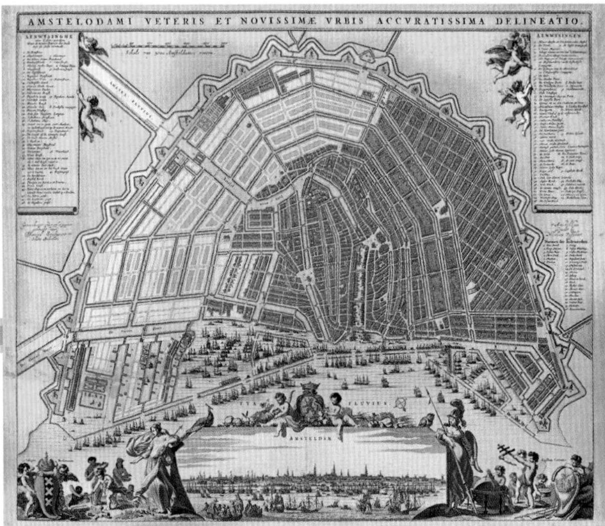

1663 The digging of a second phase of canals creates the outer ring of waterways shown on this map from the era.

1685 An influx of Huguenot refugees arrives after being forced out of their native France.

△ BETTER COCOA TRAVELS THE WORLD
In Amsterdam, Coenraad van Houten invented a new process to manufacture cocoa powder in the 19th century. This produced a better tasting product that found favor all over the world.

Thousands of workers moved to Amsterdam in the 19th century. They often lived in slums on the outskirts, where large families were constricted to one cramped room.

The ebb and flow of empire

The 18th century saw the Dutch overseas empire decline. Signs of a downturn had begun in the 1660s, when the Dutch surrendered their colony in North America to the British. New Amsterdam became New York. Nevertheless, Amsterdam itself still had a huge fleet and its ships carried on trading around the world. The waterways remained busy, and Dam Square, the great assembly point in the center of the city, was still crowded with visitors from all over Europe. With its far-reaching trading networks and embrace of individualism, Amsterdam had long been an open-minded and progressive place. This reputation for tolerance endured, with the city becoming home to many more Jews, who moved there to escape persecution.

A major blow to the Netherlands occurred when it was involved in the Fourth Anglo–Dutch War in the 1780s. The British had declared war against the Netherlands because the Dutch continued to trade and negotiate with the American colonies, Britain's enemies in the American Revolution (1775–1783). As a result of the conflict, the Dutch navy was virtually wiped out, making it impossible for them to defend either their homeland or their colonies. The French took advantage of this weakness and invaded the Netherlands in 1794. This brought an unexpected change for Amsterdam, as it became the capital of a new Dutch state, the Batavian Republic.

The city was quiet under French rule, and the Netherlands looked to be losing ground to countries such as Britain, with its expanding world empire and fast-developing industry. After Napoleon's defeat in 1813, the Dutch House of Orange returned from exile. Under the new regime, Amsterdam began to prosper once more. The city's diamond-cutting industry boomed as diamonds from South Africa became available; the port was modernized for steamships; and rail links to other Dutch cities were established. Businesses from garment manufacture to cocoa processing also did well. Another development was the advent of the bicycle, which was welcomed enthusiastically onto the flat streets of Amsterdam.

△ *AT THE JEWELER'S*, 1909
Martin Monnickendam's painting shows well-to-do shoppers inspecting diamond jewelery. In this period, Amsterdam was sometimes called the "city of diamonds."

The impact of war

Although the Netherlands was neutral in World War I, the country was hit by food shortages. In 1917, a group of women, discovering a ship loaded with potatoes in one of Amsterdam's canals, began to help themselves. The potatoes had been earmarked for the army, and soldiers were sent to stop the plundering. They opened fire, killing 6 and wounding over 100 people. The social unrest caused by incidents like this, and by the Great Depression, led many in Amsterdam to begin to support political

1751 The Stadtholder William IV dies; 40 years of unrest begin.

1780–1784 Britain destroys the Dutch navy in the Fourth Anglo–Dutch War.

1799 Depleted after the Fourth Anglo–Dutch War, the Dutch East India Company closes down.

1839 A railroad opens linking Amsterdam and Haarlem.

1860s A fresh wave of Jewish immigration begins.

1921 Het Schip is one of many housing projects to accommodate the rising population.

> **People come** here because they have the feeling that **they can do anything they want**. That is **our history**, and we have to **protect it**.

FORMER MAYOR OF AMSTERDAM JOB COHEN, QUOTED IN RUSSELL SHORTO'S *AMSTERDAM*, 2013

extremists, including the local communist and Nazi parties. The Dutch government intervened with housing projects and unemployment relief programs, such as the creation of the Amsterdamse Bos park, and Amsterdam expanded as a result. But the German army occupied the city during World War II, bringing years of oppression and the deportation of over 100,000 Jews. Amsterdam suffered as never before, with able-bodied men sent to work in German factories, serious bomb damage, and severe shortages of coal and food, before liberation finally came in May 1945.

Liberal city life

With the economy booming again by the 1950s, and the next decade ushering in a period of social and cultural change throughout the Western world, Amsterdam was primed to embrace a new libertarianism. Tolerance and acceptance were already strong pillars of city life—something that attracted many bohemians to Amsterdam, and for which it has been renowned ever since. This relatively relaxed attitude extended to the city's approach to recreational drug use and sex work. Radicalism may have become Amsterdam's trademark, but many residents moved away as social deprivation, riots, and squatting increased. The use of illegal drugs became widespread, and demonstrations and street violence gave the city a questionable reputation in the 1970s. However, there were big improvements in the following decades, with considerable investment in industry and a liberalization of the drug laws. Amsterdam began to thrive as a tourist destination and visitors flocked to the city in higher numbers than ever, charmed by the relaxed lifestyle, the beauty of the canals and streets, and the unparalleled art museums. Amsterdam was firmly back on the international map.

△ **HISTORIC ARCHITECTURE**
Amsterdam has preserved its historic canal-side architecture well, with over 9,000 listed monuments. The inner canal ring, the Grachtengordel, was made a UNESCO World Heritage Site in 2010.

Für die Zentrale für jüdische Auswanderung Amsterdam richtig übernommen:

Wachhabender

1. Für die Richtigkeit der Übernahme:
2. Verwaltung

SS-Hauptsturmführer.

zur Zahlung von 37.50 Gulden, in Worten ... Gulden.

Festgestellt ... den ... 1943.

Sachlich richtig

Polizeisekretär

SS-Sturmbannführer.

B. d. S.
Zahlstelle-Aussenstelle
Amsterdam

den 13 APR 1943. 1943.

Empfangsbescheinigung:

Von der Zahlstelle des B. d. S. — Aussenstelle Amsterdam — habe ich 37.50 Gulden, in Worten ... Gulden erhalten.
Dieser Betrag ist vorschussweise aus Judenvermögen gezahlt worden.

K 372

(Unterschrift.)

1940 The German invasion leads to the persecution of Jews in Amsterdam; initially issued with identity cards and yellow stars, many later died in death camps.

1956 The National Monument is constructed on Dam Square commemorating the casualties of World War II. It later becomes a symbol of freedom, attracting an alternative crowd.

Anne Frank's wartime diary was first published by her father Otto Frank in 1947 under the title *Het Achterhuis* (*The Secret Annex*).

1960s Tolerant Amsterdam becomes home to many hippies.

1966–1986 A period of unrest between radical youth and the city's government brings episodes of violence.

1975 New laws distinguish soft from hard drugs and decriminalize the possession of small amounts of marijuana.

2021 Amsterdam's mayor announces the relocation of the city's famous red light district.

Stockholm

CITY BETWEEN THE BRIDGES

An elegant city of bridges and islands, and one of Europe's younger capitals, Stockholm balances a medieval heritage with assured contemporary style and a sense of egalitarian openness.

Although the Mälaren valley, the watery region that stretches inland from Stockholm, has been a center of power since the 8th century CE, the city itself was only founded in the mid-13th century, when trading privileges were established with the Hanseatic port of Lübeck. Under the authority of Birger Jarl, the city's official founder, Stockholm grew as a trading station for German merchants clustered in the Gamla Stan, the medieval quarter that still remains the heart of the city.

Rise and fall

A tug of war over Stockholm with Denmark, to which Sweden was tied in the unpopular Kalmar Union, ended in the 1520s when Gustav I united rebel factions against Danish rule. Gustav graced his new royal base with a castle, and Stockholm grew rich on trade in salt and iron. In the 17th century, Sweden was elevated to the status of a great power with its own Baltic empire. Wealth from this era funded the building of aristocratic villas and the first theaters. Gamla Stan gained two new wide avenues, and a row of elegant palaces was erected along the waterfront. The population soared fivefold in half a century, reaching 50,000 by the 1670s.

Yet the good times didn't last. A series of fires, one of which wrecked the royal castle; a disastrous defeat against Russia in the Great Northern War; and an outbreak of plague in 1710 broke the back of Swedish power. Stockholm began to stagnate.

> "**Stockholm** is surely an **urban planner's dream**. Everything **works**."
>
> JANINE DI GIOVANNI, JOURNALIST

◁ *DAWN OVER RIDDARFJÄRDEN*, 1899
Heavily influenced by Edvard Munch, the nighttime paintings of Stockholm-born Eugène Jansson beautifully evoke the watery landscapes of his home city.

c.750 CE Viking traders establish the island settlement of Birka on Lake Mälaren, 18 miles (30 km) west of Stockholm.

c.1250 Stockholm is founded under the rule of the powerful nobleman, Birger Jarl. Within three decades, it is Sweden's largest city.

1520 In a massacre known as the Stockholm Bloodbath, the Danish King Christian II orders the execution of more than 80 Swedish nobles who oppose Danish rule.

1523 Gustav I liberates Stockholm from the Danish-led Kalmar Union as Sweden asserts its independence.

1612 Axel Oxenstierna becomes chancellor, an office he holds for 42 years. He implements reforms that place the monarchy on a constitutional basis.

1625 Stora Nygatan, the city's first main street, is laid out after a fire destroys much of the medieval center.

◁ CHAPEL, ROYAL PALACE
The opulent architecture of the Royal Palace is more redolent of the absolute monarchy of Gustav III, during whose reign it was built, than the comparatively modest lifestyle of the modern royal family.

A cultural rebirth

As the 18th century progressed, Stockholm began to wake from its slumbers. Work began in earnest on the new Royal Palace—on the site of the old castle—in 1727, and further fires accelerated the transformation from a city of timber to one of stone. Under the enlightened—if despotic—rule of Gustav III, the center was improved with the laying out of a grand square, Gustav Adolfs torg in Norrmalm. The construction of a string of new theaters spearheaded an awakening in cultural and artistic life. Gustav's projects ended in unfortunate fashion, though, when he was assassinated in 1792 at a masked ball at his beloved Opera House, completed just a decade earlier.

Industry and expansion

As the city grew in size through the early 19th century, life became ever tougher for ordinary Stockholmers. Many crowded into slums without running water or sewage, and outbreaks of cholera were frequent. By the 1850s, industrialization had truly begun to revive the city's fortunes. New factories provided employment for the swelling urban working class and the opening of the central railroad station allowed city dwellers an easy escape to the countryside. Farsighted urban planning ensured the burgeoning city conformed to a uniform design, with broad boulevards, parks, and well-equipped apartment blocks.

Merchants, industrial magnates, and writers mingled in the city's fashionable cafés, among them the playwright August Strindberg, whose masterpiece *Miss Julie* shocked polite society with its naturalistic portrayal of sexuality. This was the era, too, of Alfred Nobel, who made his fortune from inventing dynamite and bequeathed almost all of it to the prize fund set up in his name.

> Stockholm has everything **New York or London** has but **without the people** and the **traffic**.

BJÖRN ULVAEUS, MUSICIAN, QUOTED IN *THE GUARDIAN*, 2015

1754 The 608-room Royal Palace in Gamla Stan is finally completed. It is still the official royal residence.

1759 The Great Stockholm Fire, the city's last such large-scale disaster, destroys around 20 blocks of the city.

King Gustav III in coronation robes

1772 King Gustav III reintroduces absolute royal rule, reversing gains made by parliament, but governs according to Enlightenment principles.

1871 Stockholm's central railroad station opens.

1879 August Strindberg's *The Red Room* is published. The novel satirizes contemporary Stockholm society, and propels the author to fame.

August Strindberg's *Collected Poems*

The start of the new century saw cars and electric trams fill Stockholm's streets and the construction of some grand structures in ornate architectural styles, notably the Art Nouveau Central Post Office Building and Neo-Baroque Parliament House in Gamla Stan. In 1912, the city's profile was boosted by hosting the Olympic Games. Gold medals in cross-country running, sailing, and the tug of war reflected Swedes' enduring love of the outdoors.

Capital of cool

Sweden's neutrality in both world wars allowed Stockholm to escape the devastation inflicted across much of Europe, and thousands of Jews escaped persecution to settle in the city and beyond. A post-war boom in development—not all of it welcomed—made the city a highly desirable place to live. Meanwhile, Stockholm continued to produce artistic greats, particularly in the film world, with the actors Ingrid Bergman and Anita Ekberg following in the footsteps of Greta Garbo—who grew up in a one-room apartment in the then working-class district of Södermalm—in achieving international stardom. Benny Andersson, one of the ABBA quartet that won the Eurovision Song Contest for Sweden in 1974, was a native Stockholmer.

Though the city faced its problems—the assassination of Prime Minister Olof Palme in 1986, for example, shook the nation to the core—by the 1990s, Sweden (and Stockholm) were decidedly "cool." The emergence of telecoms giant Ericsson as a global leader in tech sealed Sweden's reputation for innovation, and in 2010 the city celebrated becoming the first European Green Capital.

Today, Stockholm remains one of Europe's most open and friendly cities, its bridges and islands a magnet for tourists, and its confident style, concern for the environment, and unstuffy egalitarianism a rare combination that is a testament to its unique history.

△ THE OLD TOWN
A medieval warren of cobbled streets, lined with fine churches and museums, Gamla Stan lies at the heart of Stockholm's complex of 14 islands linked by 57 bridges.

Stockholm's name means "log island," allegedly because its founders tossed a log into Lake Mälaren and established the settlement where it washed ashore.

1896 Alfred Nobel leaves a bequest to fund prizes in five fields to be awarded annually to those "who have conferred the greatest benefit on mankind."

1891 The Skansen open-air museum opens—the world's first—featuring examples of folk architecture from around the country.

1912 Stockholm hosts the Olympic Games. Sweden wins 24 gold medals, its highest-ever total.

T-Centralen metro station

2008 Stockholm-based Spotify is launched. Within a few years, it has transformed the global music-streaming industry.

1950 The Stockholm metro begins operation. Today, 90 of its 100 stations feature artworks, earning it the moniker "the world's longest art gallery."

Lisbon

CITY OF SEVEN HILLS

Emerging from Roman then Moorish rule, from the 15th century Lisbon was at the forefront of European exploration, exploiting its position on the western edge of Europe and becoming rich on the wealth of its empire.

Lisbon owes its existence to the Tagus, the longest river in the Iberian Peninsula. One tradition claims that the mythical Greek hero Odysseus alighted on the shore here and founded the city, although it's more likely that the settlement was begun by the Oestrimni (Latin for "people of the far west"), who arrived during the late Bronze Age and engaged in commerce from a fortified settlement on the Tagus.

> "**By day** Lisbon ... **enchants and captivates**, but **by night** it is **a fairy-tale city**, descending over lighted terraces **to the sea**.
>
> ERICH MARIA REMARQUE, *THE NIGHT IN LISBON*, 1962

From the Romans to the Moors

Archaeological finds show that the Oestrimni traded with the Phoenicians of the eastern Mediterranean, and it was likely they who called the place Alis Ubbo, meaning "peaceful harbor," which mutated into Olisipo, and later Lisbon. In 138 BCE, the settlement was absorbed by the Roman Empire. The Romans built defensive walls around the city, which stretched from what is now the Castelo São Jorge to the Tagus and, in 30 BCE, renamed it Felicitas Julia Olisipo, after Julius Caesar. But as Roman power weakened in the 5th century, various groups, including the Alans and the Visigoths, crossed the Pyrenees to rule Iberia, and a much-looted Lisbon declined.

The next invasion came from the south: an Arab and Berber army captured Lisbon in 716 CE and renamed it al-Ushbuna. It once again became a wealthy commercial hub, described by Moorish traveler al-Idrisi as a "lovely city ... defended by a ring of walls and a powerful castle." It was not until 1147 that Afonso Henriques, who eight years earlier had defeated a Moorish army and proclaimed himself king of Portugal, reclaimed Lisbon for Christian Europe.

◁ THE MONUMENT OF THE DISCOVERIES
The Padrão dos Descobrimentos, on the north bank of the Tagus, celebrates the 15th- and 16th-century explorers who established Portugal as the most powerful seafaring nation in the world.

Locals are "Lisboetas," but also "Alfacinhas" ("little lettuces"). The plant is believed to have been widely cultivated in Moorish Lisbon.

c. 1000 BCE The Oestrimni travel south from Galicia and settle across much of Portugal.

138 BCE Roman forces under Decimus Junius Brutus subdue local tribes and occupy the settlement that will become Lisbon.

409 CE Roman rule comes to an end when hordes of Alans, Sueves, and Vandals sweep over the Pyrenees and occupy Lisbon.

716 Muslim armies from North Africa conquer the city.

Tile depicting Christ assuring Afonso Henriques of victory over the Moors

1147 Afonso Henriques, the Christian king of "Portucale," captures Lisbon from the Muslims.

1279 King Dinis I begins his 46-year reign, during which medieval Portugal's economy prospers.

Portuguese ships traveled halfway around the world, bringing Moroccan dyes, West African gold, Brazilian sugar, spices from India, and Ming porcelain back to Lisbon.

City of discovery

In the mid-13th century Lisbon became the Portuguese capital and by the 15th century it was thriving, with trading partners around the Mediterranean and as far north as the Baltic Sea. The Atlantic Ocean was Portugal's frontier, and the nation grew confident enough to begin territorial expansion, first in coastal North Africa and then down the west coast of the continent. In 1497, Vasco da Gama set out from Lisbon, rounded the Cape of Good Hope, and sailed to India, giving Portugal control of Indian Ocean trade. Three years later, Pedro Álvares Cabral landed on the northeast coast of South America, in what is now Brazil, and claimed it for Portugal.

Lisbon grew rich on the wealth generated by its colonies, and became Europe's most prosperous city in the 16th century. Churches, fortresses, and palaces were built in the Manueline style, which mixed Gothic features with maritime flourishes that emphasized the source of the city's wealth. At its heart was the waterfront Paço da Ribeira, a royal palace on a vast square fronting the Tagus, flanked by administrative offices and warehouses. From his balcony, the king could watch ships arrive laden with spices and other desirable goods. The city was also the main slave-trade center in Europe, and around 150,000 enslaved Africans passed through Lisbon to be put to work in Portugal between the mid-15th and early 16th centuries.

When gold was discovered in Brazil, the proceeds triggered a boom in Lisbon. A great number of opulent buildings were commissioned by the clergy and aristocracy, including the 17th-century Church of Santa Engrácia (now the National Pantheon). The city's wealth attracted migrants, and from a city of 100,000 in 1550, Lisbon grew to accommodate 200,000 people by 1750.

A shaken capital

On November 1, 1755, a devastating earthquake struck. It occurred on All Saints' Day, when the churches were full. Much of the city came crashing down in six minutes. Panicked citizens ran down to the river to escape, only to

1415 Portugal conquers the territory of Ceuta in what is now Morocco.

1497 Vasco da Gama sets out from Lisbon, reaching India in 1498. He returns with pepper and cinnamon, prompting further expeditions.

1511 Portugal extends its sphere of influence to Malacca, in Malaysia, and establishes control of the lucrative spice trade.

16th-century scene of Lisbon harbor

c. 1695 Gold is discovered in the Portuguese colony of Brazil and the wealth that flows back funds a building boom in Lisbon.

> Crowds of **people** [were] **calling out** for **mercy**, while from the **violent and convulsive** motions of the Earth, we expected **every moment** to be **swallowed up**.

EARTHQUAKE WITNESS REVEREND RICHARD GODDARD, 1755

◁ LISBON'S PRE-EARTHQUAKE WATERFRONT
This panoramic panel of *azulejos* (tiles) shows the Tagus overlooked by a grand plaza and the domed Paço da Ribeira palace (left), in around 1700.

▽ THE GREAT LISBON EARTHQUAKE
The earthquake of 1755 was followed by a tsunami and three days of raging fire. Much of the city was destroyed and thousands were killed.

be engulfed by a tidal wave that flooded the lower city. Around three-quarters of Lisbon was destroyed, including palaces and churches, and a wealth of books and art. In the aftermath, chief minister Sebastião José de Carvalho used Brazilian gold to replace the city's mazelike medieval heart with a grid of wide, Classical-style avenues, creating the area now known as Baixa. The site of the old Paço da Ribeira became a waterfront plaza, the Praça do Comércio.

In the early 1800s, Portugal was invaded by Napoleonic France. The royal family fled to Brazil and for 13 years Rio de Janeiro was the kingdom's capital. It was the middle of the century before stability returned to Lisbon, paving the way for industrial and commercial growth. In the 1880s, a park was transformed into tree-lined Avenida da Liberdade, and the first of the city's funiculars appeared in 1884, propelled by a water gravity system; after electrification came in 1901, the city filled with electric trams. Then, in 1908, shots on Praça do Comércio signaled the beginning of the end for the monarchy.

1755 A six-minute earthquake followed by a tidal wave and fire devastates the city and kills as many as 50,000 people.

1807 Napoleon marches into Lisbon after Portugal refuses to declare war on its old ally Britain.

Lisbon's gaudy, Moorish-styled Campo Pequeno bullring opened in 1892, but the killing of the bull was outlawed in 1928.

1884 The city begins operating its first funicular trams.

1886 Avenida da Liberdade is completed. It runs north from the waterfront, and soon becomes the city's most prestigious address.

1902 The Santa Justa elevator begins operating. It connects the Baixa district with the hilltop Largo do Carmo.

Fado: the Portuguese blues

> "The **fado** is not meant to be **sung**; it simply **happens**. You **feel it**, you don't **understand it** and you don't **explain it**.

AMÁLIA RODRIGUES, FADO SINGER

△ Amália Rodrigues was Lisbon's "Queen of Fado." Born into poverty in 1920, she took the genre from the streets of Lisbon to the big screen, and to stages in Paris and New York.

◁ Fado began as the humble music of Lisbon's taverns, but poets would later write sophisticated fado lyrics.

Fado means "fate" in Portuguese, but is also the name of a form of music originating in Lisbon. It is usually performed by one singer, accompanied by dual *guitarras* (mandolin-shaped 12-string guitars) and a *viola* (Spanish guitar). Fado lyrics frequently focus on the hard realities of daily life or the trials of love. Fado is also linked with the notion of *saudade*, which is a longing for something impossible to attain. *Fadistas*, as fado singers are known, often wear a black shawl of mourning, although songs can also be upbeat.

Since the 19th century, fado has been performed in bars and clubs in working-class districts of Lisbon. It flourished during the Salazar years, before falling out of favor after the 1974 Revolution. In recent times, the genre has been rehabilitated and a new generation of musicians and singers can be heard in *casas de fado* around Lisbon, particularly in the Alfama quarter, where there is also a Museu do Fado.

1926 A military coup in Lisbon begins a long period of authoritarian rule, first under the Ditadura Nacional, then the Estado Novo (New State).

1932 Antonio de Oliveira Salazar becomes prime minister. He will rule for almost four decades.

1959 The inauguration of the Santuário de Cristo Rei, a giant statue of Jesus Christ on the banks of the Tagus River, takes place.

1966 The Ponte Salazar suspension bridge over the Tagus (later renamed Ponte 25 de Abril) is completed.

1974 The Carnation Revolution, a military coup in Lisbon, brings an end to the Estado Novo.

TIMELESS TRANSPORTATION ▷
Lisbon's trams have been climbing the city's hills for 120 years. They have declined since their 1950s heyday but remain hugely popular, and a discontinued route was revived in 2018 after a 21-year break.

Modern Lisbon

Republican sentiments had grown as the 19th century progressed. King Carlos I's 1908 assassination by gunmen meant power passed to his son Manuel II, but two years later he was deposed and fled into exile as rebel warships shelled the palace. The Republic of Portugal was proclaimed from the balcony of Lisbon's city hall.

The replacement of the monarchy with a constitutional government failed to create order. Competing local powers turned Lisbon into a battleground and in fewer than 16 years there were 45 changes of government. Yet intellectual life flourished, and the 1910s saw the first publications of Lisbon's great Modernist poet, Fernando Pessoa.

In 1926, a coup brought the authoritarian Ditadura Nacional (later known as the Estado Novo) regime to power. From its ranks, António de Oliveira Salazar emerged as prime minister in 1932. He would go on to rule Portugal in a virtual dictatorship for the next 36 years.

During World War II, Portugal remained neutral and Lisbon became crowded with refugees, many of them waiting for a visa to the US. The movie *Casablanca* hinges on "letters of transit" that will allow fugitive lovers Ilsa and Victor to reach Lisbon and a ship to safety. In the post-war era, Lisbon was the capital of an insular nation, whose citizens could be fined for letting their laundry drip. Major public works were undertaken, notably the suspension bridge over the Tagus and the Cristo Rei statue.

In 1974, a military coup brought the moribund Estado Novo era to an end and introduced democratic reforms. When fire ripped through the historic Chiado district in 1988, its elegant streets were sensitively rebuilt in time for the 1998 Lisbon World Exposition, commemorating the 500th anniversary of Vasco da Gama's voyage to India. A once-decaying stretch of waterfront hosted the event and was redeveloped as the gleaming Parque das Nações, and the same year saw the opening of the Tagus-spanning Vasco da Gama Bridge, then the longest bridge in Europe.

The 21st century has seen further grand projects, notably 2016's Museum of Art, Architecture, and Technology. With its trams, *azulejo* tiling, seafood, and fado, modern Lisbon is a deeply atmospheric place, its hills gazing down past sloping roofs and cobbled streets to the Tagus as it flows to the sea.

Lisbon is known for its *calçada Portuguesa*, pavements laid with black and white stones to create a mosaic-like image or pattern.

The 1974 coup was known as the Carnation Revolution after the flowers citizens placed in the muzzles of soldiers' guns.

1986 Portugal joins the European Economic Community. Some of the resulting funds are used to regenerate Lisbon.

1988 Fire tears through the central Chiado district, causing widespread damage.

1998 Lisbon hosts an expo to mark the 500th anniversary of Vasco da Gama's discovery of the route to India.

2004 Portugal hosts the European Football Championship. The national team reaches the final, but loses to Greece in Lisbon.

2016 The strikingly designed Museum of Art, Architecture, and Technology opens on the waterfront.

> **Fountain of courtesy**, shelter of strangers, hospice to the poor, **land of the valiant** ... a city **unique in its location and beauty**.
>
> MIGUEL DE CERVANTES, *DON QUIXOTE*, 1605

Barcelona

CITY OF COUNTS

Barcelona's stunning architecture has helped make it a world-famous cultural center. It has expanded from a compact medieval hub to a large and vibrant metropolis looking out to the shining sea.

According to legend, Barcelona was founded by a military leader from Carthage in North Africa named Hamilcar Barca. However, the Romans, who arrived in the 3rd century BCE, were the first settlers to have left a historical record. Attracted by the valuable harbor, they called the place Barcino, laid roads, and built aqueducts to create a fresh water supply. The settlement became a center for the surrounding area, where grapes were grown, and the Romans exported the local wine across their empire.

The coming of the counts

The fall of the Roman Empire was followed by several centuries of rule by the Visigoths, before the arrival of the Moors—Muslims from North Africa. In the 9th century CE, the Franks captured Barcelona, adding it to their empire. A series of local counts ruled Barcelona on behalf of the Frankish emperor, one of whom, Wilfred the Hairy (r. 878–897 CE) built fine churches and a palace, making the city a fitting capital of the County of Barcelona. His dynasty ruled for some 500 years—hence Barcelona's lasting nickname, City of Counts—conquering outposts such as Valencia, Sardinia, and Sicily. In 1137, the engagement of Count of Barcelona Ramon Berenguer IV to the heir to the throne of nearby Aragon heralded a golden age for Catalonia. The Aragonese drew wealth from Barcelona's trade, some of which was used to construct the buildings of the Gothic Quarter, the most ancient part of the city surviving today.

As the 14th century progressed, the city's fortunes began to decline. It was badly hit by the Black Death in the 1340s and then by a series of poor harvests and famines. Barcelona, where the streets once bustled with merchants and shopkeepers and the air rang with the sound of masons' chisels, was now half-empty and quiet. Local prosperity sank further after 1503, when the rulers of newly united Spain banned merchants from transatlantic trade with their recently acquired territories in the Americas.

◁ AERIAL VIEW OF BARCELONA
The Basilica of the Sagrada Família occupies one block of the grid-planned Eixample district, while the more haphazard streets of the old Gothic Quarter (far left) stretch away toward the sea.

THE VIRGIN MARY OF VECIANA ▷
This woodcarving displays an Italo-Byzantine style popular in the workshops of Barcelona in the 13th century.

230 BCE Carthaginians are believed to have founded Barcelona around this time.

218 BCE The Romans begin to conquer Catalonia, keen to exploit the region's harbor for military purposes and trade.

Roman-era relief of Medusa found in Barcelona

878 CE Wilfred the Hairy takes control of the area, becoming the first Count of Barcelona.

1137 The counts of Barcelona become kings of Aragon.

1298 Work begins on Barcelona Cathedral, a Gothic structure that takes 150 years to complete.

King Philip V bolstered his power by closing the university and banning the teaching of Catalan, to suppress potential local opposition.

War and industry

Spain's 16th-century rulers, Charles V and Philip II, were members of the powerful Hapsburg dynasty and brought the country into their huge European empire. Madrid remained their center, while Barcelona was marginalized and taxed heavily. The local population rebelled against imperial power in the 1640 Revolt of the Harvesters, a clash that led to a 12-year war. The dispute culminated in an extended siege of the city, which was forced to submit. Barcelona was also embroiled in the War of the Spanish Succession, a Europe-wide conflict between France and Austria, each vying to put their candidates on the Spanish throne. Austrian forces occupied the port and took over the city, which Philip V of Spain won back in 1714. The new king led a repressive regime, abolishing all local self-government and destroying an entire residential district to make way for an imposing fortress, the Ciutadella.

What saved the city was the coming of industry and the revival of commerce. In 1778, the long-standing ban on trade with the Americas was lifted, restoring commercial life at last, in spite of damage caused during the Peninsular War of 1808–1814. During the 19th century, the iron, wine, and cork industries expanded, followed by an increase in textile production. This brought jobs, money, and an influx of workers from the surrounding area. The city began to regain its buzz, but at a cost—still confined within the medieval city walls, Barcelona became overcrowded with workers enduring slum housing and poor sanitation. By the 1850s, it became clear that the city had to expand.

A new vision

Catalan engineer and urban planner Ildefons Cerdà devised the city's expansion, coming up with a revolutionary scheme called the Eixample (Extension), which created an entirely new city district. Cerdà saw that it was vital to give his new district better services and good roads, together with adequate ventilation, sunlight, and green space. Each intersection on his unique grid plan widened into a diamond-shaped space, easing traffic flow. The street blocks were designed to be built up on two sides only, giving access via the open sides to a central area of green space. This distinctive plan still gives much of the city center its character and navigability—even though the area

◁ *SIEGE OF BARCELONA, SEPTEMBER 11, 1714*, 1909
Barcelona fell to Philip V's forces during the War of the Spanish Succession, shown here in Antoni Estruch's dramatic painting. The city still holds an annual ceremony of remembrance.

1640 The Revolt of the Harvesters begins a long war in Catalonia and southern France.

1714 Philip V destroys much of Barcelona, forcing the city to surrender and accept him as ruler.

1808 Barcelona is occupied by the French and besieged during the Peninsular War.

1833 Poet Bonaventura Carles Aribau's *La Pàtria* heralds a literary renaissance in Catalonia.

1849 Spain's first railroad links Barcelona to Mataró, about 19 miles (30 km) along the coast.

1850 The local textile industry reaches its peak, with thousands employed in the city and nearby.

was so popular that the open sides of the blocks were soon filled in. In addition, space was provided for a large new church—the site of the future Sagrada Família, designed by Catalan architect Antoni Gaudí (see box p. 182).

A global outlook

This expansion benefited the city's industry, improved housing conditions, and helped create a sense of optimism among business owners, Catalan nationalists, writers, and artists alike. Barcelona began to make its mark on the global stage, particularly with the Universal Exposition of 1888. The city's mayor oversaw the swift construction of a number of impressive buildings. One of the most eye-catching was the Arc de Triomf at the exposition's entrance, its classical proportions offset by rich, Moorish-influenced decoration and a series of elaborate friezes which show Barcelona welcoming the participating nations and embracing the modern age.

△ PLAN OF THE EIXAMPLE, 1859
Ildefons Cerdà's plan shows the extension to the city—with its grid layout and diagonal avenues—dwarfing the old city, which is indicated in darker shading.

1854 Barcelona begins to expand beyond its city walls.

1859 Ildefons Cerdà produces the first version of the Eixample plan.

Once the city's only green space, the Parc de la Ciutadella was transformed to host the 1888 Universal Exposition.

1882 Construction work starts on the Basilica de la Sagrada Família.

1887 Lliga de Catalunya, the first party to campaign for home rule in Catalonia, is founded.

1888 The international Universal Exposition is held with the Arc de Triomf as its landmark entrance.

Antoni Gaudí

> This **man did everything** he wanted to do **with stone**.
>
> LE CORBUSIER, DURING A VISIT TO BARCELONA, 1928

Catalan architect Antoni Gaudí i Cornet (1852–1926) trained in Barcelona and spent most of his life working in and near the city. Strongly influenced by the natural world, he developed a style like no other, combining sensuously curving walls and roofs, vivid colors, and rich textures. Gaudí preferred to design every detail of his buildings and often used innovative structures, such as paraboloid arches and sloping columns. He worked slowly, producing relatively few buildings; his masterpiece, the Basilica de la Sagrada Família, is still incomplete. The dazzling Casa Batlló, decorated with kaleidoscopic tile mosaics; the curvaceous Casa Milà with its 32 wrought-iron balconies, each one unique; and the fanciful structures in Parc Güell, are all extraordinary Barcelona landmarks.

△ Casa Batlló's arched roof and tower are said to represent St. George (patron saint of Catalonia) piercing the dragon with his lance.

△ Gaudí created the mosaic-tile-encrusted Parc Güell, a public park, for his patron, industrialist Eusebi Güell.

1892 The Catalanist Union brings together Catalan nationalists and draws up a program of proposals for regional autonomy.

1901 The Catalan nationalist party, La Lliga Regionalista, is formed and wins the majority of seats in Barcelona's council elections.

1909 "Tragic Week": there are protests and bombings after a call-up for Spanish military campaigns in Morocco.

1912 Gaudí's Casa Milà, an apartment building with a facade of undulating curves, is finished.

1914 Antoni Gaudí completes Parc Güell, renowned for its mosaic-covered structures. The park is opened to the public in 1926.

A pro-Republican poster, produced during the Spanish Civil War, c. 1937

1936 The three-year Spanish Civil War begins. Barcelona is a major Republican stronghold and is heavily attacked.

After the Exposition closed, Catalan nationalism gained momentum with both the foundation of nationalist organizations and a victory at the 1901 polls. Meanwhile, the development of Barcelona's new city blocks continued and a different architectural, artistic, and literary movement evolved, known as Modernisme. In part influenced by Art Nouveau in France and Belgium, free-flowing and favoring curves over straight lines, this style was suited to the genius of Antoni Gaudí (see box). Other pioneering painters and sculptors, including Pablo Picasso and Joan Miró, made Barcelona their home in the early 20th century. Their revolutionary work, together with Gaudí's colorful architecture and concerts held at venues such as the Palau de la Música Catalana, made Barcelona a vibrant cultural center, a role the city still retains.

Conflicts and recoveries

The 20th century brought repeated political upheavals to Barcelona. One example was a week of bombings and protests against a military call-up in 1909. More damaging still was the Spanish Civil War (1936–1939), with bitter fighting bringing great loss of life and the wrecking of many buildings. The war's end brought the right-wing dictator Francisco Franco to power in Spain. Later, Franco's follower Josep Maria de Porcioles became mayor of Barcelona and remained in the post for 16 years. Porcioles' policies stimulated industry and spawned sprawling new suburbs, but the housing was often crowded and inadequate. Far more successful public works were generated by Barcelona's winning bid to host the 1992 Olympic Games. A stadium was built in the fortress-topped area of Montjuïc, and the previously run-down waterfront was transformed with city beaches, promenades, cafés, and bars. In the 21st century, continued investment in regeneration projects has boosted the city's popularity as a center for tourism and the arts—as has the high profile of its soccer team, adding sports to Barcelona's already-rich offering of unique architecture, impressive art galleries, and cutting-edge gastronomy.

Between fall 1937 and January 1939, the Republican side in the Civil War designated Barcelona the capital city of Spain.

▽ *EL PEIX*, FRANK GEHRY
Gehry created this massive golden fish sculpture in 1992 for the Olympic Games. With a shape recalling the undulating roof of a Gaudí-style building, it has become a symbol of the city.

1957 Francoist Josep Maria de Porcioles becomes mayor of Barcelona.

1979 The region of Catalonia is granted partial autonomy.

1983 The sculpture *Woman and Bird* by Joan Miró, with tiles by Joan Gardy Artigas, is placed in the Joan Miró Park.

1992 Hosting the Olympic Games, together with upgrades to the waterfront, brings new vitality to Barcelona.

2004 The first Universal Forum of Cultures, a three-yearly international cultural event, is held in Barcelona.

A survey in 2013 showed that 72.3 percent of Barcelona's residents speak Catalan; more than 95 percent understand the language.

2017 A referendum produces a majority in favor of independence, but the Spanish government imposes direct rule on Catalonia.

Venice

LA SERENISSIMA ("THE MOST SERENE")

Venice's waterside position in the Adriatic brought it trading wealth and political influence. Although no longer politically powerful, its stunning buildings and canals give it an enduring magical beauty.

No one knows for sure who founded Venice on its inhospitable lagoon site. The earliest settlers were said to be refugees fleeing Hun and Germanic incursions into Roman cities, such as Treviso and Aquileia, in the 5th century CE. Lombard invasions of northern Italy in the 6th century drove more mainlanders onto the lonely islands, which would have provided a safe, defendable haven. The settlements that grew up on the Rialto ("High Shore") and neighboring islands soon coalesced into a community. The marshy islands' natural canals were reinforced, with wooden piles sunk into the soft ground to shore up the banks and form foundations for buildings.

A growing city

As part of the Byzantine Empire, Venice was exploited as a trading port. With such a strategic position in the Mediterranean, the city's power swelled and the Venetians began to assert their independence from Byzantine rule. In the early 8th century, they chose their own governor, called the doge (a title similar to duke), and set up trading posts and colonies along the Adriatic's eastern coast.

The city's stature grew further in the 9th century when its people acquired relics—said to be the remains of St. Mark—and a new church, St. Mark's Basilica, was built to house them. As guardian of such an eminent saint, Venice gained a religious significance that underpinned its importance as a port. Wealth poured into the city, and its merchants commanded huge respect, both for their diplomacy and for their naval might. The Byzantine emperors granted Venice a measure of autonomy and, by 1100, the city was playing a major role in international affairs, supplying ships to European crusaders.

> **Sea and sky** seem to **meet half-way**, to blend their tones into a **soft iridescence** ...
>
> HENRY JAMES, *ITALIAN HOURS*, 1909

421 CE Tradition suggests refugees fleeing Gothic invasions are the first to settle on the Venetian islands.

639 The first cathedral is founded on the island of Torcello.

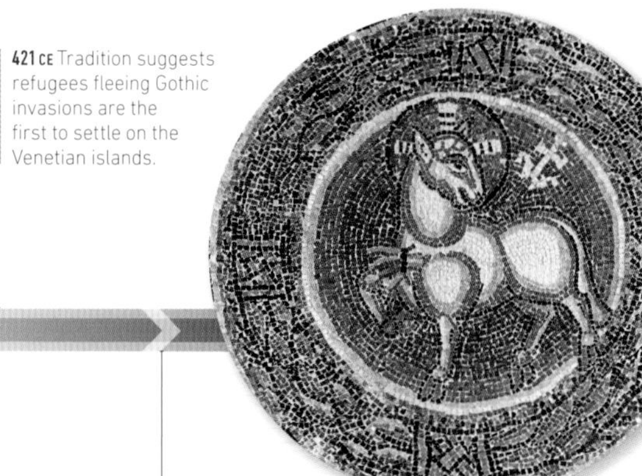

Mosaic in Torcello Cathedral showing the Lamb of God

726 The first recorded doge, Orso Ipato, comes to power and builds up Venice's navy.

828 The city acquires the relics of St. Mark and starts to build the first Venetian church dedicated to the saint.

1000 Doge Pietro II Orseolo clears pirates from the Adriatic Sea, signaling Venice's naval power.

1100 Venice is involved in providing ships for the First Crusade.

▽ *THE MIRACLE OF THE CROSS AT THE BRIDGE OF SAN LORENZO*, 1500
Venetian artist Gentile Bellini painted the miraculous recovery of a relic of the True Cross, which fell into the canal during a procession. To the right, an enslaved Moor is encouraged to retrieve the relic, but in the end only the head of the charitable body that owned it managed to save it.

△ MARCO POLO LEAVING VENICE
The 13th-century Venetian merchant Marco Polo traveled along the Silk Road across Asia. His account of the journey describes Mongolia and China in great detail.

During the Middle Ages, Venice became one of the most stable and prosperous of the Italian city-states. From 1140, as its power, influence, and territories grew, Venice restructured itself as a republic, with a strong form of government based on a council of citizens and the doge, who was elected from among the council members and took on an increasingly ceremonial role.

Fruits of trade and war

The Venetians' skill in shipbuilding gave them a formidable navy and facilitated trade. However, trading rivalry brought Venice into conflict with the Byzantine Empire, which had strong commercial links with Genoa and Pisa. The Venetians attacked Byzantine ports and, in 1204, aided by Crusader forces, captured and ransacked much of the Byzantine capital, Constantinople. This victory enabled Venice to take over many key posts in the Aegean and Greece. With their sea power secured, the Venetians could develop a lucrative trade in goods such as Far Eastern silks and spices. By the late 13th century, wealthy Venice was minting gold coins (ducats).

As the city's fortunes rose, the Doge's Palace was rebuilt with the elaborate arched Gothic facades that still stand today. St. Mark's Basilica was further adorned with spoils from Constantinople and glittering golden mosaics lining the interiors of its many domes. The city's leading families, mostly from the merchant classes, also built themselves impressive palaces, initially following the round-arched style of the buildings of Constantinople, but later adopting the fashionable pointed arches seen on the Doge's Palace itself. Many houses also served as business premises, and included warehouse space for storing spices and silks, as well as woolen fabrics bought elsewhere in Western Europe. These warehouses had direct access from the adjoining canals, allowing cargoes to be easily unloaded. The beautiful sight of pale stone and marble buildings reflected in green-tinged water became typical of the city.

The Ca' d'Oro (House of Gold) on the Grand Canal gets its name from the gilding which partly covered its exterior.

△ DOGE'S PALACE AND ST. MARK'S BASILICA
This 17th-century painting shows the waterside palace, with its ground-floor arches and upper-floor open loggia, in front of the domed Basilica of St. Mark.

In the 14th and 15th centuries, the embellishment of the city's churches and houses continued. An extension of the main Venetian shipyard, the Arsenale, enabled it to turn out warships at the rate of one per day. The Black Death of 1348–1349 took a considerable toll, but soon the population was growing again, thanks to immigration from poorer Italian cities and the declining Byzantine Empire. Trade was boosted when commercial rival Genoa suffered a military defeat. The Ottoman Turks' capture of Constantinople in 1453 ended the Byzantine Empire and created a new threat to the Venetians in the eastern Mediterranean. Even so, Venice was now the single dominant power in the area and acquired a new nickname, Queen of the Adriatic.

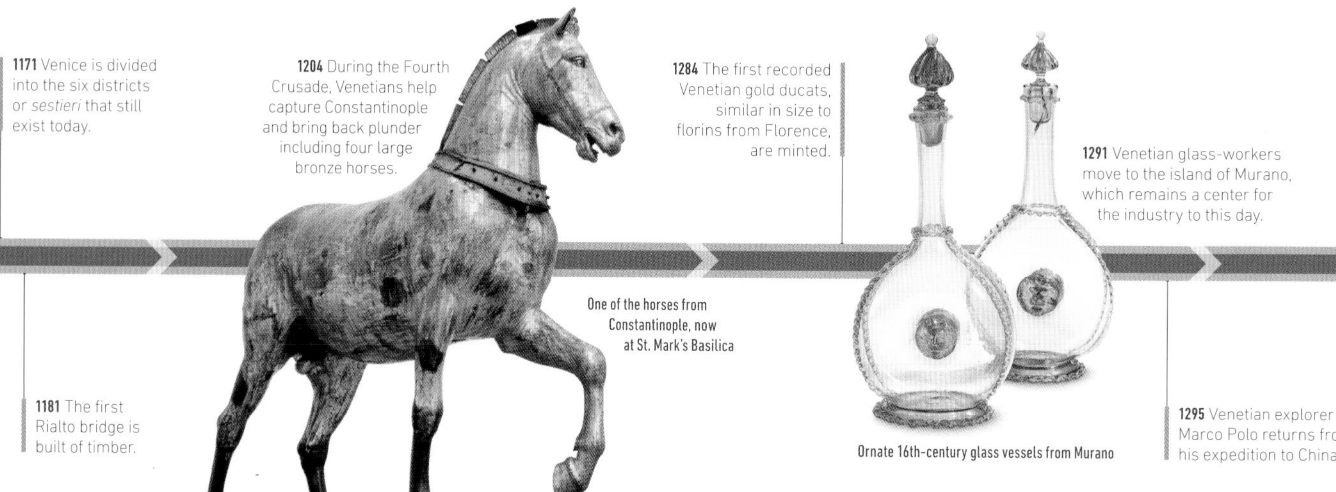

1171 Venice is divided into the six districts or *sestieri* that still exist today.

1181 The first Rialto bridge is built of timber.

1204 During the Fourth Crusade, Venetians help capture Constantinople and bring back plunder including four large bronze horses.

One of the horses from Constantinople, now at St. Mark's Basilica

1284 The first recorded Venetian gold ducats, similar in size to florins from Florence, are minted.

1291 Venetian glass-workers move to the island of Murano, which remains a center for the industry to this day.

Ornate 16th-century glass vessels from Murano

1295 Venetian explorer Marco Polo returns from his expedition to China.

The Venice carnival

△ In *The Minuet* (1754), Venetian painter Giovanni Domenico Tiepolo shows carnival-goers gathered around a couple performing a minuet, a formal dance of the period.

△ Carnival-goers sometimes wear costumes that cover them from head to foot.

> “The **mask ... liberates** the wearer—even if only for a short time—**from inhibitions** and laws ...
>
> OTO BIHALJI-MERIN, *MASKS OF THE WORLD*, 1971

The carnival, an annual festival featuring street entertainment, feasting, practical jokes, and other activities, probably began in the Middle Ages. It started as a chance for merriment in the run-up to the austerity of the Christian period of Lent. Elaborate costumes and masks both added to the fun and gave participants anonymity. Behavior that was normally banned or frowned on, such as flirting and gambling, was allowed. This gave the carnival a risqué reputation, especially in the 17th and 18th centuries, when it was at its most popular. It went out of favor at the end of the 18th century, but was revived in 1976 and now attracts visitors from all over the world. People compete to wear the most extravagant masks and enjoy the food, entertainment, costumes, and element of disguise.

△ Modern carnival masks and dresses can be both elaborate and highly theatrical.

1310 The Council of Ten, one of the Republic's main governing bodies, is formed. It is elected by the Great Council, which was founded in 1172.

1341 A rebuild of the Doge's Palace begins that will give it its ornate Gothic facades.

From the 14th century, membership of the Great Council was strictly limited to families listed in a volume called the Golden Book.

1348–1349 The Black Death cuts Venice's population roughly by half.

1380 Venice defeats Genoa at the Battle of Chioggia, winning maritime dominance of the Mediterranean.

1453 Constantinople falls to the Turks, leaving Venice the strongest power in the region.

1494 Scholar Aldus Manutius sets up his printing press in Venice.

◁ **16TH-CENTURY VENICE** Frans Hogenberg's 1572 map shows Venice isolated from the mainland in its lagoon. The Grand Canal snakes through the center, and islands such as Giudecca (lower left) and Torcello and Murano (top right) can be seen.

Venice is sited on 118 small islands, separated by over 170 canals and connected by about 400 bridges.

Venice in the 16th century remained one of the richest and most powerful cities in Europe, but it also developed its cultural credentials. The city became a center for the printing industry and home to highly original composers, such as Andrea and Giovanni Gabrieli, whose pieces combined groups of singers and brass players to create music designed specifically to resound in the vast spaces of St. Mark's Basilica. Later composers, such as Monteverdi (who was appointed *maestro di cappella*, or director of music, at St. Mark's), were renowned for the development of opera. Venice also welcomed some of Europe's finest painters, from great naturalists such as Titian and Veronese, to masters of brushwork like Tintoretto.

The city's cultural prowess was made possible thanks to merchants and churchmen, who had the funds to act as patrons to musicians and artists, and to commission new churches designed by fashionable architects, such as Palladio. Venetian trade continued, and the expensive clothes worn in many of Titian's portraits—richly worked silks and satins, together with thick furs—suggest the sheer luxury that could be glimpsed as the upper classes made their way around the city, by foot along the narrow streets and by gondola on the canals. Venice also employed large populations of skilled artisans, such as cloth-workers, carpenters, and the glass-workers of Murano, whose goods were in high demand at home and abroad.

Portrait of Leonardo Loredan by Giovanni Bellini

1501 Doge Leonardo Loredan begins his 20-year rule.

1508 Holy Roman Emperor Maximilian I and Pope Julius II form the League of Cambrai in a bid to weaken Venice.

1514 A fire destroys the Rialto bridge. It is rebuilt in stone, with work completed in 1591.

1571 At the Battle of Lepanto, a Western fleet, including many Venetian ships, defeats Turkish forces.

Turkish and Venetian ships confront each other at the Battle of Lepanto

◁ SANTA MARIA DELLA SALUTE
This large, domed church, shown in an 1850 painting by Friedrich Nerly, is in the Dorsoduro *sestiere* (district). Building began in 1631 in thanksgiving for the city's recovery from a plague outbreak that year.

△ BRIDGE OF SIGHS
The covered bridge connects the Doge's Palace, where the state inquisitors sat, with the nearby prison. Its name refers to the prisoners' sighs as they saw Venice for the last time when crossing the bridge.

A city in decline

Venice's prosperity was threatened, however, when the city found itself caught between Western Europe and the Ottoman Empire, which had strengthened its naval power and was pushing westward into the Mediterranean. Although Western forces and Venetian ships defeated the Ottomans at the Battle of Lepanto in 1571, Venice gained little from the victory and lost its important colony of Cyprus. In addition, there were devastating outbreaks of plague in the 1570s and later in 1630, causing a sharp population decline. Further colonies were lost and the Ottomans eventually took over the eastern Mediterranean, cutting off Venetian merchants' access to the lucrative spices and silks they had traded; the spice trade was increasingly dominated by newer sea powers, such as England and the Netherlands.

The final blow to Venice came in 1715, when the Venetians lost their colony in the Morea (Peloponnese), a vital toehold in the Mediterranean, to the Turks.

As a result of these territorial setbacks, Venice's economy began to stagnate. Leading families still had vast inherited wealth, and the upper classes acquired a reputation for lavish spending on fine clothes, decadent parties, and gambling. The city was still a center for the arts, especially music. Its most famous composer was Vivaldi, who wrote both for the church and for private patrons. Vivaldi also composed concertos for the all-female orchestra of the Ospedale della Pietà, an orphanage where he worked. However, as the 18th century progressed, the once-hospitable city-state seemed to turn its back on the world, the harbors and Arsenale were quiet, and Venice only became truly animated at the time of the carnival.

1577 Andrea Palladio designs the Redentore church on the island of Giudecca.

1613 Composer Claudio Monteverdi is put in charge of music at St. Mark's Basilica.

Venice lost its last eastern Mediterranean island, Crete, in a long 17th-century war with Turkey.

1630 An epidemic of bubonic plague hits Venice, killing many.

Masked 17th-century plague doctor

1708 During a hard winter, the lagoon freezes over, from the islands to the mainland.

1715 The Turks take over Venice's colony in the Morea (present-day Peloponnese), ending the city's maritime empire.

△ RAIL BRIDGE
Bringing the railroad to Venice involved building a long bridge across the lagoon to a new station, Santa Lucia, on the Grand Canal, a feat accomplished in the mid-19th century.

Research suggests that building the rail bridge and piers exacerbated flooding, now made worse by climate change.

With its empire and much of its trade gone, Venice was no longer a major power in the later 18th century. Its port still functioned—the lagoon was protected by a sea wall, finished in the 1750s—and the city remained as beautiful as ever. It was well known to European aristocrats, some of whom visited, and many of whom bought paintings by Canaletto, who recorded its canal scenes in meticulous detail, often showing the waterways almost jammed with gondolas and sailing boats. Venice acquired a new glamour for some Europeans, who appreciated its cafés, opera house, and aesthetic appeal, but it did not attract high numbers of visitors. Napoleon, sensing the city's strategic importance, conquered it in 1797, putting an end to the independent republic. Napoleon passed Venice to his allies the Austrians, who ruled it for much of the 19th century.

Under Austrian rule

The Venetians reacted against the sometimes authoritarian rule of Austria, and supporters of the Risorgimento—a radical movement that aimed to reclaim Italy for the Italians and unite it as a single state—found refuge in the city. Daniele Manin was a local leader of the movement, and soon after he was arrested by the Austrians for treason, the Venetian population staged an uprising, a rebellion that was finally forced into submission through starvation and disease. The city's political troubles meant that there was little expansion or modernization in this period, so its palaces; churches; and picturesque, winding streets were preserved.

Venice's medieval heritage brought it other allies, such as the British writer John Ruskin, who published his book about the city, *The Stones of Venice*, in 1853. Ruskin praised the beauty of its medieval churches and palaces, portraying Gothic Venice as a kind of urban paradise where craft-workers and merchants alike lived in happiness and harmony. Ruskin's writings were well known, and travelers started to add Venice to their itinerary when they visited Italy. Some upper-class visitors even rented houses in Venice for several months or even years.

The rise of tourism

Two developments raised Venice's profile higher still. A railroad line linking the city to the European mainland was followed in 1869 by the opening of the Suez Canal, which drastically cut the time it took to travel from Europe to eastern Asia by sea. Venice became a major stopping-off point for travelers from all over Europe, from wealthy tourists to those involved in running the empires of Britain, Holland, and France, who paused in the city en route to the Far East. The Venetians built an enlarged harbor for large ships, and the city's future as a transportation interchange was ensured.

1720 Caffè Florian opens in St. Mark's Square.

1725 Antonio Vivaldi, musical director at Ospedale della Pietà, writes *The Four Seasons.*

1792 Teatro La Fenice, the city's most famous opera house, opens.

1797 Napoleon invades Venice, bringing an end to the independent Venetian Republic.

GRAN TEATRO LA FENICE

The phoenix rising from the ashes, symbol of La Fenice opera house

1798 Napoleon grants Venice to Austria.

1846 A railroad line is built, connecting Venice to the mainland by a long bridge.

1848 Venice rebels against Austrian rule and the republic is restored, but only lasts for one year.

By the end of the 19th century, the cultural tourists who followed Ruskin and the long-distance travelers were joined by a further group, those who enjoyed the beaches of Venice's Adriatic Lido resort, which was made famous by books such as Thomas Mann's *Death in Venice*. The combination of an unusual island setting, the carnival, and the pleasant climate turned Venice into a highly successful tourist city, a role it adopted enthusiastically throughout the 20th century and still plays today.

However, the huge influxes of visitors that this compact city has to cope with have brought their own strains. In summer, it is often hard to move in the narrow streets, and hotel accommodation is stretched, in spite of large developments on the mainland. The crowds are also inflated by passengers from cruise ships, which frequently stop at Venice's waterside. These cause powerful waves that threaten to damage buildings which are already slowly sinking on their poor foundations. The city is also troubled by storm flood damage, especially when the tide is at its highest. Flood protection plans are underway (despite political and administrative delays) and in 2021 Italian authorities approved a ban on cruise ships entering the historic center. Meanwhile, Venice's art, history, and unique beauty still entice millions of visitors.

△ *SUPPORT*, 2017
Lorenzo Quinn's sculpture was made for the 2017 Venice Art Biennale. It represents the help needed to counter the rising sea levels caused by climate change, which threaten Venice and its fragile buildings.

1851–1853 John Ruskin's *The Stones of Venice* is published, bringing a new interest in the city's distinctive architecture.

1895 The city's first Biennale exhibition of modern art is held.

1912 Thomas Mann's novella *Death in Venice* describes the Lido in its heyday as a seaside resort.

1932 The Venice Film Festival is founded.

1951 Peggy Guggenheim opens her home, Palazzo Venier dei Leoni, to visitors, displaying her collection of modern art.

1960 Venice airport opens to the north of the city.

2003 The MOSE project, to protect the city from floods using mobile water gates, begins construction.

Cape Town

THE MOTHER CITY

This stunning city by the sea has been a colonial fueling station, an imperial outpost, a hub for gold and diamonds, and a place of segregation. Today, Cape Town looks to a multicultural future.

In 1488, Portuguese explorer Bartolomeu Dias became the first European to sail around the southern tip of Africa. The Portuguese dubbed it Cabo da Boa Esperança, or Cape of Good Hope. The ships that followed would put ashore to take on fresh water, bringing them into contact with the Khoisan people, who had lived in the region for thousands of years. A mix of Khoikhoi herders and roving San hunter-gatherers, the Khoisan eschewed permanent settlements and crossed the Western Cape on seasonal migrations.

During the 17th century, the Dutch and English challenged the Portuguese for control of the sea routes around Africa to India and beyond, and the lucrative trade in spices. In 1652, the Dutch East India Company established a permanent base at Table Bay on the Cape of Good Hope, where ships could replenish their supplies. Under Jan van Riebeeck, the Dutch began the colonization of South Africa, introducing enslaved people from West Africa and Asia to provide labor as their farmsteads grew. Expansion led to clashes with the local Khoisan, whose society crumbled in the face of European firearms and diseases. The township on Table Bay came to be known as Kaapstad, Dutch for "Cape Town."

Kaapstad

The town had five streets running parallel from the shore toward Table Mountain, intersected by five cross streets. The wide roads were planted with oak trees to give shade, and produce was sold at the large Greenmarket Square. By the 1750s, the population stood at around 5,500 Europeans and 6,700 enslaved people, the latter mostly imported from Dutch-controlled territories in the Malay Archipelago. The emerging city was already a product of multiple cultures, influenced by Asia as much as Europe and Africa.

The Cape remained a vital staging post in the European exploitation of the East. Toward the end of the 18th century, Britain challenged the Dutch for possession of the Cape Colony. It passed back and forth between the two powers before it was conclusively ceded to the British in 1814.

19TH-CENTURY CAPE TOWN ▷
Situated between the ocean and flat-topped Table Mountain, Cape Town was established as a way station for ships making the arduous voyage between Europe and Southeast Asia.

1652 Jan van Riebeeck of the Dutch East India Company establishes a settlement on the Cape for the resupplying of company ships.

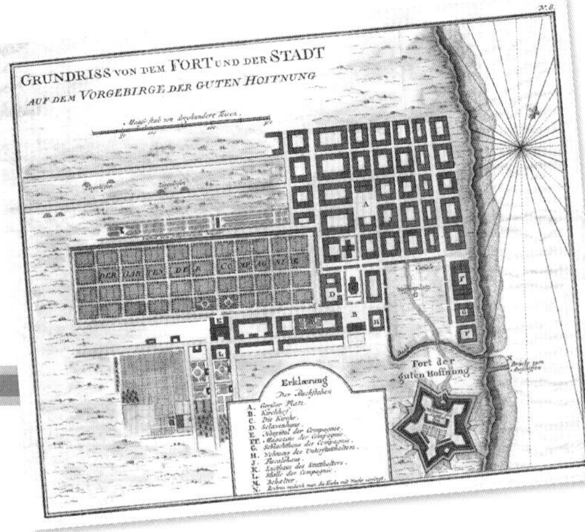

Map of Kaapstad (Cape Town) from 1750

1806 The British reoccupy the Cape Colony after the Battle of Blaauwberg, and British ownership is formalized in an 1814 treaty.

1488 Bartolomeu Dias sights Table Mountain from aboard the first European ship to round the southern tip of Africa.

1795 The British navy takes control of Cape Town and the Cape Colony territories. They are returned to the Dutch in the Treaty of Amiens in 1802.

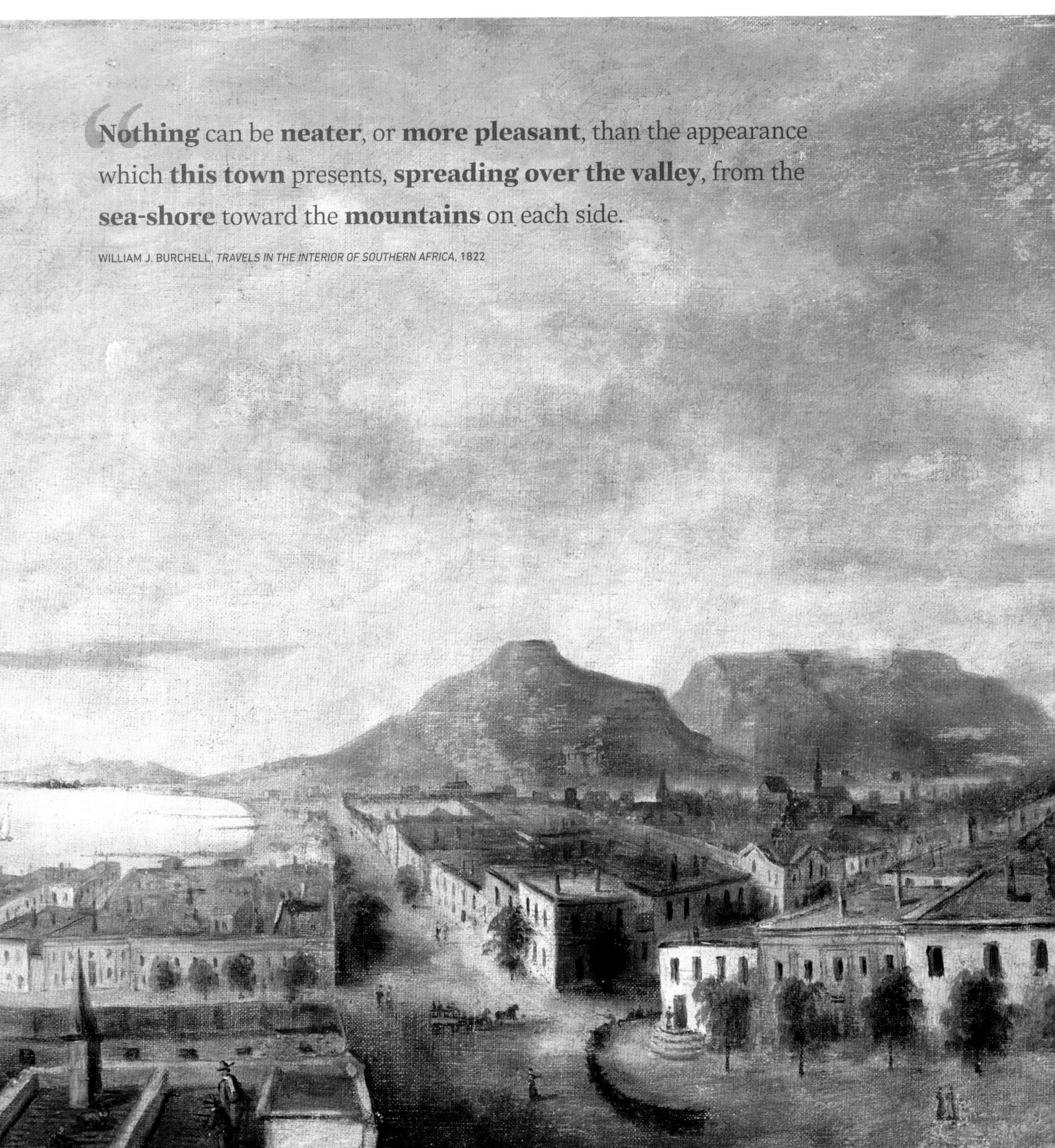

“**Nothing** can be **neater**, or **more pleasant**, than the appearance which **this town** presents, **spreading over the valley**, from the **sea-shore** toward the **mountains** on each side.

WILLIAM J. BURCHELL, *TRAVELS IN THE INTERIOR OF SOUTHERN AFRICA*, 1822

▷ **THE ENGLISH COLONIAL CITY**
In the late 19th century, Cape Town took on the appearance of a prosperous British Victorian town, as seen in this photograph of Adderley Street, with its Neoclassical General Post Office, Standard Bank building, and Grand Hotel.

Cape storms were notorious. Between 1839 and 1854 no fewer than 200 vessels were wrecked on the Cape coast in the vicinity of Table Bay.

England in Africa

Under the British, English replaced Afrikaans (the local variant of Dutch) as the official language of the Cape, and Cape culture was gradually Anglicized. In 1830, on St. George's Day (the day dedicated to England's patron saint), the city's British governor laid the foundation stone for St. George's Cathedral, and the main thoroughfare of Berg Street was renamed St. George's Street. The city gained colleges, museums, public libraries, banks, more places of worship, and a Royal Observatory, all reflecting British culture some 6,000 miles (10,000 km) to the north.

Slavery was outlawed in 1834, and formerly enslaved people established their own neighborhood, the Bo-Kaap. It remains a predominantly Muslim district today, reflecting the largely Malaysian heritage of the enslaved. However, even after they gained a semblance of freedom, many people were obliged to continue to work as indentured laborers for their colonial bosses for several years.

Many Dutch-Afrikaners were unhappy with British rule, and they abandoned the city and its environs by the thousands, intent on setting up their own state in the interior. Their mass migration led to them becoming known as Trekboers ("trekking farmers"), or simply Boers.

For much of the 19th century, Cape Town flourished, its economy boosted by regular shiploads of free-spending British colonial officers and administrators on their way to or from India. The opening of the Suez Canal in 1869 dramatically decreased shipping traffic, but any loss in the city's revenue was more than made up for by a dramatic discovery inland: great riches of gold and diamonds.

1834 In compliance with the rest of the British Empire, slavery is abolished in the Cape Colony. Formerly enslaved Asian people found their own neighborhood, the Bo-Kaap.

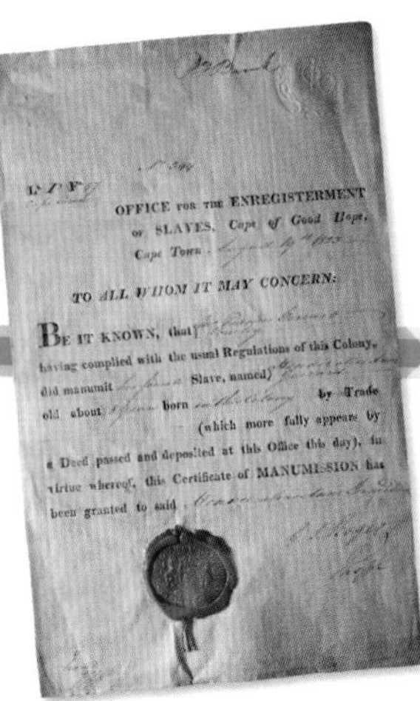

OFFICE FOR THE ENREGISTERMENT OF SLAVES, Cape of Good Hope, Cape Town

TO ALL WHOM IT MAY CONCERN:

BE IT KNOWN, that [handwritten] having complied with the usual Regulations of this Colony, did manumit [handwritten] Slave, named [handwritten] old about [handwritten] born [handwritten] by Trade (which more fully appears by a Deed passed and deposited at this Office this day), in virtue whereof, this Certificate of MANUMISSION has been granted to said [handwritten]

Slave registration document, dated 1823

1836 Dutch-descended Afrikaners embark on the Great Trek into the interior in order to live beyond the reach of British colonial rule.

1849 A petition signed by 450 citizens prevents the government in London from transporting British convicts to the Cape.

Six merino sheep, gifted by the Dutch government in 1789, launched a thriving 19th-century wool trade.

1859 The ground is broken for the colony's first railroad. The line to Wellington, 40 miles (60 km) inland, opens four years later.

A segregated city

Cape Town was flooded with fortune-seeking immigrants; from a population of around 45,000 in 1875, it reached 171,000 by 1904. The newly discovered mineral wealth, and the advent of the railroads that allowed its exploitation, meant Cape Town shifted its gaze from the sea inward into Africa. Prime Minister (and diamond-mine magnate) Cecil Rhodes instigated a land grab to control much of southern Africa. As the primary port for the region, Cape Town grew ever more wealthy, expressed most visibly in the raising of many new public buildings from the 1880s onward, including new Houses of Parliament, an opera house, and a new City Hall.

Rhodes also initiated the 1894 Glen Gray Act, which restricted Black Africans to segregated regions of the Cape and placed limitations on their land ownership. Rhodes's view was that Black people needed to be driven off their land to "stimulate them to labor." In 1901, an outbreak of bubonic plague was blamed on the city's rapidly rising Black population. By this time, an estimated 8,000 Black Africans—mainly Xhosa-speakers from the Eastern Cape—were living in Cape Town, and the disease provided an excuse for their forced relocation outside the city.

Dutch-descended Afrikaners also resented their poor status when compared with the English-speaking minority, who controlled Cape Town and the new country of South Africa, established through a union of provinces in 1910. Their discontent led to Afrikaner nationalism and the formation of the National Party. In 1948, under the leadership of D. F. Malan, the National Party won the general election, marking the beginning of the apartheid era.

Hanover Street runs through the **heart of District Six**, and along it one can feel the **pulse-beats of society**.

ALEX LA GUMA, "THE DEAD END KIDS OF HANOVER STREET," *NEW AGE*, 1956

DISTRICT SIX, 1982 ▷
District Six, the subject of this oil painting by Kenneth Baker, was a multiracial inner-city community from the mid-19th century. The "soul of Cape Town" inspired writers, artists, and a 1980s musical. Many residents were forced out under apartheid (see p. 197).

Searching for diamonds at the Kimberly Mine in the Northern Cape

1867 The discovery of diamonds and, in 1886, gold in the interior boosts the economy of Cape Town and spurs rapid growth.

1890 Cecil Rhodes becomes prime minister of the Cape Colony. His expansionist policies spark conflict with the Boers, and war is declared in 1899.

1910 The Act of Union forms the new nation of South Africa from the Cape Colony and the newly annexed Boer regions to the east.

1923 The Natives (Urban Areas) Act restricts Black people's access to Cape Town, and requires them to carry permits called "passes" at all times.

1929 The Table Mountain Aerial Cableway begins operating.

1948 The National Party comes to power. It promotes Afrikaner interests and institutes a national policy of racial segregation, or apartheid.

Discriminatory apartheid notice near Cape Town

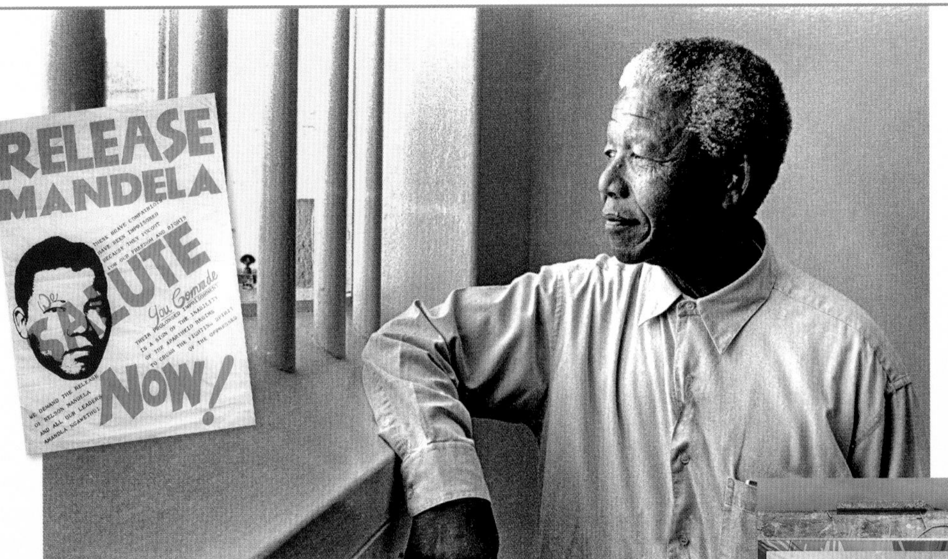

◁ Nelson Mandela, then the president of South Africa, revisits his former cell at Robben Island, where he was imprisoned for 18 of the 27 years he served behind bars.

△ This 1989 poster was part of a major international campaign for Nelson Mandela's freedom—he was eventually released in 1990.

▽ Mandela was far from the only anti-apartheid activist jailed on Robben Island, and several other prominent figures are celebrated on the island today.

Robben Island

Set in Table Bay, 7 miles (11 km) from Cape Town, small, flat Robben Island was occupied by seals and penguins before European settlers arrived. The Dutch named the island after its original residents (the Dutch word for seal is *robben*), and grazed sheep there, releasing rabbits to provide a food source for settlers. It has long served as a penal colony: historians believe the first prisoner on the island, in the mid-17th century, was Autshumato, a Cape tribal chief. The Dutch later held other political prisoners there, including royalty from their East Indian colonies. The British continued the tradition when, in 1819, they imprisoned an African Xhosa leader on the island. The most famous political prisoner of all was Nelson Mandela. He and his fellow anti-apartheid activists endured a harsh regime in cells only 44 ft (4 m) square, and were made to work in a quarry digging out limestone. Largely because of Mandela's association with the site, Robben Island, which is a 30-minute ferry ride from Cape Town, is now a popular tourist destination—former inmates act as guides.

> "**Real leaders** must be ready to **sacrifice all** for the **freedom** of their **people**.
>
> FORMER PRESIDENT NELSON MANDELA, 1998

A protest against the obligatory identity cards, 1956

1950s The previously desolate Cape Flats area is developed by the government to keep "Coloreds and Blacks" out of the city's "whites-only" center.

1964 Nelson Mandela is sentenced to life imprisonment on Robben Island.

1968 The government declares the inner-city neighborhood of District Six a "whites-only" area and forcibly relocates over 30,000 non-whites.

1986 Desmond Tutu, a powerful anti-apartheid voice, becomes Anglican Archbishop of Cape Town.

Famed jazz pianist Abdullah Ibrahim was born Adolph Brand in 1934 in Cape Town. He moved to New York in 1965.

△ TABLE MOUNTAIN AND BAY
Cape Town's spectacular natural features include Signal Hill (center), Lion's Peak (right), and Table Mountain (behind). The Cape Town Stadium (left) was constructed for the 2010 soccer World Cup.

Apartheid means the "state of being apart." The aim was to preserve the "purity" of the white race in its promised land. All South Africans were classified by race: White, Colored (Asian and mixed race, with Indians sometimes in their own category), or Black. The 1950 Group Areas Act defined where people of each ethnicity could live, and the 1953 Separate Amenities Act created separate public facilities. Black people were compelled to carry passes at all times and were prohibited from living in or even visiting many places without specific permission. In Cape Town, this led to the growth of large Black-populated shanty towns on the plains to the east of the city. Although Colored people were favored over Black citizens, they were also discriminated against. In 1968, for example, the historic Colored area of District Six was classified as a "white area"; its population was evicted and bulldozers sent in.

The rule of equality

Only hours after being released from prison in February 1990 (see box), Nelson Mandela made a public speech from the balcony of Cape Town's City Hall. It heralded the dawn of a new era for South Africa. Four years later, South Africans of all colors cast their votes in the country's first-ever fully democratic elections, and Mandela became president. In 1998, Nomaindia Mfeketo became Cape Town's first Black mayor.

In 2004, in a symbolic act, former residents evicted almost 40 years before were handed keys to new homes in District Six. Showcase events, such as the soccer World Cup of 2010, and the city's role as World Design Capital in 2014, have brought international attention. Cape Town is now known for its breathtaking natural beauty, outdoor lifestyle, gourmet dining, Afro-chic culture, and wine-growing hinterlands. Its citizens hail from a rich mix of cultural backgrounds, exemplifying Archbishop Desmond Tutu's characterization of South Africa as a "Rainbow Nation." Inequality persists, and there are still large areas of Black slums, mostly in the Cape Flats beyond Table Mountain. But Cape Town has transformed itself before, and now this dynamic city looks to the future from its grand cape-side perch.

1990 Nelson Mandela is released from prison and gives his first public speech from the balcony of the City Hall.

1994 Following democratic elections, Nelson Mandela becomes president of South Africa.

1998 After a breakdown in law and order, a vigilante organization bombs the city's V&A Waterfront. Two people are killed and 26 injured.

2003 Cape Town–born writer J. M. Coetzee wins the Nobel Prize for Literature.

2010 South Africa hosts the soccer World Cup, and eight games are played at the Cape Town Stadium, which was built for the tournament.

2015 Severe droughts see reservoir water levels decline. By 2017, officials feared city water supplies would dry up, but heavy rains in 2018 averted the crisis.

2017 The Zeitz Museum of Contemporary Art Africa (Zeitz MOCAA) opens at the V&A Waterfront.

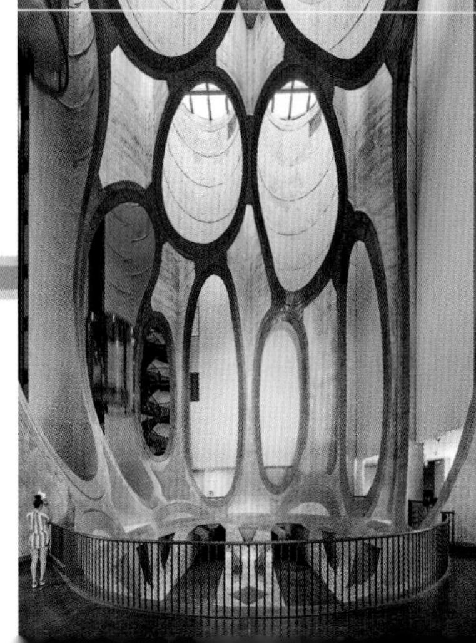

Interior of the Zeitz Museum

Shanghai

PEARL OF THE ORIENT

This former international port and playground of the elite gave birth to Chinese communism and is now a towering, futuristic global city of entrepreneurs, financiers, and visionaries.

For much of the last 200 years, Shanghai has been China's gateway to the wider world. But for centuries prior to this it was a small, isolated fishing village, with trade instead passing through Qinglong Town—now part of the Shanghai suburbs—to the west. By the 1400s, Shanghai's favorable position on the Yangtze delta, with its safe harbor on the tributary Huangpu River, saw it begin to prosper as a port. The population grew, thanks in part to migrants displaced by Mongol invasions to the north, and during the Ming dynasty it became a center for the processing and shipping of the cotton grown in the region. In the 1550s, a wall was built around the city as a defense against Japanese raids.

Prised open by opium

Half a century later, in 1603, the proselytizing Italian Jesuit Matteo Ricci became the city's first recorded Western visitor. Such arrivals were rare. Trade with Europe was carefully controlled, and mostly funneled through the southern port of Guangzhou (Canton). By the 1780s, the British East India Company came to dominate this trade due to the strength of the Royal Navy, and British desire for Chinese tea, silks, and porcelain created a trade deficit. To balance the books, the British sold increasing amounts of opium, which they cultivated in India, to the Chinese. When the Qing court tried to halt the trade, Britain responded with gunboats, triggering the First Opium War in 1839. The Chinese were defeated, and were forced to agree to the 1842 Treaty of Nanjing, which ceded Hong Kong to the British, and gave them the right to operate in five mainland cities, one of which was Shanghai.

Foreign concessions

British traders were allotted land just north of the walled city. They named their stretch of riverfront the Bund, from the Hindi for "embankment." By 1850, merchants from France, the US, and other foreign powers began to move into Shanghai, creating their own sovereign zones, known as "concessions," where they were not subject to Chinese laws.

A 21ST-CENTURY CITY ▷
The glittering bauble of the Oriental Pearl Tower is emblematic of modern Shanghai, a city where everything is bigger, faster, more expensive, and neon-drenched.

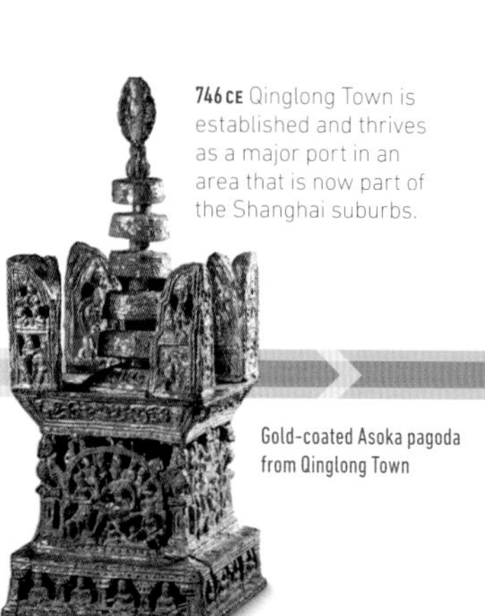

746 CE Qinglong Town is established and thrives as a major port in an area that is now part of the Shanghai suburbs.

Gold-coated Asoka pagoda from Qinglong Town

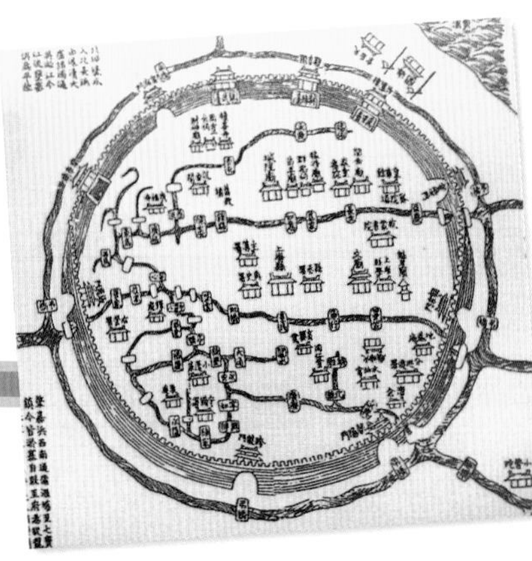

1553–1554 During the Ming dynasty, engineers encircle Shanghai with a defensive wall to protect against Japanese raiders.

1559 Pan Yunduan, the Ming-era governor of Sichuan, constructs the Yu Gardens in Shanghai for his father.

1842 Following the First Opium War, the defeated Qing court signs the Treaty of Nanjing, which opens up Shanghai to foreign merchants.

△ **THE BUND, 19TH CENTURY**
The foreign settlers turned a muddy towpath on the Huangpu River into a broad waterfront promenade lined with merchant buildings and wharves.

The 19th-century slang term to "shanghai" meant to kidnap and press someone into service as a sailor to a destination far away.

In 1850, the Taiping Rebellion plunged China into a vast civil war that set the Taiping Christian sect against the ruling Qing dynasty. When Taiping forces menaced Shanghai, they were forced back by British and French soldiers. In the wake of the unrest, the foreigners took advantage of local weakness to expand their settlements so that the Chinese became a minority in their own city. As the money poured in from trade, the European powers turned Shanghai into China's most modern city, the first in the country to have gas lights, telephones, trams, electric power, and running water.

The battle for Shanghai

Foreign influence was soon to grow. When the Chinese suffered defeat in the First Sino–Japanese War of 1895, Japan claimed the right to build factories in Shanghai, which it ran on cheap Chinese labor. In time, the situation in the city, with rich foreign capitalists exploiting uneducated but increasingly organized Chinese laborers, would have huge repercussions for the whole of China. It began with Chinese students leading anti-Japanese and anti-Western strikes, accompanied by boycotts of foreign goods. This new movement formed links with international communism and, in 1921, Mao Zedong and others held the first meeting of the Chinese Communist Party in a small house in Shanghai.

In 1932, following anti-Japanese rioting, Japanese troops invaded Chinese-administered parts of Shanghai. International condemnation forced them out, but in 1937, after a bloody three-month assault, they occupied the Chinese districts again. They completed their invasion in 1941—on the same morning as the attack on Pearl Harbor—by occupying the international concessions. The Japanese would remain in control for the next three years, until their defeat by the Americans at the end of World War II, when the whole of the city was handed back to the Chinese.

1846 Scottish merchant Peter Richards founds Richards' Hotel, the first Western hotel in Shanghai and China.

1849 The French negotiate the same settlement rights in Shanghai as the British and establish the French Concession.

1854 The British, French, and Americans create the Shanghai Municipal Council to serve their interests in the city.

1863 The British and American settlements combine to form the International Settlement.

1895 The Chinese are defeated in the First Sino–Japanese War and the Japanese win the right to exploit Shanghai.

Opium den in Shanghai

1917 An international decree outlaws opium and Shanghai becomes filled with smugglers and gangsters.

Shanghai highlife

Despite the political uncertainties, a lot of money was made in Shanghai in the 1920s and '30s. Life for the elite (known as *taipans*) revolved around members' clubs, horse races, costume balls, and nightclubs, particularly the dance palaces with their "taxi dancers"—women whose company on the dance floor was bought with a ticket. Shanghai was also a notoriously lawless city, home to a thriving sex trade, opium dens, and gun-toting gangsters. A handful of underworld bosses controlled the city, buying off the members of the Municipal Council and channeling illicit funds into respectable businesses, including their own banks. Some Chinese people prospered in this Western-dominated city, such as *compradors*, who acted as local facilitators for international businesses. But its exploitation and decadence, and the chasm between the elite and the crushing poverty of much of the native population, would trigger a backlash following Mao's takeover in 1949.

> "If **God lets Shanghai endure**, he **owes an apology** to **Sodom and Gomorrah.**"
>
> SHANGHAI MISSIONARY

▷ The Bund was a showcase for the city's foreign wealth. Its grandiose architecture was capped in 1929 by the pyramid-roofed Cathay Hotel.

◁ Shanghai's aura of glamour was popularized in images such as this 1930s graphic, which enticed visitors with the promise of exoticism and excitement.

1921 The first meeting of the Chinese Communist Party takes place in a house in Shanghai's French Concession.

1932 The Japanese Navy bombards Shanghai in response to Chinese student protests against the Japanese occupation of Manchuria.

1937 Japanese troops take control of Shanghai.

The 2020 Chinese blockbuster film *The Eight Hundred* dramatizes the desperate defense of the Sihang Warehouse during the 1937 Battle of Shanghai.

1945 American forces occupy Shanghai following Japan's surrender at the end of World War II.

1949 The Communist People's Liberation Army marches into Shanghai and Mao forms the People's Republic of China.

A flagship Chinese city

On May 25, 1949, the Mao-led Communists marched into Shanghai, taking over from the Chinese Nationalist leadership of Chiang Kai-shek. The new government singled out Shanghai as the embodiment of bourgeois excess and cracked down hard. In 1953, it was announced that all Shanghai companies were to be "owned by the people." Many foreigners had departed during the 1940s, and the last few left at the news. For the next four decades, Shanghai's economy slowed as its revenues were redirected to Beijing and used to fund regional development within China.

China grew increasingly open to market forces in the 1980s, but Shanghai had to wait nearly a decade before China's government allowed it to develop. Until the late 1980s, the city's tallest building remained the 22-story Park Hotel, built in 1934. Then, in 1990, the government in Beijing decreed that Shanghai was to become the country's new economic powerhouse. "If China is a dragon," said China's then-leader, Deng Xiaoping, "Shanghai is its head."

In the three decades since, the city has been transformed. Across the river from the Bund, a thumb of marshland was designated an investment-friendly Special Economic Zone. The area, called Pudong, saw rapid development, including the city's first skyscraper, the Oriental Pearl Tower, in 1995. Since then, Pudong has become the main financial district, home of the nation's stock market and bristling with high-rises. These include the world's second-highest building, the Shanghai Tower, which stands at 2,073 ft (632 m) and has 128 floors. Together with the Shanghai World Financial Center and Jinmao Tower (which at the time of completion contained the highest hotel in the world, occupying floors 53 to 87) it forms the world's first adjacent

◁ JING'AN TEMPLE
The city's oldest temple was first built in 247 CE but was destroyed during China's Cultural Revolution (1966–1976) and turned into a plastics factory. It was rebuilt in the 1980s.

1972 Shanghai hosts the historic meeting between Chinese Premier Zhou Enlai and US President Richard Nixon. They sign the Shanghai Communiqué, which enables the two countries to normalize relations.

1990 Shanghai's Pudong district is declared a Special Economic Zone, marking the rebirth of the city.

1995 Construction is completed on the Oriental Pearl Tower, which immediately becomes an icon of the new Shanghai.

2003 The Shanghai Maglev, the world's fastest train at 270 mph (430 kph), begins service between Pudong International Airport and the city.

2010 For the 2010 Shanghai Expo, the city builds numerous cultural venues, including the striking China Pavilion, now the China Art Museum.

◁ **PUDONG'S SUPER-TALL TRIO**
When the Jinmao Tower (center, with an illuminated spire) was completed in 1999 it was China's tallest building. It's now dwarfed by the Shanghai Tower (left) and Shanghai World Financial Center (right).

grouping of three super-tall skyscrapers. Shanghai also boasts the world's fastest commercial train, connecting Pudong International Airport with the city center.

Meanwhile, the former grand headquarters of insurance firms and banks on the Bund have become the settings for luxury brands and restaurants, where Chinese new money shops for Italian suits, French fashion accessories, and Swiss watches, and grazes on tasting menus prepared by the world's top chefs. Many of the historic Art Deco gems of the former French Concession have been preserved and repurposed into more stylish restaurants and hotels. Since the city hosted the Shanghai Expo in 2010, it has also been graced with a large number of significant new cultural institutions including art museums, theaters, and concert halls.

Back in the early 20th century, Shanghai used to be referred to as the "Paris of the East" for its lifestyle and beauty. These days, any comparisons with other cities are redundant: Shanghai is out on its own, racing into the future.

> "**New York** may be the **city that never sleeps**, but **Shanghai** doesn't even **sit down**, and not just because there is **no room**.
>
> PATRICIA MARX, *NEW YORKER*, 2008

2016 Shanghai Disneyland opens as the first Disney park in mainland China.

2017 Work finishes on the Shanghai Tower, at 2,073 ft (632 m) the world's second-tallest building. It has the world's fastest elevators.

In 2019, Shanghai had over 24 million residents, making it China's most populous city—and the third-largest in the world.

Sydney

HARBOR CITY

Born as a British penal colony on Aboriginal lands, today Sydney is one of the world's most international cities, with a glorious harbor and beachside lifestyle.

In 1770, the British ship HMS *Endeavour* dropped anchor in what would become known as Botany Bay. Its captain, James Cook, in the company of some 40 men, was rowed ashore to be met by two Aboriginal people, whose ancestors had lived in the area for tens of thousands of years. "They called to us," recorded the naturalist Joseph Banks, "very loud in a harsh-sounding language," of which the crew "understood not a word." What some historians believe the original inhabitants of the Sydney area said was, "Warra warra wai!"—meaning "Go away!"

Penal settlement

Instead, 18 years later, on January 26 (a date still marked as Australia Day), the First Fleet of 11 British ships arrived just north of Botany Bay in Sydney Cove, which they named for Lord Sydney, the British Home Secretary. A party led by Captain Arthur Phillip planted a British flag and claimed possession of the territory before unloading 732 convicts who had been deported from the United Kingdom. These convicts, along with their guards and a handful of officials, established the colony that would become Sydney, the founding settlement of the new entity of Australia.

Two years later, the Second Fleet arrived, bearing more convicts. Subsequent vessels also brought free settlers, who Phillip believed were vital to the colonization of the new land. The Europeans carried smallpox with them, devastating Aboriginal communities. They had no immunity to the disease, and were forced off their lands. Sydney's story would be written not by Australia's Indigenous people, but by their colonizers.

▽ *SYDNEY HARBOR*, 1907
Australian Impressionist Arthur Streeton painted this view of Sydney Harbor – the busy seaport dotted with sailboats, clippers, and steamships – on his return to Australia after a decade spent in Europe.

From 45,000 BCE Aboriginal people live in the area that would become Sydney, according to the dating of tools found in the region.

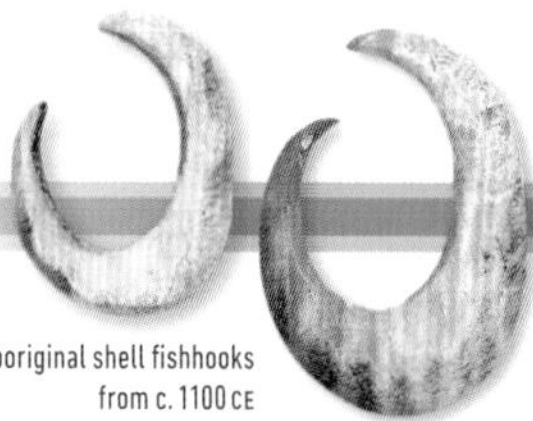

Aboriginal shell fishhooks from c. 1100 CE

1770 CE HMS *Endeavour*, commanded by Captain James Cook, is the first European ship to chart this part of the Australian coast, making land at Botany Bay.

1788 The British colony of New South Wales is established with the arrival of the First Fleet under Captain Arthur Phillip.

1790 The Second Fleet arrives. More than a quarter of its 1,006 convicts had died during the long voyage.

1797 After tension with colonists, 100 Aboriginal people attack a farm at Parramatta, west of Sydney, and suffer heavy losses.

> "We had the **satisfaction** of finding the **finest harbor in the world**, in which a thousand **sail of the line** may ride in the most **perfect security**.

GOVERNOR ARTHUR PHILLIP, MAY 15, 1788

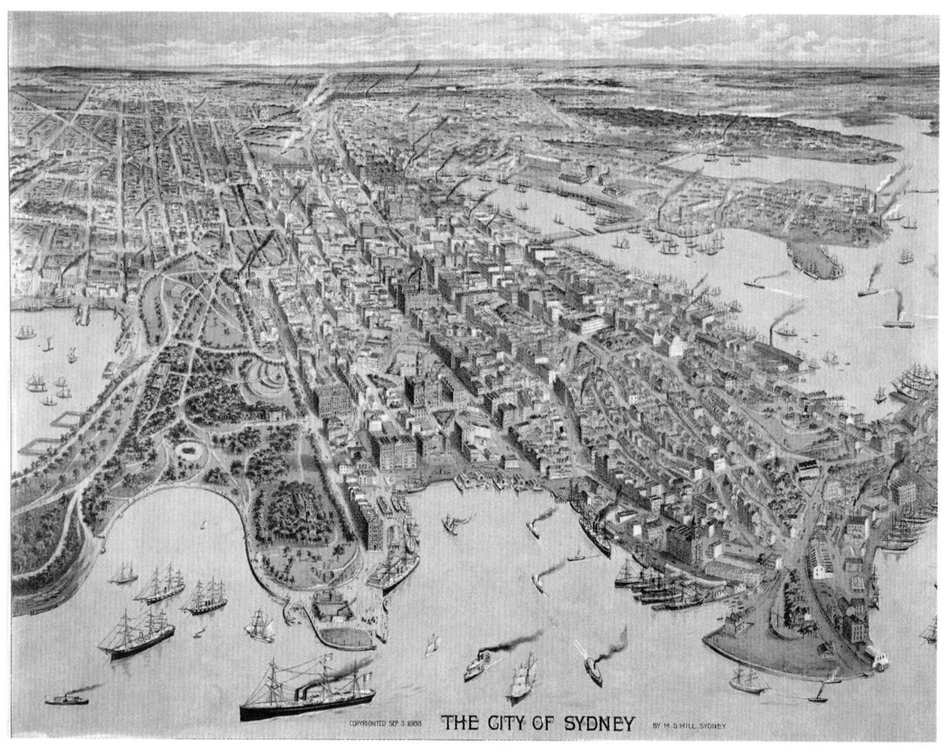

△ *THE CITY OF SYDNEY*, 1888
The first European settlement was established at Sydney Cove, which is at the centre of this map by M.S. Hill celebrating the city's centenary. The area is now known as Circular Quay..

On December 28, 1809, a new governor, Lachlan Macquarie, arrived from Britain and stepped ashore at Sydney Cove. He took up his duties on the first day of the new year. Macquarie later wrote that the town was "barely emerging from a state of infantile imbecility," with few roads and public buildings, and with commerce still in its "early dawn." He laid the groundwork for modern central Sydney, based on his own street plan. The grandest street, home to some of the most prestigious buildings—including what is now Parliament House—he named after himself.

Australia's first city

In 1840, the British government largely ended convict transportation to mainland Australia, and in November that year, the *Eden* was the last convict ship to arrive in the bay. Sydney started to shape a future that would erase its penal origins. Within a decade, free settlers outnumbered convicts in the city, a trend that massively accelerated in the 1850s, when gold was discovered inland and prospectors rushed to Sydney from all over the world.

Sydney Cove continued to reflect the city's history, with the governor's residence in its botanical garden setting on one side and, across the water, the narrow streets, pestilential slums, brothels, and drinking dens of "the Rocks" on the other. Between them, a sober Victorian city was taking shape. The rapidly swelling population necessitated massive building projects. In 1868, Sydney's first royal visitor, HRH Prince Alfred, Duke of Edinburgh, laid a foundation stone for a new town hall inspired by Paris's Hôtel de Ville. The same year, Archbishop Polding laid the foundation stone for the magnificently Gothic St. Mary's Cathedral beside the expansive Hyde Park.

By now, Sydney's residents could attend university, go to the museum, or take horse-drawn omnibuses out into the country. Australia's first rugby club was founded in Sydney in 1863 and the inaugural first-class cricket match at the Sydney Cricket Ground was played between New South Wales and Victoria in 1878. (The first actual recorded cricket match in Australia had taken place in Sydney way back in 1803.)

Reporting on the centenary celebrations in 1888, the *Sydney Morning Herald* noted that the city was full of visitors from the Australian colonies and New Zealand,

1799 Government House is constructed in Parramatta for Governor John Hunter. It remains Australia's oldest public building.

1810 The 11-year rule of Governor Lachlan Macquarie begins. He oversees Sydney's transition from a penal colony to a free society.

1831 The *Sydney Herald* newspaper begins publication. It is renamed the *Sydney Morning Herald* in 1841.

1840 The Sydney City Council is established. Two years later the former colonial settlement is officially recognized as a township.

An 1850s game inspired by the Australian gold rush

1851 Gold is discovered in the Sydney hinterlands and large numbers of immigrant miners pour into the city, swelling the population from 39,000 to 200,000 within 20 years.

1868 Sydney's first royal visitor, Prince Alfred, Duke of Edinburgh, lays the foundation stone of Sydney Town Hall.

> “The **best things** about Sydney are free: the **sunshine’s free**, and the **harbor’s free**, and the **beach is free**.
>
> RUSSELL CROWE, ACTOR, 2015

with upward of 50,000 spectators present for the unveiling of a statue to Queen Victoria. Absent, however, would have been Sydney’s remaining Aboriginal people, who in the 1880s were removed to a reserve far from the center. That same centenary year, several boats carrying Chinese immigrants into Sydney were turned away. Chinese people had been arriving in the city since the 1840s, but protests against cheap Chinese labor were beginning to have an effect, culminating in the 1901 White Australia policy, a set of acts and policies which largely prevented people of non-European ethnic origin, especially Asians and Pacific Islanders, from moving to Australia. For the first half of the 20th century, preference was given to British immigrants above all others.

BONDI BEACH ACROBATICS ▷
Sydney beach culture boomed in the early 20th century. It was a great form of cheap entertainment, and up to 50,000 people visited Bondi Beach on summer days.

Invitation to the opening of the Queen Victoria Building

1878 The inaugural cricket match at the Sydney Cricket Ground is played between New South Wales and Victoria.

1879 The city holds the Sydney International Exhibition to showcase its industrial, scientific, and cultural achievements to the world.

1898 The city’s landmark Queen Victoria Building (QVB) is completed.

1900 Bubonic plague arrives in Sydney and kills 103 people. It is most virulent in the waterfront slums and leads to demolition and rebuilding in the Rocks.

1901 With the inauguration of the Commonwealth of Australia on January 1, Sydney becomes the capital of New South Wales.

1907 The world’s first surf lifesaving club is founded at Bondi Beach.

1915 Duke Kahanamoku of Hawaii introduces surfing to Sydney.

Post-war arrivals

△ Immigrants on the MV *Toscana* about to depart Trieste in 1954.

△ An Assisted Passage advertisement.

In 1947, Australia opened its doors to wartime refugees from Southern Europe to provide the labor needed for a booming economy. Tens of thousands took the opportunity to start a new life, with Sydney becoming the final destination of a large majority of them. The flow of new arrivals was augmented by the Assisted Passage program, which saw the Australian government offer to subsidize the fares of people across Europe who wanted to escape post-war austerity and find a new life on the other side of the world. All the immigrants would have to pay was the equivalent of £10. The scheme attracted over one million people from Great Britain alone—they became known as the "£10 poms." The immigrant intake dramatically increased Sydney's population, which rose by over 120,000 between 1946 and 1951.

> "To be **Australian** is ... a representation of our **shared history**, whether you **landed here by boat or by air**, or have had your ancestry rooted here for **thousands of years**.

PRITIKA DESAI, A FIRST-GENERATION CITIZEN OF AUSTRALIA, OF INDIAN ORIGIN, 2017

Opened in 1935, Sydney's Luna Park is one of only two amusement parks in the world that are protected by government legislation.

1930 At the Sydney Cricket Ground, legendary batter Don Bradman enters the record books with 452 runs not out in 415 minutes.

1932 Following eight years of construction, Sydney Harbor Bridge opens to traffic.

1934 The city's Anzac War Memorial in Hyde Park is raised to the memory of 60,000 Australians who lost their lives in World War I.

HARBOR BRIDGE FIREWORKS ▷
Fireworks displays using the pylons, arch, and catwalk of the Harbor Bridge have been a Sydney signature since the 1980s, notably each New Year's Eve and for the 2000 Olympics.

Leaving Europe behind

In the early 20th century, a city improvement board recommended workers move from the center to the suburbs. The wealthy, who had already planted their villas on the headlands and bays fringing the harbor, were joined by developments of low-rise bungalows. Increasingly, habits no longer mimicked those of Britain: the suburban Sydneysider enjoyed a relaxed, outdoor-oriented lifestyle, echoing that of Southern California, which shared a similar climate. The city's second most-famous landmark, the Harbor Bridge, was built in 1932 to facilitate expansion on the north side of the harbor.

There is no better symbol of the shift in the city's identity than the Opera House. When it was completed in 1973, the arts venue looked like nothing else—perhaps a flock of gulls on the wing or soaring sails. It was the work of Danish architect Jørn Utzon, but it owed nothing to European traditions. This fresh, forward-looking building, in the words of US architect Frank Gehry, "changed the image of an entire country."

Meanwhile, with the abolition of the White Australia policy in the mid-1960s, the flow from Europe was eclipsed by arrivals from Asia. Sydney rapidly transitioned into one of the world's most multicultural cities. Today, almost half of its citizens were born overseas, and in parts of the city you are as likely to hear Arabic, Mandarin, Cantonese, or Vietnamese as you are English. This diversity is a symbol of the city, celebrated in festivals and in the opening ceremony of the Sydney-set 2000 Olympics, which highlighted immigration and Aboriginal culture. With its semitropical climate, glorious harbor, multiethnic tapestry, and pervasive air of opportunity, the bay to which Britain once banished its undesirables is now one of the world's most admired cities.

The large granite pylons framing the Harbor Bridge have a purely aesthetic function.

1947 The Australian Government launches an ambitious immigration program that results in a population boom in Sydney.

1973 The Sydney Opera House officially opens. During 14 years of construction its cost rose from AU$7 million to AU$102 million.

1988 An estimated 2.5 million gather around Sydney Harbor to celebrate Australia's bicentennial with a First Fleet reenactment and fireworks.

2000 Sydney hosts the Olympic Games and wows the world with memorable opening and closing ceremonies.

2016 Sydney's population passes five million.

2019 The first line of the Sydney Metro opens.

Presidio Ave California
& Market
Streets

San Francisco

GOLDEN GATE CITY

The ultimate boom or bust city, San Francisco is a bayside beauty that has seen earthquakes, fires, and gold rushes. It's been a cradle of countercultural cool—and has also been shaped by floods of money.

Human habitation in the area that is now San Francisco Bay dates back to at least 3000 BCE. When the first Spanish ship entered the bay in 1775, it was the home of the Yelamu people, who moved seasonally between several villages along the coast. Recognizing the large, sheltered natural harbor's strategic significance, the Spanish dispatched an overland expedition from Mexico under Captain Juan Bautista de Anza, who established a military garrison, or *presidio*, on the headland in 1776.

Later that year, Franciscan priest Father Francisco Palóu found a site 3 miles (5 km) to the southeast for a mission (Misión San Francisco de Asís, or simply Mission Dolores) that would spread Christianity to the Yelamu. The mission employed Indigenous conscript workers, many of them forcibly relocated. They were housed between the *presidio* and the mission, on a site that became known as Yerba Buena ("good herb"), after the aromatic local plant.

◁ UPHILL RIDES
Installed in 1873, San Francisco's now-iconic cable cars, shown in this 1950s poster for airline TWA, were inspired by the cable-hauled carts used in California's gold mines.

The Americans and the gold rush

In the decades that followed, Yerba Buena became a town of a few hundred people. Despite the deaths of many of the Indigenous workers to European diseases, it expanded from the original workers' settlement down to the cove where ships moored. California became part of Mexico when the country gained its independence from Spain in 1821, before being captured by the US during the Mexican–American War in 1846. The Americans renamed the town San Francisco after the original mission, and in 1848 a discovery was made that would transform its fortunes: a laborer named James Marshall spotted gold in the water flowing through the sawmill where he worked.

San Francisco's Filbert Street is one of the world's steepest major streets, with a gradient of up to 31.5 percent.

> One day **I'll go to Heaven** and **I'll look around** and say, 'It ain't bad **but it ain't San Francisco.**'
>
> HERB CAEN, HUMORIST AND JOURNALIST

3000 BCE The Ohlone people are already settled on the Northern California coast, living in small hunter-gatherer villages. The Ohlone group that live in the San Francisco Bay are known as the Yelamu.

1775 CE The Spanish packet-boat *San Carlos* is the first European ship to sail into what will later be called San Francisco Bay.

1776 Spanish colonizers, including Captain Juan Bautista de Anza and Franciscan priest Francisco Palóu, arrive at the future site of San Francisco and build the *presidio* and Mission Dolores.

1835 The US attempts to buy Northern California from Mexico. The Mexicans instead try to sell it to Britain.

1846 The US Navy captures the small settlement of Yerba Buena. The following January, they rename it San Francisco.

1848 A laborer spots a glint of gold in a stream. When the find is publicized it triggers the California Gold Rush the following year.

◁ 1906 EARTHQUAKE
Buildings that survived the initial devastation were then subject to several days of raging fires caused by broken gas pipes and torn electric cables.

△ A CITY REBORN
The Panama–Pacific International Exposition of 1915 was held ostensibly to celebrate the Panama Canal, but it announced the post-quake rebirth of San Francisco.

The California Gold Rush transformed San Francisco from a wild frontier post to a booming and even wilder city on the make. Eager prospectors arrived via the port city, raising the population from less than a thousand in 1848 to 25,000 by the end of 1849 and 56,000 10 years later. San Francisco transitioned from a city of tents and flimsy shacks to one of brick and stone. The once-bare plaza at the heart of Yerba Buena was now Portsmouth Square, location of a new City Hall and the Hall of Justice. Along with these grand civic edifices came merchants, bars, brothels, and gambling dens to relieve any successful gold diggers of their earnings. The seeds of San Francisco's multiculturalism were sown at this time, notably with the arrival of thousands of Chinese people, who came to build the transcontinental railroad that would connect the boom city to the rest of the US. They settled near Portsmouth Square and what is now Grant Avenue, which became the city's official Chinatown—the only part of town where Chinese people were legally allowed to live and inherit property.

The earthquake

By 1900, the population had grown to over 300,000. On the morning of April 18, 1906, many of them were shaken awake by a massive earthquake. The tremors lasted less than a minute, but tore the city apart, destroying buildings, causing fires, killing an estimated 3,000, and leaving half the population homeless.

Remarkably, within just 10 years San Francisco bounced back. The earthquake's devastation was used as an opportunity for regeneration. Streets were widened and the city gained a new civic center complex, capped by a 1915 Beaux-Arts City Hall, with a dome higher than that of its model, the US Capitol in Washington, D.C. While the rest of the country suffered in the Great Depression of the 1930s, San Francisco carried on building. It gained its grand Opera House in 1932 and Museum of Modern Art in 1935. The next year saw the completion of the San Francisco–Oakland Bay Bridge, followed six months later by the Golden Gate Bridge, at the time the longest and the tallest—and perhaps the most beautiful—suspension bridge in the world.

1864 Samuel Clemens, better known as Mark Twain, settles in the city and finds work on a local paper. He calls his new home "the liveliest, heartiest community on our continent."

1906 San Francisco is hit by a devastating earthquake that destroys over 80 percent of the city.

1915 An ambitious rebuild is capped by the completion of an imposing new City Hall.

1934 A former military jail on a craggy island in the bay is converted into a federal penitentiary named Alcatraz.

1937 Workers complete the Golden Gate Bridge, which connects the city with Marin County. Its main span stretches for a record-breaking 4,200 ft (1,280 m).

1953 Lawrence Ferlinghetti opens the City Lights bookstore, establishing San Francisco as a locus for Beat Generation writers, poets, and thinkers, including Allen Ginsberg (right).

1963 Alcatraz closes as a federal penitentiary. The following year it is occupied by Native American activists, part of a rising tide of protests for Indigenous rights.

CITY OF DREAMS ▷
Commenting on San Francisco's inspirational qualities, musician Paul Kantner of Jefferson Airplane once memorably described the city as "49 square miles surrounded by reality."

Capital of counter culture

During World War II, the city remained buoyant as more than 1.5 million troops passed through on their way to the Pacific, most of them bent on having a good time before they shipped out. After the war, a feeling of disillusionment with the mainstream, as well as the influences of jazz and mysticism, shaped a group of writers, artists, and agitators who became known as the Beat Generation. With Lawrence Ferlinghetti's City Lights bookstore as their headquarters, the Beats made San Francisco the nonconformist capital of the US. In the mid-1960s, the baton passed to the hippies, who turned the Haight-Ashbury district into the center for 1967's drugged-up, psychedelic "Summer of Love," soundtracked by the Grateful Dead, Janis Joplin, and Jefferson Airplane. The city remained radical in the 1970s through its associations with the LGBTQ+ social movement.

In 1989, the city was hit by a terrible earthquake, almost as severe as that of 1906. Several freeways collapsed, along with part of the Bay Bridge's upper deck, and more than 19,000 homes were destroyed. Again, city officials seized the chance to improve civic facilities, notably replacing the damaged Embarcadero Freeway, an eyesore that had divided the waterfront from downtown, with a smaller boulevard and a thriving waterfront promenade and plaza.

"**San Francisco itself is art**, above all **literary art**. Every block is a **short story**, every **hill a novel**."

WILLIAM SAROYAN, WRITER

Home of tech giants

Since the 1990s, the San Francisco area has been central to the tech boom. The presence of global giants such as Google, Apple, Facebook, Instagram, and Twitter has helped the city attract bright young minds. San Francisco has become a pioneer in environmental consciousness, often topping surveys of the greenest cities in the US. The trajectory of this most unpredictable city is like one of its famed cable cars: no one knows whether it is going to keep climbing or take a sudden plunge, but it's an incredible ride.

The rainbow flag was first used as a symbol of LGBTQ+ pride at a 1978 Gay Freedom Day parade in San Francisco.

A poster for concerts held during the Summer of Love

1966 Scott McKenzie records *San Francisco (Be Sure to Wear Flowers in Your Hair)*, and the following year the city leads the world into the so-called "Summer of Love."

1978 Mayor George Moscone and San Francisco Supervisor and LGBTQ+ rights activist Harvey Milk (right) are shot and killed in the City Hall.

1989 The Loma Prieta earthquake hits the San Francisco Bay Area, killing 63 people and causing over $5 billion in damages.

1995 Craigslist and eBay are founded in the Bay Area. They're part of a major dotcom boom in the region: Google follows in 1998.

2013 Activists protest against private "tech buses" that ferry employees to out-of-town corporate campuses, fueling the feel of a divided city.

New York City

THE BIG APPLE

In just 400 years, New York City has developed from a tiny settlement to one of the most culturally diverse, dynamic, and influential cities in the world—a living symbol of the US.

The forested island of Manhattan was home to the Lenape people when Dutch settlers arrived on the coast in 1624. The Lenape grew maize to supplement their hunting and fishing, and knew the island as *manahāhtaan*, or "the place for gathering wood to make bows."

The Dutch set up the New Amsterdam trading post, took over the entire island from the locals, and began to build haphazard streets of houses on its southern tip. One street, wider than the rest, followed the route of an existing Native American trail: it became known as Broadway. However, after 40 years of trading, the Dutch colonists had earned less profit than they had hoped for. When four hostile English ships sailed into New Amsterdam's harbor, the Dutch governor, Peter Stuyvesant, surrendered. In 1665, the English renamed the city New York.

New York prospers

Under the British, New York expanded and grew wealthy. Immigrants arrived from England, France, and Germany, as did an increasing number of enslaved people from West and Central Africa. Money poured in, especially to the island's corn millers, shipbuilders, and merchants, who built impressive houses along an expanding network of winding streets. By the 1770s, New York was North America's second-largest city and was heavily taxed. Locals were frustrated at being taxed without having any representation in the British Parliament, and the city became one of the first to resist colonial rule.

New York suffered badly in the ensuing Revolutionary War. The rebels held it during the conflict's early days, but the British occupied the city, and its important harbor, between late 1776 and 1783, when American troops marched triumphantly back into New York.

> "There is **no place like it**, no place within an atom of its **glory**, **pride**, and **exultancy**.
>
> WALT WHITMAN, WRITING IN THE *BROOKLYN EAGLE*, c. 1847

◁ *NEW YORK SKYLINE*, 1921
Manhattan's distinctive skyline rises over the harbor and the Hudson River, in one of American painter and printmaker Joseph Pennell's many cityscapes.

1524 CE Italian explorer Giovanni da Verrazzano sails into Upper New York Bay.

1624 The Dutch found the settlement of New Amsterdam as a base for fur traders.

1626 Dutch governor-general Peter Minuit buys Manhattan from the Lenape, exchanging it for goods such as tools, cloth, and shell beads.

1664 The English take over the settlement, which consists of a few curving streets protected by a wall and a fort.

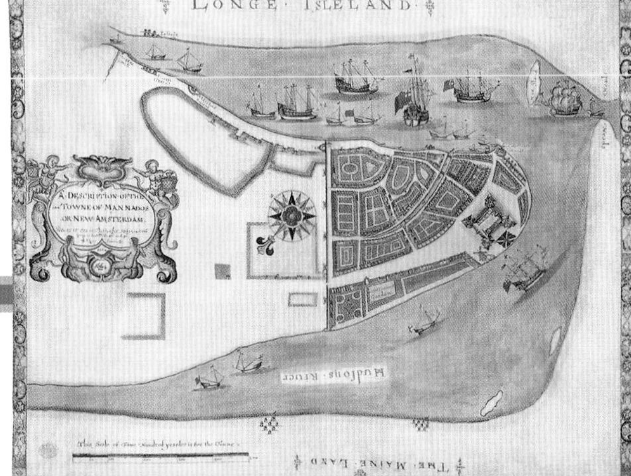

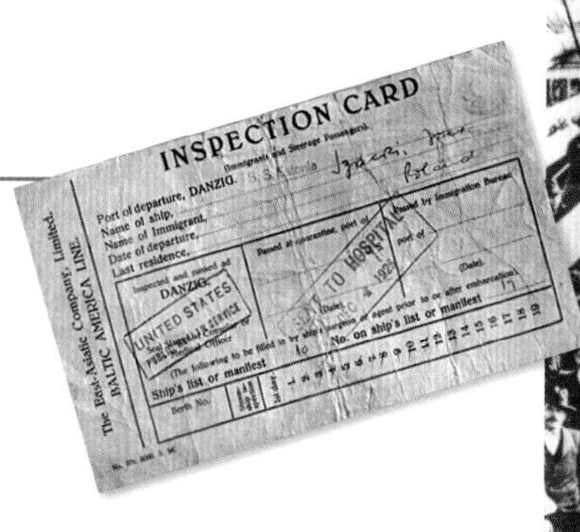
INSPECTION CARD
Port of departure, DANZIG
Name of ship.
Name of Immigrant.
Date of departure.
Last residence.
BALTIC AMERICA LINE.
The East Asiatic Company, Limited.

▷ ELLIS ISLAND INSPECTION CARD
Immigrants passing through Ellis Island were issued with cards like this to show they had been vaccinated, disinfected, and passed health inspections.

IMMIGRANTS GATHER ON DECK ▷
Many who arrived in the city by sea in the 19th and early 20th centuries were hoping for a more prosperous life than had been possible in Europe.

New York City's oldest surviving building is a Dutch timber-frame house built in Canarsie, Brooklyn, in 1652 by Pieter Claesen Wyckoff.

After independence, New York continued to grow. Its island site made it ideal for shipping. With the introduction of steamboats, the creation of the Erie Canal in 1825, and later the railroad, transportation links with the Midwest were strong, enabling trade and industry to thrive more than ever. Increasing wealth brought benefits such as the city's first hospital, free state schools, and an enduring newspaper, the *New York Post*. The city's prosperity also helped it weather disaster. In 1835, a devastating fire wiped out much of old New York, but rebuilding was soon underway, and this time the city benefited from a proper city plan. This grid of regular, standard-width streets and avenues began to spread across the whole of Manhattan. With great foresight, the planners left a large tract of land free from development, and from 1858 this became Central Park, still one of the largest city-center parks in the world.

◁ *CENTRAL PARK*, c. 1903
Maurice Prendergast's painting shows a crowd gathering on July 4 to celebrate American Independence. The park was a popular place for walks, carriage trips, concerts, and ice skating.

Home of Liberty

New York's harbor was the main point of entry for immigrants from Europe. Large groups from Germany and Ireland came in the 1840s and 1850s. Later waves arrived from Eastern and Southern Europe, many of them leaving famine and persecution behind, and hoping to start a new life in a country offering freedom and opportunity. Many started businesses, in everything from shopkeeping to garment manufacture, adding further to the city's growth. New York's inventiveness and drive was showcased at the

1789–1790 New York City is the US's first national capital; the role next passes to Philadelphia, then Washington, D.C.

1811 A grid plan is drawn up for much of Manhattan.

1823 New York City, now more populous than Boston or Pennsylvania, becomes the US's largest city.

1835 The Great Fire destroys many city blocks and hundreds of buildings.

By the 1850s, around one quarter of New York City's population was Irish. Many had left home due to the Irish Potato Famine, and settled in neighborhoods including the Bronx and Lower Manhattan.

1853–1854 A World's Fair is staged in the specially built Crystal Palace exhibition building.

1858 Central Park, designed by landscape architect Frederick Law Olmsted, opens.

1868 Built on iron viaducts above the city streets, the first elevated railroad eases street congestion.

1870 John D. Rockefeller founds Standard Oil.

1853 World's Fair, a bustling modern event that caught the imagination of the world. By the 1890s, newcomers were arriving via Ellis Island, sighting the Statue of Liberty as they approached a city where fortunes could be made.

A gilded age

In the second half of the 19th century, the city's businesses were expanding, and merchants and tycoons—who employed many of the new arrivals—became enormously rich. Families like the Astors, Vanderbilts, and Carnegies made millions from real estate, railroad-building, shipping, and steel manufacture. The richest people built themselves mansions on Fifth Avenue; others lived in tall, terraced houses made from distinctive brown stone. The great tycoons were famous for their lavish lifestyles, furnishing their homes luxuriously, throwing huge parties, and collecting paintings and sculptures. The extravagance of the era was reflected in Mark Twain's 1873 novel *The Gilded Age*, and the name stuck. The rich families also benefited New York, paying for railroads, museums, and galleries; the Metropolitan Opera; and other public buildings that gave the city a lasting legacy.

However, the city was no utopia. Some of the upper class were corrupt—businessman and politician William "Boss" Tweed stole vast sums of public money. New York still suffered many social problems, with much poverty, slum housing, and a high crime rate. By the end of the century, the streets were so crowded with houses, shops, factories, and offices that developers started building upward. Taking advantage of a large workforce and a ready supply of steel, they began to construct skyscrapers, like the famous Flatiron Building, that took the city to a new level.

1886 The Statue of Liberty, a gift from France to the US, is opened.

1896 Movies are first shown in New York City.

1902 The Flatiron Building, a 21-story skyscraper on a narrow, triangular site at the meeting point of Broadway and 5th Avenue, is completed.

Capital of jazz

> "The **Cotton Club** was the most **prestigious** showcase for **black musical talent** in **New York**.
>
> CONSTANCE VALIS HILL AND GREGORY HINES, *BROTHERHOOD IN RHYTHM*, 2000

▷ Dorothy Dandridge sang at the Cotton Club early in her career, before becoming a successful film actress.

△ A poster for Duke Ellington, who played regularly at the Cotton Club during the 1920s and '30s with his orchestra.

△ The entrance to Harlem's famous Cotton Club was lit with bright neon signs. The venue was initially open only to white patrons, although the entertainers were Black jazz musicians.

Jazz, Black American music born in New Orleans, blended African and Caribbean elements with European dance rhythms. After World War I, many jazz musicians moved to New York City: Black musicians such as singer Cab Calloway, trumpeter Louis Armstrong with his Hot Five and Hot Seven groups, and bandleader Duke Ellington played in clubs in Harlem. Another group, The Original Dixieland Jass Band, who came to New York from New Orleans, were the first to make a jazz record; one of their disks sold a million copies. Such successes brought more people to the bars and clubs of Harlem, and helped New York catch the eyes and ears of the world.

1920 National Prohibition begins, driving the sale of alcohol underground, where it is controlled by gangsters in big cities like New York.

1925 The first edition of the *New Yorker* magazine is published.

1926 Flamboyant, corrupt politician Jimmy Walker becomes mayor, and illicit "speakeasies" flourish.

1929 A stock market crash leads to mass poverty and unemployment.

1930 The Chrysler Building, one of the world's most stunning Art Deco skyscrapers, is completed.

1931 The 1,454 ft (443 m) Empire State Building opens.

1933 Prohibition comes to an end; Fiorello La Guardia is elected mayor.

1936 Eleven state-of-the-art outdoor swimming complexes are created by the city authorities.

◁ *WORKERS OF AMERICA*, 1930–1931
One of the ten sections of Thomas Hart Benton's *America Today*. This mural celebrates construction workers. The newly built Empire State Building is shown in the background.

The high life

As New York prospered, arts and culture flourished. Although there was a national ban on alcohol from 1920, many New Yorkers ignored it, buying drink illegally and indulging their love of theater, sports, and good food, and dancing to live music. Many made fortunes, although Prohibition also brought crime. The 1920s was a golden era of Broadway musicals, the cinema came of age, and New York set a new standard of modernity as more and more skyscrapers rose into the dusty city air. Black Americans, excluded from clubs and theaters downtown, opened their own venues, which played host to the newest, most dynamic music of the age—jazz. Soon, white Americans were also listening to jazz (see box), and the Harlem Renaissance saw the city's Black poets and artists gain recognition. New York was becoming a world-renowned cultural capital.

The Great Depression

In 1929, the New York Stock Exchange plummeted, and the US was plunged into depression. Fortunes were lost overnight, the power of the Gilded Age families was reduced, and countless workers lost their jobs. Many people had to line up for benefits or food handouts, while others squatted in shacks in Central Park, or waited hopelessly for work at the docks or on construction sites. But the city did not lose its optimism. New Yorkers elected a reforming mayor, Fiorello La Guardia, who established public housing schemes and projects to provide jobs and welfare. Skyscrapers were completed, public art projects proliferated, and many companies began to recover. When a World's Fair was held in 1939–1940, 44 million people visited. New York was still one of the world's greatest cities.

At the height of Prohibition, it is estimated there were somewhere between 20,000 and 100,000 speakeasies in New York.

In the 1920s, builders across the US raced to put up the world's tallest building. The Empire State was the winner, and remained the world's tallest from 1931 to 1970.

1939 Rockefeller Center is completed in Midtown.

1940 Queens–Midtown Tunnel opens, relieving congestion on many bridges of the East River.

1941 The US enters World War II after the bombing of Pearl Harbor, Hawaii.

1942 Times Square, famous for its neon signs, is blacked out to test whether New York City could go dark if there were air raids.

△ *CAMPBELL'S SOUP CANS*, 1965
New York–based artist Andy Warhol produced numerous paintings and prints inspired by items that symbolized the mass consumer culture of 1960s America. Warhol's vivid, almost neon colors seemed to represent the vibrancy of New York itself.

Winners and losers

During World War II, New York bustled with troops and incoming refugees—some 900,000 locals served in the military. Industries from shipbuilding to garment-making made vital contributions to the war effort, and after the war the city boomed. The influx of returning GIs and the arrival of new immigrants created demand for housing. Robert Moses led numerous projects as Construction Coordinator, building new highways and bridges, as well as Lincoln Center and Shea Stadium. As a result, the construction business prospered and many new glass and steel towers went up, sometimes replacing much-loved older buildings. The newly important service industries boomed, too, especially finance, tourism, and law, fueling rises on the New York Stock Exchange and turning the city into one of the world's key financial centers. New York buzzed with confidence, and its importance was confirmed when the United Nations built its headquarters in the city.

But not everyone was a winner. Manual industries such as shipbuilding and dock-working, which had been so important to New York, went into decline and many of the city's poor got poorer. Lower-income areas, such as the Bronx, suffered from crime and dilapidation. Districts like Harlem, with its large Black population, had to deal with the effects of segregation and police violence. In July 1964, Harlem and Bedford-Stuyvesant saw six nights of rioting after police shot dead a Black student, James Powell.

△ WARHOL AND BASQUIAT, 1984
Two icons of New York art, Andy Warhol and Jean-Michel Basquiat collaborated in the 1980s and became close friends.

1955 Work begins on Lincoln Center, a high-profile arts complex in a previously run-down area.

1959 The Solomon R. Guggenheim Museum opens in a striking new building designed by veteran American architect Frank Lloyd Wright.

1963 The elaborate Pennsylvania Station, a 1910 Beaux Arts building, is demolished, bringing calls for the preservation of historic landmarks.

1963 Release of *The Freewheelin' Bob Dylan*; the album cover features a New York street.

1964 Race riots break out in Harlem and Brooklyn's Bedford-Stuyvesant.

1969 The Stonewall Riots take place in Greenwich Village.

1973 The World Trade Center opens.

1973 Rock club CBGB opens in the East Village. Regulars include the Ramones, Patti Smith, and Blondie.

> "Once you have **lived** in **New York** and it has become **your home**, no place else is **good enough**. All of **everything** is concentrated here.
>
> JOHN STEINBECK, *THE NEW YORK TIMES*, 1953

A cultural capital

The post-war period also saw New York become the Western world's artistic capital. Jackson Pollock produced vibrant abstract works by dripping paint onto the canvas; Andy Warhol pioneered Pop Art; while Jean-Michel Basquiat, one of the first world-famous Black artists, drew on Expressionism and street art to make paintings that explored race and class. New York's music was vibrant, too. Jazz was still developing, and the arrival of singers such as Bob Dylan bolstered a major folk revival. Disco, punk, and hip-hop followed in later decades.

Greenwich Village, on the west side of Manhattan, became well known as a haunt of artists, bohemians, and other non-mainstream groups, including LGBTQ+ people, who faced discrimination and persecution. The Stonewall Inn, a gay bar in the Village, was, like other LGBTQ+ venues, often raided by the police. Police violence during one such raid in July 1969 met a robust resistance from the bar's patrons and sympathizers, and the resulting Stonewall Riots became famous as a key stage in the gay rights movement.

◁ *WILD STYLE*, 1982
This cult movie celebrates hip-hop, which was born in 1970s New York. Break dancing, DJing, graffiti, and rapping were the pillars of a street culture that took over the world.

By the 1970s, the city's prosperity had plunged after richer people moved out of town, taking tax revenue with them, while social problems remained. The city authorities took on heavy debts, bringing near-bankruptcy. A large federal loan in 1975 staved off disaster, and the following decade saw another boom, with state money enabling regeneration in the Bronx and other poor neighborhoods, and the stock market fighting back. The finance and real-estate sectors did well in the 1980s. Later, leaders such as David Dinkins, who was mayor in the early 1990s, tried to redress the city's social balance by tackling racial inequality and crime. New York still faced trials: the 9/11 attack on the World Trade Center was the deadliest terrorist attack in history. Yet the city's spirited recovery, via rebuilding and memorials, impressed the world, proving that this creative, vibrant, and optimistic city has always bounced back.

The 1990s sitcom *Friends* showcased the bustle of modern Manhattan to a massive global audience—although, aside from a few exterior shots, it was filmed in a studio in California.

1975 A financial crisis brings the city close to bankruptcy.

1990 David Dinkins becomes New York City's first Black mayor.

1994 Rudy Giuliani becomes mayor and begins a crackdown on crime.

2001 The World Trade Center is destroyed when terrorists fly airplanes into its twin towers.

2009 The High Line, a park constructed on former tracks of an elevated railroad, opens.

2012 Hurricane Sandy brings floods, subway closures, and power blackouts to the city.

▽ *TRIBUTE IN LIGHT*
This installation, consisting of searchlights that shine upward to form two vertical beams, has been lit annually since 2002 to commemorate those lost in the 9/11 attack on the twin towers.

Havana

CITY OF COLOR

Havana has been the gateway to Spanish America, a playground for the US Mafia, and the capital of Fidel Castro's socialist experiment. Its story is a historical roller coaster, full of drama, hardship, and glamour.

When the Spanish arrived in the late 15th century, Taíno people occupied most of Cuba, and several Indigenous villages existed in the region under a *cacique* (chief) called Habaguanex. Havana was founded on the western shores of the Puerto de Carenas in November 1519, the last of seven Spanish *villas* (colonial towns). This sheltered natural harbor was to define the city. Its strategic location as a stop-off point for ships shuttling between Europe and the newly colonized lands of New Spain would make the fledgling trading port rich—and highly coveted.

Pirates and treasure fleets

By 1550, the native population had been decimated by European diseases and Spanish brutality. Meanwhile, a thriving Havana, its port crowded with galleons weighed down by New World silver, became a target for opportunistic pirates, among them Frenchman Jacques de Sores, who sacked the town in 1555, leaving most of it in ruins. In response, the Spanish strengthened Havana's defenses, building two sturdy forts to protect the jaws of the harbor and a wall 3 miles (5 km) long with nine bastions and 11 heavily guarded gates. In 1592, Havana was granted city status, and in 1607 it replaced Santiago de Cuba as colonial capital.

Havana's new defenses kept out buccaneers, but proved less effective against better organized European invaders. In 1762, during the Seven Years' War, the British amassed the largest-ever transatlantic battle fleet, capturing the city's Morro fort after a 44-day siege. Havana's fall ushered in a short but momentous 11-month British occupation, during which the city was opened to freer trade.

Building a colonial city

The Spanish regained Cuba in exchange for Florida in 1763, and embarked upon an ambitious building program whose fruits are still visible today. The city's Baroque cathedral and the formidable ramparts of La Cabaña, then the second-largest fort in the Americas, were erected. Street grids were laid out to the west incorporating new inventions such as gas lighting, trams, and the electric telegraph, while the port was busy with sugar and tobacco. Graceful buildings hosted the latest plays and a flourishing social scene, and Havana became known as the Paris of the Caribbean. It was largely spared during Cuba's 19th-century independence wars, but tragedy struck in 1898, when the American battleship USS *Maine* mysteriously exploded in the harbor, killing most of its crew. The Americans blockaded Cuba, and war soon followed.

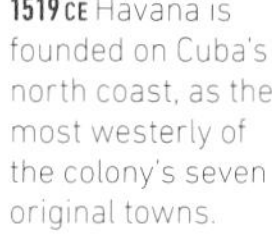

1519 CE Havana is founded on Cuba's north coast, as the most westerly of the colony's seven original towns.

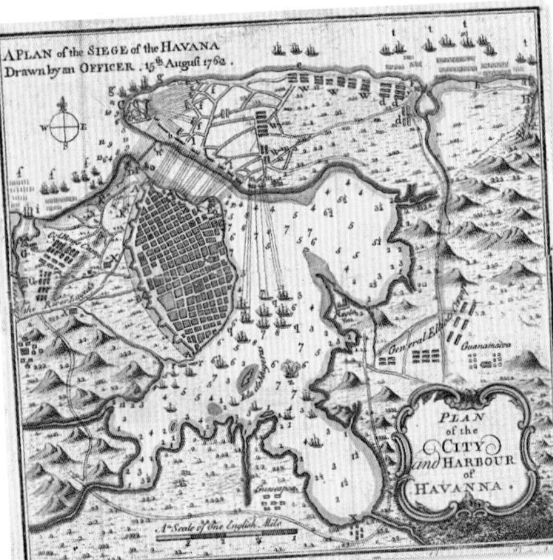

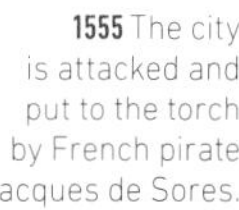

1555 The city is attacked and put to the torch by French pirate Jacques de Sores.

1762 Siding with France in the Seven Years' War, the Spanish lose Havana to the British.

1768 The *Santísima Trinidad*—then the largest warship in the world—is built in Havana.

Havana is one of the **great cities of the world**, sublimely tawdry yet stubbornly graceful, like **tarnished chrome**—a city, as a young **Winston Churchill** once wrote, where "**anything might happen**."

JONATHAN MILES, AMERICAN JOURNALIST, 2003

▽ OLD HAVANA
Havana evolved as a maritime city based around four main squares, with muscular forts protecting an expansive natural harbor. Neoclassical buildings with distinctive arches and columns were added in the 19th century.

"In a **revolution**, one **wins or dies**— if it is a **real one**.

CHE GUEVARA, FAREWELL LETTER TO FIDEL CASTRO, 1965

American power and mob rule

The Spanish-American War was short but decisive, and proved the death knell for Spanish power in Cuba. Spain relinquished its colony in 1898, and in 1902 Cuban independence was confirmed by the Treaty of Paris. Yet Cuba was too great a prize to be left to its own devices. The US maintained a naval base in Guantanamo Bay, and would influence the country—and its flourishing capital—for decades to come.

Havana had now expanded well beyond its demolished walls. The city spread into the former forest enclave of Vedado and snaked west along the coast on an elegant sea-drive where fashionable locals paraded nightly. When an early-20th-century sugar boom gifted the government with a seemingly bottomless pit of money, successive presidents sponsored a grandiose construction campaign. President Gerardo Machado was particularly influential, commissioning extravagant buildings such as the Art Deco Hotel Nacional, and Havana's Neoclassical Capitolio.

But all was not well. An increasingly autocratic Machado was forced out in 1933, and power repeatedly changed hands until former army sergeant Fulgencio Batista staged a coup in 1952, and promptly cut a deal with the US Mafia, opening the Cuban capital to rampant development. For the next seven years Havana barely slept, as millions of American tourists flew in to savor a cocktail of casinos, racetracks, and nightclubs. Frank Sinatra and John F. Kennedy came along for a party that was lubricated by rum with a soundtrack of mambo and rumba.

While tourists and rich Cubans prospered, most of the country got short shrift. Tired of corruption, angry and alienated workers channeled their frustration through the

◁ **CASTRO AND CHE GUEVARA, 1959**
In January 1959, Fidel Castro, Che Guevara, and their army of bearded guerrillas entered Havana to proclaim the so-called "Triumph of the Revolution" amid a wave of popular support.

1853 Birth of José Martí in Havana. The poet, philosopher, and journalist helped inspire the Cuban independence movement.

1898 The explosion of USS *Maine* in Havana harbor kills 261 and leads to the Spanish-American war.

Cuba had a railroad before Spain, and was the first Latin American country with a track. The 1837 line linked Havana to Bejucal.

1902 Cuba gains independence and Havana spreads west, creating the new American-influenced Vedado neighborhood.

1926–1929 Havana's domed national assembly (Capitolio) is built using money from Cuba's post–World War I sugar boom.

1933 The overthrow of dictator Gerardo Machado leads to a shoot-out in Havana's Hotel Nacional.

◁ *PAISAJE DE LA HABANA*, 1961
René Portocarrero was a self-taught Modernist artist active between 1934 and 1985. His abstract cityscapes of Havana in the 1950s and '60s burst with tropical color.

> In **Cuba** and **specifically in Havana** there's a **sort of energy** that turns every situation into **something unexpected**.
>
> FERNANDO PÉREZ, CUBAN FILM DIRECTOR, 2012

Officially known as San Cristóbal de la Habana, Havana is named after Saint Christopher, the patron saint of travelers, and Habaguanex, a Taíno chief who was active in the area when the Spanish arrived.

nationalist cause of Fidel Castro, who emerged from Cuba's eastern mountains with Argentinian doctor-turned-soldier Che Guevara to march on Havana. Castro's revolutionaries arrived in January 1959 to virtually no opposition as Batista and the Mafia, realizing history was against them, had packed their bags and fled. The revolutionaries celebrated their victory in the Havana Hilton, and a new age dawned.

Socialist Havana

Castro's reign as prime minister and president lasted 50 years, and profoundly shaped Havana. With the capitalist world held at arm's length, the city took a unique path through the modern age. Its development was put on hold as the government concentrated on national issues such as inequality, education, and health care. As Cuban-American relations soured and the US trade embargo, first instituted by President Kennedy in 1960, was tightened, ordinary people suffered. Many left, some sailing on flimsy rafts to the US. This economic stagnation protected Havana's historic streets from development, but also ensured their neglect. A city that had once been defined by trade metamorphosed into a stuck-in-time museum replete with crumbling buildings and antediluvian American cars, although jazz, salsa, and street art continued to flourish.

Keen to alleviate its economic woes, the government welcomed a new wave of tourists from Europe and Canada in the 1990s, beginning Havana's rehabilitation. Today, with bureaucracy relaxed and restaurants thriving, Old Havana is a romantic and atmospheric place; its graceful squares and cobbled streets partially restored and enjoying a second life, its resolute spirit undimmed.

1952 A coup by Fulgencio Batista opens Havana to the Mafia, gambling, and mass US tourism.

1959 Fidel Castro enters Havana and sets up a temporary government headquarters in the Havana Hilton.

1982 Old Havana is made a UNESCO World Heritage Site, accelerating the process of historical restoration.

1991 Collapse of the Soviet Union and beginning of the "special period," a decade of austerity and shortages.

2011 A loosening of restrictions on private enterprise sees a blossoming of Havana's long-neglected restaurant scene.

2016 US president Barack Obama makes a historic visit to Havana, but does not meet Fidel Castro, who dies later in the year.

CENTENARIO REVOLUCION
MAYO 1810-1910
Registrado

Buenos Aires

LA REINA DEL PLATA ("THE QUEEN OF SILVER")

Proud, self-assured Buenos Aires is a vibrant mix of European splendor and Latin exuberance. This grand port city gave birth to the tango, and its culture and architecture have been shaped by waves of immigrants.

Hundreds of years before the arrival of the Spanish, Indigenous Querandí and Charrúa people lived in nomadic tented camps across the grasslands of southeastern South America, catching fish and hunting deer, guanacos, and rhea.

The Spanish arrived in what is now Peru in the 1530s, and were captivated by the nearby gold and silver, but the land to the south initially held little interest. Explorer Pedro de Mendoza founded a settlement called Santa María del Buen Ayre on the southern shores of the La Plata River in 1536. But it was crippled by lack of food and conflict with the Querandí, who used their hunting *bolas* (throwing weapons) in battle against the Spanish cavalry.

△ **CITY MAP OF BUENOS AIRES, 18TH CENTURY**
Buenos Aires's rigid street grid dates back to the city's foundation in the late 16th century.

Isolated outpost

A second, more successful attempt was made in 1580. Conquistador Juan de Garay sailed downriver from Asunción and set up a town that became a nexus for beef and contraband. But, with commerce channeled through Lima, Buenos Aires remained a backwater. Its fortunes were turned around in 1776, when it became capital of the new Viceroyalty of Río de la Plata, which encompassed much of the southern half of South America. Increasingly pushed to the margins, the Querandí and Charrúa retreated inland or took jobs on ranches. In the city, the loosening of laws encouraged trade, and the economy grew.

◁ **A FESTIVE PLAZA DE MAYO**
The monumental Plaza de Mayo during a 1910 festival celebrating the centenary of the May Revolution, in which Argentina gained its independence from Spain.

1516 Iberian explorer Juan Díaz de Solís, the first European to explore the La Plata River, meets local resistance and is killed, either by the Charrúa, or the northern Guaraní people.

1536 The first European settlement in the area is established by Pedro de Mendoza, but is abandoned only five years later.

1580 Buenos Aires is established for the second time by Spaniard Juan de Garay.

1776 Buenos Aires is made capital of the Viceroyalty of Río de la Plata (containing most of present-day Argentina, Chile, Bolivia, Paraguay, and Uruguay).

◁ THE MAY REVOLUTION
This commemorative postcard shows the personalities involved in the 1810 May Revolution and its aftermath, including general and war hero José de San Martín; Cornelio Saavedra, the country's first president; and Manuel Belgrano, creator of the Argentinian flag.

The city matures

In the decades that followed, Buenos Aires grew rich thanks to its vibrant port. As the city spread from its riverside hub, distinct neighborhoods developed in the growing suburbs, anchored around gossip-filled *pulperías* (taverns and stores). But tensions rose between the free-trading city, and the stagnating provinces. In 1852, Buenos Aires seceded from the confederation, and functioned for nine years as a de facto independent state. Order was only restored in 1861, when Buenos Aires's troops defeated the Argentine Army to win the Battle of Pavón, and the city was reinstated as capital, its dominance assured.

War and independence

Despite increasing prosperity, years of isolation had fueled bitterness among the city's inhabitants. When the British attacked in 1806 and 1807, they were driven back not by the Spanish army, but by local militias, their victory adding to a sense of empowerment. After the Spanish monarchy was deposed by Napoleon in 1808, Buenos Aires' *criollos* (Latin Americans with Spanish ancestry) replaced their viceroy with a locally elected junta. The May Revolution of 1810 triggered a protracted liberation struggle and, in 1816, the region declared its independence. After a brief spell as capital of the United Provinces of the Río de la Plata, in 1831 the city became capital of the Argentine Confederation, a precursor to the modern state.

A golden age dawns

From the late 19th century, Buenos Aires prevailed as Argentina's magnetic main city; a proud metropolis whose personality reflected its location between grasslands and river estuary: dockers crammed the port, while ranchers supplied the burgeoning steakhouses and fanned an emerging equestrian culture. Its mix of cultures spawned a hot new dance called tango (see box) and writers like Jorge Luis Borges. The physical landscape of the city changed, too. Much of Buenos Aires's architecture dates from the era beginning in the 1880s, when idealistic architects used the capital's ever-expanding street grid as a blank canvas for creations such as the Eclectic Casa Rosada, the Neoclassical National Congress building, and the Beaux-Arts City Hall.

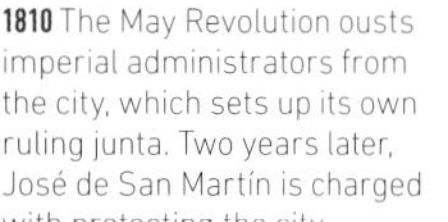
1810 The May Revolution ousts imperial administrators from the city, which sets up its own ruling junta. Two years later, José de San Martín is charged with protecting the city.

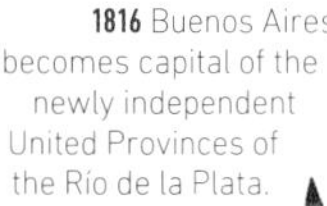
1816 Buenos Aires becomes capital of the newly independent United Provinces of the Río de la Plata.

1821 Buenos Aires University, Argentina's top educational establishment, is founded. It lists 17 former Argentinian presidents among its alumni.

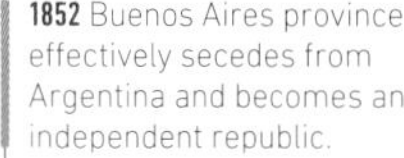
1852 Buenos Aires province effectively secedes from Argentina and becomes an independent republic.

The roots of tango

> **Tango** was an **immigrant music**, so it does not have a **nationality**. Its only **passport is feeling.**
>
> CARLOS GAVITO, ARGENTINIAN DANCER

The tango has its roots among the poor and dispossessed of Buenos Aires. It was born in the brothels and dive bars of the working-class immigrant neighborhoods of La Boca and Barracas in the late 19th century, a cultural collision of *candombe* (a dance developed by the descendants of enslaved Africans in Uruguay) and European polka dances and minuets. Considered the music of immigrants in its early years, it was later appropriated by the bohemian upper class, who introduced it to Paris and New York in the 1910s, where it became an instant sensation. These days, tango's sensuous moves and graceful athleticism are widely appreciated everywhere from expensive dinner shows to private dance schools, not just in Buenos Aires, but all over the world.

△ Tango's intimate embraces were initially considered vulgar by the establishment, and the dance was not seen as respectable until it became popular in Europe.

◁ French-born Carlos Gardel (1890–1935), nicknamed "the song thrush," was a tango singer extraordinaire whose music helped define the art.

1858 Café Tortoni opens. This elegant, iconic coffee house becomes a tango venue, a haunt of writers, and a hive of city gossip.

Mass immigration meant that by the late 1870s, half of Buenos Aires's population was foreign-born, the majority of them Spanish and Italian.

1861 With Buenos Aires's victory over the Argentine Confederation in the Battle of Pavón, the city becomes the nation's capital again, and dominates the new administration.

1882 After a general strike, the Italian La Boca neighborhood briefly secedes from Argentina and flies the Genovese flag.

1898 The Casa Rosada, the ornate office of the Argentinian president, is officially inaugurated.

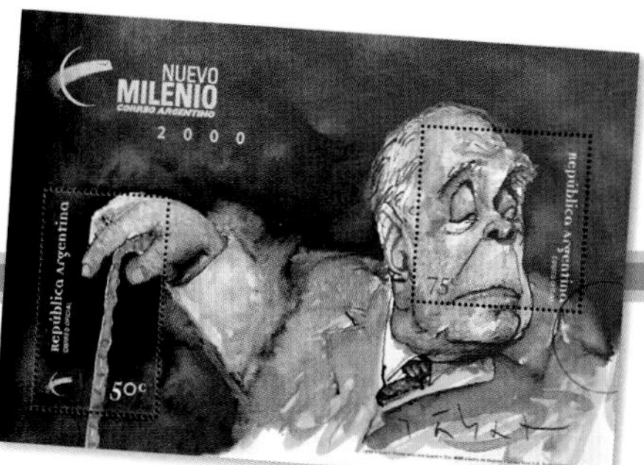

Argentinian postage stamp featuring Jorge Luis Borges

1899 The great Argentinian writer Jorge Luis Borges is born in Buenos Aires.

△ **EVA PERÓN AT A RALLY, c. 1952**
Eva Perón's huge popularity was reflected in outdoor speeches in which she addressed thousands of supporters, many of them drawn from the city's working classes, in the Plaza de Mayo.

Between 1870 and 1910, Buenos Aires's population grew an astronomical 786 percent, thanks largely to mass immigration from Spain and Italy. The demographic boom ushered in a golden age, and the new arrivals helped give Buenos Aires a discernible Southern European flavor. By the advent of World War I, Argentina was one of the 10 richest countries in the world, and its illustrious capital was a breeding ground for art and fashion. Never shy in expressing their views, its self-assured residents were celebrated for being extroverted and sophisticated.

The growth of individual wealth saw the expansion of rich suburbs, like the Barrio Norte, punctuated with French-style mansions and smart polo clubs. Elsewhere, vast civic projects such as the building of the Teatro Colón opera house in 1908 and the opening of the subway (the first in South America) earned Buenos Aires the moniker "the Paris of South America."

Juan and Eva Perón

However, fraud and corruption at high levels, as well as periods of social unrest, meant Buenos Aires was often less enlightened than it looked. And for all its riches, the city was still peripheral on the world stage. Change came in 1946, when General Juan Perón rose to power on a tidal wave of working-class populism. Perón built his political base among the city's urban poor—migrant workers

1910 In Argentina's centennial year, Buenos Aires enters its golden age with elegant new buildings such as the Galería Güemes.

1913 The Subte subway opens. It is the first underground railroad in Latin America.

1925 A new port facility, the Puerto Nuevo, opens in the city's Retiro neighborhood.

1936 A giant obelisk is raised on Avenida 9 de Julio to celebrate the 400th anniversary of the city's founding.

Adolf Eichmann and an estimated 300 other Nazis took exile in Argentina after World War II. Eichmann lived in Buenos Aires for eight years.

1951 A crowd of up to two million gather on Avenida 9 de Julio to implore Eva Perón to run as Vice President.

PUENTE DE LA MUJER ▷
The opening of this landmark pedestrian bridge in 2001 helped promote Buenos Aires as a slick, modern, 21st-century city.

who had flocked to Buenos Aires since the early 1930s to live in crowded *villas miserias*, or shanty towns. He initiated huge infrastructure projects, investing heavily in railroads, hydroelectric dams, hospitals, schools, and public-sector homes.

Perón's appeal was augmented by his wife Eva (also known as Evita), an actress from a poor village in the Pampas, whose empathetic speeches to crowds of adoring *descamisados* ("shirtless ones") quickly morphed into mass rallies. Eva Perón helped make Buenos Aires world famous.

Highs and lows

By the late 20th century, Buenos Aires, like the wider nation, was stuttering. In 1976, a right-wing military junta overthrew the government, and the next seven years were marred by state violence and repression as the military hunted down and killed their opposition in the Guerra Sucia ("dirty war"). Eva Perón's exuberant rallies were replaced by vigils held by the Madres de Plaza de Mayo, the mothers of left-wing radicals who had been killed or "disappeared."

Soccer, which had been brought to Argentina by British immigrants in the 1860s, offered some respite, with glory in the form of World Cup wins in 1978, when Buenos Aires hosted the final, and in 1986, when local son Diego Maradona brought the trophy back from Mexico.

Democracy returned in the 1990s, and Buenos Aires entered the 21st century in the midst of a regeneration project on a scale not seen since the 1880s. The focus was Puerto Madero, a neglected port area that was ingeniously replanted with residential skyscrapers and ritzy cultural facilities. Despite an economic meltdown in 2001, the city managed to cling onto its vivacious spirit with a dynamic new dining scene and a resurgent interest in tango. Buenos Aires may have suffered ups and downs since the days of colonization and independence, but it has never lost its poise or passion.

In Puerto Madero, every street is named after a woman, from activist Azucena Villaflor to writer Juana Manso.

> “If I have to apply **five turns** to **the screw** each day for the **happiness of Argentina, I will do it.**
>
> EVA PERÓN

1960 Diego Maradona, one of the world's greatest soccer players, is born. He grows up in the poor suburb of Villa Fiorito.

1978 Argentina, playing at home, win the World Cup for the first time, at Buenos Aires's El Monumental stadium.

1999 Work begins to regenerate the degraded Puerto Madero area with hotels, cultural centers, offices, theaters, and restaurants.

2013 Local-born Cardinal Jorge Mario Bergoglio becomes Pope Francis. He is the first South American pope and the first pontiff from outside Europe since 741 CE.

MORE GREAT CITIES

Belfast

Titanic City

In the 19th century, Belfast was one of the great shipbuilding ports, assembling the vessels that maintained Britain's empire. The city's modern origins date to 1611, when Baron Chichester built a castle on the Lagan River. By the 17th century the castle was gone, but Belfast was a center for the linen industry and a busy port, and then, with the Industrial Revolution, came shipbuilding. When Ireland was divided in 1921, the city became capital of Northern Ireland, but was blighted by years of sectarian violence. Since the 1998 peace accord, Belfast has blossomed, attracting visitors to *Titanic* Belfast, a museum to the city's most famous creation.

Copenhagen

City of Spires

One of Europe's smaller capitals, Copenhagen punches well above its weight, particularly with regard to environmental issues and the well-being of its citizens. From its origins as a Viking fishing village, established in the 10th century, it rose to become capital of Denmark in the early 15th century. Much of the city dates to the early 19th century, when Copenhagen experienced a period of cultural creativity known as the Danish Golden Age, which brought a Neoclassical look to the city's architecture. Since 2000, the Danish capital has been connected to the Swedish city of Malmö by the 9-mile (15-km) Øresund Bridge, cementing Copenhagen's role as a cultural and geographic link between the Nordic countries and the rest of Europe.

Marseille

The Phocean City

The port of Marseille is one of the oldest cities in Europe, founded in about 600 BCE and known to the Greeks as Massalia. It was an important trading point between the ancient civilizations of the Mediterranean and northern Europe and has retained that role even today, which explains its size as the second-largest city in France. Its status as a major port in the Mediterranean has also made it a natural center for immigration; the city has a sizable population with African heritage and the third-largest Jewish community in Europe after London and Paris. A reputation for criminality has been tempered in the 21st century by massive investment, and today Marseille is said to have the most museums in France after Paris.

Naples

City of the Sun

First settled by Greeks in the 1st millennium BCE, Naples is one of the world's oldest continuously inhabited cities and has been the site of a commercial port since the 9th century BCE. It was conquered by the Romans, followed by the Ostrogoths and Byzantines, and was later governed by Normans, Swabians, Angevins, Spanish, Austrians, and French, only becoming part of the Kingdom of Italy in 1861. This tumultuous history and exchange of cultures is reflected in the rich fabric of the city. At the same time, with its densely packed, ungentrified old quarter of narrow alleys and weathered facades, no other city feels quite so "Italian." Naples is also the home of pizza, as well as several other epicurean highlights, but arguably its best asset is the magnificent view of the city from the water.

Lagos

Las Gidi

Its name meaning "lakes" in Portuguese, Lagos originated as home of the Yoruba people and later a port, becoming a key center during the years of British colonial rule. From 1914 until 1991 it was Nigeria's capital. While no longer the seat of political power, Lagos is the most populous city in Nigeria (and second-largest in Africa) and the country's economic and cultural center, famous for its entrepreneurial spirit, music scene, movie industry, and nightlife—as well as its gridlocked traffic. The city sprawls around a lagoon and several islands. To its 21 million residents, Lagos is Nigeria.

△ **Copenhagen** An 18th-century lithograph showing the busy port.

△ **Naples** Mount Vesuvius looms over the Bay of Naples.

Osaka

City of Water

If Tokyo is the glittering capital and Kyoto the city of temples and culture, Osaka is Japan's gritty, hard-working, commercial and industrial third city. As Naniwa, it was Japan's capital from 645 to 745 CE. When the imperial court moved to Kyoto, Osaka continued to play an important role as a hub for land, sea, and river-canal transportation, during which time it was known as the "Nation's Kitchen" for its role in distributing rice. Numerous global companies, such as Panasonic, Sanyo, and Sharp, are headquartered in modern Osaka. The city is also known for its food scene and has been feted as one of the world's culinary capitals.

Vancouver

Rain City

Set amid snow-capped mountains on an ocean inlet on Canada's Pacific coast, Vancouver benefits from a picturesque setting. The region around it was inhabited by Indigenous Coast Salish people when Europeans set up a trading post, Fort Langley, in 1827. The mid-19th-century Gold Rush brought thousands of hopeful arrivals and the settlement was founded as a city in 1886, named after English navigator George Vancouver. The city developed as Canada's main Pacific port, and with trade has come an influx of East Asian immigrants. Vancouver's rich mix of nationalities has made the city one of Canada's most cosmopolitan.

Boston

Beantown

Boston's legacy is built on its role in the American Revolution. The city-to-be was first settled in 1630 by Puritans from England. Trading in tobacco, rum, salted cod, and enslaved people enriched the city, but taxes levied by the British sparked a revolt, and in 1770 British soldiers fired on the crowd, an event called the Boston Massacre. Three years later, the city's citizens threw a shipment of English tea into the harbor, and the aftermath triggered the American Revolution. In the 19th century, Boston became a center of liberal arts and education, regarding itself as an "Athens of America." The modern city retains a legacy of independence and education.

Miami

The Magic City

Miami is the only major US city founded by a woman. Julia Tuttle was a citrus grower who convinced railroad magnate Henry Flagler to extend his Florida East Coast Railway to the region, kick-starting the growth of the city. Northerners were drawn by the climate, and Miami experienced a property boom in the 1920s. After Fidel Castro's revolution in 1959, many wealthy Cubans relocated to Miami, and it is now the second-largest city in the US with a Spanish-speaking majority. The city's pastel-colored Art Deco buildings, wide sandy beaches, and party culture make it a tourism hub for both US and international visitors, second in the country only to New York.

Cartagena

Heroic City

Founded by the Spanish in 1533 on the Caribbean coast of what is now Colombia, Cartagena was once among the most important trading ports in the Americas, connecting Spain with its New World empire. The city was fortified with walls of mined coral and a castle to defend against pirates, and adorned with cathedrals and churches. Cartagena's historic beauty, its proximity to beaches, its citizens' zest for life, and a charm that was an inspiration for writer Gabriel García Márquez mean that the city exerts an influence that far exceeds its modest size.

Rio de Janeiro

Marvelous City

Although neither its country's capital nor its largest city, Rio de Janeiro is emblematic of Brazil. Its spectacular natural setting, squeezed between mountains and sea; its beaches, such as Copacabana and Ipanema; the highly distinctive Sugarloaf Mountain; and the statue of Christ the Redeemer are national icons. Founded in 1565 by the Portuguese, Rio prospered when gold and diamonds were discovered inland in the late 17th century and shipped out through its port. It was the capital of Brazil until the founding of Brasília in 1960. Today, Rio remains one of the most naturally beautiful and culturally vibrant cities in the world.

△ **Osaka** The port of Osaka is Japan's principal seaport.

△ **Rio de Janeiro** The statue of Christ the Redeemer stands atop Mount Corcovado.

Washington, D.C. p.258

St. Petersburg p.236

Philadelphia
Edinburgh
Palmanova
Valletta
Alexandria
Baghdad
La Plata

Brasília p.264

Isfahan p.242

CHAPTER 4
CITIES BY DESIGN

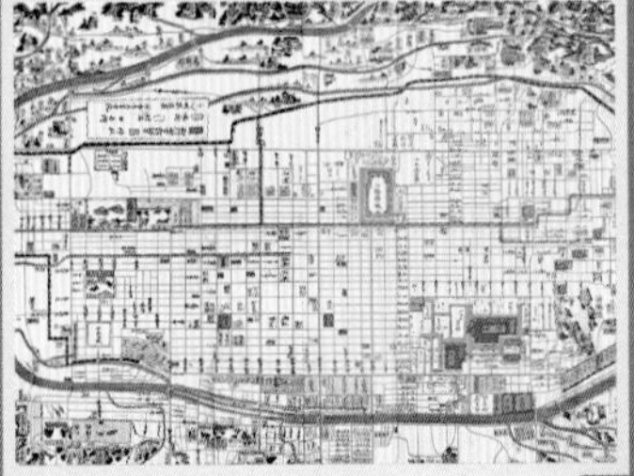

Kyoto p.252

Chandigarh

Jaipur

Canberra

Singapore p.246

St. Petersburg

WINDOW ON EUROPE

Inauspiciously located on a boggy delta, St. Petersburg was conceived and built as Peter the Great's vision for a new capital. It has long held a reputation as Russia's most cultured and sophisticated city.

In the early 17th century, the region around what would become St. Petersburg fell into Swedish hands. A century later, determined to establish a northern port for his empire, Russia's ambitious young ruler Peter I ("the Great") captured the strategically important Nyenschantz fortress from the Swedes. Here, he decided to build a new city, named in honor of his patron saint, St. Peter.

> "**St. Petersburg**, the most abstract and **intentional** city on the **entire globe**.
>
> FYODOR DOSTOEVSKY, *NOTES FROM UNDERGROUND*, 1864

A city rises

A modernizing, Western-oriented leader, Peter wanted his new city to be his "window on Europe." Inspired by Venice and Amsterdam, canals were to be its main arteries and, in contrast to Moscow's organic structure, the layout was planned from the outset: Peter wanted straight streets and buildings made of stone. Architects and craftsmen were drawn from far and wide to realize his vision. Yet conditions for the 40,000 serfs brought in to drain the marshy land and dig the canals were appalling, and the death toll led to the later claim that the city was built on human bones. In 1712, Peter moved the capital to St. Petersburg, and two years later the Summer Palace, the city's first, was finished.

After Peter's death in 1725, his successors continued to extend the city. Especially influential was the extravagant Empress Anna, under whom the imperial court began to look and feel very similar to those of Western Europe, with fashion and ballet imported from France and opera from Italy. Her successor was the astute Elizabeth. Similarly Europhile, Elizabeth's tastes favored the Baroque, and she employed the Italian architect Bartolomeo Rastrelli to redesign the riverside Winter Palace on a lavish, monumental scale. Like Anna, Elizabeth also encouraged the arts, setting up the Russian Academy of Arts in 1757.

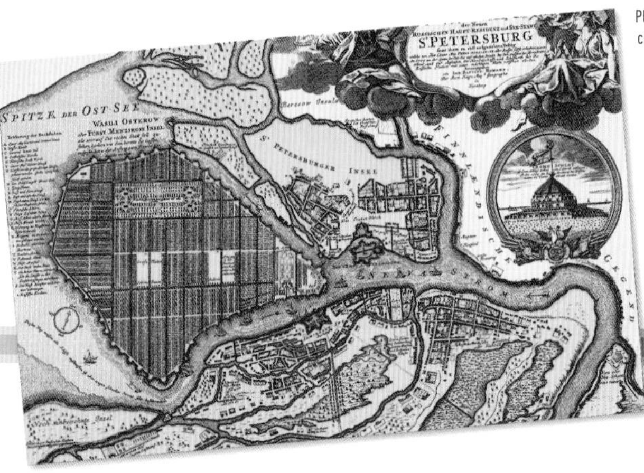

Plan of Peter's idealized city, c. 1720

1703 Peter the Great founds St. Petersburg, initially as a fortress and naval base.

1712 Never a fan of Moscow, Peter declares St. Petersburg his new capital, while the city continues to take shape.

1721 The city legally becomes part of Russia after Sweden cedes sovereignty at the Peace of Nystad.

1730 Empress Anna comes to the throne and promotes Western European culture.

1754 Work starts on the enlarged, opulent Winter Palace, masterpiece of the Italian architect Bartolomeo Rastrelli.

▽ *WINTER PALACE BY NIGHT*, 1857
Now part of the Hermitage Museum, the Winter Palace was the official home of Russia's rulers from 1732 to 1917. Originally built for Peter the Great, it was reconstructed for Empress Elizabeth to show off Russia's imperial might.

Catherine the Great

Although born in Prussia, the daughter of a German prince, Catherine the Great had lived for years in Russia by the time she succeeded her husband, the boorish Peter III, as ruler in 1762. Intelligent and ambitious, Catherine expanded her empire and pushed through much-needed reform, modernizing the administration and presiding over a period in which St. Petersburg took its place at the heart of European culture. She continued the work of her predecessors in inviting the best artists and architects of Western Europe to the capital, building the Neoclassical Marble Palace for her lover Grigory Orlov, extending the royal residence at Tsarskoye Selo (just outside the city), and ordering the addition of the Hermitage wing to the Winter Palace to house her growing collection of books and paintings. A firm follower of Enlightenment philosophy, with its emphasis on reason, she also founded the Smolny Institute—Russia's first educational establishment for women—and the country's first public library.

◁ For this 1770 portrait by court painter Fyodor Rokotov, Catherine posed in traditional Russian dress.

◁ Catherine ordered an exact copy of Raphael's Vatican loggias for her Hermitage collection.

1762 Catherine II ("the Great") begins her 34-year reign as empress.

1764 The Smolny Institute for Noble Maidens is founded in St. Petersburg.

1789 The Neoclassical Academy of Sciences building is completed on the Neva waterfront.

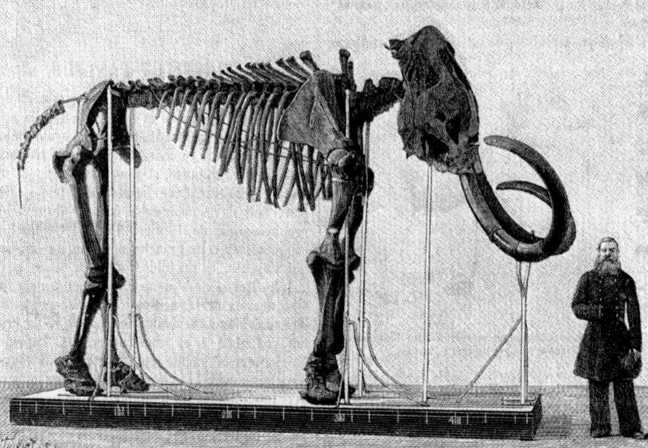

Mammoth skeleton, Academy of Sciences

1812 Russians defeat Napoleon's invading army; Alexander I orders a new public building campaign in celebration.

1825 Rebels agitating for a constitutional monarchy are shot dead in Peter's Square (now Senate Square) in the Decembrist Revolt.

1851 The railroad linking Moscow and St. Petersburg opens; the New Hermitage is completed.

By the time Catherine the Great came to power in 1762, an unpromising, mosquito-infested swamp had been transformed into the showpiece capital of Peter's imagination: an elegant city of bridges and islands, studded with fine churches and grand waterfront palaces. During Catherine's reign, underpinned by the wealth of the expanding empire, it evolved into one of the great cultural centers of Europe (see box). Catherine also greatly influenced the look of the capital, overseeing a shift from Baroque to a more restrained Neoclassical style.

A Russian culture

In the early 19th century, wars with Napoleon threatened the peace of the capital, but Russia (helped by the bitterly cold weather) managed to hold back the French. After the defeat of Napoleon, Alexander I ordered a vast construction program in the French-influenced "Empire" style, shown in grand edifices such as the Russian Museum building and Kazan Cathedral. Yet a distinctly Russian culture also began to emerge. The poet Alexander Pushkin founded the influential literary and political magazine *The Contemporary* in 1836, and novelists Nikolai Gogol and Fyodor Dostoevsky found inspiration in the city. In the other arts, St. Petersburg was developing an increasingly Russian outlook as a revival of traditional Russian architecture—seen in buildings like the Church of the Savior on Spilled Blood, with its striking multicolored domes—gathered strength.

Three revolutions

The city kept its reputation for luxury, especially among the aristocracy. However, courtiers in the finest furs and immaculately booted officers were jostled on the streets by beggars in rags and down-at-heel servants and workers. It was a place of extreme social contrasts, where some ate caviar and others lacked even bread.

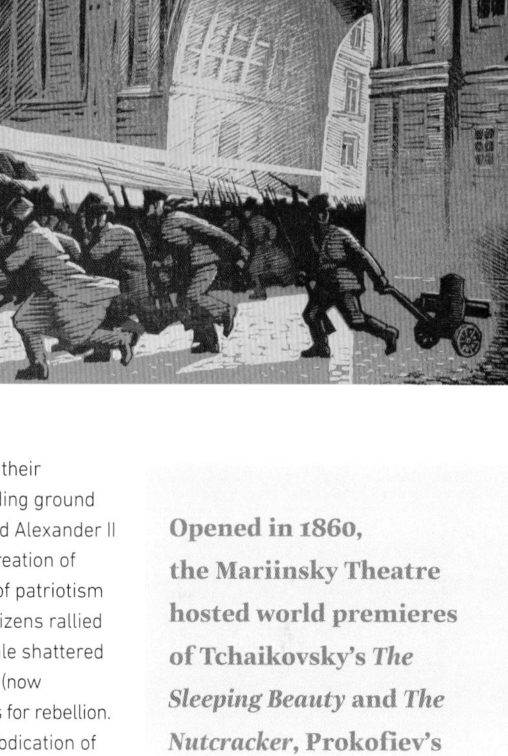

▷ OCTOBER REVOLUTION
The Bolsheviks' storming of the Winter Palace in October 1917 attacked the core of imperial power. It proved a pivotal moment in Russian history.

In 1861, the emancipation of the serfs broke the bonds between Russia's peasants and their landlords. Many moved to cities such as St. Petersburg, to work in textile and metalworking factories. Russia's industry developed quickly, helped by newly built railroads, but while some workers prospered many found they had to put up with squalid housing, with little prospect of change under their autocratic rulers. The capital became a breeding ground for revolutionary politics. Rebels assassinated Alexander II in 1881, and a revolution in 1905 led to the creation of Russia's first parliament, the Duma. A wave of patriotism greeted Russia's entry into World War I as citizens rallied to the imperial cause, but by 1916, with morale shattered by horrifying war losses, the streets of the city (now renamed Petrograd) once more rang with calls for rebellion. Violent clashes in February 1917 led to the abdication of Emperor Nicholas II, but the new provisional government's failure to end the war fed support for more radical change. In October 1917, Bolshevik revolutionaries (the "Reds") stormed the Winter Palace and removed the government.

Opened in 1860, the Mariinsky Theatre hosted world premieres of Tchaikovsky's *The Sleeping Beauty* and *The Nutcracker*, Prokofiev's *Romeo and Juliet*, and Aram Khachaturian's *Spartacus*.

1866 Fyodor Dostoevsky's *Crime and Punishment* is published; set in crowded taverns and gloomy tenements, the novel reflects the city's impoverished side.

1883 Construction of the Church of the Savior on Spilled Blood begins on the site of Alexander II's murder.

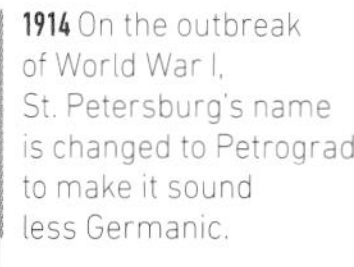

1905 The Bloody Sunday massacre of peaceful demonstrators sparks a wave of strikes and mutinies, leading to the foundation of the first Duma (parliament).

1914 On the outbreak of World War I, St. Petersburg's name is changed to Petrograd to make it sound less Germanic.

Fabergé's Lilies of the Valley egg

1916 The Fabergé company produces the last of its series of imperial Easter eggs.

1917 The imperial regime falls in March; eight months later, Bolsheviks seize power by storming the Winter Palace.

◁ THE SIEGE OF LENINGRAD
Many of the civilian casualties of the Siege of Leningrad suffered from starvation, particularly during the harsh winter of 1941–1942.

As the Bolsheviks, led by Vladimir Lenin, ended Russia's involvement in World War I and secured their grip on power, a loose counterrevolutionary coalition of moderate republicans and staunch pro-monarchists (the "Whites") mobilized in opposition to the new regime, with international support. Fearing a German attack on Petrograd, Lenin moved the capital to Moscow. As the country's opposing factions became engulfed in a bitter civil war, the city remained under Bolshevik control, fiercely defended by Lenin's Red Army. But the war's effect on the city was devastating. Thousands died as part of the nationwide wave of mass executions known as the "Red Terror," as the Bolsheviks brutally suppressed all opposition, and with the economy grinding to a halt many more died of starvation. By 1920, the population had shrunk by two-thirds, to around 750,000. Recovery set in after the Bolshevik victory, and on Lenin's death in 1924 the new Soviet Union's second city was renamed Leningrad in his honor.

> "I thought of every **uneaten bowl of soup**, every **crust of bread thrown away**, every potato peeling, with ... **remorse** and **despair**.
>
> DMITRI LIKHACHEV, SOVIET DISSIDENT, ON THE SIEGE OF LENINGRAD

Leningrad

The city grew rapidly in the 1920s as it served at the forefront of the Soviet industrial program, and the expanding suburbs were filled with utilitarian mass housing for the workers. But the assassination of the Leningrad Communist Party leader Sergei Kirov in 1934 commenced another tragic chapter. Lenin's successor, the authoritarian Joseph Stalin, used Kirov's murder (widely believed to have been ordered by Stalin himself) as a pretext to unleash another wave of violent purges. Leningrad, as home of the alleged opposition, was particularly brutally targeted. Those branded as "enemies of the people"—including many of the city's political and military elite—

1918 Russia descends into civil war; Moscow becomes the capital.

1919 In the Battle of Petrograd, the Red Army led by Leon Trotsky fends off the forces of the Whites.

Red Army propaganda poster, with the slogan "We will not give up Petrograd," 1919

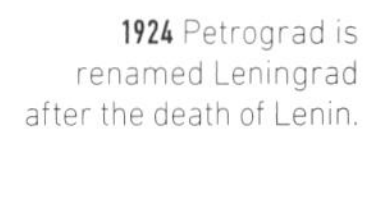

1924 Petrograd is renamed Leningrad after the death of Lenin.

Statue of Lenin in Lenin Square

1934 Sergei Kirov, the Communist Party leader in Leningrad, is assassinated.

1936 Stalin's Great Purge of wealthy peasants, ethnic minorities, and political opponents begins.

1941–1944 From September 8, 1941, to January 27, 1944 (a total of 872 days), the Nazis blockade Leningrad.

were arrested and sent to forced labor camps, and many were killed. Those who could, escaped to freedom in Western Europe or the US. They left behind a city in which spying and persecution were rife, and fear was universal.

In a depleted state following Stalin's purges, the Red Army was ill-prepared when the Soviet Union entered World War II and Leningrad found itself encircled by Nazi forces. The 28-month blockade was one of the greatest tragedies of the war, with supplies of food and fuel cut off and conditions almost unbearable in the severe cold of winter. At least 670,000 civilians lost their lives, and by 1944 the city lay in ruins. The exceptional bravery and suffering of ordinary men and women during the siege led to Leningrad being awarded the accolade of the Soviet Union's first "Hero City," but that was not enough to stop further Stalinist purges in the post-war period.

City of the future

Reconstruction took decades. Large-scale new housing was built on the city fringes, and the metro, begun before the war, reached completion in 1955. But despite productive industries, such as engineering, metalworking, and shipbuilding, Leningrad remained underfunded in favor of the capital, with a wide gap between rich and poor. As the sclerotic Soviet system veered toward collapse in the late 1980s, city dwellers took advantage of their new freedoms, holding vast demonstrations to expedite its demise.

Although inequality remains a serious issue, the 21st century has seen huge growth in the economy and urban regeneration. And as eye-catching new buildings take their place alongside the beautifully restored *grandes dames* of old, this richly historical city is embracing the future with as much vigor as at any time in its past.

△ **FONTANKA EMBANKMENT**
The writers Alexander Pushkin, Ivan Turgenev, and Anna Akhmatova are among the many cultural figures who have lived in the elegant 18th- and 19th-century palaces and houses flanking the Fontanka River.

1942 Dmitri Shostakovich's stirring 7th Symphony (the "Leningrad") helps inspire resistance while the city is under siege.

1948–1950 During the "Leningrad Affair" many members of the city's government are arrested on false charges; some are executed.

1991 The Soviet Union is dissolved; the people of Leningrad vote to restore the name St. Petersburg.

2008 The Constitutional Court of Russia moves to St. Petersburg from Moscow.

2019 The 87-story Lakhta Center, at 1,516 ft (462 m) Europe's tallest building, is completed.

Isfahan

HALF THE WORLD

Four hundred years ago, as the glittering capital of Safavid Persia (now Iran), Isfahan was larger than London, more cosmopolitan than Paris, and more beautiful than Rome.

History is full of instances of kings, emperors, sultans, and shahs commissioning imposing monuments and palaces, but rarely has their ambition stretched to creating an entire city. Such was the achievement of Shah Abbas, the Persian monarch who in just 30 years, from 1598 to 1629, established a glorious new capital that inspired the rhyming proverb *"Isfahan nesf-e jahan,"* or "Isfahan, half the world."

A city of lost heads

Isfahan predated Abbas: historians suggest that when Cyrus the Great, the founder of the first Persian Empire, captured Babylon in the 6th century BCE and declared that its Jews could return to Jerusalem, some of them instead chose to settle in Isfahan. The city was conquered by Islamic armies in 642 CE and grew to prosperity under first the Persian Buyid dynasty and then the Seljuk Turks. After the fall of the Seljuks it declined, but visiting in 1327 the great Arab traveler Ibn Battuta could still remark that, "The city of Isfahan is one of the largest and fairest of cities, but it is now in ruins for the greater part." The ruin was caused by the Mongols, who had launched repeated attacks in the 13th century. Worse was to come: in 1387, Isfahan surrendered to the Mongol warlord Timur. The Isfahanis revolted and, in retribution, Timur ordered a massacre of its residents. His soldiers killed 70,000 citizens and built 28 towers out of their heads.

◁ MASJID-E SHAH
Shah Abbas conceived his immense public mosque to be without equal. Referring to the most sacred site in Mecca, its foundation inscription reads, "A second Kaaba has been built."

> The **epitome** of the world is **Iran**, the **epitome** of Iran is **Isfahan.**
>
> MULLAH SALIH QAZVINI, 17TH-CENTURY PERSIAN SCHOLAR

559 BCE A town called Gabae exists on the future site of Isfahan during the Achaemenid era.

642 CE A Muslim Arab army captures the town and makes it a regional capital.

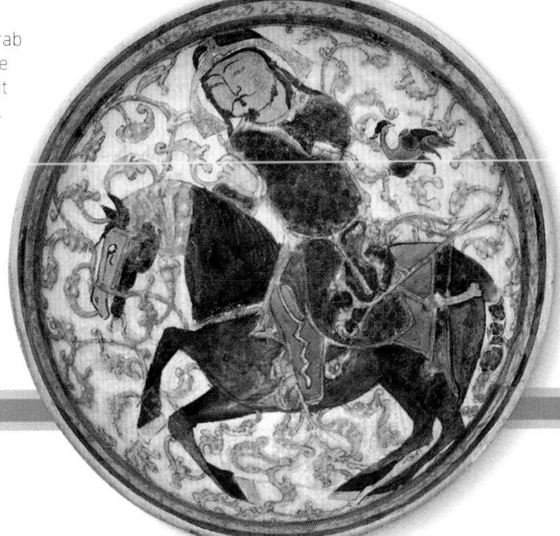

Seljuk ceramic bowl, 12th–13th century

1051 Toghril Beg, founder of the Turkic Seljuk dynasty, makes Isfahan his capital.

1072 The reign of Malik Shah I begins. He commissions the Masjid-e Jami, the city's oldest surviving mosque.

1387 Turkic-Mongol warlord Timur captures and plunders Isfahan, then slaughters its citizens.

△ SHEIKH LOTFOLLAH MOSQUE
Once the preserve of the royal court, the Lotfollah Mosque is decorated inside and out with multicolor patterned tiling.

△ MAYDAN-E NAQSH-E JAHAN
In the time of Shah Abbas, this vast square (shown here in the 1840s) was used to host horse-racing, polo matches, and other festivities. Anchored by the Masjid-e Shah mosque, it was also a shopping hub, with exotic goods from the Silk Road laid out on merchants' stalls.

Safavid glories

The Safavids were followers of the teachings of celebrated Sufi ascetic Sheikh Safi-al-Din, from whom they took their name. They originated in northwestern Iran, and following a series of victories on the battlefield their leader, Ismail, a 14-year-old descendant of the sheikh, proclaimed himself shah (king) in 1501. Abbas, who came to power in 1588 at the age of 17, was the fifth of the Safavid shahs. His predecessors had ruled first from Tabriz and then Qazvin, but both cities were vulnerable to incursions from the Ottoman Turks to the west, and so Abbas moved the seat of Safavid power southeast to Isfahan. There, he planned to create a capital that would exemplify the greatness of the Safavid Empire. Rather than remodel the existing city, he laid out a new city beside the old, between the extant walls and the Zayanderud River.

Image of the World Square

The focal point for the new city was a vast public plaza, the Maydan-e Naqsh-e Jahan ("image of the world square"). This was cut with water channels for coolness, and enclosed by a perimeter of arcaded shops with rows

> "The **people of Isfahan** are very **open with ... foreigners**, having to **deal every day** with people of other nations.
>
> ANTONIO DE GOUVEA, 17TH-CENTURY PORTUGUESE AMBASSADOR

1598 The Safavid Shah Abbas I makes Isfahan his capital and sets about building a regal new city.

1602 The 33-arch Si-o-se Pol, officially the Allahverdi Khan Bridge, is built across the Zayanderud River, serving as both a bridge and a dam.

1629 Workers complete the Masjid-e Shah, or Shah Mosque, which anchors the south side of Abbas's grand central square.

1722 Afghan tribesmen defeat a Safavid army and capture Isfahan.

▷ THE GARDENS OF ISFAHAN
In the Safavid period, visitors often compared the city to a forest because of its profusion of trees and flowering gardens, as enjoyed by the small group gathering for a picnic in this Safavid-era tiled panel.

of plane trees for shade. The square's purpose was both ceremonial and functional, hosting market traders, public entertainment, and military parades. The arcade on the north side linked with the old bazaar, while a grand gate set in the western arcade led through to the royal gardens and magnificent Ali Qapu Palace, the shah's official residence. Facing the gate across the square was the Sheikh Lotfollah Mosque, an exquisitely decorated place of worship reserved for the shah and the women of the court: it was connected to the palace via a tunnel. The grand public mosque, the stupendous Masjid-e Shah, sat on the fourth side of the square.

Beyond the square, Abbas's city included broad, tree-lined promenades; parks and gardens with terraces and shallow pools in which bobbed cut roses; and multiple viewing pavilions from which to appreciate all this splendor. To conduct the royal road into the city, the shah had his engineers construct the Si-o-se Pol, or "bridge of 33 spans," which Britain's Lord Curzon, visiting in 1889, thought "the stateliest bridge in the world."

The fall of Isfahan

By the mid-1600s, Isfahan had a population of around 600,000—larger than London—with an open intellectual climate and a cosmopolitan outlook. After Abbas, however, a succession of progressively weaker Safavid shahs made few further contributions to Isfahan's magnificence.

In 1722, Afghan invaders laid siege to the city for six months, and its citizens were reduced to cannibalism before the last of the Safavid shahs surrendered. The Afghans responded to the surrender with a fury of killing and devastation. The fall of Isfahan ended the most brilliant period in Iranian history. Much of the city was left in rubble, and new rulers eventually moved the capital to Tehran. Renovation did not properly begin until the early 19th century, when governor Hajji Mohammed Hossein Isfahani began an extensive rebuilding campaign.

Isfahan began to grow in the early part of the 20th century, its population swollen by migrants from the south, and again in the 1980s by those fleeing the border during the war against Iraq. Today, the city is Iran's third-largest metropolis, and growing fast: between just 2000 and 2021 its population leapt from 1.4 million to 2.2 million. And while modern Isfahan is known as the site of Iran's premier nuclear research facility, care has been taken to preserve the legacy of Abbas. The heart of the city remains a showcase for the greatest ensemble of Islamic architecture ever created.

Since its creation in the early 17th century, the only significant change to the Maydan-e Naqsh-e Jahan, Isfahan's central square, has been the addition of fountains.

1736 Isfahan loses its status as the capital of Persia, as Mashhad in the northeast and then Tehran become the new centers of power.

1920 The status of Isfahan has dwindled to such a degree that its population stands at just 80,000.

1979 Following a popular revolution focused on the figure of Ayatollah Khomeini, Iran becomes an Islamic republic. One of the city's main streets is renamed after him.

1980 The eight-year Iran–Iraq War begins, during which Isfahan swells with migrants escaping the border.

2015 Isfahan Metro starts operating.

Singapore

LION CITY

Singapore is an island, a city, and a state—and one of the world's strongest economies. Once a duty-free harbor surrounded by swamps, this multiethnic metropolis is now a picture of verdant prosperity.

By the 8th century CE, the Malay Peninsula was controlled by Sumatra's Srivijaya Empire. Yet the island at its tip remained a backwater, and is barely mentioned in histories until the end of the 13th century, when legend tells of a Sumatran prince who, after spotting a big cat, proclaimed the land Singapura ("lion city" in Sanskrit) and established a port. Chinese traders arrived to export hornbill ivory, laka wood, and tin, and established communities alongside local Malays. The town, which was probably sited near Fort Canning in modern Singapore, welcomed Mongolian, Indian, and Arab merchants, and the seeds of multicultural life were planted.

By the end of the 14th century, empires based in Malacca, northwest of Singapore, and Thailand were competing over the region, and Singapore declined. In 1511, the Portuguese, who dominated the spice trade between Europe and Asia, took Malacca, and in 1613 they destroyed Singapore's port.

In the 17th century, naval power slipped from the Portuguese to the Dutch. But another empire was growing increasingly ambitious. The British were eager to expand, not least because the lucrative opium trade between China and British India passed through the archipelago.

Port prosperity

Lieutenant Thomas Stamford Raffles stepped onto the island in 1819, and saw opportunity in its forested swamps. He struck treaties with the local rulers, who allowed the British to establish a trading base.

Raffles turned the small settlement into a free port with a deep-water harbor, and divided it into ethnic districts that remain visible today. In the 1820s, a series of treaties gave the British control of the whole island and, in the absence of tax and restrictions, trade soared. Between 1819 and 1824, the population swelled from 1,000 to 10 times that number as Chinese, Malay, and Indian workers made the port their home. Further growth came in 1869, when the Suez Canal slashed transportation times between Europe and Asia. Trade tripled in a decade, and soon boats laden with rubber grown on the peninsula sailed around the world.

GARDENS BY THE BAY ▷
This lush park in the Marina Bay district features the Flower Dome, the world's largest glass greenhouse (left), and the OCBC Skyway (foreground), whose walkways wind around vertical gardens.

Singapore is the oldest archaeologically confirmed area of Chinese settlement outside of China.

c. 1299 CE According to tradition, a Sumatran prince takes control of a fishing village and names the island Singapura.

1613 Portuguese raiders burn down Singapore town, and the island is neglected for 200 years.

1819 Thomas Stamford Raffles strikes treaties with chieftains to convert the island's swampland into a deep-water harbor.

1826 With Penang and Malacca, Singapore forms part of the Straits Settlements, controlled by the British East India Company (and later a British Crown colony).

Rubber tree plantation in Singapore, c. 1890

1860s Trade accelerates under the British, with spices, tin, and later rubber passing through Singapore's increasingly busy port.

△ SINGAPORE, 1931
Singapore attracted workers, merchants, and British high society. This illustration by Donald Maxwell comes from Rudyard Kipling's book *East of Suez*.

The British and the Chinese

By the end of the 19th century, Singapore was a busy frontier town. Rickshaws dashed between the docks, trading firms, narrow shophouses, and Chinese temples. Workers labored in fields of pineapple and rubber trees, or in fish and tin processing plants. Some locals sought solace in opium and gambling dens, and Singapore became known for its lawlessness, while diseases such as cholera and smallpox ripped through the cramped poorer districts.

The wealthier parts of town were a magnet for the British elite. Colonial buildings rose, and the Raffles Hotel offered an elevated level of service to match its guests' aspirations. Electric lights and fans brought comfort, while the Singapore Sling was invented in the hotel's Long Bar. The cocktail made it acceptable, and downright elegant, for high-society ladies to sip alcohol in public under the guise of a pink fruit drink. Elsewhere, baskets of noodles on poles bounced through the streets to feed Chinese dock workers, and portable stoves perched in Indian construction sites.

Chinese people had formed the largest ethnic group in Singapore since 1827, but until the 1930s, most were temporary male workers who sent money back to China. Once they began to stay and start families, their culture became an increasingly important part of the island's identity. Hokkien and Mandarin helped give Singaporean English its idiosyncratic sound, while Cantonese-speakers brought *wayang* (Chinese street opera) to neighborhood temples. Every week, silk-robed actors performed traditional dramas, often based on folk tales, as the air filled with the sound of cymbals and the waft of incense.

1887 Raffles Hotel opens, named after Singapore's British founder. Bartender Ngiam Tong Boon develops the Singapore Sling cocktail here by 1915.

1942 The Japanese occupy Singapore for three years. Europeans are imprisoned and thousands of Chinese men are executed.

1950s *Wayang* (Chinese street opera), performed for a century on temple grounds, declines with the postwar economic downturn.

Wayang street performers, 1960

1959 Singapore elects its first prime minister, Lee Kuan Yew of the People's Action Party (PAP). He rules for 31 years, transforming the nation.

Singapore was largely unaffected by World War I, but the British were wary of Japanese power, and after the conflict they built a huge dry dock. Defended by heavy guns, it was part of a first-rate naval infrastructure. Yet the British were not prepared for an assault from the north. When World War II began, the Japanese army marched through the Malay Peninsula, crossing the narrow Straits of Johor and taking Singapore in 1942. Under Japanese occupation, Chinese men endured particular persecution, and many were executed. The British returned to govern in 1945, but their failure to protect Singapore led to a rise in nationalism, and in the 1950s the island moved toward self-government.

Independence

In 1959, Singapore elected its first prime minister, Lee Kuan Yew (see box, p. 250). He faced serious problems, including social unrest and poor, overcrowded housing. Singapore briefly joined Malaysia in 1963, but negotiations collapsed amid violence, and in 1965 it became an independent state. It was a bold move. The country had half the land area of London and no natural resources.

Lee's laws were draconian (he restricted press freedom and expanded corporal punishment) but business-friendly, and attracted international investment. He also wanted to provide home ownership to all, and the government began buying up land via the Housing & Development Board (HDB). Villages and shophouses—two- or three-story apartments above shops—were torn down and replaced with self-contained, affordable residences, which were landscaped and connected to new local shops and services. City life became high-rise and high-density, and by the 1980s, more than 80 percent of Singaporeans lived in HDB apartments.

> **Singapore** is the **meeting place** of a **hundred peoples.**
>
> BRITISH WRITER SOMERSET MAUGHAM, *THE LETTER*, 1926

NEOCLASSICAL BUILDINGS NEAR MARINA BAY ▷
This 1960s photograph shows the Fullerton Building (top) and the Victoria Memorial Hall and Clock Tower (right). These colonial edifices would soon be joined by towering HDB apartments.

1960 The Housing & Development Board (HDB) is established to deal with the housing crisis.

1963 Malaysia becomes a new country, incorporating Singapore.

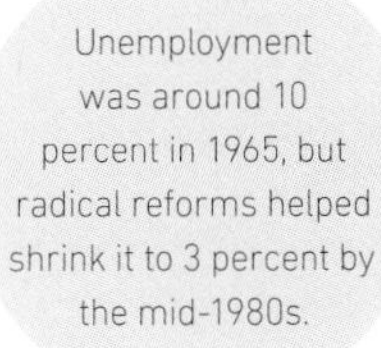

Unemployment was around 10 percent in 1965, but radical reforms helped shrink it to 3 percent by the mid-1980s.

The Age

SINGAPORE IS OUT OF MALAYSIA

Split may lead to stability

Swift bid for 'relations' by Indonesia

Racial rivalry

STOP PRESS

1965 Singapore becomes an independent state. English, Malay, Mandarin, and Tamil are declared the official languages.

1967 National Service requires all men to serve two years of active military duty.

Lee Kuan Yew

> **Nobody** doubts that if you **take me on**, I will put on **knuckle-dusters** and catch you in a **cul-de-sac**.

LEE KUAN YEW, SINGAPORE'S FIRST PRIME MINISTER, 1994

Singapore prospered because of its first prime minister. Lee Kuan Yew governed for an astonishing 31 years, from 1959 to 1990. He restricted freedoms and kept a tight grip on power, but helped transform Singapore into one of Asia's wealthiest countries.

Lee was third-generation ethnic Chinese and studied law at Cambridge. His first language was English, and he did not start learning Mandarin until he was 32. He advocated Confucian values of loyalty to the family and state, and pushed for English and Mandarin bilingualism. Lee slashed public holidays and imposed heavy fines for vandalism, while his anti-corruption bureau could investigate the bank accounts of anybody, including the children of officials—living beyond your means was seen as evidence of a bribe. Lee's government built excellent public housing and propelled Singapore from a struggling island to an international finance and tourism hub.

△ Lee Kuan Yew visiting the housing projects he famously introduced. Lee brought affordable home ownership to the vast majority of Singaporeans.

△ Lee celebrating his first election as prime minister, 1959.

1970 Singapore's population reaches two million.

1971 Hawker carts are gradually licensed and resettled in centers created by the HDB. The popular spaces function as community dining halls.

1973 Singapore Zoo opens. It uses modern, landscaped enclosures rather than visible cages for its 270 species.

1978 All currency exchange controls are abolished, laying the way for a foreign exchange that by 2013 overtakes Japan to become Asia's largest.

Singapore's MRT railroad opened in 1987, and is now used by over three million people a day.

1987 All schools are directed to conduct lessons in English, solidifying Singapore as a primarily English-speaking country.

1990 Goh Chok Tong becomes the second prime minister of Singapore, with slight relaxation of state control.

Hawker halls and green shoots

For centuries, hawkers have been whipping up hot dishes to give Singapore's workforce a taste of home. But hawkers also strayed through each other's territories, shaping a unique cuisine. Malaysian satay skewers and Indian curry puffs borrowed each other's spices and *rojak buah* combined Singaporean pineapple with Chinese doughnuts.

To fix low cleanliness standards on congested streets, from 1971 the government began pushing hawkers into food halls attached to new HDB towns and imposed hygiene ratings. Over the decades, they have become respectable enough for one hawker stand to be awarded a Michelin star for its soy-sauce chicken—the first street-food vendor in the world to receive the accolade.

In 1978, all currency exchange controls were abolished, and by the end of the decade a quarter of the country's GDP derived from finance. Changi Airport opened in 1981 to match the still-thriving port. Locals zipped across the city on the new MRT rail network, from cramped one-room HDB flats in Jalan Kukoh to the multilingual cries of Tekka Wet Market and the glittering office blocks of Orchard Road. Tourists arrived in droves to sample the city's cuisine, shops, galleries, ultra-modern infrastructure, and major resorts such as Universal Studios.

Between 1980 and 2010, Singapore's population doubled from 2.5 to 5 million. In the 2010s, as HDB residences stretched taller than ever, this urban island brought nature into its architecture with the futuristic Gardens by the Bay nature reserve. By 2020, the Singapore Food Agency was sketching its vision for rooftop farms atop lofty parking lots, glistening with fresh produce to meet nearly a third of the population's needs. Singapore appeared as multiethnic as ever, a prosperous world leader with a future that is as green as it is gleaming.

△ MARINA BAY SANDS
The triple towers of this resort in Singapore's commercial center contain a casino, hotel, museum, exhibitions, and the world's longest elevated pool.

The lion-headed, fish-shaped "Merlion" is the symbol of Singapore—a Merlion fountain stands in the park of the same name.

2009 The 50-story "Pinnacle" residential development opens with two sky gardens that stretch 1,600 ft (500 m)—the longest ever built on skyscrapers.

2013 Drama *Ilo Ilo* wins the Caméra d'Or at the Cannes Film Festival, a first for a Singaporean feature film.

2012 Gardens by the Bay opens. The futuristic botanical garden seeks to bring greenery into Asia's second-smallest country.

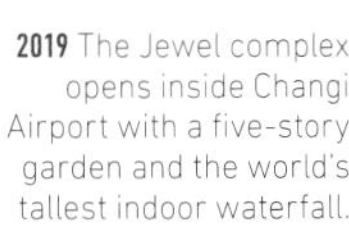

2019 The Jewel complex opens inside Changi Airport with a five-story garden and the world's tallest indoor waterfall.

2020 Hawker culture is added to the Intangible Cultural Heritage list by UNESCO.

▽ **MAP OF KYOTO, 19TH CENTURY**
Modern Kyoto retains much of its original grid design, as seen in this 19-century woodblock print, which also shows the mountains surrounding the city. Note that due north is not at the top, but on the left side of the map.

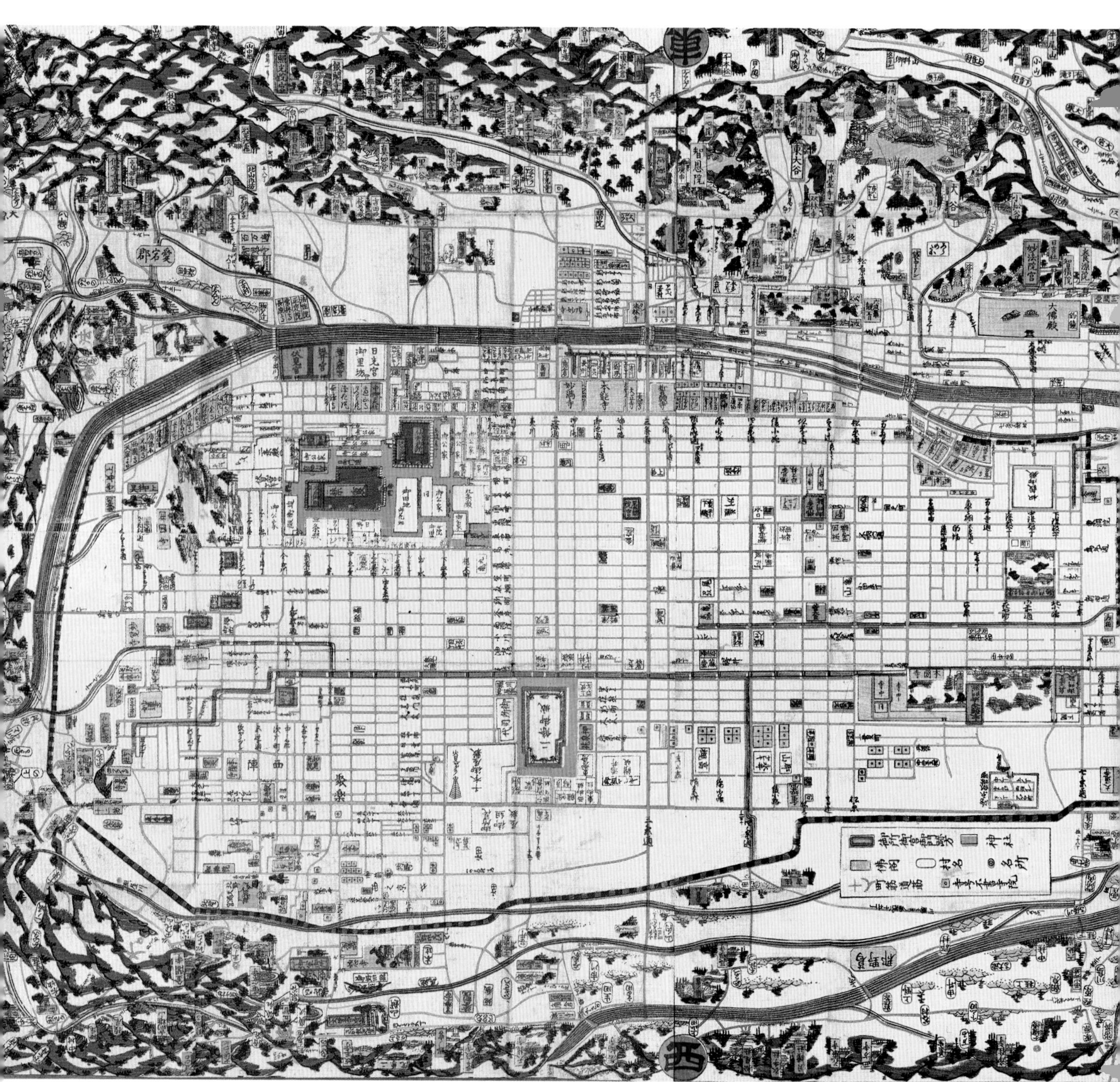

Kyoto

THE THOUSAND-YEAR CAPITAL

Kyoto was Japan's imperial capital for over a millennium. The setting for both the golden Heian age and a medieval renaissance spurred by Zen Buddhism, the city shaped Japanese culture as we know it today.

For many centuries, Japan was occupied by a patchwork of clans, but from around the 4th century CE, an imperial dynasty gradually gained power over the main island of Honshū. Its court initially changed location after each ruler, as death was taboo in the local Shintō religion. In the 700s, however, this practice gave way to the idea of a fixed capital, most likely inspired by interactions with Korea and China and the influence of Buddhism. After a few fits and starts, Heian-kyō—later called Kyoto—was founded in central Honshū in 794 CE. It would remain the imperial capital for centuries to come.

Heian-kyō: a model city

Heian-kyō was modelled after Chang'an (present-day Xi'an; see pp. 60–65), the capital of Tang-dynasty China and the largest city in the world at the time. It was laid out in a grid on a north–south axis: at the top was the Imperial Palace compound, from where a grand boulevard led through the city to the main gate, Rashōmon. Smaller, numbered avenues ran east–west. The powerful clans which made up the nobility were allotted land according to status: the higher the rank, the greater the plot size and, more importantly, the closer to the Imperial Palace. Heian-kyō was a city where status mattered more than anything: to live below Rokujō (Sixth Avenue) was unacceptable for an aristocrat.

Heian-kyō's layout wasn't just geometrical: it also followed ancient Chinese geomancy (otherwise known as feng shui). The palace compound was oriented to the North Star and the main boulevard—running south from the palace and, crucially, from the emperor's perspective —was named Suzaku ("vermilion bird") for the creature that represents summer and the south. The city's location, in a basin surrounded on three sides by mountains, was also auspicious. Especially important was the presence of the 2,782-ft (848-m) Mount Hiei to the northeast – a direction associated with evil in Chinese geomancy. The mountain, and the Buddhist monastery of Enryaku-ji built atop it, would protect the city.

794 CE Emperor Kammu establishes the imperial capital at Heian-kyō. The city is renamed Kyoto in the 11th century.

805 The monk Saichō establishes the Tendai sect of Buddhism, centered on Mount Hiei.

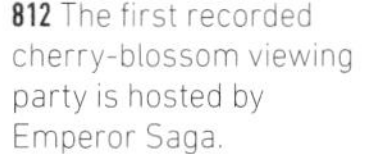

812 The first recorded cherry-blossom viewing party is hosted by Emperor Saga.

869 A procession conducted as a purification ritual against the plague is the origin of Kyoto's famous Gion Matsuri festival.

Founder of the Fujiwara clan, Fujiwara no Kamatari

900s The Fujiwara clan solidifies its grip on the court with a succession of strategic marriages and regencies.

△ *THE TALE OF GENJI*
Written in installments in the 11th century by Heian-kyō lady-in-waiting Murasaki Shikibu, *The Tale of Genji* was a hit in its own time. It is also an invaluable record of the culture of the imperial court, and famous scenes have inspired countless artistic representations, like this 19th-century woodblock print by Hiroshige.

The culture of Heian-kyō

Heian-kyō means "capital of peace and tranquility," and its founding ushered in the Heian era (794–1185), four centuries that laid the foundations for Japanese culture. Wars took place at the fringes of the empire, which would grow during this time to encompass all of present-day Japan save for the islands of Hokkaidō and Okinawa. But for the city's courtiers it was largely a peaceful time, one that allowed a rich culture to develop. The capital was everything for this elite class—there were no executions in Heian-kyō, as banishment to the provinces was considered punishment enough.

The court paid tribute to the powerful empire of China, and Japanese emissaries brought back the latest ideas on statecraft, technology, and the arts. But the Tang dynasty crumbled in the late 800s, and from this point on the culture of the court—and by extension the city and empire—developed with little outside influence. Refined aesthetics, in tune with the subtle changes of nature, evolved. The nobility delighted in excursions to see flowers in bloom or hear birdsong. Poetry—the greatest art of the era, composed for lovers or contests held at court—was judged by how well it captured a scene in a particular moment.

This was a golden age for culture. Japan developed its own Buddhist iconography, in the form of statues and mandala paintings, as well as new writing scripts and lacquerware techniques. Yet life for ordinary people was hard. By the 1100s, unprecedented fires and natural disasters, followed by bloody succession battles—and eventually a full-blown civil war—spelled the end of peace and tranquility, and the beginning of the feudal era.

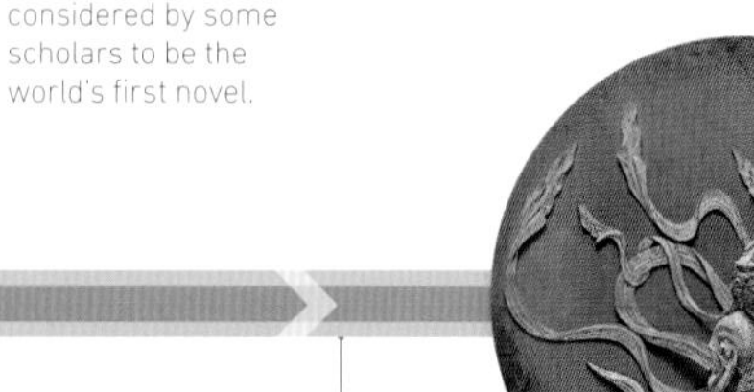

1000s Murasaki Shikibu writes *The Tale of Genji*, considered by some scholars to be the world's first novel.

1053 Jōchō, known as the father of Japanese Buddhist sculpture, carves the Amida Nyorai ("the Buddha of Limitless Light"), his most famous work.

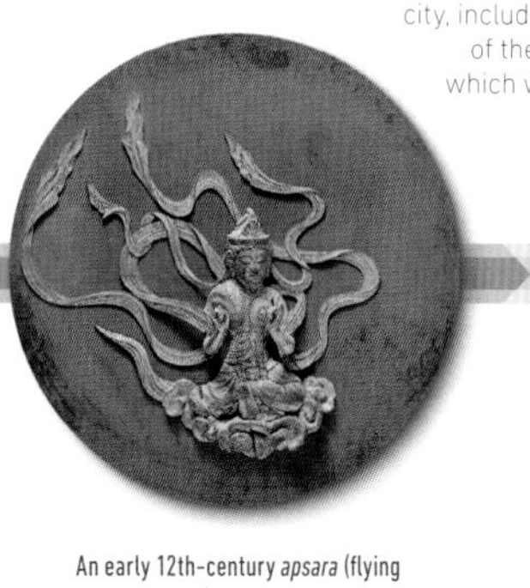

An early 12th-century *apsara* (flying celestial being) sculpture from Kyoto

1177 The Great Angen Fire destroys a large part of the city, including the Great Hall of the Imperial Palace, which was never rebuilt.

1180 The Genpei War begins, bringing an end to the largely peaceful Heian era.

1192 General Minamoto Yoritomo, victor of the Genpei War, declares himself the first shogun of Japan.

The Tale of Heike, a 14th-century epic account of the Genpei War

Buddhism in Kyoto

△ Saichō founded Tendai Buddhism, based on Chinese teachings, in Japan in 805 CE.

"Though you **wipe your hands** and brush off the **dust and dirt** from the vessels, what is the use of all this fuss if **the heart is still impure?**

TEA MASTER SEN NO RIKYŪ, 16TH CENTURY

Kyoto, from its inception, was inseparable from Buddhism, which arrived in Japan via Korea in the 6th century CE. During the Heian era, distinctly Japanese sects emerged, notably Tendai Buddhism, to which the great monastery on Mount Hiei belongs. Tendai Buddhism was patronized by the Heian imperial court, where its rituals were performed, and it was common for members of the imperial family to study and train at Mount Hiei. Its most important contribution to Japanese culture was a doctrine that allowed the native Shinto belief system to coexist with Buddhism.

In the 12th century, Japanese monks went to China to study, only to discover that a whole new sect had emerged: Chan Buddhism, which would become Zen in Japan. Zen entered the country just as feudalism was taking root and Zen Buddhism, with its emphasis on discipline, found followers among the ascendant warrior class. Its focus on minimalism and mindful rituals would shape tea ceremonies—Japan's most famous tea master, Sen no Rikyū, was a student of Zen. Indeed, throughout Japan's medieval period, the monasteries of Kyoto would have a profound influence on culture, architecture, and the arts.

△ Japan's two main Zen sects are Sōtō and Rinzai. These monks, pictured in the 1930s, follow Rinzai, which is more prominent in Kyoto. Rinzai temples feature the dry landscape gardens with rocks, moss, and carefully raked gravel so associated with Zen.

1202 Kyoto's first Zen temple, Kennin-ji, is established by the monk Eisai, who introduces Zen teachings to Japan, as well as popularizing tea drinking.

By the 1200s much of Kyoto, including the Rashōmon gate, was decaying. This is the backdrop for Akira Kurosawa's film *Rashōmon*.

1212 Poet Kamo no Chōmei writes "An Account of a Ten-Foot-Square Hut," a work known for its expression of *mujō* (the Buddhist concept of impermanence), inspired by recent fires and earthquakes in Kyoto.

1319 Daitoku-ji is founded. One of Kyoto's largest and most important Zen temples, this is where tea master Sen no Rikyū studied.

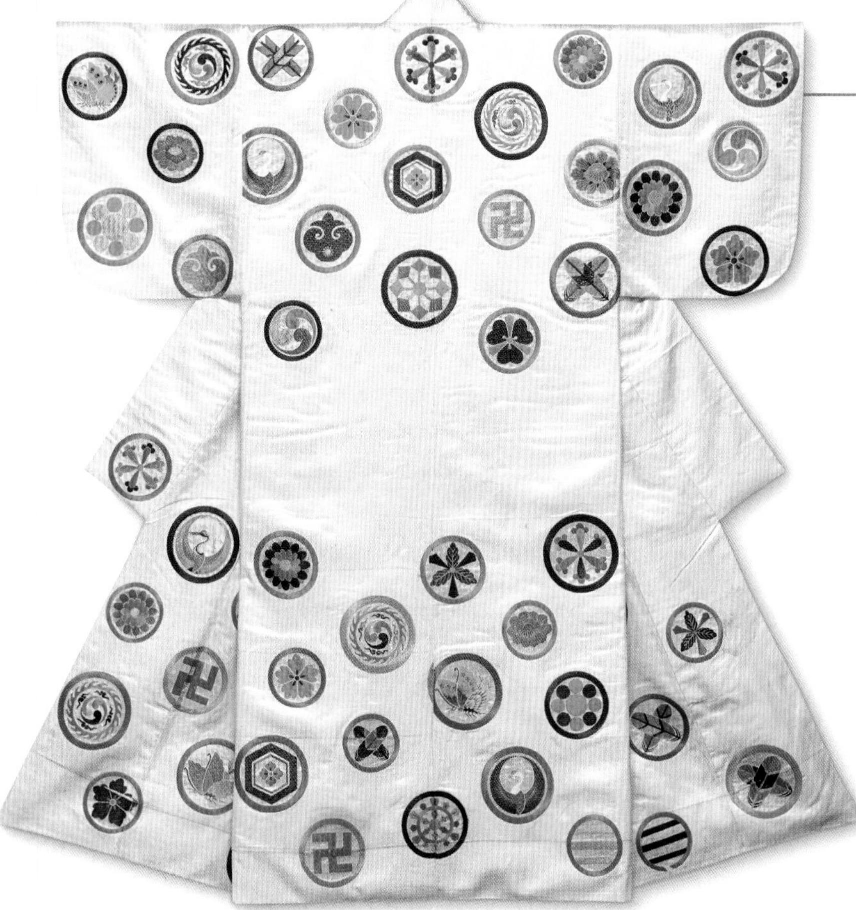

◁ NŌ COSTUME FROM THE EDO PERIOD (1603–1868)
Nō dance theater blends popular entertainment, older folk rituals, and courtly music. It was developed in the late 14th century by actor and musician Kan'ami and further established by his son, Zen'ami—considered among Japan's greatest dramatists. It is still performed today by *nō* actors wearing ornately embroidered robes.

Medieval Kyoto

After the civil war, the emperor remained ruler in title, but authority had shifted to a new figure: the shogun, or "supreme commander." In 1185, the ruling shoguns made Kamakura, a village far from Kyoto, their political capital. Yet the emperor and court stayed in Kyoto, and when the Kamakura shogunate fell to the forces of General Ashikaga Takauji in 1333, Kyoto became Japan's full capital again—a title it would hold for 200 years to come.

The Ashikaga weren't great rulers—they allowed regional warlords to gain too much power—but they were fine patrons of the arts, and *nō* plays and *sadō* ("the way of tea") emerged during their reign. In the 1500s, a new style of *sadō* that prized imperfection, impermanence, and a rustic minimalism grew in popularity. It would have a lasting impact on the arts, influencing forms as diverse as pottery, flower arrangement, and architecture.

This creativity took place amid turmoil: the infamous Ōnin War of the late 15th century left Kyoto in ruins, erasing all that remained of the Heian era, and kicking off a century of near-constant warfare. The period saw the city rebuilt, but the conflict dealt another blow to Kyoto: the victor, Tokugawa Ieyasu, formed a new shogunate in a village called Edo, which would later be known as Tokyo.

"In **Kyoto**,
hearing **the cuckoo**,
I long for **Kyoto**.

"IN KYOTO", MATSUO BASHO, 1690 (TRANSLATED BY JANE HIRSHFIELD)

1397 The third Ashikaga shogun commissions the construction of Kyoto's famous Golden Pavilion.

1467 A succession dispute triggers the start of the 10-year Ōnin War, which all but destroys Kyoto.

The late 16th century saw great artistic progress; the tea ceremony reached its zenith.

1573 Powerful warlord Oda Nobunaga overthrows the Ashikaga shogunate.

1600s The Katsura Imperial Villa, considered by many to be the pinnacle of Japanese architecture, is constructed over several decades.

Modern Kyoto

The Meiji Restoration of 1868 (see p. 297) brought about the return of the emperor's authority. But it also ushered in the end of Kyoto's reign as imperial capital. The court moved to Tokyo, and its artists followed. The city lost a third of its population in less than a decade. Kyoto retained a certain cachet in the coming decades: it had, after all, been the imperial capital for over a thousand years. Goods produced here—from turnips to sumptuous textiles—bear the suffix "kyo" and are considered the height of good taste. Rebuilt over the centuries, the city's temples are outstanding examples of traditional aesthetics and architecture, and the practice of the arts from the medieval era, from tea ceremonies to *nō* theater, continues to this day. Kyoto is where Japanese people go to learn about their culture, a living city that echoes with the past.

△ HIGASHIYAMA DISTRICT
Higashiyama is one of the best-preserved districts in Kyoto, with many traditional buildings made of stucco and wood. The temples Kiyomizu-dera and Ginkaku-ji are here, as is the Gion neighborhood, where most of the city's *geiko* (geisha) houses are located.

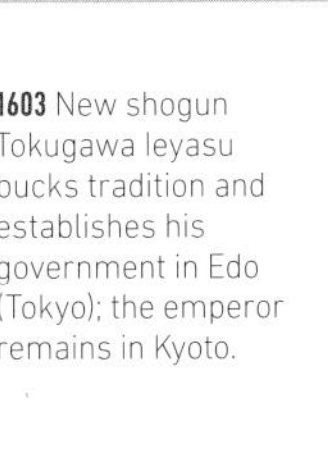

1603 New shogun Tokugawa Ieyasu bucks tradition and establishes his government in Edo (Tokyo); the emperor remains in Kyoto.

1800s Kyoto's *geiko* (the Kyoto dialect word for geisha, women skilled in traditional arts and entertainment) become the height of fashion.

1868 Following the Meiji Restoration, the emperor moves to Tokyo, and that city's castle is refashioned into a new imperial palace.

1894 Kyoto celebrates its 1,100th year with the construction of the great hall at the Heian Shrine, a reproduction of the original Heian Imperial Palace.

1994 Kyoto's historic monuments gain UNESCO World Heritage status, with Shinto shrines and Buddhist temples honored.

1997 Representatives from nations around the world meet in Kyoto to sign a treaty on climate change, popularly known as the Kyoto Protocol.

Washington, D.C.

THE AMERICAN ROME

Specially planned in the 18th century as the grand capital of the newly independent United States, Washington, D.C., has played a unique role in American history and remains a focal point for global attention.

Rich in natural resources, the area of Chesapeake Bay that would become Washington, D.C., had long been a flourishing trade center for the Indigenous Nacotchtank people before the arrival of European colonists in the early 17th century. After establishing the settlement of Jamestown in the Colony of Virginia in 1607, the English explorer John Smith led a crew up the Potomac River the following year; the expedition mapped the region and reached the river's furthest navigable point, later settled as Georgetown. The English newcomers traded fur and set up plantations of tobacco and corn across the region, forcing enslaved Africans to do the backbreaking work of harvesting the crops, and gradually suppressed the Indigenous population, with whom regular disputes arose over land ownership.

The first fort in what is now the District of Columbia was built in 1697, but it was not until the mid-18th century that the Potomac ports of Georgetown (now a historic neighborhood in the northwest of Washington, D.C.) and Alexandria, 7 miles (12 km) across the river to the south, were formally established.

A new capital city

Within a few years, both towns were thriving communities attracting a growing stream of settlers, lured by the booming transatlantic trade in tobacco and other goods. The towns were laid out on a grid plan and soon populated with churches, schools, banks, and taverns.

Meanwhile, conflict was brewing between the American colonists and their British overlords over the issue of taxation. Full-scale war erupted in 1775, initially going the way of the British—Georgetown was occupied by British troops for almost a year—but by 1783 the Americans had prevailed. In the resulting Constitution of the newly independent United States of America, ratified in 1788, a key provision was the creation of a new, purpose-built capital city, to be located on land "not exceeding 10 miles square" (26 sq km). The land was not to form part of any of the existing states, and Congress was to agree the location.

WASHINGTON, D.C., c. 1856 ▷
From the outset, Washington, D.C., was planned on a monumental scale. Capitol Hill was so named by Thomas Jefferson, then the nation's first Secretary of State, in 1793, in reference to the Capitoline Hill, one of the seven hills of Rome.

John Smith's 1612 map of Virginia

1607 Captain John Smith lands in Chesapeake Bay and founds the settlement of Jamestown.

1619 The first enslaved Africans are brought to the Colony of Virginia and forced to work on the plantations.

1748 Land is granted for the town of Alexandria, sited on the Potomac's western bank.

1751 The construction of Georgetown begins on the eastern bank of the Potomac River.

1788 The Constitution of the United States is ratified; it sets down conditions for a new capital city, governed independently of the states of the Union.

"It is ... called the **City of Magnificent Distances**, but it might [better] be termed the **City of Magnificent Intentions**.

CHARLES DICKENS, *AMERICAN NOTES*, 1842

> We have built no **national temples** but the **Capitol**. We consult no **common oracle** than the **Constitution**.

RUFUS CHOATE, LAWYER AND REPRESENTATIVE FOR MASSACHUSETTS, 1833

△ **SOUTH PORTICO, WHITE HOUSE**
Originally called the President's House, the White House was rebuilt after being burned down during the War of 1812. The bow-shaped South Portico was added in 1824.

The grand plan

When Congress met in 1789, a fight quickly emerged between the Northern and Southern states over which would be beneficiary of the new capital. In the end, Alexander Hamilton and Thomas Jefferson brokered a deal allowing it to be built in the South on the condition the government settled the North's war debts. President George Washington chose the site, a parcel of land to be ceded from Maryland and Virginia that included both Alexandria and Georgetown—and was handily close to his Mount Vernon estate.

A team under surveyor Andrew Ellicott was selected to survey the site, and the president appointed Pierre Charles L'Enfant, a French-born architect, to produce a master plan for the city's layout. The new city was named after the president, and the federal land became the Territory (later District) of Columbia, in honor of Christopher Columbus.

L'Enfant's novel design, influenced in part by André Le Nôtre's garden designs at Versailles, was for a traditional gridiron street plan to be cut through diagonally by sweeping avenues, with large public circles and plazas to be built at the intersections. The city was to radiate out from the President's House and the Capitol, and would be built on a grand scale that would impress competing nations.

A time of optimism

L'Enfant's plans were revised by Ellicott, construction progressed slowly, and it was not until 1800 that the government moved to the new Capitol. By this time, work on the new Palladian-style mansion for the head of state, designed by Irish-born architect James Hoban, was sufficiently advanced for the second president, John Adams, and his wife Abigail to move in. Construction of the rest of the city continued, but there was soon a major setback. In 1812, a major war broke out between the US and Britain. Two years later, the British defeated the Americans at nearby Bladensburg, entered the city, and set fire to the Capitol, President's House, and other important buildings.

After the war ended in a truce in 1815, Washington began to boom. The reconstruction was accompanied by a rise in business activity as the American West began to open up and transportation was improved. A railroad line to Baltimore was completed in 1835, ultimately extending

1790 Congress passes the Residence Act for a new federal capital to be established on the Potomac River.

1791 Andrew Ellicott begins surveying the site of the new capital and Pierre Charles L'Enfant produces his plan for the "Federal City."

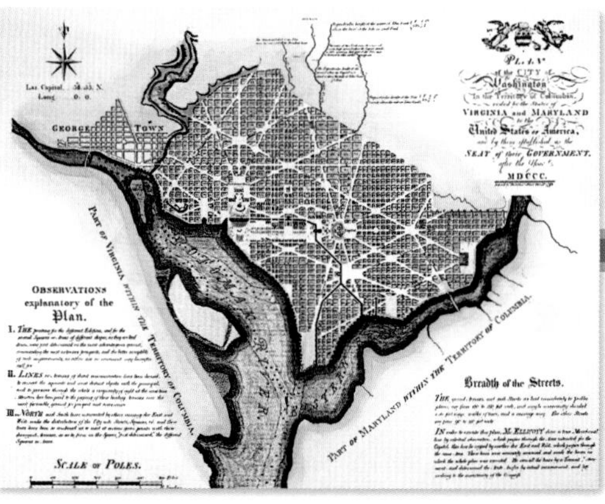

Andrew Ellicott's revised city plan

1792 Construction of the President's House (later the White House) begins. Workers include enslaved Black people and stonemasons from Edinburgh.

1800 The seat of government is transferred from Philadelphia to Washington, D.C.

1814 British troops set fire to Washington during the War of 1812.

1824 The semi-circular South Portico is added to the White House.

to New York and other cities, and the Chesapeake and Ohio Canal brought coal to the capital from the Appalachians. Tourists arrived with the railroads, and Washington grew as the civil service expanded under President Andrew Jackson. As more and more states joined the US, the number of legislators outgrew the Capitol building; extensions in the 1850s more than doubled its length.

Civil War and reconstruction

By the mid-19th century, the open sore of slavery had begun to threaten the unity of the country. Formed from two slave-owning states, the city's history had been tied to the slave trade from its inception, and it grew to become one of the most active slave depots in the country. Groups of enslaved people chained together could be seen on the streets from the Capitol, and even at the White House most servants were enslaved. Nonetheless, in the decades leading up to the Civil War, Washington became a center of abolitionism. Confrontations between pro- and antislavery factions made the place increasingly tense, and outbreaks of violence and rioting were common.

In 1861, the Civil War erupted. Volunteers lined up by the thousands to fight for the Union. The capital—never far from the front line—was heavily fortified, and hospitals were set up to tend to the wounded. After the District-wide abolition of slavery in 1862, freedmen and women from across D.C. began to congregate in the city. Victory for the Union came three years later, but within days the nation was in mourning when President Abraham Lincoln was shot at a Washington theater, and died the following day.

△ **GRAND REVIEW OF THE ARMIES**
In May 1865, some 150,000 soldiers marched along Pennsylvania Avenue from the Capitol to the White House in a parade held to celebrate the end of the Civil War.

1835 The Baltimore and Ohio Railroad links Washington, D.C., with Baltimore, Maryland.

1847 Tensions between Alexandria (a slave-trading center) and increasingly abolitionist Washington lead to Alexandria being returned to Virginia.

In 1848, a group of 77 enslaved people attempted to escape Washington by boat. All were recaptured.

1855 Smithsonian Castle, the first home of the Smithsonian Institution, is completed.

1859 The Senate Wing of the Capitol is completed.

1862 Slavery is abolished in the District of Columbia.

The presidential order abolishing slavery in all states

1865 John Wilkes Booth assassinates President Abraham Lincoln at Ford's Theatre.

The City Beautiful

△ A symbolic focus for many Americans, the Lincoln Memorial makes a fitting western end point to the National Mall.

> "The civic center's **beauty** would **reflect the souls** of the city's inhabitants, inducing **order, calm, and propriety** therein.
>
> WILLIAM H. WILSON, *THE CITY BEAUTIFUL MOVEMENT*, 1989

In the late 19th century, the squalid conditions endured by the working classes, who were often crammed into unsanitary tenements in cities such as Washington, led social reformers toward a new fashion in city planning: the City Beautiful movement. Proponents believed that beautification would sweep away social ills and encourage civic harmony. Borrowing heavily from the Beaux-Arts style popular in Paris, and emphasizing the importance of parks and green spaces, the new style was embraced enthusiastically in the 1902 McMillan Plan for Washington, D.C. Under the plan, slums near the Capitol were demolished and the National Mall was redeveloped as a grand processional way, flanked by harmonious Neoclassical cultural institutions and culminating in the stately Lincoln Memorial, which was eventually completed in 1922. Though never fully implemented, the McMillan Plan continues to inform city development today.

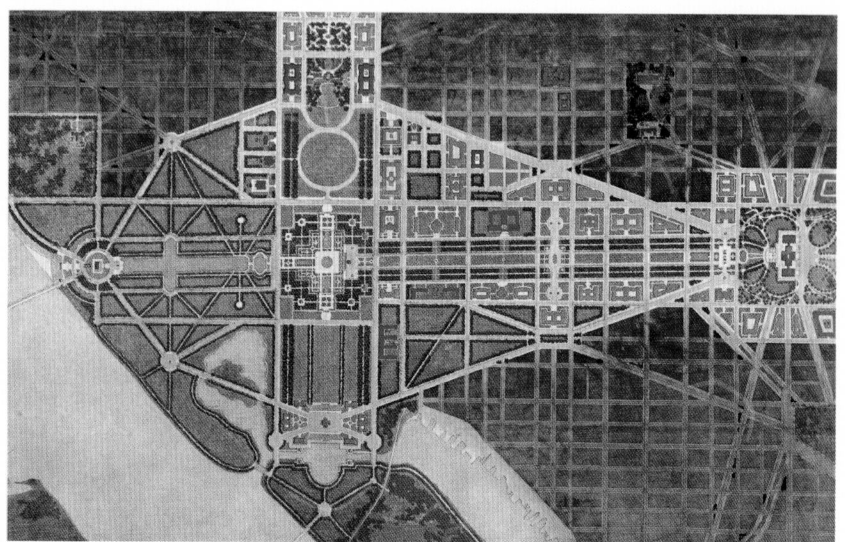

△ Under the McMillan Plan of 1902, the National Mall was laid out on an east–west axis, with a branch to the north linking it to the Ellipse park in front of the White House.

1867 Howard University is set up for Black students.

1884 The 555 ft (169 m) Washington Monument is completed.

1902 Under the influence of the City Beautiful movement, the McMillan Plan is launched to improve Washington, D.C.

1919 White mobs attack Black people on Washington's streets, leading to six days of unrest.

1929 The Great Depression begins; many unemployed people come to the city to protest about the lack of government support.

◁ "I HAVE A DREAM"
In 1963, Civil Rights Movement leader Martin Luther King, Jr., gave his famous "I have a dream" speech in front of the Lincoln Memorial. King's assassination five years later led to widespread rioting, and parts of the city burned for four days.

After the Civil War, the Freedmen's Bureau was set up to help those freed from slavery find housing and work. One of its jobs was to found the first university for Black students, leading to the creation of Howard University in 1867. As the city's population mushroomed, growing fourfold in the 1860s to 132,000 by 1870, Washingtonians began to agitate for improved services. Large municipal projects of the 1870s included better sewers, street paving and sidewalks, and improved public parks. But while new, comfortable suburbs were built for wealthier citizens, the poor remained in the backstreets and alleys of the city center—one of the inspirations for the McMillan Plan (see box).

Cauldron of tensions, beacon of hope

As US power rose inexorably in the early 20th century, so Washington, D.C., blossomed, with new art galleries, concert halls, and museums opening. Black culture in particular began to thrive. The U Street Corridor became a center for jazz, and figures such as Duke Ellington and poet Langston Hughes became prominent. In the 1930s, the population surged as President Roosevelt's New Deal brought workers into the city in the wake of the Great Depression.

However, discrimination was still rife and tensions between rich and poor, and Black and white, only increased after World War II as economic migrants moved up from the South. The city was a fitting focal point for the Civil Rights marches of the 1950s and '60s. By the 1990s, urban neglect had worsened, and the city had gained a reputation as the "murder capital" of the US. Yet revitalization was not far away: in the 21st century, investment and new infrastructure have breathed life into long-overlooked districts, and the city is once again a magnet for tourists. And while Washington remains a focus for the nation's simmering tensions—evidenced by the invasion of the Capitol in January 2021—its role as the beacon of US democracy feels more important than ever.

If legislation were passed to make Washington, D.C., a separate US state, it would rank 51st by area, 49th by population size (before Vermont and Wyoming), and first for GDP per capita.

Washington, D.C.'s population soared by 300,000 between 1940 and 1943 as federal employees flocked to the capital.

1954 Racial segregation of public places is declared illegal.

1963 Around 250,000 people join the March on Washington for Jobs and Freedom.

1998 Mayor Anthony A. Williams is elected; his policies help reduce unemployment and crime and improve public services.

2009 More than a million people crowd onto the Capitol's West Front to watch the inauguration of President Barack Obama, setting a record for any event in the city.

2016 The National Museum of African American History and Culture opens.

Brasília

CAPITAL OF HOPE

One of the world's youngest cities, Brasília was purpose-built as Brazil's capital and as a symbol of the country's determination to succeed. The result, a futuristic metropolis, is renowned for its Modernist architecture.

Built entirely from scratch in the 1950s, to a single plan in the Modernist style, Brasília's breathtaking buildings and sweeping vistas made it immediately world famous. It was constructed at staggering speed, in less than four years, but its story goes back much farther.

Brazil was claimed by the Portuguese in 1500, but by the late 18th century an independence movement was gathering strength. One of the movement's leaders, physician and revolutionary Joaquim José da Silva Xavier, proposed that when Brazil won its independence it should have a new capital to replace the colonial capital of Rio de Janeiro, which was identified with foreign rule. When Brazil became independent in the 1820s, its government quickly decided on a name for the new city, Brasília. However, the nation had to wait well over 130 years for the money and political will to build its new capital.

◁ NATIONAL CONGRESS OF BRAZIL
The Chamber of Deputies, with its bowl-shaped roof, adjoins the twin office towers at the center of the National Congress building. This stunning complex was completed in 1958.

The turning point

The decisive moment came during Brazil's 1955 election. One of the three presidential candidates was Juscelino Kubitschek de Oliveira, whose campaign promised to modernize the country, open up the economy, and create the long-awaited new capital. Soon after Kubitschek won the election, celebrated Brazilian architect and planner Lúcio Costa secured first place in a competition to draw up a master plan, and Oscar Niemeyer, who had previously worked for Costa and with the president, became the architect of the city's main buildings.

> "... a **new society** was being **born**, with all the **traditional barriers** cast aside.
>
> OSCAR NIEMEYER, INTERVIEW IN *THE GUARDIAN*, AUGUST 1, 2007

1789 Joaquim José da Silva Xavier, known as Tiradentes, suggests that Brazil should have a new capital.

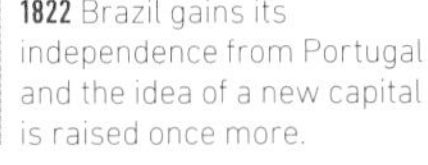

1822 Brazil gains its independence from Portugal and the idea of a new capital is raised once more.

1891 The intention to found a new inland capital is incorporated into Brazil's constitution.

1955 Elections in Brazil are won by Juscelino Kubitschek de Oliveira, with the slogan "Fifty Years' Progress in Five."

1956 Juscelino Kubitschek is inaugurated as president, with a commitment to realize Brasília.

△ OSCAR NIEMEYER
The architect with a model of the hourglass-shaped cathedral, designed in 1956.

△ CATHEDRAL OF BRASÍLIA
Oscar Niemeyer's design features 16 steel columns that converge to form a vast crown. Bronze statues of the Four Evangelists stand near the entrance.

The chosen site of the capital was in Goiás state, on Brazil's central plateau. Extensive clearing, building of roads, and installation of basic services had to take place before construction could begin. Meanwhile Costa devised a visionary master plan with a symbolic shape, based on a cross. Viewed from the air, the city's layout most resembles an airplane, bird, or dragonfly. Twin avenues trace the body of the airplane from east to west, making a Monumental Axis (Eixo Monumental), which leads to the Square of the Three Powers. This axis is the site of the city's major legislative, executive, and judiciary buildings, including elegant Modernist structures such as the Supreme Federal Court, National Congress, and Presidential Palace. Running roughly from north to south, through the airplane's "wings," is a broad expressway, home to the city's residential and commercial blocks.

These areas are precisely zoned, with houses, apartments, shops, and schools arranged together in *superquadras* ("superblocks"), where the provision of facilities is intended to correspond with the number of residents. Niemeyer and Costa took care to provide both luxury and less costly housing, including accommodation specifically built for the many foreign diplomats posted to Brasília.

Brasília's architecture

Niemeyer's designs, with their bold use of concrete to create a combination of forms—from towers to shallow domes—immediately attracted worldwide attention. Strongly influenced by the pioneering

1956 Work on the new capital's site begins, at a location 620 miles (1,000 km) from the coast.

1957 Lúcio Costa wins the competition for conceiving a master plan for the city.

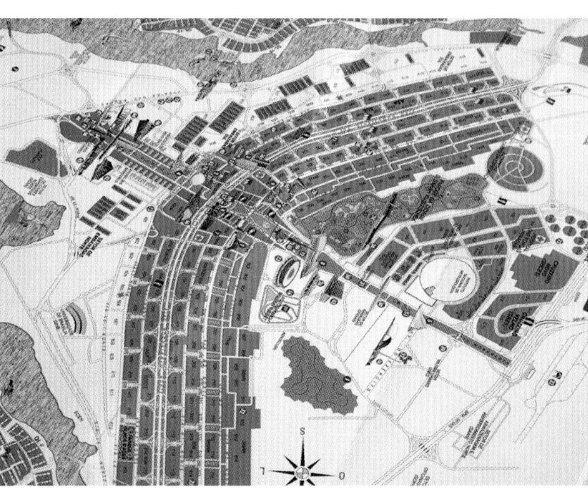

April 22, 1960 The city is officially inaugurated by President Kubitschek.

1961 *Justice by* Alfredo Ceschiatti, principal sculptor of the capital, is positioned outside the Supreme Federal Court.

Swiss-French architect Le Corbusier, Niemeyer shared the utopian ideals of the Modernist movement. By rejecting ornament in favor of minimalist, curvilinear designs, his buildings heralded a new way of urban living. Perhaps the most striking example of all is the almost transparent, crown-like cathedral, finished years after the main city was completed. All of these spectacular structures are set off by the surrounding spaces, which were the work of the notable Brazilian landscape architect Roberto Burle Marx. Both buildings and landscaping are enhanced by the local terrain, which is flat, allowing for long and dramatic vistas.

Success and expansion

Brasília was an instant success and an inspiration for Brazilians, who saw the city's modernity as a statement of their country's hope for the future. Architects and planners were similarly enthused, keen to emulate aspects of the design when remodeling urban areas around the world. The population began to increase, too, as more and more people moved to the city. They filled not only the superblocks, but also several satellite towns built outside the central area. These towns, not designed by Niemeyer, are more haphazard and sometimes crudely built, with shops, apartments, and workplaces crammed into small spaces. In contrast, many of the affluent inhabitants of the upmarket city center leave Brasília during the weekends, often heading to the bright lights of Rio de Janeiro.

Brasília remains a unique achievement and a singular manifestation of Modernist principles, designated by UNESCO as both a World Heritage Site and a City of Design. As a model of urban planning and a symbol of Brazil's ambition, it is renowned all over the world.

△ PRESIDENTIAL PALACE
The president's official residence (also known as the Palace of the Dawn) lies on the shores of the artificial Paranoá Lake, another element of the city plan.

Brasília was designed as a city for around 600,000 people; the population is now nearer 3 million.

1962 The University of Brasília opens.

1970 After a struggle to secure funds, the Cathedral of Brasília reaches completion.

1987 The city receives the designation of UNESCO World Heritage Site.

2000 The population of Brasília's Federal District exceeds two million (triple the planned number).

2006 The National Museum of the Republic, with its sculptural white concrete dome, is opened.

2014 Brasília is one of the cities to stage the 2014 FIFA World Cup, in the extended Estádio Nacional Mané Garrincha.

2017 UNESCO names Brasília a City of Design, recognizing design as a key part of the city's industry and culture.

MORE GREAT CITIES

Edinburgh

Auld Reekie ("old smoky")

In the mid-18th century, Edinburgh's grandees noted the civic improvements being carried out in the industrial cities of England, compared them to the teeming—and often unsound and unsanitary—tenements that filled their own city, and decided something had to be done. Lord Provost George Drummond launched a Commission of Proposals for Public Works in order to "improve and enlarge the city and to adorn it with public buildings which may be for the national benefit." In 1766, the council ran a competition, selecting a plan by architect James Craig for the "New Town." Informed by a love of Classical architecture, Craig devised a gridiron plan of wide streets with broad, solidly constructed buildings in white sandstone. The New Town came to be defined by its open spaces, light, and order, transforming the city from Auld Reekie into the Athens of the North.

Palmanova

Star-Shaped City

The most distinctive aspect of Palmanova can only be fully appreciated from the air: the city is laid out in the shape of a nine-point star. It was constructed by the Republic of Venice in 1593, designed as a defense against Ottoman Turks. The outline of the star was etched into the landscape with a moat. This surrounded a nine-sided city with nine fortified bastions. There were three concentric defensive walls, pierced by three large gates. Despite the elegant layout, Palmanova was more fort than town, and no one wanted to live there. Venice resorted to populating it with pardoned criminals.

Valletta

Il-Belt ("the city")

In 1565, the Knights of Malta, commanded by their Grand Master Jean Parisot de la Valette, withstood an Ottoman siege for four months. Such was the gratitude of Europe for the knights' heroic defense that money poured into the island, allowing de Valette to construct a new fortified city, named after himself. The knights, aided by military engineers, built the city on a narrow peninsula surrounded on three sides by water. It had a uniform grid plan within high, fortified walls that followed the rocky coastline. There was only one city gate, which was in the land wall, and from there a main street ran to the fortress of St. Elmo at the tip of the peninsula. Some monuments were lost to 19th- and 20th-century development, but modern Valletta still retains its skyline and form from the 16th century.

Baghdad

Round City

In a region rich in ancient settlements, Baghdad is a relative newcomer. It was founded in 762 CE by the Abbasid Caliph Al-Mansur as the new seat of his Islamic empire. According to legend, the caliph himself drew up the plans for a round city to be constructed beside the Tigris River. Its massive brick walls had a circumference of 4 miles (6.4 km), were 80 ft (24 m) high, and were ringed by a deep moat. The walls contained four great gates from which straight roads, lined by vaulted arcades, ran toward the center of the city. At the heart of Baghdad was the royal precinct, with military barracks and state offices ringing the two most important buildings: the Great Mosque and the caliph's Golden Gate Palace. No traces of this remarkable geometric city remain in modern Baghdad.

Alexandria

Lost City

In his quest to spread Hellenic culture to the ends of the Earth, the brilliant general Alexander the Great founded at least 20 cities that carried his name, including Alexandria in Egypt. Alexander selected the site on the Mediterranean coast, and his architect, Dinocrates, conceived the plan, laying out his vision on the ground in grain. It followed the typical pattern of many Greek cities as prescribed by the great urban planner Hippodamus, but

△ **Palmanova** An aerial view of the star-shape fortress city.

△ **Baghdad** A 19th-century European rendering of the walled Iraqi city.

exceeded them in the creation of a causeway linking the mainland to the island of Pharos to create two immense, sheltered harbors. Alexander died within a decade and never saw his new city. Almost all traces of the ancient city have vanished, shattered by earthquakes and either submerged under the sea or buried beneath the concrete of the modern Egyptian city.

Chandigarh

The City of Beauty

In the bloody partition that split India in 1947, the state of Punjab lost its capital to Pakistan. Indian Prime Minister Jawaharlal Nehru decided to build a new capital city, designed to express what he called "the nation's faith in the future." The initial plans came from American architects Albert Mayer and Matthew Nowicki, but were developed by celebrated architect Le Corbusier. The result is a city laid out on a grid, divided into 56 sectors, each designed as a self-contained neighborhood with schools, entertainment, and shops. Parks and tree-lined avenues soften the effect of its blocklike concrete buildings, and today Chandigarh is claimed to be the cleanest city in India.

Jaipur

Pink City

When Maharaja Sawai Jai Singh II's hilltop city of Amber began to suffer from congestion and water shortages, he decided to build a new city on a flat plain nearby. With help from architect Vidyadhar Bhattacharya, Singh created a blueprint for the city based on an ancient Hindu doctrine called *vastu shastra*, meaning the "science of architecture." Construction began in 1726 and took four years. The resulting city was divided into nine blocks, two containing state buildings and palaces, the rest public, and the whole surrounded by fortified walls with seven gates. One of the city's notable features was the Jantar Mantar observatory, with the world's largest stone sundial. When Britain's Prince of Wales visited in 1853, the king ordered all the buildings to be painted pink; those in the historic center remain pink today.

Canberra

Bush Capital

In 1901, when the new Commonwealth of Australia was formed, Sydney and Melbourne were in dispute over which of them should be the national capital. The compromise was to build an entirely new capital city. An international competition resulted in the selection of Chicago architect Walter Burley Griffin as the designer of the city; his plan was distinguished by its incorporation of vegetation. Construction began in 1913 and the Australian parliament took up residence in 1927. Although Canberra initially remained small, its growth stunted by the 1930s Great Depression and World War II, from the 1950s the city grew quickly and within a couple of decades became the international capital it was designed to be.

Philadelphia

City of Brotherly Love

Philadelphia began as one of America's earliest commercial developments. The original settlement was devised in 1682 by Englishman William Penn, who wished to create a refuge in the colonies for Quakers and other persecuted religious groups. On a tongue of land between the Delaware and Schuylkill Rivers, he sketched out a grid of streets with a large central square, surrounded by four satellite squares. Gridded plots made it easier to sell property "sight unseen" to potential immigrants back in Europe.
The city would go on to play a key role in the American Revolution as the site of the signing of the Declaration of Independence in 1776. It was the nation's largest city until overtaken by New York in 1790 and the home of many US firsts, including the first library, hospital, zoo, and stock exchange.

La Plata

City of Diagonals

In 1880, it was decided the wealthy Buenos Aires province needed a capital distinct from the city of the same name, which was also the national capital. No existing city was considered large enough, so the solution was to build a new one from scratch. Engineer Pedro Benoit planned a perfect square grid, 36 by 36 blocks. From each corner of the grid, grand diagonal avenues converged at the center's large public square, overlooked by a grand Neo-Gothic cathedral.
For decades the city was under-populated, but in the 21st century it has become a thriving city with beautiful architecture, green spaces, and a vibrant college scene.

△ **Jaipur** The Jantar Mantar observatory, a UNESCO World Heritage Site.

△ **Canberra** Australia's national parliament building, Parliament House, dating from 1988.

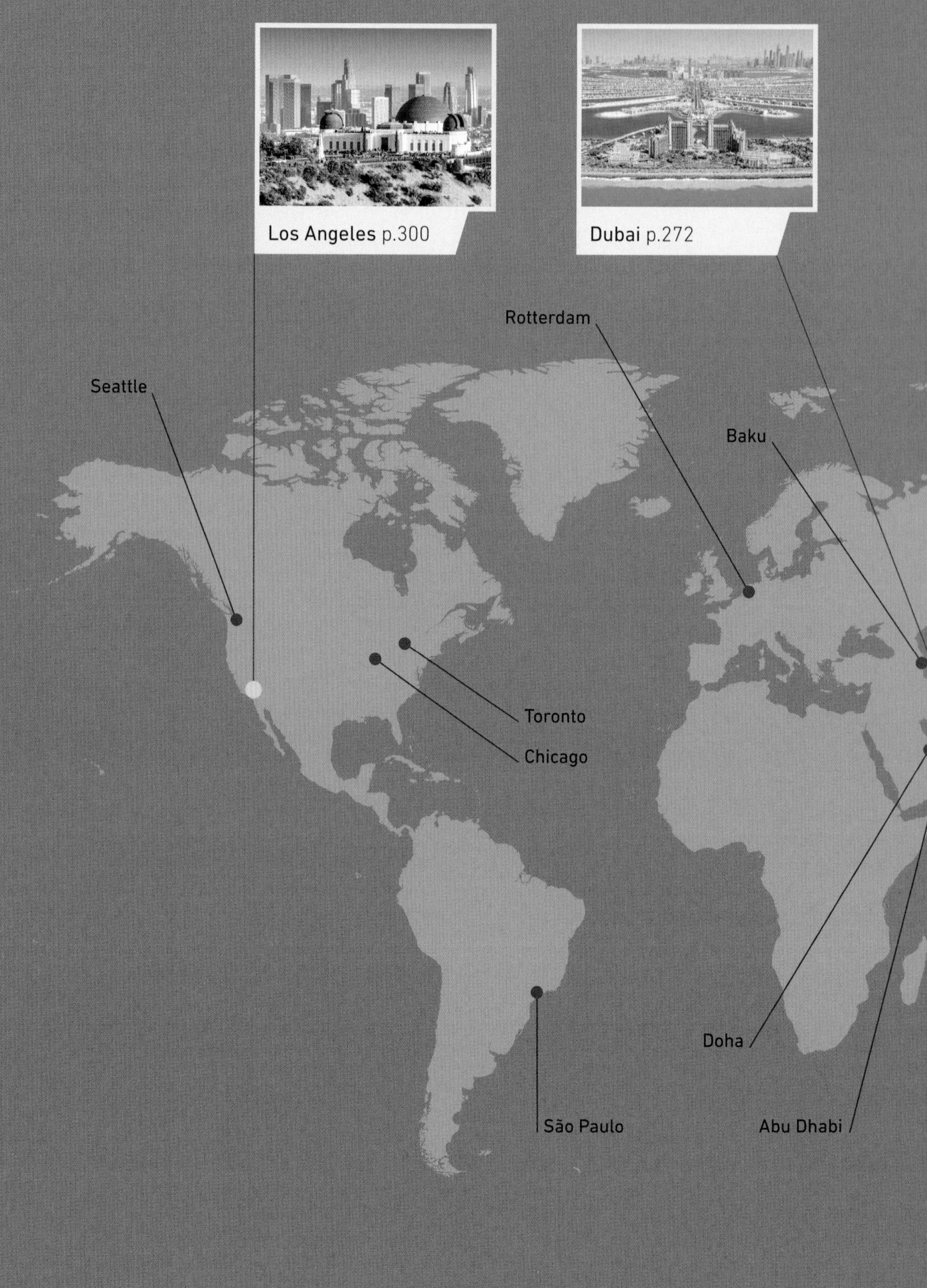
Los Angeles p.300
Dubai p.272
Rotterdam
Seattle
Baku
Toronto
Chicago
Doha
São Paulo
Abu Dhabi

CHAPTER 5
MODERN METROPOLISES

Hong Kong p.284

Beijing p.276

Seoul p.288

Tokyo p.294

Kuala Lumpur

Nur-Sultan

Dubai

PEARL OF THE GULF

Once an obscure pearling village bowing to British imperialism, Dubai has risen in the space of a generation to become a glitzy, wealthy city of the future, attracting more tourists than many much-larger countries.

The beginnings of the futuristic developments and urban sprawl that make up modern Dubai could not be more humble. Up until the mid-18th century, there is scant mention of even a settlement in the place the city now occupies. When Muslims from the west of the peninsula conquered the region in the 7th century, they spoke of inhabitants at Al Jumeirah, but said nothing of Dubai.

The pearling village

The earliest recorded mention of a place called "Dibei" was by the state jeweler for Venice, Gasparo Balbi, who came to the region in around 1580 to investigate the local pearling industry. Like many settlements along the banks of the Persian Gulf at this time, Dubai would have been a small pearling and fishing village, comprising a handful of simple homes made of wood and reed, called *arish*.

◁ AERIAL VIEW OF DUBAI
The Palm Jumeirah, Dubai's luxury island residence, was created in the Persian Gulf from reclaimed land. Viewed from the air, it resembles a stylized date palm.

About 250 years after Balbi's visit, the Al Bu Falasah, a large family within the region's ruling tribe of Bani Yas, fell out with the tribe's new leaders in Abu Dhabi. As a result, the Al Bu Falasah headed north toward the Dubai creek, where they soon became the new rulers of the settlement. The saltwater inlet of the creek no doubt appealed as a rich resource of fish and as a natural harbor, where traders of spices, gold, and textiles could easily alight.

The Al Bu Falasah family maintained good relations with both the surrounding sheikdoms and the British, who during the 19th century used a series of treaties and agreements to help serve their own commercial and military ambitions in the region.

Over the course of the next century, the new rulers of Dubai slowly turned their little coastal settlement into a thriving port by making it tax-free for merchants and traders. Even when the invention of the Japanese cultured pearl left Dubai's natural pearling industry in tatters in the 1930s, the port continued to attract traders from all over the world. The stage for Dubai's future as an international hub had been set.

1580 Venice's state jeweler, Gasparo Balbi, visits Dubai (Balbi calls it "Dibei") and notes the high quality of the settlement's pearls.

c. 1830 Members of the Al Bu Falasah family (a branch of the ruling Bani Yas) settle by the creek in Dubai to establish Al Maktoum rule in the emirate.

c. 1800–1900 The pearling industry prospers as Dubai's pearls are sold to markets in India and Europe.

1820 The General Treaty of Peace between the British and the Sheikh of Dubai (and other emirate sheikhs) creates the Trucial States.

1928 First crop of commercial Japanese cultured pearls is produced, leading to the collapse of the natural pearling industry in Dubai.

◁ AL MAKTOUM BRIDGE
In 1963, Sheikh Rashid cut the ribbon on Dubai's first bridge, connecting the Dubai and Deira sides of the creek. The bridge greatly improved circulation and commerce in the fledgling city.

One theory about the origin of "Dubai" is that it comes from "dabaa," describing how water "creeps" into the creek.

The modern era

The man credited with laying the foundations of modern Dubai is Sheikh Rashid bin Saeed Al Maktoum, whose time in power (1958–1990) coincided with the British withdrawal from the Persian Gulf in 1968, and with the emirate striking black gold (oil) in 1966.

A year into his rule, Sheikh Rashid recruited John Harris, a British town planner, to turn the collection of settlements scattered around the port into a functioning urban space. Harris oversaw the introduction of Dubai's very first water pipes, telephone lines, and electricity grid, and the opening of the state-of-the-art Al Maktoum hospital. From 1969, armed with new-found wealth from oil, Sheikh Rashid accelerated the modernizing process. His most visionary project was the development of shipping ports, in particular the Jebel Ali Port. Finished in 1979, it saw the once-small village of Dubai transform into the biggest and busiest commercial port in the Middle East. That same year, Dubai's first skyscraper, Sheikh Rashid Tower (now part of the Dubai World Trade Center complex), loomed into view at a height of 489 ft (149 m). The transition from port to glamorous city of the future really began, however, when Sheikh Rashid passed away in 1990 and his triumvirate of sons took over.

Future-proofing the city

Sheikhs Maktoum, Hamdan, and Mohammed managed the development of Dubai with the same far-sightedness as their father. Appreciating that oil money would one day run out, they continued to invest in large infrastructure projects, including the city's two international airports, and free trade zones, such as the Dubai Internet City.

As the end of the 20th century approached, the brothers future-proofed their capital by establishing high-speed internet and advanced telecommunications. They also relaxed traditionally conservative laws (allowing foreigners to drink alcohol, for example) and began construction of the skyscrapers that would make Dubai famous. The Etisalat Tower, with its distinctive "golf ball" pinnacle, was completed in 1992, closely followed by the National Bank of Dubai Tower, its curved shape inspired by the traditional *dhows* (sailing boat) that used to ply the Dubai creek. The wavelike Jumeirah Beach Hotel opened in 1997, as well as a new airport terminal in 1998, boldly announcing Dubai's emergence as a tourist destination.

In the shadow of Dubai's multitude of cranes, gleaming skyscrapers, and glitzy designer malls, however, lie company-run shanty towns, where migrant construction workers live in overcrowded and unsanitary conditions.

1968 With the British withdrawal from the Persian Gulf, discussions begin about the formation of a federation of emirates.

1969 First export of oil from Dubai commences, providing the emirate with the wealth to modernize at pace.

Stamp celebrating Dubai's underwater oil storage

1971 The United Arab Emirates is formed, with Dubai's Sheikh Rashid as vice-president and first prime minister.

The population of Dubai today is more than 30 times what it was in the early 1970s.

1979 With the opening of Jebel Ali Port, the largest artificial harbor in the world, Dubai becomes the Middle East's major commercial port.

> Dubai will **never settle** for anything less than **first place**.
>
> MOHAMMED BIN RASHID AL MAKTOUM, *MY VISION: CHALLENGES IN THE RACE FOR EXCELLENCE*, 2004

These workers, mostly from the Indian subcontinent, first arrived in the 1960s during the early days of Dubai's oil boom, with numbers rising from the 1980s onward.

Something old, something new

In the 21st century, Dubai has made headlines as the home of the world's largest artificial islands—the Palm Jumeirah opened in 2006—as well as the biggest malls, huge international sporting events, grass golf courses in the desert, and the globe's busiest international air travel hub. North of the strips lined with skyscrapers and neat rows of palm trees, and close to the location of the original pearling village, *abras* (wooden boats) once again sail on the Dubai creek. Rather than pearls and exotic spices, their cargo is now wealthy tourists, who disembark to wander through refurbished souks and historic villages, where traditional artisans and heritage museums sit in reconstructed mud-baked houses. When the metro system opened in 2009—the same year the world's tallest building, the Burj Khalifa, was completed, realizing a dream of Sheikh Mohammed—it was the first in the Persian Gulf, enhancing Dubai's reputation as the most foreigner-friendly city in the region.

Add to this low crime rates and a burgeoning cultural scene, and it is easy to see why Dubai entices international professionals and a growing number of celebrities, such as British power couple, David and Victoria Beckham, and Bollywood royalty, Abhishek and Aishwarya Rai Bachchan.

△ **CITY SKYLINE**
Dubai's ultra-modern skyline rises above the desert dunes, dominated by the soaring silhouette of Burj Khalifa.

▽ **MALL CITY**
Dubai boasts the world's largest retail mall, Dubai Mall, which encompasses an enormous aquarium, an ice rink, and theme parks, as well as over 1,000 shops.

1999 The world's only "seven star" hotel, Burj al Arab, opens in Dubai.

2000 Opening of Dubai Internet City, a free economic zone where tech giants Nokia, Microsoft, Google, and Cisco set up regional offices.

2001 Work begins on Palm Jumeirah, the first of the Palm Islands, artificial luxury archipelagos aimed at increasing residential capacity and tourism to Dubai.

2009 The launch of *Slaves of Dubai*, a documentary exposing the plight of migrant workers, coincides with the opening of Burj Khalifa, the world's tallest building.

2020 Dubai is set to host Expo 2020 (delayed to 2021 due to COVID-19), with the theme "Connecting Minds, Creating the Future."

Beijing

NORTHERN CAPITAL

China's capital is a city where monuments from an imperial past are juxtaposed with the futuristic buildings of the world's most dynamic economy, creating an irresistible blend of tradition and modernity.

Lying just north of the Yellow River plain, the Beijing region was settled as early as 500,000 BCE by a form of *Homo erectus* known as Peking Man. Although the mythological Yellow Emperor, one of China's great cultural heroes, was said to have won a victory at nearby Banquan, the city only emerges from legend as the site of the capitals of Ji and Yan, two of the kingdoms that vied for control of China during the Warring States period. At this point, it was known as Yanjing. After Yan's absorption into a unified China by the Qin in the 3rd century BCE, Yanjing remained a provincial capital on the empire's periphery for the next 1,000 years.

The Tang and Jin city

Under the Tang dynasty, the city—now renamed Youzhou—became an important garrison center, and the Fayuan Temple, Beijing's oldest Buddhist shrine, was built in the mid-7th century CE. Although far from the main dynastic capitals, Youzhou had for centuries been vulnerable to attacks by the nomads on China's northern borders. In 938 CE, one of these groups, the Khitan, took it as the southern base of their Liao Empire and called it Nanjing, or "southern capital." They remodeled the city, punctuated its walls with eight gates, and built still-surviving landmarks, including the Tianning Temple and Niujie Mosque. Yet another name change—to Zhongdu ("central capital")—took place under the Jin, who reconfigured and further enlarged the city, and graced it with a string of palaces. The city was flourishing as never before.

> "[The city] is ... **planned out** with a degree of **precision** and **beauty** impossible to describe.
>
> MARCO POLO, *THE TRAVELS OF MARCO POLO*, c. 1300

BEIJING'S MODERN CITYSCAPE ▷
The gravity-defying headquarters of China Central Television (CCTV) loom over Beijing's business district, one of the innovative new buildings that complement the city's more traditional landmarks.

c. 1200 BCE Yanjing is founded as the walled capital of Yan, the first state around Beijing.

226 BCE The Yan state is absorbed by the Qin state under Shi Huangdi, the first emperor of a united China.

314–534 CE Renamed Youzhou, the city is controlled by nomadic invaders, including the Xianbei.

938 The city comes under the control of the Khitan Liao dynasty and is renamed Nanjing.

1127 The Jin (Jurchen) establish themselves in the city—now called Yanjing—and later rename it Zhongdu.

1179 The Jin build the Daning Palace on Taiye Lake in what is now Beihai Park.

The Forbidden City

△ This 19th-century painting shows attendant officials to the imperial court in full court garb. Now designated a UNESCO World Heritage Site, the imperial palace was the residence of 24 emperors.

The Forbidden City, the new imperial palace complex ordered by the Yongle Emperor in 1406, took around 15 years to construct. Built on a north–south axis, the entire complex was enclosed by a wall 2 miles (3.5 km) in length and a moat. Inside, the imperial buildings—containing, according to legend, 9,999 rooms—were laid out following strict feng shui principles. Three magnificent halls lay at its core. Grandest of all was the Hall of Supreme Harmony, where the emperor held court during the Ming era; later, during the Qing, it was used for major state occasions such as the enthronement of a new emperor. To the north, through the Gate of Heavenly Purity, lay the emperor's private quarters and, at the northern end of the complex, the Imperial Garden, a space for private retreat. All but closed off to the outside world, the Forbidden City remained the residence of the emperors, increasingly secluded from the political realities of their realm, until the eventual collapse of imperial rule in 1912. Twelve years later, the doors were thrown open to the public and the complex became a museum.

1215 The Mongols take Zhongdu, damaging it severely and causing its near abandonment.

1266 Kublai Khan orders the reconstruction of Zhongdu as the Mongols' southern capital, renaming it Dadu.

1275–1292 The Venetian merchant Marco Polo travels in China, later writing an account including a description of Mongol Dadu.

1368 After driving the Mongols out, the Ming begin rebuilding the section of the Great Wall to the north of the city.

1403 The Yongle Emperor renames the city Beijing; three years later, the construction of the palaces and halls of the Forbidden City begins.

It took over a million laborers and 100,000 specialized craftsmen to complete the construction of the Forbidden City.

The Mongol city

In 1215, disaster struck Zhongdu. The Mongols, recently united by Genghis Khan, swept down from Mongolia, breached the walls, and engaged in an orgy of looting. The city smoldered for a month and remained a ruin for decades until Genghis's grandson Kublai, persuaded by his advisers that his vast new realm required a base closer to China's heartlands, ordered a new capital built just to the north of Zhongdu's remains.

△ TEMPLE OF HEAVEN
The Temple of Heaven complex was the main place of worship for emperors in the city during the Ming and Qing eras.

Work began on Dadu ("the great capital") in 1267. The city was laid out on a square grid intersected with *hutongs*, or alleys lined by secluded courtyard houses—a feature of Beijing's old quarters ever since. Kublai Khan's luxurious royal palace in the southern part of the city, described by the Venetian traveler Marco Polo, was lavishly adorned with marble, gold, and silver, and surrounded by a hunting park and a series of lakes channeled from the city's rivers. In the commercial areas, clustered shops and markets were packed with goods brought in by barge up the Grand Canal, the broad waterway linking northern and southern China that Kublai ordered to be repaired. The city was protected by a wall that Marco Polo claimed was 24 miles (40 km) long.

The Ming reconstruction

Dadu's prosperity was not destined to last. Succession disputes, floods, and plagues sapped Mongol power and sparked a number of revolts. In 1368, the rebel leader Zhu Yuanzhang drove the last Mongol ruler from the city. The Ming dynasty he founded initially based itself at Nanjing, more than 620 miles (1,000 km) to the south, leaving Dadu to slide back into obscurity. Only when one of his younger sons, then the governor of the old state of Yan, seized the throne did the city return to center stage. The new Yongle Emperor officially renamed his home base Beijing ("northern capital"), and ordered a massive reconstruction, establishing the Zijincheng (Forbidden City) as its heart (see box). The city became the Ming capital in 1421. The emperor also restored the Grand Canal, and further palaces and pavilions were added by his successor, the Zhengtong Emperor.

By the mid-15th century, Beijing's population had swollen to a million. To serve these increasing numbers, the imperial government built *langfang*, premises from which merchants could trade in everything from donkeys to books—the latter bought by aspiring bureaucrats studying at the Guozijian, the Imperial College. Outside influences reached China to a very limited extent, through foreign merchants and, from the start of the 17th century, through Jesuit missionaries such as Matteo Ricci.

△ HALL OF PRAYER
Within the Temple of Heaven complex, the Hall of Prayer for Good Harvests was built entirely of wood, without nails. First constructed in 1420, it was rebuilt in 1889 after a lightning strike.

1421 With the completion of the Forbidden City, the capital is transferred from Nanjing to Beijing.

Jiajing-era wucai jar

1521–67 The Jiajing Emperor neglects the government, devoting himself to Daoism, and chooses to live in isolation outside the Forbidden City. The production of *wucai* "five-enamel" porcelain jars reaches new heights of refinement.

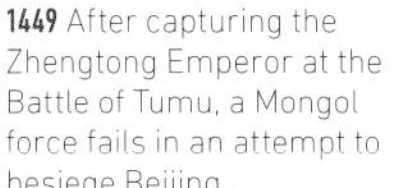

1449 After capturing the Zhengtong Emperor at the Battle of Tumu, a Mongol force fails in an attempt to besiege Beijing.

1553 In response to continued Mongol raids, a wall is built around Beijing's Outer City.

1601 The Jesuit Matteo Ricci establishes a mission in Beijing, adopting Chinese dress as a means of gaining acceptance at court.

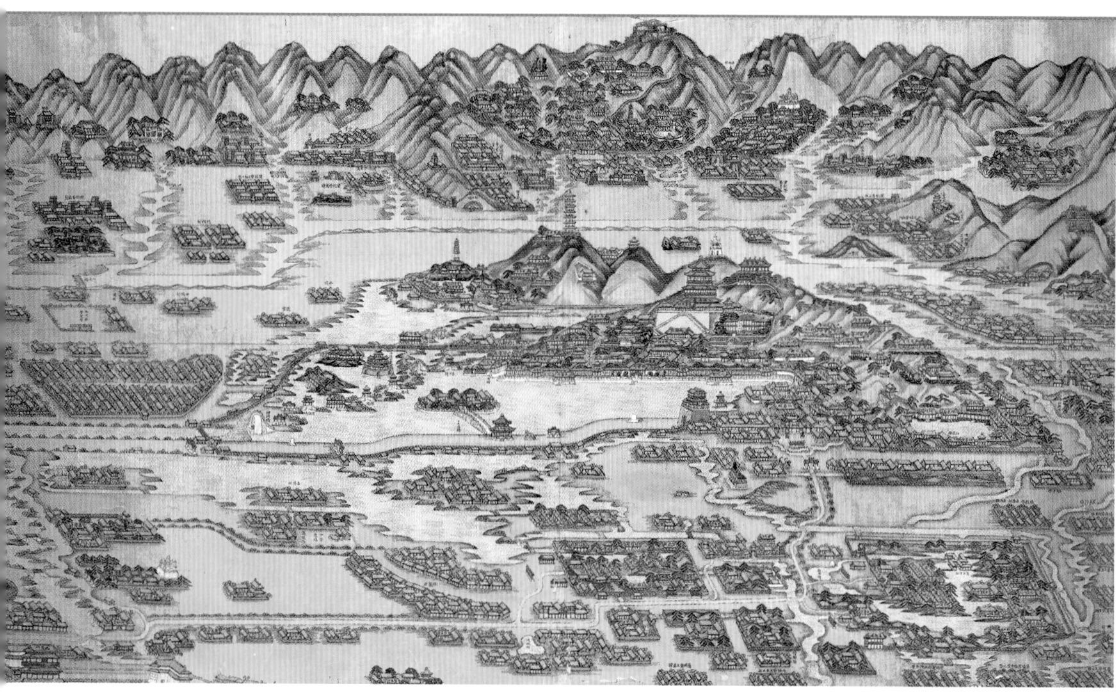

△ SUMMER PALACE, 1888
The Yiheyuan (Summer Palace) was built as an imperial retreat from the Forbidden City's stifling summer heat. It became the main residence of the Empress Cixi before its partial destruction by the Eight-Nation Alliance during the Boxer Rebellion.

The rule of the Qing

Just as the Mongols had at the end of their rule, the Ming faced widespread rebellion. As one of the rebel leaders, Li Zicheng, stormed into the Forbidden City in 1644, the Chongzhen Emperor, the final Ming ruler, hanged himself from a tree in Jingshan Park. Li did not last long, however: within weeks another nomad group, the Manchus, seized Beijing, where they established the new Qing dynasty.

The Qing formally divided Beijing into two: the Inner City, comprising the Forbidden City and the northern quarters, was now reserved for the Manchu "bannermen" (hereditary warriors and their families), while the Chinese were confined to the Outer City in the south. The Qing enforced segregation harshly and imposed Manchu customs on the Chinese, such as the *queue*, a long pigtail with a shaved head for men.

The long reigns of the Kangxi, Yongzheng, and Qianlong emperors, which stretched over 130 years, gave Beijing, and China, a new sense of stability. Though continuing the Ming dynasty's isolationism, tentative connections were made with the West. The Jesuits helped the court with calendrical calculations, and in 1650 were given permission to construct a church next to the imperial elephant stables. Around the same time, the Dutch joined the Portuguese in being permitted to send trade missions (though only once every eight years), and in 1694 the "Russian House," the first foreign embassy, was established in Beijing.

The life of court and city

The Qing emperors built palatial gardens, including the Yuanmingyuan ("garden of perfect brightness"), or Old Summer Palace, to Beijing's north as a retreat from the heat and noise of the city, and in 1750 the Qianlong Emperor erected the even-larger Yiheyuan (new Summer Palace). New halls were added to the Forbidden City, and grand military parades and ice-skating competitions among the bannermen enlivened the life of the court. In 1790, the court entertainment office invited an operatic troupe from Anhui (in eastern China) to perform for the emperor, which eventually developed into the tradition of the Peking opera.

The bulk of the population rarely saw the emperor, save at special parades outside the Forbidden City. Ordinary people lived in simple brick single-story courtyard houses, a refuge from life on the crowded streets, where food vendors noisily hawked roast chestnuts and steamed

1644 The rebel Li Zicheng takes Beijing, but the Manchu enter and drive him out, founding the Qing dynasty.

1661 The Kangxi Emperor ascends the imperial throne; his 61-year rule begins a period of prosperity for Beijing.

1709 Under the Kangxi Emperor, construction of the Yuanmingyuan (Old Summer Palace) begins; the palace and gardens are expanded several times.

1730 An earthquake causes considerable damage to the Forbidden City.

1750 The Qianlong Emperor orders the construction of the Yiheyuan (Summer Palace).

In 1774, the imperial government banned the opening of any more theaters in the Inner City, fearing they promoted immorality.

1793 A British mission led by Lord Macartney visits Beijing, but fails to establish trading relations.

1854 Taiping forces set off to capture Beijing but turn back before reaching the city.

BOXERS IN BEIJING ▷
Soldiers of the "Righteous and Harmonious Fists" militia (or "Boxers") were a convenient reservoir of anti-European feeling for Qing traditionalists, but their attacks on foreign targets backfired on the court.

dumplings, and policemen patrolled nightly, enforcing the curfew that was rung out from the Drum and Bell towers in the city center.

The collapse of the imperial system

The later Qing period ended Beijing's time of security. In 1854, 30,000 families fled the oncoming Taiping rebels, an army inspired by religious fervor that aimed to storm Beijing but in the end failed to reach the city. Even so, the cost of fighting the rebels helped trigger a major financial crisis that left many starving. Six years later, during the Second Opium War, British and French troops attacked the city, and ransacked the Old Summer Palace complex.

The shock of these tumultuous events promoted the cause of modernization, but as foreign influence grew, conservatives grouped around the Dowager Empress Cixi launched a counterreaction. In 1899, Cixi supported a violent uprising by the xenophobic "Boxer" movement (who adopted the slogan "Support the Qing, Destroy the Foreigners"). The Boxers entered Beijing and subjected the foreign legations there to a two-month siege, before an eight-nation expeditionary force (including Americans and Japanese, as well as Europeans) arrived to fight back, causing the imperial court to flee to Xi'an. The Qing's prestige was shattered and despite further fitful reforms, including a promise to adopt constitutional government, the regime collapsed in 1912 when the last emperor, Puyi, was deposed.

The new republican government struggled to establish its authority, and the mass of urban poor and activist students provided a potent mix that fueled radical politics and sparked large demonstrations. Though Western-style buildings sprouted in Beijing, the collapse of the country into warlordism and the move of the national capital to Nanjing in 1927 left it neglected (its name was even downgraded, to Beiping, or "northern peace"). In 1937, war broke out with Japan and under Japanese occupation the city suffered terrible privations. Even when it was liberated at the end of World War II, shortages continued, as civil war between Nationalist and Communist forces wracked the country. Beijing's reconstruction would have to wait.

THE LEGATION QUARTER ▷
After China's defeat in the Second Opium War, the Qing were forced to allow foreign legations to set up in Beijing. By 1900, the Legation Quarter was home to delegations from 11 countries.

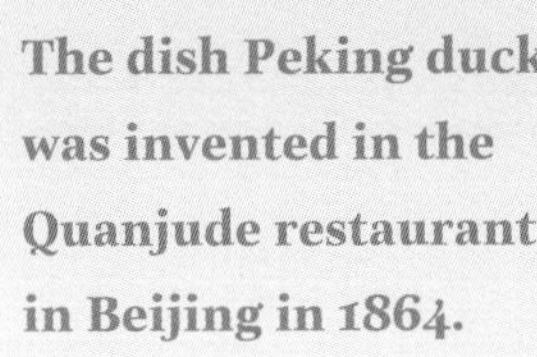

The dish Peking duck was invented in the Quanjude restaurant in Beijing in 1864.

1860 Anglo–French forces occupy Beijing and destroy the Old Summer Palace.

1861 On the death of her husband the Xianfeng Emperor, the Dowager Empress Cixi assumes effective control, dominating the government until her death in 1908.

1900 The Boxer militia occupies Beijing and besieges its foreign legations, provoking intervention by an eight-nation coalition.

1912 The six-year-old Emperor Puyi is forced to abdicate and Yuan Shikai becomes President of the Republic of China.

1928 Beijing is occupied by Nationalist forces of the Kuomintang.

1937 War breaks out between Japan and China. Beijing is occupied by Japanese troops.

△ BIRTH OF THE PEOPLE'S REPUBLIC
At 3 p.m. on October 1, 1949, Mao Zedong announced the birth of the People's Republic of China to a large crowd gathered in Tiananmen Square. The date became China's national day, with celebratory events held in the square ever since.

During the course of its 3,000-year history, Beijing has held no fewer than 16 different official names.

The People's Republic

In January 1949, People's Liberation Army forces entered Beijing, marking the virtual end of the Chinese Civil War and a new era for the city (which now had its old name restored). In October 1949, Communist Party leader Mao Zedong announced the foundation of the People's Republic of China (PRC) from a platform on Tiananmen Square. So began a wholesale transformation of both city and country.

Tens of thousands of party and government workers moved into Beijing, marking the most radical shift in its demography since the coming of the Manchu, and the restoration of the city as national capital made it the centerpiece of new socialist political and economic policies. The Inner City walls were largely demolished to allow freer flow of traffic on wide avenues—a process completed in 1965 when the Outer City walls were pulled down to allow the building of an underground rail system. *Dayuan*—large apartment buildings—were built to house the growing population and state-controlled department stores replaced neighborhood markets.

Reshaping the city

As part of the 10th anniversary celebrations of the People's Republic, an even more ambitious program of reshaping the city was undertaken. Tiananmen Square was expanded in order to accommodate mass gatherings and massive new buildings, combining Soviet-style architecture with more traditional Chinese forms, were constructed: among them, the Great Hall of the People on Tiananmen Square; the Cultural Palace of Nationalities; and the new Beijing train station. This initiative was part of the Great Leap Forward program, which set up people's communes to administer workplaces and schools, although the promotion of "backyard furnaces" in a rapid attempt to industrialize proved to be ineffective. In the 1960s, another of the struggles between tradition and change that had long characterized Beijing's history took place in the form of the Cultural Revolution, spearheaded by young Red Guards who targeted what they saw as conservative elements, including intellectuals, teachers, and even cultural sites across the city.

The death of Mao Zedong in 1976 marked the beginning of a new phase in Beijing's history. Under the leadership of Deng Xiaoping and his successors, economic reforms

Emblem of the People's Republic of China

1949 Nationalist troops in Beijing surrender to the Communists. Mao Zedong establishes the People's Republic of China (PRC).

1959 The Great Hall of the People and nine other major buildings are built to celebrate the 10th anniversary of the PRC.

1969 The Beijing underground system opens.

1976 Mao Zedong dies and is laid to rest in a mausoleum in the center of Tiananmen Square.

Workers' monument outside Mao's mausoleum

> The **Beijing Olympics** represent China's grand entrance onto the **world's stage** and confirmation of its ... **superpower** status.
>
> MA JIAN, WRITER, 2008

were implemented that allowed limited private ownership. New shopping malls began to spring up across the city, and a number of high-tech zones were set up—including Zhongguancun, now regarded as China's Silicon Valley. The boundaries of the city extended steadily, with a series of new highways constructed (now totaling seven) and more subway lines built to cope with the burgeoning population of a capital city of an economy that by the 1990s was growing at over 10 percent a year.

The transition to modernity was not without its difficulties. Anxieties about the rate of change were among the factors that led to a widespread student protest movement in 1989, and the city had to overcome tensions caused by an influx of migrant workers from the countryside and the demolition of many of the *hutongs* and older neighborhoods of Beijing to make way for gleaming skyscrapers. Meanwhile, pollution problems worsened as the number of vehicles in the city mounted.

The 21st century

By the 2000s, Beijing was transformed, taking its place as a city at the forefront of modern architectural styles with innovative structures such as the egg-shaped National Center for the Performing Arts and the CCTV Headquarters. None came to greater global attention than the extraordinary "Bird's Nest" stadium, built for the city's hosting of the 2008 Olympic Games. The Games were the boldest statement yet of the new China: the nearly 7 million people who attended them live and 3.5 billion people who watched them worldwide were treated to China's first-ever tally-topping medal performance and a jaw-dropping opening ceremony that celebrated both the country's traditional culture and its status as a modern economic leviathan. It was a fitting theme for a city with roots in the ancient past, but whose dizzying dash toward modernity leaves visitors with the feeling that in the blink of an eye, the whole landscape may be transformed once more.

▽ **OLYMPIC STADIUM**
The original inspiration for the design of the Beijing National Stadium (or "Bird's Nest") came from Chinese glazed ceramics and the veining on scholar's rocks.

1978 Deng Xiaoping becomes Communist Party leader and begins a process of economic reform.

1987 Bernardo Bertolucci's *The Last Emperor* is filmed in the Forbidden City.

1989 Martial law is imposed after student demonstrations.

In 1995, there were more than 8.3 million bicycles on Beijing's roads.

2007 An ad-hoc artists' enclave is transformed into the 798 Art District by a redevelopment plan.

2008 The Olympic Games are held in Beijing; China tops the medal tally.

2008 The Beijing–Tianjin high-speed railroad opens, operating at speeds of up to 220mph (350kph).

Hong Kong

PEARL OF THE ORIENT

Coming into its own as a merchant port, Hong Kong blended Chinese and British influences to become the archetypal Asian metropolis, a symphony of sky-high architecture, unabashed commerce, and restless energy.

Long before Hong Kong's incarnation as an island metropolis, it was the home of various tribes known as the Yue, who had body tattoos, short hairstyles, and were experts at offshore fishing. After the first emperor of the Qin dynasty annexed southern China—including modern-day Hong Kong and Guangdong—in 214 BCE, a number of Han Chinese were forced to settle in the region, and the Yue were gradually assimilated into Han Chinese culture.

During the Tang era (618–907 CE), the Tuen Mun district of what is now the New Territories is believed to have served as a port and a base for salt production and pearl fishing. In the 12th century, members of the Tang clan, whose descendants still hold political sway in Hong Kong today, first began to settle in the region. Over the following centuries, they were joined by the Hau, the Pang, the Liu, and the Man, collectively making up the Five Great Clans of the New Territories.

◁ HONG KONG AT NIGHT
Chinese junk boats date back to the Han dynasty, from 220 BCE. The vessels are an iconic sight on Victoria Harbor, juxtaposed against the backdrop of Hong Kong Island's skyscrapers.

Foreign traders

The Ming dynasty (r. 1368–1644) neglected the islands of Hong Kong, viewing the region as uncivilized. The Portuguese, who installed themselves in nearby Macau in 1557, were the first Europeans to bring trade, and were later followed by the Dutch, French, and British. During the subsequent Qing era, all foreign trade was channeled solely through Guangzhou (or Canton) on the mainland, and Hong Kong remained an undeveloped backwater. However, in 1842 China was forced to hand over Hong Kong Island to the British after losing the First Opium War; foreign trade could now be opened up, and for the new landlords the island's deep harbor presented a great opportunity.

> "**Hong Kong** has created one of the **most successful societies** on **Earth**.
>
> QUEEN ELIZABETH II, 1997

c. 1100 CE Over several centuries, five clans of Han Chinese arrive from nearby Chinese mainland provinces, driving out local inhabitants, and building walled villages on the barren, hilly land.

1557 The Portuguese establish Macau, setting up the first European trading port in the region.

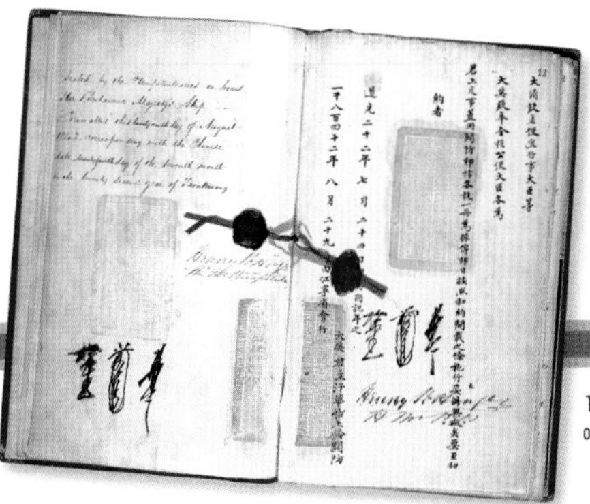

The Treaty of Nanjing

1842 China hands Hong Kong Island to the British "in perpetuity" in the Treaty of Nanjing, after losing the First Opium War.

1880 Hong Kong thrives as a merchant port, overseeing about a third of mainland China's imports and exports. Silk and jade are popular goods.

△ COLONIAL ERA
The British introduced double-decker trams in 1912 and double-decker buses in 1949. Today Hong Kong has the world's largest fleet of double-decker trams.

> **Every inch of space was used**. As the road narrowed, signs receded upward ... **Hong Kong** had the knack of building **where others wouldn't dare**.
>
> JONATHAN GASH IN *JADE WOMAN*, 1989

Hong Kong under the British

The British set up merchant houses in the new colony, and trade in silk and jade soon developed. They built a city on the north coast of the island, which they named Victoria, with the Central district—the focus for business and administration—at its heart; soon cricket fields sat alongside tea houses. Without an adequate legal system or policing, life in its early days was lawless, however, and opium dens and prostitution proliferated, giving the new settlement a reputation for vice.

For the expansionist British, control of Hong Kong Island alone was never enough. After victory in the Second Opium War—a war forced by the British in order to improve their trading concessions further—they were granted a portion of the Kowloon peninsula and Stonecutters Island under the 1860 Convention of Peking. More was to follow: after China's humiliating defeat in the First Sino-Japanese War, European powers pressed the crumbing Qing dynasty into yet another loss of land, and in 1898 Britain was leased the New Territories—almost all the remainder of Kowloon, plus 200 outlying islands—for a period of 99 years. The Chinese were left the tiny walled city of Kowloon, and even that fell into British hands with the fall of the Qing dynasty in 1912.

Neon city

Hong Kong's population grew rapidly through the second half of the 19th century, and by 1900 had reached 370,000. Further waves of incomers followed the 1911 Chinese Revolution and the onset of war with Japan in 1937.

The Japanese took Hong Kong in 1941, sparking an exodus, but the population surged again after the establishment of the People's Republic of China (PRC) in 1949. This created a huge pool of cheap labor for a thriving textiles and clothing industry. During the next prosperous decades, the city stepped onto the world stage. By the 1970s, Hong Kong dazzled with neon lights, as business owners vied for attention with huge billboards.

As Hong Kong boomed, so, too, did its distinctive culture. For many audiences in the West, the first glimpse of the city was in Bruce Lee's martial arts movie *Enter the Dragon*. Lee's celebrity ushered in two decades of successful Hong Kong cinema and Asian-chart-dominating Cantopop. Meanwhile, China set up a string of Special Economic Zones on the mainland close by, making Hong Kong—long an established financial hub—an international trading gateway to the PRC. By 1990, Hong Kong's GDP was the largest in Asia after Japan.

1898 China agrees to lease the New Territories (200 small islands) for 99 years to the British.

1941 Japan takes Hong Kong during World War II. The population shrinks from 1.6 million to 500,000 in less than four years.

1973 *Enter the Dragon*, filmed in Hong Kong, is an international hit, making Hong Kong–American actor Bruce Lee a worldwide star.

1980 China sets up Special Economic Zones near Hong Kong, with its modern port, intended to attract international trade and investment and boost exports.

1997 Celebrations take place as Britain returns the New Territories, Kowloon, and Hong Kong Island to China, which designates them a Special Administrative Region.

Hopes after handover

With much fanfare from mainland China, Britain returned not only the New Territories, but also Kowloon and Hong Kong Island to the Chinese in 1997. China agreed to follow a "One Country, Two Systems" principle for 50 years, allowing, it was hoped, political freedom and capitalist trade to continue for Hong Kong. The decade leading up to the handover had been an uneasy one, with almost a million residents emigrating. Yet the territory was left to flourish. Building projects turned Hong Kong into a great world metropolis, and today the city often tops the global ranking for the number of buildings over 492 ft (150 m) tall. Soon, mainland Chinese tourists began venturing to Hong Kong for a glimpse of unfettered Chinese capitalism. This trend was fast-tracked in 2018 when the Hong Kong–Zhuhai–Macau Bridge opened, allowing mainlanders to pop into Hong Kong in less than an hour. There have been tensions over China's increasing control of Hong Kong's affairs, and how the city continues to integrate with the mainland remains to be seen. Yet Hong Kong has long inspired incomers to conjure fortunes from its infertile land, and its independent streak lives on in its politics, soaring skyline, and intoxicating island-metropolis way of life.

△ NEON SIGNS IN KOWLOON
Hong Kong was ablaze in neon from the 1950s to the '80s during economic boom times. Many signs have disappeared and there is now a push to preserve the remaining examples as heritage pieces.

Hong Kong has over 15,000 restaurants, one of the highest densities in the world, partly because few homes have large kitchens.

1998 Chek Lap Kok Airport opens after six years of construction and at a cost of $20 billion, making it one of the world's most expensive airport projects.

2004 "A Symphony of Lights" opens. High-tech light shows are projected nightly onto the walls of 20 buildings on Hong Kong Island's North Shore.

2018 The world's longest sea bridge, the Hong Kong–Zhuhai–Macau Bridge, opens, allowing China's mainlanders to drive to Hong Kong.

Seoul

SOUL OF ASIA

Originally a small riverside settlement, Seoul sprinted into modernity from the late 20th century. High-speed internet and architectural daring feed its designer skyline and 24-hour lifestyle, which offer a preview of the future.

The site of present-day Seoul was first settled as early as 4000 BCE. Four millennia later, a village sprang up around the shared border of three kingdoms along the Han River. This community built earthen walls and tombs for their deceased, but it was the much-later construction of two palaces that drew more settlers to the area. First, King Munjong of Goryeo built a summer palace in 1068. Then, in 1392, King Taejo founded the Joseon dynasty and ordered the construction of the Gyeongbok Palace. This "palace of shining happiness" would be home to the Joseon monarchs for nearly 200 years. At this time, the city was known as Hanseong. King Taejo also built a defensive wall along the ridges of the four surrounding mountains. Protecting the inhabitants from wild tigers and other animals, the wall also limited contact with foreigners, sealing off the city from the West and other outside influence. The government kept its politics and culture close to China's and followed a Confucian ideology. Over the next 500 years, four more palaces were built by the Joseon dynasty, and together they became the Five Grand Palaces.

Language and learning

Cultural life in Hanseong blossomed during the 30-year reign of King Sejong from 1418. His Jiphyeonjeon Hall, within the Gyeongbok Palace, became a center of scholarship, leading advances in science, literature, and agriculture. Frustrated that the average citizen could not read the Chinese characters used by the elite, Sejong masterminded the development of a new phonetic written script, *hangul*, which promoted widespread literacy and continues to be used today.

◁ *MAGPIE AND TIGER*, 19TH CENTURY
In this example of *minhwa* (Korean folk art), the comical tiger satirizes Joseon authority while the magpie stands for the common man.

▷ DONGDAEMUN DESIGN PLAZA (DDP)
The huge and striking DDP, a cultural complex designed by Zaha Hadid Architects and opened in 2014, is clad in 45,000 aluminum panels.

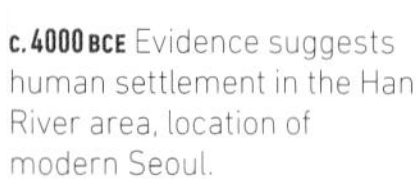

c. 4000 BCE Evidence suggests human settlement in the Han River area, location of modern Seoul.

1392 CE King Taejo names Hanseong (later Seoul) as the capital of the Joseon state and constructs the Gyeongbok Palace.

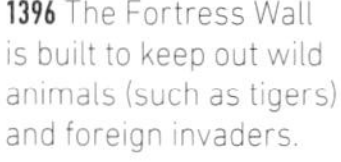

1396 The Fortress Wall is built to keep out wild animals (such as tigers) and foreign invaders.

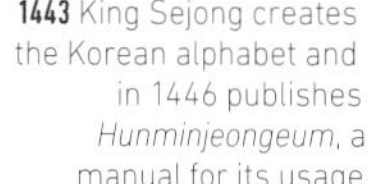

1443 King Sejong creates the Korean alphabet and in 1446 publishes *Hunminjeongeum*, a manual for its usage.

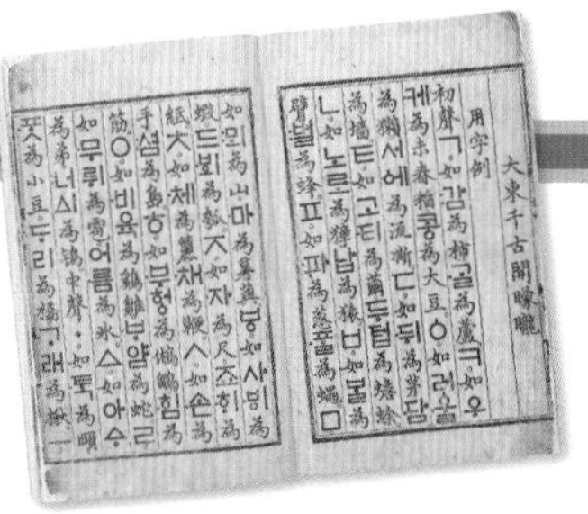

1669 The Honcheonsigye is invented, an astronomical clock showing the position of celestial bodies.

design
shop
살림터 D1

◁ GYEONGBOK PALACE
The Joseon dynasty palace, dating from 1392, was regarded as the heart of Seoul. Major restoration work was undertaken from 1867, and again from 1989.

For 60 years, a network of trams trundled through Seoul from downtown to outlying neighborhoods. Trains and buses replaced the tram system in 1968.

A new era dawned in the late 19th century. King Gojong, the final monarch of the 500-year Joseon dynasty, declared the start of the Great Korean Empire in 1897. He was determined to modernize the country and end centuries of isolation by opening up relations with Western powers, following the example of neighboring China and Japan. Thanks to joint ventures with the US, in 1902 the city became the first in East Asia to have telephones, the telegraph, trams, electricity, and water systems.

With its eyes on this up-and-coming metropolis, Japan annexed Korea and occupied its capital for 35 years from 1910. The Japanese renamed the city Keijō (Gyeongseong in Korean) and imposed measures intended to eradicate Korean identity, including banning the speaking of the national language. A series of mass demonstrations against Japanese rule in 1919 spread from the capital across the country. The March First Movement, as it became known, resulted in thousands of deaths and arrests, but also fostered a clear "Seoulite" identity and strengthened national unity.

The Japanese did, however, invest heavily, improving roads and ports, introducing trains, expanding neighborhoods, and constructing Neoclassical Western-style buildings. They also enthusiastically promoted the city as a tourist destination in East Asia. High-quality guidebooks and magazines gushed about the architecture, parks, and museums of Keijō. With its wonders shared and a new train line connecting the city to China, the capital of the former hermit kingdom was now open to visitors.

War and recovery

By the time Korea finally gained independence from Japan in 1945, its capital was one of the most industrialized cities in East Asia. Japan's surrender at the end of World War II led to the division of Korea into North and South protectorates, overseen by the Soviet Union and the US respectively. As Cold War tensions led to a breakdown in negotiations about this temporary division, elections were held in South Korea and the First Republic of Korea was declared in 1948.

1867 Gyeongbok Palace is reconstructed as a royal complex of 5,792 rooms, after being burned to the ground around 1597.

1897 King Gojong declares the start of the Great Korean Empire, taking the title of Emperor Gwangmu.

1905 The Japan–Korea Treaty is signed in Seoul, establishing a Japanese protectorate over Korea. It becomes effective in 1910.

1910 The Japanese annex Korea and occupy Seoul, renaming the city Keijō.

1915 The Joseon Industrial Exhibition is held in the grounds of the Gyeongbok Palace.

The March First Movement against Japanese rule, which started in Seoul in March 1919, is today marked with a national holiday.

Seoul was adopted as the Republic's capital. It was only at this point that the city's name was officially established, although it had been in use for some time: "Seoul" was derived from a Korean term for capital.

Stability was some way off, though. In June 1950, North Korean forces crossed the mountains at the edge of Seoul and invaded, starting the Korean War. Seoul was devastated by a three-month occupation, during which the South Korean government fled the city and moved the capital to Busan in the south. Over the next three years, the city changed hands multiple times. American troops entered Seoul in 1950 as part of a UN counterattack. Entire districts were bombed out and leafy, store-lined avenues were turned into battlegrounds.

By the end of the war in 1953, Seoul was left in ruins. Poverty, hunger, and crime were compounded by a series of coups, dictatorships, and rebellions. As North Korean refugees arrived in the city, fleeing even worse conditions, its population swelled by 1.5 million to 2.5 million in less than a decade. The military-controlled government of President Park Chung-hee oversaw rapid urban development and the Seoul suburbs began to sprawl. The Gyeongbu Expressway, constructed from 1968, and the Hannam Bridge, opened in 1969, linked the south of the Han River to the old city center. This created a new residential and business district in an area of former rice paddies known as Gangnam. Development was so rapid that this period is now known as the "Miracle on the Han River." Over several decades, a modern city emerged from the post-war rubble, one that was invested in technology, electronics, and science, rather than agriculture.

American influence

The presence of the US military introduced new kinds of food to the Korean palate. Some of the most well-known Korean dishes today started as American imports. Spam, a canned cooked meat from Minnesota, found its way into "army stews" in Seoul's restaurants. Chicken used in Korean soups was now served battered and fried, Kentucky-style, with mayonnaise on the side.

American Peace Corps volunteers, who began arriving in Seoul in 1966, influenced local culture in other ways, promoting the virtues of volunteering and democracy.

▽ NAMDAEMUN GATE, 1930s
During the first half of the 20th century, Seoul's cityscape saw Joseon-era gates sit alongside new Western-style buildings and trams.

As **Paris** was for **France**, **Seoul** was not simply Korea's largest town. **It was Korea.**

GREGORY HENDERSON, FOREIGN SERVICE OFFICER IN KOREA, 1968

1925 The occupying Japanese finish construction of the Neoclassical-style Seoul Station and, in 1926, Seoul City Hall.

1945 At the end of World War II, Korea gains independence from Japan.

1948 The First Republic of Korea is proclaimed and the capital is officially named Seoul for the first time.

1950 During the Korean War, Seoul changes hands between North and South Korea four times.

The Statue of Brothers at the War Memorial of Korea

Olympic regeneration

> We created an even more **festive atmosphere** for what is ... the greatest **international festival of peace.**

CHYUN SANG JIM, DEPUTY SECRETARY GENERAL OF THE SEOUL OLYMPIC ORGANIZING COMMITTEE, 1987

△ The motto for the 1988 Seoul Olympic Games was "Harmony and Progress."

▷ Construction of the Grand Olympic Bridge over the Han River began in 1985, but was not completed until 1990.

Seoul hosted the Olympic Games in 1988, investing heavily in urbanization projects in the seven-year lead-up to the event. The aim was to raise the profile of Seoul and make it an economic and cultural hub for East Asia. The government pulled money, people, and other resources from elsewhere in the country and employed them all in developing the city. Residents of some Seoul neighborhoods earmarked for Olympic redevelopment were forced to relocate. Workers from other regions gravitated toward the capital, often attracted by new jobs in the automotive and consumer electronics industries. Other regeneration projects included new housing and new metro lines and, most notably, a scheme to beautify the long-neglected Han River. Upgraded paths were laid along its course and locals started to cycle and stroll its length again. The Games were a major success and their infrastructure delivered a long-term legacy, with parks, stadiums, and other venues still playing a part in Seoul's daily life.

1971 The 774-ft (236-m) N Seoul Tower is built at the summit of Namsan mountain, overlooking Seoul. The observatory deck opens to the public in 1980.

1974 Seoul's first metro line—Subway Line 1—opens, serving nine stops.

1988 Seoul hosts the Olympic Games, spurring major housing and riverfront regeneration.

1996 The 75-ft (23-m) Maitreya Buddha at Bongeunsa Temple in Gangnam district is completed.

2002 Seoul hosts the FIFA World Cup in its purpose-built Seoul World Cup Stadium, designed in the shape of a Korean kite.

Seoul regularly tops the charts for having the fastest internet access in the world—more than triple the global average speed.

SEOUL CITYSCAPE ▷
Seoul sits in a valley ringed by mountains and the Fortress Wall, completed in 1396. Large sections have been restored following damage during the 20th century.

Seoul came of age in 1988: nationwide anti-government protests resulted in democratic national elections, and the city hosted the Olympic Games (see box). Seoulites embraced the event and rushed to volunteer. The capital courted more international business, and firms such as Samsung partnered with universities in Seoul for research and development into consumer electronics.

Fast, multifaceted future

Technology was the great hope for a modern Seoul of the future. Through the '90s, young Seoulites would hunker down in dimly lit internet cafes (or "PC bang") to play popular online games. This drove the adoption of internet use at home in South Korea, which was double that of the US by 2001. Seoul's high population density made it easy to install a broadband network. By 2010, over 90 percent of its residents could connect to high-speed internet.

Efforts were also made to create green space and boost the city's cultural life. The reclamation of the Cheonggyecheon stream was a case in point: after the Korean War, it had been paved over with roads and an elevated expressway, but in 2005 it was brought back into use as a waterway, lined with nearly 7 miles (11 km) of pedestrian-only paths. Herons, fish, and the tinkle of flowing water returned to the city. The Seoul Metropolitan Government also identified disused buildings and areas to "activate" for public use and recreation. Old train lines were reborn as parks. Abandoned factories buzzed as new art spaces. In addition, the five royal palaces and the city's *hanok* (traditional wooden houses) were restored. A renewed Seoulite identity began to emerge, which took pride in its unique, layered, Asian-meets-Western past.

In 2012, singer Psy and his hit song "Gangnam Style" brought the wealthy Seoul neighborhood of Gangnam to international attention. Popular K-dramas (South Korean–made television series) flaunt the city's futuristic buildings, such as the Dongdaemun Design Plaza (DDP) in the fashion district. Yet traditional values endure alongside 21st-century developments. A landmark of Gangnam itself is the towering Maitreya Buddha statue at the ancient Bongeunsa Temple, completed in 1996. Today, futuristic skyscrapers—monuments of glass and polished steel, the headquarters of internationally powerful companies—share the limelight with Seoul's Five Grand Palaces.

Seoul's Lotte World Tower, opened in 2017, boasts the world's highest glass-bottom observation deck, the loftiest swimming pool, and the fastest elevator.

2005 The Cheonggyecheon stream reopens as a waterway and pedestrian-only public space.

2012 The song "Gangnam Style" by Seoul singer Psy is the first YouTube video ever to top one billion views, putting K-pop and the city's affluent Gangnam district on the map.

2015 Seoul claims the world's top fiber-optic broadband provision, with free Wi-Fi in 10,430 public places. The aim is free Wi-Fi coverage in all public places by 2022.

2019 The film *Parasite*, set in Seoul, explores class divisions and discrimination. It goes on to become the first non-English-language film to win the Academy Award for Best Picture.

2020 The population of Greater Seoul hits nearly 26 million, meaning that for the first time more than 50 percent of South Koreans live in the city.

FUJIMAK
SUPER

Tokyo

EDO ("MOUTH OF THE BAY")

Tokyo grew from a strategic castle town to become the world's largest city. It's an ambitiously built metropolis that in recent decades has captured the global imagination as a city of tomorrow.

For most of its history, Tokyo was called Edo ("mouth of the bay"). This area of tidal flats and reed beds, where the Sumida River meets Tokyo Bay, has been inhabited for at least 10,000 years, according to archaeological records. Far from Kyoto, the imperial capital, Edo didn't enter the history books until the beginning of the feudal era, in the late 12th century, when a minor warrior clan, who took the name Edo, built a fort on a hill here.

The shogun's city

Fifteenth-century Japan was a time of near-constant warfare as regional warlords called *daimyō* vied for influence and land. In 1600, General Tokugawa Ieyasu won a decisive battle with the backing of some key *daimyō*, unifying the country and becoming shogun, the de facto ruler of feudal-era Japan. Unlike previous shoguns, Ieyasu set up his power base in Edo, far from the entrenched influences of Kyoto, where the emperor—by now little more than a figurehead—and old noble families still lived.

Edo was a strategic choice. The Edo family had lost it to the powerful Uesugi clan, who chose the losing side in the war, leaving it in Ieyasu's grasp. Tokyo Bay was a natural harbor and the Sumida River would make it easy to ferry goods into the city, while a plateau overlooked the bay, the tidal flats, and the plains beyond—perfect for a castle. And Edo's proximity to Mount Fuji, worshipped as a god since ancient times, was auspicious. Like Kyoto, the city was designed with geomantic principles in mind, and guardian temples were built northeast and southwest of the castle, the two directions that portend evil.

The early Tokugawa shoguns were enthusiastic and resourceful urban planners, overseeing the construction of an extraordinary network of moats, canals, aqueducts, and sewers. All were dug by hand, with clans who had opposed Ieyasu obliged to provide laborers.

Tokyo is still a medieval city by design: wide boulevards and neat grids are rare; narrow, meandering roads are more common.

◁ TOKYO SKYLINE
Where one- and two-story wooden buildings stood less than a century ago, central Tokyo is now awash with skyscrapers. Tokyo Tower, which resembles the Eiffel Tower in shape but not in color, is an icon of the city.

1457 The first Edo Castle is built by a vassal of the powerful Uesugi clan.

c. 1200 CE The Edo clan establishes a fortification on Tokyo Bay, laying claim to the area.

1603 Tokugawa Ieyasu, the son of a minor warlord who rose to become shogun of Japan, chooses Edo for his capital.

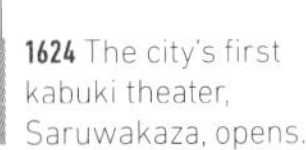

1624 The city's first kabuki theater, Saruwakaza, opens.

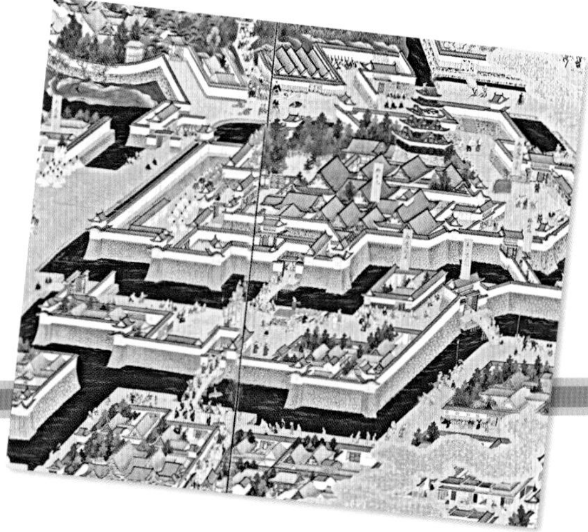

1636 The construction of Edo Castle is completed; at the time, Edo was the world's largest fortified town.

To solidify his power and discourage dissent, the shogun required *daimyō* to spend every other year in Edo, and their wives and families to stay permanently. The large retinues required to maintain their villas in Edo, along with the artisans and merchants who followed to supply goods and services, caused the city's population to quickly swell.

◁ KAJI-HAŌRI
This woolen *kaji-haōri* (literally "fire coat") with family crest was designed for a woman of samurai rank to wear in the event of fire.

Life and culture in Edo

Japan under Tokugawa rule was relatively peaceful, but freedoms were limited. The country was largely sealed off from the rest of the world and there was a strict class hierarchy. At the top were the *daimyō* and their retainers, known as samurai. Farmers were held in some esteem—rice was required for survival, after all. At the bottom were artisans and the merchants, the classes that made up the townspeople of Edo. Women, following the neo-Confucian values of the era, were considered subservient to men, though many worked to survive or support their families.

In Edo, the *daimyō* had their villas on the highland plains, where they were safer from earthquakes and floods. The townspeople lived along the Sumida River delta, mostly in wooden tenements that often went up in flames—a famous saying from the era proclaimed that "fires and quarrels are the flowers of Edo." The city's firemen, drawn from the merchant classes, were local heroes, lauded for their bravery, stamina, and skill.

In peacetime, the samurai saw their incomes dry up, while some merchants became incredibly wealthy. Strict laws prohibited them from flaunting their riches (anything decorated with gold leaf or thread, for example, was forbidden), but they improvised their own culture, patronizing kabuki (a stylized dance-drama) theaters and sumo-wrestling tournaments. They also spent lavishly on banquets and courtesans—prized for their beauty, wit, and skill in the arts—in the city's licensed pleasure quarters.

The most evocative examples of Edo's rich culture are the woodblock prints (*ukiyo-e*) produced in the 18th and 19th centuries. Great artists like Hokusai and Hiroshige created works that celebrated everyday life in Edo, capturing the charm and swagger of kabuki stars (the influencers of their day), and depicting scenes outside the city at a time when movement was strictly regulated.

△ SAPPORO BEER POSTER, EARLY 1900s
Beer was introduced to Japan in the late 19th century. It was a luxury item, far more expensive than sake.

The making of a "modern" city

The 1868 Meiji Restoration (see box), which ended feudalism in Japan, gave Edo a new name and a new purpose. Edo was a city that served the shogun; Tokyo, as the capital of an aspiring modern nation-state, needed to serve a different purpose. And while Edo had its own kind of sophistication, Japan wanted to show the world that it could be modern in the Western sense, too. This was a strategic move by a new government, ruled by a young emperor and largely made up of high-ranking lords and samurai from the rebel provinces, to project strength and ward off would-be colonizers.

1657 The Great Meireki Fire kills an estimated 100,000 people and destroys more than half of the city, including the castle.

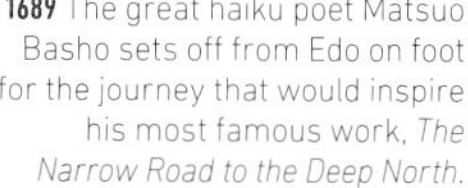

1689 The great haiku poet Matsuo Basho sets off from Edo on foot for the journey that would inspire his most famous work, *The Narrow Road to the Deep North*.

1707 Mount Fuji erupts, covering Edo, 62 miles (100 km) east of the volcano, in several inches of ash.

1721 Edo's population surpasses one million, making it the world's largest city.

1832 Hokusai finishes his iconic *Thirty-Six Views of Mount Fuji* series; until the age of skyscrapers, the mountain was visible from the city streets.

Meiji Restoration

△ Yōshū Chikanobu's 1885 woodblock triptych, *Horse Track at Shinobazu*, shows one of the popular new diversions introduced after the Meiji Restoration.

By the mid-19th century, after 250 years of rule, the Tokugawa shoguns' hold on power was growing increasingly tenuous. Ambitious *daimyō* (regional warlords) in the southwest of the country were agitating for reform, and American ships in Tokyo Bay were demanding Japan open its ports. Civil war broke out in 1867 between the rebel *daimyō* and Tokugawa loyalists; while not without bloodshed, it didn't upend life as much as the constant wars of the 15th century. But when it ended the following year, there was a dramatic power shift: there would be no more shoguns, and full power reverted to the emperor, in what came to be known as the Meiji Restoration.

Meiji means "enlightened rule" and the new head of state, a 16-year-old boy whose father had died abruptly the year before, would take the title of Emperor Meiji.

The court moved from Kyoto to Edo, the castle was transformed into an imperial palace, and the city renamed Tokyo ("eastern capital"). As feudalism ended, so did restrictions on movement and social class. Ports were opened, and ideas and technology from the US and Europe began to stream into the capital, which had a profound effect on politics, the arts, and—as electricity, trains, and factories arrived—on the lives of ordinary citizens.

1868 The Meiji Restoration restores rule to the emperor and Edo is renamed Tokyo.

1909 Tokyo's population passes two million.

1914 Tokyo Station, the city's main rail terminus, which is modeled on Amsterdam Centraal, opens.

1918 Neon lights go on in Tokyo's Ginza district.

Nihombashi, a canal bridge now overshadowed by the city's elevated highway, is considered Tokyo's center; all distances from the capital are measured from this point.

Tokyo was transformed into a model city for the new Japanese empire, which would include Korea, Taiwan, and Manchuria as Japan embarked on its own colonization project. With feudalism over, cooperative *daimyō* were offered something like severance packages (perhaps a provincial governorship) and their lands in Tokyo were taken by the state for new purposes. Museums, parks, universities, hospitals, and military training facilities were built, often modeled on developments in Paris, Berlin, or London. Some villas were also purchased by wealthy merchants, who could finally acquire status symbols long prohibited to them.

At first, Western ideas were limited to the capital's elite, but as the 20th century began they started to reach the emerging middle class. The new trading companies and department stores had work for young men and women, who commuted on the new tram lines and adopted Western dress and hairstyles. It was a heady, disorienting time, when certain parts of Tokyo more closely resembled Europe than the rest of Japan; at the same time, many residents still lived in wooden tenements, adhering to a way of life that little reflected the great changes elsewhere in the city.

▽ MODERN GIRLS IN GINZA, 1928
Ginza—the first Tokyo district to get electric street lights and brick buildings—became the flourishing center of the new "modern" culture. This was the place to see and be seen in the latest Western fashions.

The Great Kantō Earthquake

In 1923, on a windy September day at noon, when stoves all over the city were alight for lunch, the Great Kantō Earthquake shook Tokyo to its core, and did more to transform the city than any Meiji government project. Fires swept through the city, in particular the tightly packed former merchant quarters, causing far more casualties and damage than the initial quake.

◁ OLYMPICS POSTER
The 1964 Tokyo Summer Olympics, the first to be held in Asia, were a global showcase for a progressive post-war Japan.

Tokyoites (like the *edokko*, or "children of Edo," before them) were used to fires, and many quickly rebuilt their properties—so quickly that the city had little chance to institute urban planning. However, many also decided to settle in the far west of the city, in districts that had been village-like but were transforming into commuter towns. As the 20th century wore on, it was these western districts—Shinjuku, Shibuya, and Harajuku, for example—that became more developed and culturally relevant.

World War II, occupation, and the Olympics

An expansionist Japan, which had already annexed parts of China, officially entered World War II on the Axis side in 1940. In Tokyo, daily life was one of increasing scarcity, and many children were evacuated to the countryside. The city was bombed over a hundred times by Allied forces and once again was laid to ash. When Japan surrendered, what remained of the citizenry was war-weary and hungry, with little energy to resist the Allied occupation that followed. Illicit markets thrived and people struggled to survive.

By the 1960s, life was returning to a new normal—one touched by American influences like blue jeans, jazz, and aspirational consumerism. Like cities around the world, Tokyo was the site of major student protests during this era, largely targeting the terms of Japan's military alliance with the United States.

And the city did what it had always done: it rebuilt. The 1964 Tokyo Summer Olympics were viewed at the time as Tokyo's comeback, and much of the city's current infrastructure dates to the frantic construction

1923 The Great Kantō Earthquake (magnitude 7.9) strikes the coast south of Tokyo.

1927 The first section of the Tokyo Metro (the first underground railroad anywhere in Asia) opens.

1944 A single night of firebombing, the deadliest in history, kills an estimated 100,000 people and destroys nearly half the city.

1952 The Allied occupation of Japan, led by the United States and headquartered in Tokyo, ends.

1958 The Tokyo Tower, a symbol of the city's post–World War II reconstruction, is completed.

1964 The *shinkansen* (bullet train) makes its debut with a route connecting Tokyo and Osaka.

1964 Tokyo hosts the Summer Olympics, the first games held in Asia and the first to be internationally televised.

that took place in the preceding years: the *shinkansen* (bullet train) and the elevated highway, but also the covering up of the canals of the shogun era. Now rather fetid and unused, they were considered eyesores.

Contemporary Tokyo

Boom or bust, Tokyo kept on building. The city's destruction after the Great Kantō Earthquake and during World War II meant there weren't many noteworthy old buildings to save, and centuries of fires had contributed to the idea that buildings weren't really permanent anyway. Old structures were torn down and built anew. Skyscrapers and a staggering new city hall went up in Shinjuku. Building on Edo-era land reclamation projects, artificial islands in Tokyo Bay were refashioned into leisure and commercial districts.

In the 1980s, when Japan's economy was soaring, the capital became a source of global fascination, its colorful neon streets, dense crowds, and giant video advertisements becoming a kind of visual shorthand for the city of tomorrow, and an inspiration for cyberpunk aesthetics everywhere. During the height of Japan's economic bubble (which burst in the early 1990s), land in Tokyo's Ginza neighborhood was among the most expensive in the world.

While many still associate Tokyo with a kind of cityscape made famous in films like *Blade Runner* (1982), the city has already moved on. More recent developments feature glittering glass towers, terraced green spaces, wooden latticework (reminiscent of traditional architecture), and revitalized waterways—the features of a city hoping once again to be seen as a beacon of the world to come.

△ SHINJUKU AT NIGHT
The Shinjuku neighborhood of Kabukichō is Japan's largest nightlife district. Its neon visuals are a symbol of modern urban life.

In 2020, Tokyo's population topped 14 million. The Greater Tokyo Metropolitan Area, home to over 37 million people, is the world's largest conurbation.

1967 Yoyogi Park, a military barracks during the Allied occupation, and later the Olympic Village, is refashioned into a green public space.

1995 A religious cult releases toxic nerve gas on the Tokyo Metro during the morning commute, killing 13 and injuring thousands.

2012 Construction is completed on the Tokyo Skytree, which becomes the tallest tower in the world.

Los Angeles

LA-LA LAND

Creative, bold, and not always angelic, sunny LA has spent the last 240 years transforming itself from a tiny Spanish pueblo into the world's largest dream factory, a storied cityscape of movies, music, and industry.

Los Angeles's first-known citizen was a diminutive female in her early 20s known as La Brea Woman. Her fractured skull and part of her skeleton were found at the La Brea tar pits in LA's Miracle Mile neighborhood in 1914. She lived around 10,000 years ago, and research suggests she ate stone-ground grains.

The Chumash people had arrived by 5000 BCE and established a sophisticated artisan culture in the Ballona wetlands, just south of present-day Venice Beach. From around 200 CE, they were gradually displaced by the Tongva, hunter-gatherers who had migrated from the arid interior. The most influential of several local peoples, they built sea-going vessels for fishing and lived in small villages, several of which survived well into the colonial period.

The Spanish arrival

Juan Rodríguez Cabrillo, a veteran of Hernán Cortés's Aztec campaigns (see p. 69), was the first European to explore the Californian coast. Sailing north from New Spain (modern-day Mexico), he landed on Santa Catalina Island in October 1542. Despite several hundred years of Tongva settlement, Cabrillo claimed the island for Spain, exploring San Pedro and Santa Monica bays on the mainland before heading further north. For the next 200 years, California was mostly ignored by Europeans, save for a mapping mission by explorer Sebastián Vizcaíno, who spent 1602 looking for safe harbors along a shoreline that many Spaniards still considered to be the western edge of a Californian island.

> "**Tip the world over** on its side and **everything loose** will **land in Los Angeles**.
>
> FRANK LLOYD WRIGHT, ARCHITECT

GRIFFITH OBSERVATORY ▷
Built in 1935, the Griffith Observatory has space exhibits and a planetarium, and offers views of the city and the Hollywood Sign. It has featured in films including *Rebel Without a Cause*.

5000 BCE A Chumash culture in the Los Angeles area is practicing basketry and using tar for waterproofing.

1000 BCE Chumash people settle along the coast, where they engage in fishing and build boats.

Tongva woman, 1905

200 CE The Tongva people begin a gradual western migration into the Los Angeles Basin.

1542 Juan Rodríguez Cabrillo lands on Santa Catalina Island and surveys San Pedro Bay. It is the area's first European contact.

In the early 1500s, around 25 Tongva villages existed in the area, with a combined population of about 500.

1602 Spaniard Sebastián Vizcaíno tracks the coast looking for safe harbors.

GRIFFITH OBSERVATORY

◁ SAN GABRIEL ARCÁNGEL MISSION
Founded in 1771 by the Franciscan order as the fourth of 21 Spanish missions in California, the San Gabriel Mission moved to its present site in 1775.

Indigenous people suffered as the city grew. Villages were uprooted and local laws allowed Indigenous "vagrants" to be bought as servants.

The Spanish missions

Keen to outmaneuver their British, French, and Russian competitors, the Spanish began to strengthen their presence in the frontier lands of California in the late 18th century by building a network of Catholic missions. In 1769, a reconnaissance party led by California's first governor, Gaspar de Portolá, set out from Loreto, New Spain, and traveled north through present-day Los Angeles County. Stopping to camp by a river that meandered past a Tongva village, they named the waterway El Río de Nuestra Señora la Reina de Los Ángeles de Porciúncula, and the seed of a city was born.

San Gabriel Arcángel, the first Franciscan mission in the Los Angeles area, was founded in 1771. Six years later, after establishing the town of San Jose to the north, near San Francisco Bay, new Spanish Governor Felipe de Neve proposed the foundation of a settlement close to San Gabriel to act as a bulwark against Spain's colonial rivals.

El Pueblo de Nuestra Señora la Reina de los Ángeles ("The Town of Our Lady the Queen of the Angels," shortened to "El Pueblo") was laid out in 1781 and settled with 44 pioneers from what is now northwest Mexico. They were chosen for their resourcefulness, and only two of them were white.

Mexican takeover

The village gradually developed into a self-sufficient farming community, with Indigenous people employed as paid laborers. A second mission was established at nearby San Fernando in 1797, but the settlement faced sporadic flooding and a powerful earthquake in 1812. When Mexico gained its independence from Spain in 1821, it took over a year for news of the revolution to reach the isolated pueblo. After swearing allegiance to the Mexican cause, LA was granted city status in 1835.

The missions were loyal to the Spanish church and, wary of their influence, the Mexican government broke up the estates, many of which became cattle ranches. Settlers began to arrive from the fledgling United States, while the Tongva and other Indigenous peoples became increasingly marginalized. But a greater upheaval was to come: in 1846 the Mexican–American War began. There was fighting in and around the city, but by January 1847 Mexican resistance in California was over, and in 1850, it was incorporated into the United States.

1771 The San Gabriel Arcángel mission is built in the LA area using forced Indigenous labor.

1781 El Pueblo de Nuestra Señora la Reina de los Ángeles is founded by 44 settlers from New Spain.

Cross marking the site of the original pueblo of LA

Between 1781 and 1850 LA's population grew remarkably slowly, from 44 inhabitants to around 2,000.

1821 With Mexican independence, the region is no longer under the control of Spain.

1833 The Spanish missions are secularized, leaving land open to ranchers.

> **Thousands of men** ... began to "**ride the rails**," stowing away in **empty boxcars** and **jumping trains**.
>
> HADLEY MEARES ON THE IMPACT OF THE SANTA FE RAILWAY, *LA CURBED*, 2017

Under new government, development accelerated. LA's street names were anglicized and tensions brewed between Spanish-speakers and newer Anglo immigrants. Many arrivals were attracted to ranching, which remained the region's key industry, especially during the California Gold Rush of the 1840s and '50s, when beef fed thousands of prospectors. Yet, with a population of around 2,000, LA itself still wasn't much larger than a village. For the next two decades it remained a shady, lawless place where gangs roamed the streets. And then everything went boom.

The golden age dawns

LA's population exploded 20-fold between 1870 and 1900. Growth was spurred by the building of railroads and the 1892 discovery of oil. Electric streetcars began rattling around the increasingly sophisticated city center, as the city spawned a fire department, a public library, newspapers, and churches of several different denominations. Meanwhile, city promoters set about hyping LA as the promised land, with its warm climate, cheap and fertile land, and California sun.

The most crucial of several new railroads was the long-distance Santa Fe Railway, which linked the growing city with the rest of the nation in 1887. With it came migrant workers—Chinese, Irish, Germans, and Americans from the east coast—who added diversity to the growing hub. Around the same time, LA made plans to acquire its first proper seaport in the form of San Pedro, the muddy bay that Juan Cabrillo had explored two centuries before. It was dredged in 1871, breakwaters were built to protect the harbor, and the city of San Pedro was incorporated into LA in 1909.

Beautiful buildings were also joining the city's functional early structures. Beaux-Arts offices and theaters rose in Downtown, and the Bradbury Building, noted for its ornate interior and iron balustrades, opened in 1893. Rugged Griffith Park, one of the US's largest urban spaces, was established in 1896.

Oil had first been pumped to the surface in 1892. By the 1920s, the region was producing 25 percent of the world's supply, a deluge that fueled its 20th-century motorcar addiction. The first car in a city that would soon become jammed with them hit the road in 1897. That year, LA made its first motion picture, a grainy 25-second street scene featuring horse-drawn carriages and men in bowler hats.

In 1910, a 17-minute silent short called *In Old California*, directed by D. W. Griffith, was shot in the village-like district of Hollywood, 7 miles (11 km) northwest of Downtown. The new art form would transform LA and change the US forever.

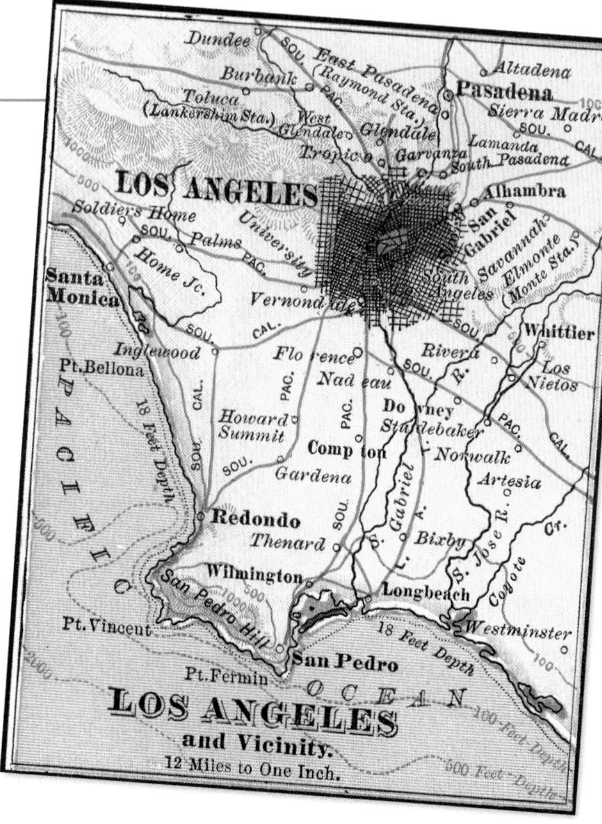

△ **1900s MAP OF LOS ANGELES**
By 1900, LA's population had just broken 100,000. It had yet to engulf surrounding settlements such as Santa Monica, which it was connected to by an electric railroad.

1846 US marines occupy Los Angeles at the start of the Mexican–American War.

1887 The Santa Fe Railway links LA to Chicago and opens the city to mass migration.

1887 Real-estate agent Harvey Henderson Wilcox buys 160 acres (65 hectares) of land northwest of LA and names it Hollywood.

1907 LA's port opens after the dredging of the San Pedro mudflats.

1910 Hollywood is incorporated into LA and the district's first movie is shot.

D. W. Griffith, Hollywood's first movie director

The golden age of Hollywood

◁ Marilyn Monroe was born in LA in 1926. A huge star in the 1950s, she has come to epitomize fame, glamour, and the ephemeral nature of Hollywood.

▽ Hollywood stars have been imprinting their hands (and feet) into the cement on Hollywood Boulevard since the 1920s.

△ The Hollywood Sign was erected in 1923 as a temporary real-estate advertisement but quickly became iconic. The "land" suffix was removed in 1949.

Hollywood's golden age began around 1912, when the first big film production company, Universal, started operating in the LA suburb. The era lasted around 50 years and saw huge technological advances—from sound and color to crosscuts and special effects—and an abundance of talent concentrated in one place. Actors like Clark Gable and Greta Garbo became the epitome of the movie star. However famous, most actors worked within a studio system in which eight big production companies exercised tight control. In the early 1960s, the rise of television and antitrust regulations dented the popularity of movies and the power of the studios, but later in the decade, the "New Hollywood" era ushered in a more independent approach to filmmaking, headed by directors such as Francis Ford Coppola and Sidney Lumet. The 21st century has seen a lucrative revival dominated by sequels and superheroes.

> "That's what **Hollywood** is—a **set**, a glaring, gaudy, **nightmarish set**.
>
> ETHEL BARRYMORE, ACTRESS, 1942

1913 Completion of Los Angeles Aqueduct, which diverts water from farmland.

1923 The iconic Hollywood Sign is unveiled on Mount Lee in the Hollywood Hills.

1929 The first Academy Awards are held at the Hollywood Roosevelt Hotel.

1939 Raymond Chandler's LA-based novel *The Big Sleep* is published. It later becomes a movie starring Humphrey Bogart and Lauren Bacall.

1943 The Zoot Suit Riots see baggy-suited Latino and Black men targeted by white servicemen.

Freeways began to appear in LA from 1940, culminating in the opening of the world's first directional interchange in 1953.

SUNSET BOULEVARD ▷
Sunset Boulevard runs roughly east–west for 22 miles (35 km) from Downtown LA to the Pacific Ocean, passing through West Hollywood and Beverly Hills. It began its life as a cattle trail.

The birth of Tinseltown

Hollywood became the quintessence of LA as the movie industry entered its golden age (see box), and soon the whole city was known as "Tinseltown." Movie stars and the rich and famous flocked to live in deluxe new suburbs as the city, powered by oil and entertainment, grew five-fold between 1900 and 1920, swallowing up numerous surrounding towns. Decorated by ornate movie palaces like Million Dollar Theater and entertainment venues such as the Hollywood Bowl, and presided over by politicians whose relationship with organized crime was often cozy, it seemed as if everyone was living in a Raymond Chandler novel: talking sharp, while wading waist-deep in corruption.

World War II was only a minor blip in LA's meteoric ascent. Shipbuilding and airplane manufacture kept the economy buoyant even as social problems arose: 1943 saw a grim wave of violence as white servicemen turned on fashionably dressed Mexican and Black people in the Zoot Suit Riots.

California dreaming

Post-war LA embraced the motorcar with unbridled zeal. Freeways multiplied, suburbs sprawled, and smog coated everything in a dirty film. As the Baby Boomers boomed, so did LA's industry, assembling cars, making furniture, and stitching clothes, while the movie business matured, and real-estate agents got rich subdividing land.

There was music, too. LA's '60s musical awakening began on the coast with surf pop and the addictive harmonies of the Beach Boys, before migrating to the more bohemian confines of Laurel Canyon in the Hollywood Hills, where it spawned the likes of the Byrds; the Doors; Joni Mitchell; and Crosby, Stills & Nash.

Modern growing pains

By the mid-1980s, the hangover had started to hit hard as deprivation and violence rose in parts of the city. The changing mood saw hippie harmonies and soft rock replaced by mostly Black hip-hop that engaged with city life and racial injustice. The videotaped beating of a Black man, Rodney King, by LAPD officers in 1991 sparked the 1992 LA riots, and marginalized areas like Compton and Watts saw high crime and drug use.

Meanwhile, poor urban planning resulted in traffic congestion and smog, and forest fires became fiercer and more regular. Out-of-control blazes in the 2010s destroyed many properties and threatened still more.

But LA is changing. In the next decade, the growing Latinx community is set to become a majority for the first time since the 1850s. In the economic sphere, the city has diversified through tourism, aerospace engineering, and computer manufacturing. The arts remain upbeat, with a still-buoyant movie industry, dazzling new architectural projects, and a strong international influence. In 2028, LA will become only the third city to host the Olympic Games three times. America's dream factory is as dynamic as ever.

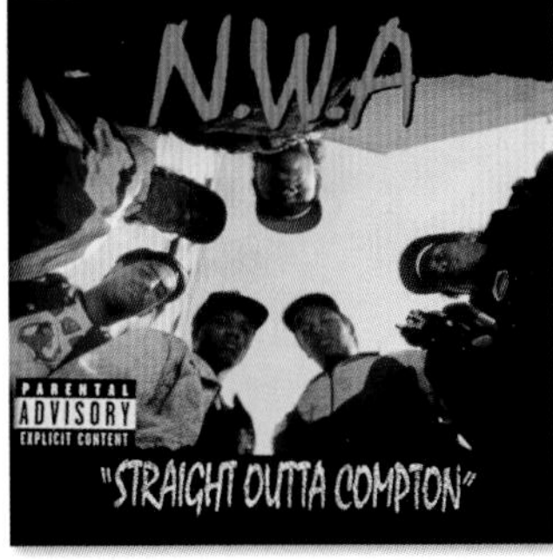

△ *STRAIGHT OUTTA COMPTON*
In 1988, N.W.A. put gangsta rap and the city of Compton on the map. Other rappers from the LA area include Snoop Dogg and Kendrick Lamar.

1957 The Troubadour opens. The hugely influential club helps cement the careers of the Byrds, the Eagles, and Guns N' Roses.

1984 LA becomes the only US city to host the Summer Olympic Games twice.

1991 Rodney King is beaten by police, sparking riots in 1992.

1994 The Northridge earthquake kills around 60 people and causes over $20 billion of damage.

1997 The Getty Center, an architectural marvel and one of the US's most-visited museums, opens.

2017 The Me Too movement exposes sexual harassment in Hollywood. Film producer Harvey Weinstein is later convicted of rape and jailed.

2017 *La La Land*, a joyous tale of love and dreams in LA, directed by Damien Chazelle, wins six Academy Awards.

The US poster for *La La Land*

2018 Woolsey wildfire progresses through Malibu to singe the cusp of the city of LA.

MORE GREAT CITIES

Rotterdam

Manhattan on the Meuse

Rotterdam has been called the "ultimate city of reconstruction." The city was founded in the mid-13th century, but bombing by the German air force during World War II almost completely destroyed the center. The municipality saw it as a once-in-a-lifetime opportunity to reimagine the city as a more functional and beautiful place. It became one of the world's leading laboratories for design and architecture, pioneering prototypes that were later adopted across Europe and America, such as the world's very first pedestrianized shopping street. It remains a work in progress.

Baku

City of Winds

Baku has a history that stretches back to at least 885 CE, and encompasses periods of rule by the Persians and Ottomans, and both Imperial and Soviet Russia. However, the period following the 1991 collapse of Moscow rule has seen the Azerbaijani capital reborn. Paid for by the revenue of Caspian Sea oil fields, 21st-century Baku is a city of glitzy architectural showpieces, such as the wave-shaped Heydar Aliyev Center designed by British–Iraqi architect Zaha Hadid and the trio of skyscrapers known as Flame Towers, meant to represent tongues of flame shooting up from the earth—they flicker at night with LED lights.

Doha

Pearl City

As recently as the middle of the 20th century, even though it was the chief settlement in Qatar, Doha was no more than a small fishing and pearling village. It was founded sometime in the 1820s. A century later it had a population of about 12,000, but this diminished when the pearl trade was devalued by the advent of cultured pearls in Japan and the Great Depression of the 1930s. When oil was discovered in 1940, the country was transformed. Today, Doha is a city of 2.4 million people and is in constant flux with the construction of ever-taller skyscrapers, dazzling cultural centers, and other investment projects befitting the capital of one of the world's richest countries.

Abu Dhabi

Manhattan of the Middle East

Archaeological evidence shows that the area around Abu Dhabi was settled as far back as 3000 BCE. The modern city began when Bedouin of the Bani Yas tribe settled here in the 1790s. Abu Dhabi ("father of gazelle"—the animals were abundant here at one time) remained a minor settlement until the discovery of oil in the mid-20th century. When the United Arab Emirates was formed in 1971, Abu Dhabi was made its capital, but despite its status and new-found wealth, the town modernized slowly. In the 21st century, Abu Dhabi is in the process of transforming itself into a modern, forward-thinking metropolis, with projects like Masdar, a self-contained sub-city powered by renewable energy, and the Saadiyat Island cultural zone, with branches of the Louvre and Guggenheim museums.

Nur-Sultan

City of Peace

The capital of Kazakhstan was renamed in 2019 after former President Nursultan Nazarbayev, and has a history of name changes. The city was originally founded on the Ishim River in 1830 by Siberian Cossacks as Akmolinsk. During the Soviet era it was a small regional center known as Tselinograd, reverting to a variant of its original name, Akmola, after the regime's collapse. When the city took over the role of capital from Almaty in 1998, it became Astana. Since then, oil wealth has been spent on international planners and architects with the aim of creating an audacious showpiece for the independent nation. The resulting cityscape features a slew of remarkable buildings, many of which reference Kazakh heritage, such as the Baiterek tower, inspired by the Kazakh "tree of life."

△ **Rotterdam** The striking Market Hall in central Rotterdam.

△ **Doha** The city's skyscrapers include the cylindrical Doha Tower (second from right).

Kuala Lumpur

KL

Meaning "muddy river confluence" in Malay, Kuala Lumpur was founded by Chinese tin miners in 1857. Despite its malaria-infested jungle location, it prospered and became capital of the Federated Malay States in 1896. When Malaya (later Malaysia) declared independence from Britain in 1957, Kuala Lumpur continued as the new nation's capital. Since that time, it has ridden the Southeast Asian economic boom to become a sprawling city bristling with skyscrapers, most notably the Petronas Towers, once the tallest buildings in the world and still the tallest twin towers. Although the majority of the population is Malaysian Chinese, the city is a mix of cultures in which mosques and temples mix with high-rises, Chinese shophouses, and Malay *kampungs* (villages).

Seattle

Emerald City

The city that gave the world Starbucks and the grunge band Nirvana was officially established in 1869 on the shores of Elliott Bay. It was named in honor of Chief Si'ahl of the local Duwamish and Suquamish Indigenous peoples. It boomed during the first years of the 20th century following the Klondike Gold Rush, and again in the latter part of the century thanks to the presence of the Boeing aircraft factory and the advent of mass air travel. In recent times, it has been a center for new tech, home to the likes of Microsoft and Amazon. Its status as a major Pacific port has also made it a hub for immigration, especially from Asia; more than 15 percent of its approximately 3.9 million residents are of Asian descent. The city has a reputation for liberalism, and it has one of the largest LGBTQ+ communities in the US.

Chicago

Windy City

The largest city in the American Midwest occupies land once roamed by native Fox, Miami, Potawatomi, and Sauk peoples. In 1803, the US Army built Fort Dearborn on the south bank of the Chicago River. In 1837, its population reached 4,000 and Chicago was incorporated as a city. Despite a fire in 1871 that destroyed a third of the city, Chicago flourished as a center for manufacturing and meatpacking, and as a transportation hub. In 1885, Chicago gave the world its first skyscraper and, following an influx of African Americans from the south in the 1920s and '30s, it nurtured a particular strain of Chicago jazz and blues. In recent times, industry has been replaced as the economic backbone by finance and technology, but the city retains its blue-collar image and a reputation for rough-and-tumble politics.

Toronto

The 416

The Toronto area has been inhabited for more than 10,000 years, but the city was founded by the British as York in 1793. It was renamed in 1834 to distinguish it from New York. As a major destination for immigrants to Canada, Toronto grew rapidly through the remainder of the 19th century. Today, it is the most populous city in Canada and still a magnet for immigration: more than half of its residents belong to a minority population group. A popular urban myth has it that the United Nations rated Toronto as "the most multicultural city in the world." That may not be true, but the City of Toronto public transit helpline provides a service in over 80 languages. While not the nation's capital, the city is home to the Stock Exchange and the headquarters of the country's five largest banks.

São Paulo

Sampo

Founded by Jesuit missionaries in 1554, São Paulo is the largest city in Brazil and second most-populous in the entire Southern Hemisphere, with over 21 million in its metropolitan region. It was overshadowed by Rio de Janeiro until the end of the 19th century, when it experienced an economic boom based on the export of coffee. On the back of this, the city welcomed waves of immigrants from Europe, the Middle East, and Asia. It is today the major economic centre of not only Brazil but all of South America. It is also ethnically diverse, with sizable Italian, Arab, and Jewish communities and the largest Japanese population outside Japan. São Paulo has few historical buildings or beauty spots, but it is dynamic and industrious.

△ **Kuala Lumpur** The Petronas Towers are the world's tallest twin towers.

△ **Toronto** The CN Tower dominates the Toronto skyline.

Index

Page numbers in **bold** refer to main entries.

Acknowledgments

Dorling Kindersley would like to thank the following:
Alexandra Beeden for proofreading; Amy Child for design assistance; Steve Crozier for retouching; Abigail Ellis for language advice; Abigail Mitchell for editorial assistance; Helen Peters for indexing; Managing Jackets Editor Saloni Singh.
"In Tokyo" by Matsuo Basho, translation © Jane Hirshfield 2011; used by permission of Jane Hirshfield, all rights reserved.

The publisher would like to thank the following for their kind permission to reproduce their photographs:

(Key: a-above; b-below/bottom; c-center; f-far; l-left; r-right; t-top)

1 Alamy Stock Photo: Chronicle. **2 AWL Images:** Michele Falzone. **3-4 Getty Images / iStock:** E+ / raisbeckfoto. **6 Mary Evans Picture Library:** © The Pictures Now Image Collection. **8 Alamy Stock Photo:** CPA Media Pte Ltd / Pictures From History (b). **Bridgeman Images:** © Zev Radovan (cl). **9 Alamy Stock Photo:** Christopher Scott (b). **10 Bridgeman Images:** © Leonard de Selva (tc). **Getty Images:** De Agostini / DEA PICTURE LIBRARY (cl). **George Steinmetz:** George Steinmetz Photography (tl). **11 akg-images:** (r). **12 Bridgeman Images:** © Brooklyn Museum of Art / Bequest of Alexander M. Bing (t). **Getty Images:** The Image Bank / Fraser Hall (br). **13 Alamy Stock Photo:** Andrew Fare (tl). **Bridgeman Images:** (cl). **14 AWL Images:** Michele Falzone (tc). **Bridgeman Images:** © Detroit Institute of Arts, USA (tl). **Dreamstime.com:** Beatrice Preve (bc). **Getty Images:** De Agostini / DEA / W. BUSS (br); Hulton Fine Art Collection / Heritage Images (tr). **Picfair.com:** Diego Lezama (cla). **Shutterstock.com:** Gianni Dagli Orti / © Banco de México Diego Rivera Frida Kahlo Museums Trust, Mexico, D.F. / DACS 2021. (clb). **SuperStock:** DeAgostini (bl). **15 akg-images:** Suzanne Held (tc). **Alamy Stock Photo:** imageBROKER / Peter Schickert (bl). **Bridgeman Images:** © British Library Board. All Rights Reserved (tl). **16 akg-images:** Mondadori Portfolio / Electa (bl). **16-17 Bridgeman Images:** © Detroit Institute of Arts, USA (t). **17 Bridgeman Images:** (br). **18 akg-images:** (br). **Bridgeman Images:** (bl); Alinari (t). **19 Alamy Stock Photo:** Jam World Images (b). **Bridgeman Images:** (cra); © Look and Learn (cr). **Dreamstime.com:** Petr Zamecnik (tl). **20 akg-images:** (bc). **Alamy Stock Photo:** Hemis.fr / René Mattes (tl). **Bridgeman Images:** © Germanisches National Museum (bl). **21 Alamy Stock Photo:** Granger Historical Picture Archive, NYC (b). **Bridgeman Images:** Alinari (t). **Getty Images:** Hulton Archive / Heritage Images (cra). **22 Bridgeman Images:** (tl). **Getty Images:** Popperfoto (bc). **23 akg-images:** View Pictures Ltd / Francesco Russo (bc). **Alamy Stock Photo:** AA Film Archive (cr); Collection Christophel / © Riama Film / Gray-Film / Pathé Consortium Cinéma (t). **24-25 AWL Images:** Michele Falzone. **25 akg-images:** jh-Lightbox_Ltd. / John Hios (br). **26 4Corners:** Luca Da Ros (t). **Alamy Stock Photo:** Azoor Photo (bl); Peter Horree (br). **27 Alamy Stock Photo:** North Wind Picture Archives (t). **Bridgeman Images:** (bc). **28 4Corners:** Gianluca Santoni (t). **Bridgeman Images:** The Stapleton Collection (br). **29 Alamy Stock Photo:** Chronicle (bc); Peter Eastland (t); Jeremy Hughes (crb). **30-31 Getty Images:** Hulton Fine Art Collection / Heritage Images. **31 Getty Images / iStock:** PaulaConnelly (crb). **32 akg-images:** (tl). **Alamy Stock Photo:** Classic Image (cla); WBC ART (cb). **Bridgeman Images:** The Stapleton Collection (bl). **33 © The Metropolitan Museum of Art:** Rogers Fund, 1912 (br). **Shutterstock.com:** OPIS Zagreb (t). **34 akg-images:** Roland and Sabrina Michaud (bc); New Picture Library / De Agostini Picture Lib. / G. Dagli Orti (tl). **Alamy Stock Photo:** Max Right (tr). **35 Architectural Firm: Adnan Kazmaoğlu Mimarlık Araştırma Merkezi:** Photography Agency: Studio Majo, Engin Gerçek & Aras Kazmaoğlu, Photographer: Engin Gerçek & Aras Kazmaoğlu (br). **Getty Images:** Corbis Historical / swim ink 2 llc (bl). **36-37 Dreamstime.com:** Beatrice Preve. **37 Alamy Stock Photo:** Peter Horree (bc). **Bridgeman Images:** (crb). **38 Getty Images / iStock:** Brasil2 (tl). **Getty Images:** LightRocket / Marji Lang (br). **39 Alamy Stock Photo:** www.BibleLandPictures.com / Zev Radovan (cb). **Getty Images:** De Agostini Picture Library (tl). **40 Alamy Stock Photo:** Chronicle (bc); www.BibleLandPictures.com / Zev Radovan (bl). **Bridgeman Images:** Everett Collection (l). **41 Bridgeman Images:** © Andrusier (br). **Nat Geo Image Collection:** (tc). **42 Alamy Stock Photo:** John Frost Newspapers (br); Sueddeutsche Zeitung Photo / Scherl (tl). **43 Getty Images:** Hulton Archive / Yael Ilan / GPO (br); Lior Mizrahi (t). **44 Getty Images:** De Agostini / DEA / W. BUSS. **45 Bridgeman Images:** (br). **Getty Images:** De Agostini / DEA / W. BUSS (bc). **46 Alamy Stock Photo:** National Geographic Image Collection (t). **SuperStock:** DeAgostini (bl). **47 Alamy Stock Photo:** Heritage Image Partnership Ltd / Werner Forman Archive (cr); The Picture Art Collection (bc). **Bridgeman Images:** (ca). **48 Alamy Stock Photo:** Robertharding / Peter Barritt (bc). **Getty Images:** De Agostini / DEA / Biblioteca Ambrosiana (bl). **48-49 Bridgeman Images:** © British Library Board. All Rights Reserved. **50 Alamy Stock Photo:** Dinodia Photos RM (t); The Picture Art Collection (br). **Bridgeman Images:** Pictures from History (cl). **51 Alamy Stock Photo:** Agefotostock / Dinodia (crb); Classic Collection (t). **52 Alamy Stock Photo:** ART Collection (t); Matteo Omied (bc). **53 Alamy Stock Photo:** Dinodia Photos RM (cl); Historic Collection (br). **Bridgeman Images:** (tl). **54 Alamy Stock Photo:** REUTERS / B Mathur (t). **Getty Images:** Picture Post / Central Press (bl). **Shutterstock.com:** Lefteris Papaulakis (br). **55 4Corners:** Günter Gräfenhain (t). **Getty Images:** LightRocket / Marji Lang (br). **56 Alamy Stock Photo:** imageBROKER / Peter Schickert. **57 Alamy Stock Photo:** CPA Media Pte Ltd / Pictures From History (br). **58 Alamy Stock Photo:** IndiaPicture / Khazanchi BN (bl). **Bridgeman Images:** © British Library Board. All Rights Reserved; © Cincinnati Art Museum / John J. Emery Fund (br). **59 Alamy Stock Photo:** VTR (bc). **Shutterstock.com:** Waj (t). **60-61 akg-images:** Suzanne Held. **61 Alamy Stock Photo:** World History Archive (bc). **62 Alamy Stock Photo:** Album / British Library (br); The Picture Art Collection (l). **63 Bridgeman Images:** (tl); Pictures from History (br). **64 akg-images:** Laurent Lecat (cl). **Getty Images:** De Agostini / DEA / J. E. BULLOZ (br); Sygma / Daniele Darolle (tl); Moment / Weiming Chen (bl). **65 Getty Images:** E+ / Terraxplorer (br); Moment / Eastimages (t). **66-67 Shutterstock.com:** Gianni Dagli Orti / © Banco de México Diego Rivera Frida Kahlo Museums Trust, Mexico, D.F. / DACS 2021. **67 Dreamstime.com:** William Perry (br). **68 Alamy Stock Photo:** Heritage Image Partnership Ltd / Werner Forman Archive / N.J. Saunders (bl); Icom Images (t). **69 Alamy Stock Photo:** Lanmas (bc); Lebrecht Music & Arts / Derek Bayes (t). **Shutterstock.com:** Gianni Dagli Orti (bl). **70 Alamy Stock Photo:** SOTK2011 (br). **Shutterstock.com:** Gianni Dagli Orti (t); Vadim Petrakov (bl). **71 Bridgeman Images:** Jean Pierre Courau / © Estate of Juan O'Gorman / ARS, NY and DACS, London 2021.; © Duvallon (bc). **72 Alamy Stock Photo:** Granger Historical Picture Archive, NYC (bc). **Dreamstime.com:** Witr (t). **73 Alamy Stock Photo:** Juan Romero (br); Vintage_Space / © Banco de México Diego Rivera Frida Kahlo Museums Trust, Mexico, D.F. / DACS 2021. (cr). **Bridgeman Images:** Luisa Ricciarini / © Banco de México Diego Rivera Frida Kahlo / © DACS 2021 (c). **74-75 Picfair.com:** Diego Lezama. **75 Shutterstock.com:** Gianni Dagli Orti (br). **76 4Corners:** Giovanni Simeone (br). **Alamy Stock Photo:** INTERFOTO / History (tc). **Bridgeman Images:** Jean Pierre Courau (cl). **77 Alamy Stock Photo:** Realy Easy Star (bl). **Getty Images:** The LIFE Picture Collection / Fritz Goro (tr). **78 SuperStock:** DeAgostini. **79 Alamy Stock Photo:** Rubens Alarcon (br); Heritage Image Partnership Ltd / Werner Forman Archive / Museum fur Volkerkunde, Berlin (clb). **80 Alamy Stock Photo:** INTERFOTO / History (bl); World History Archive (tl); North Wind Picture Archives (br). **81 Alamy Stock Photo:** Zoonar GmbH / Pawel Opaska (t). **Getty Images:** De Agostini / DEA / G. DAGLI ORTI (br). **82 Alamy Stock Photo:** CPA Media Pte Ltd / Pictures From History (br). **Shutterstock.com:** Angela Meier (bl). **83 Bridgeman Images:** © Archives Charmet (bl). **Getty Images:** Moment / Punnawit Suwuttananun (br). **84 Alamy Stock Photo:** Classic Image (ftl); The Print Collector / Art Media / Heritage Images (fbl); World History Archive (bl); Historic Collection (br). **Jennifer Branch:** https://JenniferBranch.com (clb). **Bridgeman Images:** Luisa Ricciarini / © Estate of George Grosz, Princeton, N.J. / DACS 2021.(tl); © Leonard de Selva (cla). **Getty Images / iStock:** E+ / Mordolff (tr). **SuperStock:** DeAgostini (tc, bc). **85 Alamy Stock Photo:** Robertharding / Luca Tettoni (tc). **Getty Images:** narvikk (tl). **86-87 Alamy Stock Photo:** Classic Image (t). **86 Alamy Stock Photo:** Chronicle (bl). **Getty Images:** Museum of London / Heritage Images (br). **87 Alamy Stock Photo:** © Museum of London / Heritage Image Partnership Ltd. **88 Alamy Stock Photo:** AF Fotografie (cla); World History Archive (tc). **Bridgeman Images:** © Philip Mould Ltd, London (bc). **89 Alamy Stock Photo:** Granger Historical Picture Archive (bc). **Bridgeman Images:** © Guildhall Art Gallery (t). **90 akg-images:** © Sotheby's (tl). **Alamy Stock Photo:** David Dixon (tr). **Bridgeman Images:** (br); © St. Paul's Cathedral Library (cra). **91 akg-images:** (tr). **Alamy Stock Photo:** Chronicle (br). **Bridgeman Images:** © Westminister Archives (bl). **92 Alamy Stock Photo:** GL Archive (bc). **Bridgeman Images:** (tl). **93 akg-images:** Interfoto / Friedrich (cr). **Bridgeman Images:** © Malcolm English (t). **Getty Images:** Chris Gorman (br). **94 Alamy Stock Photo:** The Print Collector / Art Media / Heritage Images. **95 Alamy Stock Photo:** SuperStock (br). **Getty Images:** De Agostini / DEA PICTURE LIBRARY (bl). **96 Alamy Stock Photo:** Chronicle (t). **Bridgeman Images:** © Look and Learn (bl).

97 Alamy Stock Photo: World History Archive (cr). **98 Bridgeman Images:** The Stapleton Collection (bc). **Getty Images:** Roger Viollet (ca). **99 RMN:** (C) Musée d'Orsay, Dist. RMN-Grand Palais / Patrice Schmidt (tr). **100 Alamy Stock Photo:** Shawshots (bl). **© Heringson, Archiv Schmölz+Huth www.schmoelz-huth.de:** (tl). **101 Alamy Stock Photo:** Michael Jacobs / Architectural Works by Gehry Partners, LLP. **102 Getty Images:** Franco Origlia (l). **102-103 Alamy Stock Photo:** World History Archive. **103 Bridgeman Images:** © Raffaello Bencini (clb, bl). **104 Alamy Stock Photo:** The Picture Art Collection (t). **Bridgeman Images:** © Dario Grimaldi (bc). **105 Bridgeman Images:** © Museumslandschaft Hessen Kassel / Ute Brunzel (bl); © Nicolò Orsi Battaglini (tl); Luisa Ricciarini (cra). **106 Bridgeman Images:** © Royal Collection / Royal Collection Trust © Her Majesty Queen Elizabeth II, 2021 (tl). **Getty Images:** Hulton Archive / Heritage Images / Ashmolean Museum (bc). **107 Getty Images:** Corbis Historical / swim ink 2 llc (cr); Moment / Suttipong Sutiratanachai (t); Paris Match Archive / Gerard Gery / Georges Menager (bc). **108-109 SuperStock:** DeAgostini. **109 Bridgeman Images:** © Lobkowicz Collections (bc). **110 Alamy Stock Photo:** Prisma Archivo (t). **Getty Images:** Hulton Archive / Imagno (bc). **111 The City of Prague Museum:** (br). **112 akg-images:** (clb). **Dreamstime.com:** Photosimo (cla). **Getty Images:** Hulton Archive / Heritage Images (tl). **113 Alamy Stock Photo:** CTK (tr). **Getty Images:** Archive Photos (bc). **114 Alamy Stock Photo:** Heritage Image Partnership Ltd / © Fine Art Images (cb). **114-115 SuperStock:** DeAgostini. **115 Bridgeman Images:** (br). **KHM-Museumsverband:** (bc). **116 Alamy Stock Photo:** Art Kowalsky (br). **Bridgeman Images:** (t, bc). **117 Getty Images:** Hulton Archive / Imagno (tr); Moviepix / Movie Poster Image Art (bc). **118-119 Bridgeman Images:** Luisa Ricciarini / © Estate of George Grosz, Princeton, N.J. / DACS 2021. **119 Alamy Stock Photo:** Agencja Fotograficzna Caro / Frank Sorge (br). **120 Bildarchiv Preußischer Kulturbesitz, Berlin:** Deutsches Historisches Museum / Arne Psille (bl). **Bridgeman Images:** © DACS 2021 (tl). **121 Alamy Stock Photo:** ARCHIVIO GBB (crb). **Getty Images:** Hulton Archive / Stringer / Express (tr). **122 4Corners:** Sabine Lubenow / Fosters + Partners (r). **Getty Images:** Tom Stoddart (tl); ullstein bild (bc). **123 Getty Images:** ullstein bild / Ulrich Hässler (bl); ullstein bild / Schöning (br). **124 Getty Images / iStock:** Oleg Elkov (bc). **124-125 Getty Images / iStock:** E+ / Mordolff. **126 akg-images:** (bc). **Alamy Stock Photo:** Heritage Image Partnership Ltd / © Fine Art Images (t). **127 Alamy Stock Photo:** Everett Collection Historical (cra); Heritage Image Partnership Ltd / © Fine Art Images (bl). **128 Alamy Stock Photo:** Rob Atherton (br). **Dreamstime.com:** Marcorubino (tl). **The Federal State Budget Institution of Culture Shchusev State Museum of Architecture:** (clb). **129 Alamy Stock Photo:** domonabikeCzech (bc); Vyacheslav Lopatin (cr). **130 Alamy Stock Photo:** Jose Lucas (bc). **130-131 Alamy Stock Photo:** Historic Collection. **132 Alamy Stock Photo:** Heritage Image Partnership Ltd / © Fine Art Images (bc). **Getty Images:** DigitalGlobe / ScapeWare3d (cra); Keystone-France / Gamma-Keystone (cla). **133 Alamy Stock Photo:** The Picture Art Collection (r). **© The Metropolitan Museum of Art:** Gift of J. Pierpont Morgan, 1917 (bl). **134 Alamy Stock Photo:** Archive Farms Inc / Burton Holmes Historical Collection (t). **Bridgeman Images:** Buyenlarge Archive / UIG (br). **135 Getty Images:** AFP / Marwan Naamani (t); AFP / Khaled Desouki (bc). **136 akg-images:** Heritage Images / Heritage Art (cb). **136-137 Getty Images:** narvikk. **138 Alamy Stock Photo:** Nick Bobroff (br). **Bridgeman Images:** © Christie's Images (tl). **139 Alamy Stock Photo:** Godong (tl). **Indian PostsTelegraph Department, GOI:** Department of Posts, Ministry of Communications, Government of India (bc). **Shutterstock.com:** clickedbynishant (cr). **140-141 Alamy Stock Photo:** Robertharding / Luca Tettoni. **141 Alamy Stock Photo:** Antiqua Print Gallery (bc). **142 Alamy Stock Photo:** Sharad Raval (l). **Copyright by Thailand Post. All rights reserved.:** (bc). **Getty Images / iStock:** thitivong (tr). **143 Alamy Stock Photo:** CPA Media Pte Ltd / Pictures From History (br). **Bridgeman Images:** © Luca Tettoni (bl). **Getty Images:** Hulton Archive / Print Collector (tr). **144-145 Getty Images:** Moment / Mongkol Chuewong (t). **144 Alamy Stock Photo:** Mr.Black&White (bc). **Getty Images:** Bettmann (clb). **145 Getty Images:** Moment / Suttipong Sutiratanachai (bc). **146-147 Bridgeman Images:** © Leonard de Selva. **147 Alamy Stock Photo:** Artokoloro (bc). **Getty Images:** Universal Images Group / Picturenow (br). **148 Alamy Stock Photo:** World History Archive (bl). **148-149 Getty Images / iStock:** E+ / georgeclerk (t). **149 akg-images:** Akpool Gmbh / Arkivi (bl). **Mary Evans Picture Library:** Retrograph Collection (cr). **150 Alamy Stock Photo:** Granger Historical Picture Archive (bl). **Library of Congress, Washington, D.C.:** 2001620435 (bc). **150-151 Jennifer Branch:** https://JenniferBranch.com. **152 Alamy Stock Photo:** Everett Collection Historical (bl). **Andrew LaMar Hopkins:** (cra). **153 Alamy Stock Photo:** LocalColor Photo (br). **Getty Images:** Archive Photos / G. D. Hackett (tr); Hulton Archive (bl). **New Orleans Jazz & Heritage Foundation Archive:** (tl). **154 akg-images:** (bl). **Alamy Stock Photo:** Heritage Image Partnership Ltd / Fine Art Images (br). **155 Getty Images:** EyeEm / Nathanael Hovee (br); Moment / Copyright by 8Creative.vn (bl). **156 akg-images:** Africa Media Online / Iziko Museum (br). **Alamy Stock Photo:** Artepics (tr); World History Archive (ftl); Steve Speller (clb). **AWL Images:** Michele Falzone (fbl). **Dreamstime.com:** Kmiragaya (cl). **Getty Images:** Corbis Historical / Fine Art Photographic (tc). **Mary Evans Picture Library:** Grenville Collins Postcard Collection (bl); © The Pictures Now Image Collection (cla). **© National Gallery of Ireland:** Photo Copyright National Gallery of Ireland (tl). **SuperStock:** DeAgostini (bc). **157 Alamy Stock Photo:** The History Collection (tc). **Photolibrary:** Photographer's Choice / Tom Bonaventure (tl). **158-159 © National Gallery of Ireland:** Photo Copyright National Gallery of Ireland. **158 Bridgeman Images:** © Boltin Picture Library (bl). **160 Alamy Stock Photo:** Phil Behan (t); Pictorial Press Ltd (bl). **Getty Images:** Mondadori Portfolio (br). **161 Dreamstime.com:** Ericlaudonien (cr). **Getty Images:** Hulton Archive / Culture Club (bl). **162-163 Getty Images:** Corbis Historical / Fine Art Photographic. **164 Alamy Stock Photo:** Art Collection 2 (t). **Rijksmuseum, Amsterdam:** On loan from a private collection (br). **165 Alamy Stock Photo:** The Picture Art Collection (br). **Rijksmuseum, Amsterdam:** (cra); On loan from the City of Amsterdam (t). **166 Alamy Stock Photo:** World History Archive (bl). **Getty Images:** Popperfoto (tl). **Rijksmuseum, Amsterdam:** Gift of the Stichting Vrienden van de schilder Martin Monnickendam (tr). **167 Bridgeman Images:** (bl). **Getty Images:** Moment / George Pachantouris (cra). **168-169 Alamy Stock Photo:** Artepics. **169 Alamy Stock Photo:** Lebrecht Music & Arts (br). **170 Alamy Stock Photo:** Europe (tl); incamerastock / ICP (bc); Historic Collection (br). **171 4Corners:** A Tamboly (bc). **Alamy Stock Photo:** Akademie (clb); Kavalenkava Volha (t). **172 Alamy Stock Photo:** Steve Speller. **173 Alamy Stock Photo:** Album (bc). **Getty Images:** Hulton Archive / Stringer (br). **174 akg-images:** Bruno Barbier (tl, tc). **Alamy Stock Photo:** Granger Historical Picture Archive, NYC (bl). **Getty Images:** Bettmann (bc). **175 akg-images:** Bruno Barbier (tl). **Alamy Stock Photo:** North Wind Picture Archives (cr). **Getty Images:** Popperfoto / Paul Popper (br). **176 Alamy Stock Photo:** kristof lauwers (br). **Bridgeman Images:** Photo © LIMOT (cl). **Fado Museum:** Cover of the music sheet "Fadista", by Pedro F. Ribeiro d' Almeida and Fernando Corte Real, Sassetti & C.ª, Fado Museum Collection (ca). **Getty Images:** ullstein bild Dtl. (bl). **177 Alamy Stock Photo:** Aron M (tr); Kim Petersen (br). **178-179 AWL Images:** Michele Falzone. **179 akg-images:** Joseph Martin (br). **Alamy Stock Photo:** World History Archive (bc). **180 Alamy Stock Photo:** Album (br). **SuperStock:** Album / Ramon Manent (cl). **181 Alamy Stock Photo:** Vintage Archives (t). **Getty Images / iStock:** Starcevic (br). **182 Alamy Stock Photo:** Stefano Politi Markovina (tl). **Bridgeman Images:** Pictures from History (br); Prismatic Pictures (tc). **183 Alamy Stock Photo:** Agefotostock / Javier Larrea (cr); Hemis.fr / Ludovic Maisant (bc). **184 akg-images:** Cameraphoto Arte (bl). **184-185 SuperStock:** DeAgostini. **186 akg-images:** Cameraphoto Arte (tr); Van Ham / Saša Fuis, Köln (br). **Alamy Stock Photo:** World History Archive (tl). **Bridgeman Images:** © Derek Bayes (bl). **187 Alamy Stock Photo:** Peter Horree (tl). **Bridgeman Images:** (tr). **Shutterstock.com:** poidl (cr). **188 Alamy Stock Photo:** Album (br); The Protected Art Archive (t); Heritage Image Partnership Ltd / The Print Collector (bl). **189 akg-images:** (t, cra). **Alamy Stock Photo:** The History Collection (bc). **190 Alamy Stock Photo:** Theo Moye (cb). **Bridgeman Images:** (bl); © Look and Learn (t). **191 akg-images:** Starsinvenice Di Carlo Pecatori / Archivio Cameraphoto Epoche (br). **Alamy Stock Photo:** Samantha Ohlsen (t). **Getty Images:** Corbis Historical / Duffy GraphicsDaniel McInnis LLC (bl). **192 Alamy Stock Photo:** The Picture Art Collection (bc). **192-193 akg-images:** Africa Media Online / Iziko Museum. **194 Alamy Stock Photo:** Reuters / Mike Hutchings (bl). **Bridgeman Images:** © Look and Learn (t). **195 Bridgeman Images:** © Look and Learn (bl). **Getty Images:** Hulton Archive / Keystone (br). **The Cape Gallery: / Bobby Moore:** Kenneth Baker (cr). **196 akg-images:** Africa Media Online (tl). **Alamy Stock Photo:** Marek Poplawski (cr). **Bridgeman Images:** Nationaal Archief / Collectie Spaarnestad / Anefo / Fotograaf onbekend (bl). **Getty Images:** Jurgen Schadeberg (t). **197 Alamy Stock Photo:** Hufton+Crow-VIEW / With permission from Heatherwick Studio (br). **Getty Images / iStock:** Ben1183 (t). **198 Alamy Stock Photo:** CPA Media Pte Ltd / Pictures From History (bc). **Shanghai Museum:** (bl). **198-199 Photolibrary:** Photographer's Choice / Tom Bonaventure. **200 Alamy Stock Photo:** Contraband Collection (br); CPA Media Pte Ltd / Pictures From History (t); Historic Images (bl). **201 Bridgeman Images:** Pictures from History (cl). **Mary Evans Picture Library:** (cra). **202 Alamy Stock Photo:** Everett Collection Inc / CSU Archives (bl); Jon Arnold Images Ltd (tl); View Stock (br). **203 Getty Images:** Moment / Xiaodong Qiu (l). **204 Australian Museum:** (bl). **204-205 Alamy Stock Photo:** The History Collection. **206 National Museum of Australia:** Lannon Harley (bc). **State Library of New South Wales:** (bl); Hill, M. S. The City of Sydney [a Bird's-Eye View] [Cartographic Material] / M.S. Hill. [S.n.], 1888. (tl). **207 Alamy Stock Photo:** History and Art Collection (clb). **State Library of New South Wales:** George Caddy (tr). **208 Australian National Maritime Museum:** (bc); collection gift from Barbara (tl). **images reproduced courtesy of Powerhouse Museum:** Collection:Museum of Applied Arts and Sciences. Purchased 1985 (cl). **209 Getty Images / iStock:** africanpix (bl). **Getty Images:**

Allsport / Matt Turner (tr). **210 Mary Evans Picture Library:** © The Pictures Now Image Collection. **211 Getty Images:** Archive Photos / Fotosearch (br). **212 Alamy Stock Photo:** Dale Smith (crb). **Getty Images:** Universal Images Group / Universal History Archive (t). **Mary Evans Picture Library:** © Thomas Cook Archive (cl). **213 Alamy Stock Photo:** Lebrecht Music & Arts / Odile Noel (bl); TCD / Prod.DB / © Nicoletta (bc). **Getty Images:** Moment / Dan Kurtzman (tr). **214-215 Alamy Stock Photo:** World History Archive. **215 Alamy Stock Photo:** Universal Images Group North America LLC / PicturesNow (br). **216 Alamy Stock Photo:** Contraband Collection (tc); Everett Collection Historical (tr). **Bridgeman Images:** © Christie's Images (clb). **217 Alamy Stock Photo:** Francois Roux (r). **Mary Evans Picture Library:** Grenville Collins Postcard Collection (bl). **218 Alamy Stock Photo:** IanDagnall Computing (tr); Science History Images / Photo Researchers (cla); Red Poppy (bc). **National Museum of African American History and Culture:** Collection of the Smithsonian National Museum of African American History and Culture, Gift of Vicki Gold Levi, © 1933 by Mills Music Inc., NYC, renewed 1985 (cra). **219 Photo Scala, Florence:** The Metropolitan Museum of Art / Art Resource / The Metropolitan Museum of Art, Gift of AXA Equitable, 2012 (2012.478a–j) / © The Metropolitan Museum of Art (tl). **Shutterstock.com:** AP (bc). **220 Bridgeman Images:** © 2021 The Andy Warhol Foundation for the Visual Arts, Inc. / Licensed by DACS, London. (t); © Ben Buchanan (cr). **Courtesy of Sony Music Entertainment:** (bc). **221 Alamy Stock Photo:** Collection Christophel / © Wild Style (ca). **Getty Images / iStock:** Michael Ver Sprill (br). **222 Alamy Stock Photo:** History and Art Collection (bc); Niday Picture Library (bl). **223 Dreamstime.com:** Kmiragaya. **224 Bridgeman Images:** United Archives GmbH (l). **Dreamstime.com:** Sergei Nezhinskii, with Permission from Hungarian Post (bl). **225 Bridgeman Images:** © Christie's Images (tl). **Greg Young Publishing, Inc.:** Original artwork by Kerne Erickson, © Greg Young Publishing, inc, www.gregyoungpublishing.com. (bl). **226-227 Mary Evans Picture Library:** Grenville Collins Postcard Collection. **227 Alamy Stock Photo:** Album (cra); Wolfgang Diederich (bc). **228 Alamy Stock Photo:** The Picture Art Collection (tl); World History Archive (bl). **Getty Images / iStock:** michal812 (bc). **229 Alamy Stock Photo:** Constantinos Iliopoulos (tl); Bernardo Galmarini (c); Neftali (br). **230 Alamy Stock Photo:** Carmen Jost (bl); PictureLux / The Hollywood Archive (t). **231 4Corners:** Reinhard Schmid (t). **Alamy Stock Photo:** PA Images / Peter Robinson (bl). **232 Bridgeman Images:** © Leonard de Selva (bl). **Dreamstime.com:** Giuseppe Esposito (br). **233 4Corners:** Günter Gräfenhain (br). **Getty Images:** Moment / wichianduangsri (bl). **234 akg-images:** (tr). **Alamy Stock Photo:** Archive Images (tl). **Bridgeman Images:** © Lucien Herve / Artedia (bl); The Stapleton Collection (br). **235 Alamy Stock Photo:** Andrew Fare (tc). **Shutterstock.com:** S-F (bc). **236 akg-images:** (bl). **236-237 akg-images**. **238 Bridgeman Images:** Portrait de l'imperatrice Catherine II de Russie (1729-1796). Peinture de Fedor (ou Fiodor) Stepanovitch Rokotov (1736-1809), 1770. Huile sur toile. Russie, Moscou, Musee National d'Histoire ©Electa/Leemage pse155689 (c); Stefano Bianchetti (bc). **Getty Images / iStock:** Nigel Jarvis (t). **239 Bridgeman Images:** (tr). **Mary Evans Picture Library:** John Massey Stewart Collection (bc). **Shutterstock.com:** (br). **240 akg-images:** (bl). **Alamy Stock Photo:** ITAR-TASS News Agency (t). **241 Alamy Stock Photo:** Lebrecht Music & Arts / Music-Images (bl). **Getty Images / iStock:** unclepodger (br). **Shutterstock.com:** Parsadanov (t). **242-243 Bridgeman Images:** The Stapleton Collection. **243 © The Metropolitan Museum of Art:** Harris Brisbane Dick Fund, 1951 (bc). **244 Alamy Stock Photo:** Nick Fielding (tr); The Granger Collection (clb). **Getty Images:** De Agostini / DEA / ICAS94 (br); Universal Images Group / Sepia Times (tl). **245 Avalon:** Francesco Tomasinelli (bc). **© The Metropolitan Museum of Art:** Rogers Fund, 1903 (t). **246 Library of Congress, Washington, D.C.:** LC-USZ62-120357 (b&w film copy neg.) (bc). **246-247 Shutterstock.com:** S-F. **248 Alamy Stock Photo:** Rolf Richardson (bl). **Getty Images:** Archive Photos / Jim Heimann Collection (clb); Archive Photos / Herbert (br). **Mary Evans Picture Library:** (t). **249 Getty Images:** Popperfoto / Paul Popper (cr). **Mary Evans Picture Library:** © John Frost Newspapers (bc). **250 Alamy Stock Photo:** Matt Merritt (bl). **Getty Images:** AFP (crb); The LIFE Picture Collection / Larry Burrows (cl). **251 Alamy Stock Photo:** Everett Collection Inc / © Film Movement (clb). **Shutterstock.com:** Chanchai Duangdoosan (br); Melinda Nagy (t). **252-253 Alamy Stock Photo:** Andrew Fare. **253 Alamy Stock Photo:** Art Collection 3 (bc). **Integrated Collections Database of the National Institutes for Cultural Heritage, Japan:** https://colbase.nich.go.jp/collection_items/tnm/H-758?locale=en, Gift of Japan Delegate Office for World's, Columbian Exposition, Chicago, Tokyo National Museum (br). **254 Alamy Stock Photo:** CPA Media Pte Ltd / Pictures From History (br). **Bridgeman Images:** The Stapleton Collection (t). **© The Metropolitan Museum of Art:** Mary Griggs Burke Collection, Gift of the Mary and Jackson Burke Foundation, 2015 (bl). **255 Alamy Stock Photo:** CPA Media Pte Ltd / Pictures From History (tl); MeijiShowa (cra). **Marser:** (bl). **256 Bridgeman Images:** (br). **© The Metropolitan Museum of Art:** H. O. Havemeyer Collection, Bequest of Mrs. H. O. Havemeyer, 1929 (tl). **257 Bridgeman Images:** Pictures from History / Kusakabe Kimbei (bc). **Dreamstime.com:** Sean Pavone (t). **258 Getty Images:** De Agostini / DEA PICTURE LIBRARY (bl). **258-259 Alamy Stock Photo:** Archive Images. **260 Alamy Stock Photo:** Granger Historical Picture Archive, NYC (bc). **Getty Images:** Archive Photos (cl). **261 Getty Images:** Archive Photos / Kean Collection (t); Universal Images Group / Sepia Times (bl); Universal Images Group / Universal History Archive (br). **262 Alamy Stock Photo:** Robertharding / Frank Fell (tl). **Getty Images:** Bettmann (br). **Library of Congress, Washington, D.C.:** G3852.M3G45 1915 .M3 (cr); LC-DIG-stereo-1s07887 / Moulton, J. W. (Joshua W.) (bl). **263 Alamy Stock Photo:** Robertharding / Frank Fell (br). **photo:Bob Adelman:** (t). **264-265 Bridgeman Images:** © Lucien Herve / Artedia. **265 Alamy Stock Photo:** GL Archive (br). **Shutterstock.com:** rook76 (bc). **266 Alamy Stock Photo:** Pedro Luz Cunha (br). **Bridgeman Images:** Jean Pierre Courau (bl). **Dreamstime.com:** Tacio Philip Sansonovski (tl). **Getty Images:** The LIFE Picture Collection / Frank Scherschel (tr). **267 Alamy Stock Photo:** Cro Magnon (t). **AWL Images:** Ian Trower (bc). **268 Alamy Stock Photo:** Sunny Celeste (br). **Getty Images:** De Agostini / DEA / U. Colnago (bl). **269 Dreamstime.com:** Taras Vyshnya (br). **Getty Images / iStock:** ferrantraite (bl). **270 AWL Images:** Tom Mackie (bc). **Shutterstock.com:** PureSolution (tr). **271 4Corners:** Susanne Kremer (tr). **Getty Images / iStock:** Yongyuan Dai (bl); E+ / ispyfriend (tl); TwilightShow / Courtesy of Zaha Hadid Architects and Courtesy of Zaha Hadid Architects (tc). **272-273 Shutterstock.com:** PureSolution. **273 Muharraq Forever:** https://www.flickr.com/photos/muharraq (bc). **274 Ludwig Hejze:** (tl). **Shutterstock.com:** rook76 (bc). **275 Alamy Stock Photo:** Frederic Reglain (br). **AWL Images:** Jon Arnold / (bl). **Getty Images / iStock:** adrian825 (t). **276 Alamy Stock Photo:** World History Archive (bc). **276-277 Getty Images / iStock:** E+ / ispyfriend. **278 Alamy Stock Photo:** Granger Historical Picture Archive, NYC (t). **Getty Images:** De Agostini / DEA PICTURE LIBRARY (bl). **279 AWL Images:** Steve Vidler (tr). **Bridgeman Images:** © Indianapolis Museum of Art / Gift of Mr and Mrs Eli Lilly (bc). **Getty Images:** De Agostini / DEA / Biblioteca Ambrosiana (tc). **SuperStock:** Universal Images Group (br). **280 Alamy Stock Photo:** The History Collection (bl). **Bridgeman Images:** Pictures from History (t). **281 Alamy Stock Photo:** Photo12 / Ann Ronan Picture Library (bc); The Protected Art Archive (tr). **Bridgeman Images:** Pictures from History (tc). **282 Alamy Stock Photo:** Melvyn Longhurst China (bl). **Bridgeman Images:** © Archives Charmet (t). **Getty Images / iStock:** paulmerrett (br). **283 Alamy Stock Photo:** Bjanka Kadic (br). **Dreamstime.com:** Xi Zhang (cr). **284-285 Getty Images / iStock:** Yongyuan Dai. **285 Alamy Stock Photo:** CPA Media Pte Ltd / Pictures From History (bc). **286 akg-images:** Paul Almasy (tl). **Alamy Stock Photo:** Heritage Image Partnership Ltd (br). **Shutterstock.com:** Concord / Warner Bros / Kobal (bl). **287 Alamy Stock Photo:** Sean Pavone (t). **Getty Images:** Visual China Group / Ma Honghai (br). **288-289 Getty Images / iStock:** TwilightShow / Courtesy of Zaha Hadid Architects and Courtesy of Zaha Hadid Architects. **288 Getty Images:** Universal Images Group / Sepia Times (cb). © **Kansong Art and Culture Foundation:** (bc). **290 Alamy Stock Photo:** Nattee Chalermtiragool (t); World History Archive (bl). **291 Alamy Stock Photo:** Chronicle (cra); Ivan Vdovin (bc); Pavel Dudek (br). **292 Alamy Stock Photo:** Paul Brown (bc); Retro AdArchives (tl). **AWL Images:** Ian Trower (cra). **293 Alamy Stock Photo:** BFA (bc); Sean Pavone (t). **Shutterstock.com:** SS pixels (bl). **294 4Corners:** Susanne Kremer. **295 Alamy Stock Photo:** ART Collection (br); GL Archive (bl). **296 Alamy Stock Photo:** Art Heritage (br); CPA Media Pte Ltd / Pictures From History (cl). **Integrated Collections Database of the National Institutes for Cultural Heritage, Japan:** https://colbase.nich.go.jp/collection_items/tnm/I-2959?locale=en, Tokyo National Museum (tc). **297 Getty Images:** Hulton Archive / Culture Club (bl); Universal Images Group / Sepia Times (t). **298 Alamy Stock Photo:** Retro AdArchives (tc); Sueddeutsche Zeitung Photo / Scherl (cl). **Bridgeman Images:** Pictures from History (bc). **299 Alamy Stock Photo:** P. Batchelder (t). **Getty Images:** Moment / falcon0125 (br). **300 Alamy Stock Photo:** The History Collection (bl). **300-301 AWL Images:** Tom Mackie. **302 Alamy Stock Photo:** The History Collection (t). **Los Angeles Public Library:** Security Pacific National Bank Collection (bc). **303 Alamy Stock Photo:** Everett Collection Historical (br). **Collection of Dan Pope:** (bl). **Shutterstock.com:** Encyclopaedia Britannica / Uig (tr). **304 Alamy Stock Photo:** PictureLux / The Hollywood Archive (bc). **Getty Images:** Archive Photos / MPI (tl); Michael Ochs Archives (tc); De Agostini / DEA / W. BUSS (cra). **305 4Corners:** Giovanni Simeone (tr). **Alamy Stock Photo:** CBW (cr); Everett Collection Inc / © Summit Releasing / Ron Harvey (br). **Getty Images:** Corbis Historical / Ted Soqui (bc). **306 Alamy Stock Photo:** Allard Schager (bl). **Getty Images:** Moment / Matteo Colombo (br). **307 Getty Images:** EyeEm / Rosley Majid (bl). **Getty Images / iStock:** Elijah-Lovkoff (br)

All other images © Dorling Kindersley
For further information see: www.dkimages.com